The development gap

The development gap

A spatial analysis of world poverty and inequality

J.P. Cole
Professor of Geography,
University of Nottingham

JOHN WILEY & SONS
Chichester · New York · Brisbane · Toronto

British Library Cataloguing in Publication Data:
Cole, J.P
  The development gap.
  1. Economic development
  2. Equality
  3. Geography, Economic
  I. Title
  330.9   HD82   80-40284

  ISBN 0 471 27796 7

Typeset by Photo-Graphics, Yarcombe, Honiton, Devon
and printed in the United States of America.

Preface

The present book was written in 1978 and revised in 1979 before being given to the publisher. Many of the numerical data are for the period 1974-76 as this was the latest time when a fairly complete set of data was available for the world as a whole.

The main aim of the book is to look at the question of inequality and development in the world from a spatial viewpoint and to give equal emphasis to natural resources and to production. Many sets of data are no more than estimates. Undiscovered mineral reserves, by definition, can only be a matter of speculation. It is felt that the wide disparities revealed in the book in the distribution of natural resources and of production according to population would have emerged with any reasonable method of estimation.

The author wishes to thank several years of Geography students at Nottingham University whose ideas and comments have been invaluable during the running of a Developing World course. He is very grateful to Paul Mather for his assistance in the computing of principal components and linkage analysis in Chapter 4. The help of his two sons in reading the manuscript was invaluable as was a discussion about the contents of the book with Dr Bryan E. Coates of the Geography Department, Sheffield University. The help of his father in both checking the text and drawing certain illustrations is appreciated. The maps and diagrams were produced by Carol Walter. Finally, the comments of an anonymous referee, provided by the publisher, were as far as possible taken into account as the text was redrafted.

Contents

1

Introduction

1.1 The aim of the book

The inhabitants of some parts of the world have much higher material living standards than those of other parts. The contrast between rich and poor regions has existed and has been commented on for a very long time. Only since the Second World War has widespread concern been expressed about the disparity and about the ways of changing it.

There is no straightforward, widely accepted way of measuring different levels of living standards. The level of consumption of material goods such as steel and sugar can be measured numerically with reasonable accuracy. The level of provision of services such as education and health is more difficult to quantify. The availability and enjoyment of happiness, peace of mind, and environmental attractiveness virtually defy numerical measurement. In the present book the terms rich and poor refer largely to the consumption of goods and services that can be measured numerically.

The gap between rich and poor may be viewed at the level either of single individuals or of groups of people. The aggregation of individuals may be based on a demographic, economic or cultural criterion, producing such groups as old-age pensioners, coalminers or Sikhs. Alternatively, individuals may be grouped according to the regions, such as counties or provinces, in which they happen to live. The present book is concerned mainly with contrasts in standards of living between groups of people living in distinct regions of the world.

It appears that the gap between rich and poor individuals and between rich and poor regions has tended to widen in the last few hundred years. Presumably in the very distant past, in pre-agricultural societies, everyone everywhere had a very low level of consumption. In predominantly agricultural societies there was scope for some people to become rich. Today the contrast between a primitive food gatherer in the Amazon forest and a Texan multi-millionaire is enormous. Similarly, even the average standard of living of each citizen of the U.S.A. is perhaps a hundred times that of the average inhabitant of the Amazon region of South America. The main aim of this book is to examine the feasibility some time in the future of narrowing, if not closing, the wide gap between rich and poor regions of the world.

1.2   The matters to be considered

The level of consumption of goods and services of the inhabitants of a given region depends to a large extent on the productivity of its economically active population. Productivity per person employed is largely related to two influences or factors. It depends firstly on the *efficiency* of means of production used and secondly on the *accessibility* of natural resources.

The above assertion may be illustrated by a simple example. In a given locality there are two coal seams, one thin, dipping, and faulted, the other thick, horizontal, and not contorted. The coal may be extracted either with pick and shovel or by a mechanical cutter. The level of productivity per worker is determined firstly by the means of extraction used and secondly by the accessibility of the coal. The smallest amount produced per worker in a given time will come from manual extraction in the unfavourable seam. The largest amount will be obtained by mechanical extraction in the favourable seam. The idea behind the above situation, with suitable modifications, can be applied to various sectors of production such as agriculture, manufacturing, and transportation.

The *efficiency* of the means of production in a given region is related to the level of mechanization and technology available and to the level of education and skill of persons employed. The *accessibility* of the natural resource influences the level of

Plate 1.1 (Opposite top) Three Mexican cultivators weed a small field of maize (corn). The oxen are muzzled to keep them from eating the maize. Such low productivity infuriates American tourists visiting developing countries

Plate 1.2 (Opposite bottom) Slow retail sales turnover in a South Mexican market in a country town. In the larger towns, supermarkets are taking over some of the retail trade

productivity achieved in its extraction or use. The *quantity* of the natural resource available per inhabitant determines how long the reserves will last at a given rate of extraction if they are non-renewable.

Great regional disparities occur in the world in the amount of goods and services produced per inhabitant. Great regional disparities also occur in the availability of natural resources per inhabitant. Examples in the form of familiar countries may be given. Australia and Canada are countries in which productivity per economically active person is very high in most sectors of the economy. Both are also well endowed with natural resources per inhabitant. The U.K., Japan, and, even more strikingly, Hong Kong, are countries with high worker productivity but comparatively few natural resources of their own. The inhabitants of the Amazon forest region of South America mostly have a low level of productivity yet considerable natural resources. Finally, Northeast Brazil, Bangladesh, and Java (Indonesia) are three examples of regions with very low productivity *and* a very unfavourable ratio of natural resources to population.

In spite of the great contrasts in levels of productivity and in the availability of natural resources between different parts of the world referred to above, the expectation or hope has been widely expressed that the gap in living standards between different parts will be narrowed, if not closed. Increasingly in the 1970s, however, the prospect that the gap can be closed has been questioned. One reason often given is that there are not enough natural resources even for the high standards of living of the rich countries to be maintained, let alone for the poor countries to move out of their present low levels. It is also evident that it would be very difficult for the productivity gap to be eliminated since the means of production in poor countries generally lag in efficiency very far behind those in the rich countries.

Even if the two above views are not correct it has been argued that the present political system of the world makes any massive international redistribution of population or of products very unlikely. The rich countries intend to maintain their high levels of production and consumption and will not make substantial sacrifices. In addition, the countries with very large natural resources at their disposal seem increasingly reluctant to allow their reserves to be used up too quickly. For example Venezuela cut

Plate 1.3 (Opposite) There is plenty of forest still in Amazonia for the few inhabitants but extracting wild rubber from the thinly dispersed *Hevea brasiliensis* tree is time-consuming. Source: Lau (1969). Reproduced by permission of Instituto Brasileiro de Geografia e Estatística

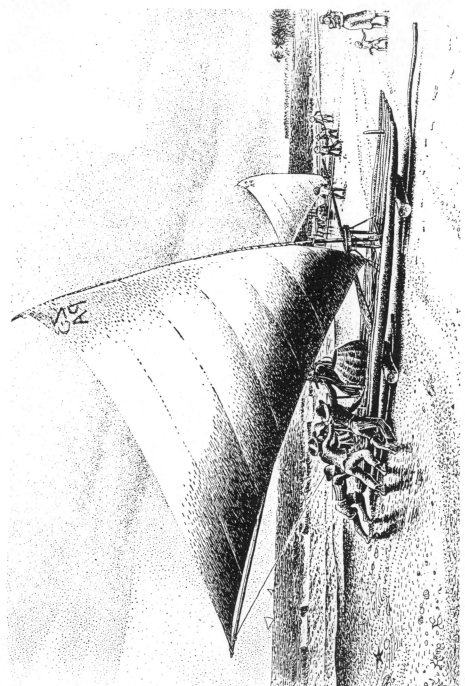

Plate 1.4 Vessels used for fishing in the Atlantic Ocean off Northeast Brazil. They are not only dangerous but also ill-equipped to catch more than small quantities of fish. Source: Lau (1969). Reproduced by permission of Instituto Brasileiro de Geografia e Estatistica

its oil production by nearly half in the mid-1970s after huge increases in the price of oil, Australia is concerned about the depletion of its vast mineral reserves, and Mexico apparently intends to extract its newly found large oil reserves quite slowly.

The main theme of the present book is one that has not received much serious attention in studies of world production and natural resources. It will be argued that even if there are no long-term problems regarding the availability of natural resources and the productivity gap and even if there were no political barriers to the redistribution of population and of products in the world it would still be impossible to achieve equality throughout. The reason is that even with a powerful, centrally controlled world state the international redistribution of people or of products (or both) that would be needed to provide the basis for uniform living standards throughout the world would be so great that it would be physically or geographically impossible to achieve them for many decades to come.

1.3   Some terms used in the book

A particular word is conventionally defined by other words. These in turn are defined by yet more words (or even by the original word). In this section some of the terms to be used in the book will be explained with the help of examples rather than by strict definitions. Four areas of terminology will be referred to: geographical, development, wealth (and income), and money.

(i) *Geographical* information is often in some way related to the location of features in area and to distance between them. A given feature may have a general *position* in the world and also a more specific *site,* the actual locality in which it is situated. For example the position of New York is on the east coast of North America while the site of the original European settlement is at the southern end of Manhattan Island. Features on the earth's surface can mostly be represented symbolically on maps as dots, lines or patches. On a world scale, for example, towns would be dots, rivers and railways lines, and countries patches.

Distances between places may be measured in various ways (see Figure 1.1). The shortest geometrical distance between two places may be a Euclidean straight line, but on the spherical surface of the earth the shortest distance between two places that are some distance apart is along a *great circle* (one cannot travel through the earth). In practice it may be necessary to travel between two places along a transportation link considerably in excess of the shortest distance (see Figure 1.1). Distances between places can also be assessed in time travelled and in cost and in even more abstract ways. One may, for example, hear it said in Britain that New Zealand and Australia are the closest countries to us (in a cultural sense). In fact they are the farthest in space distance.

The present book refers frequently to areal units. The expression *sovereign state* is technically the term to use with reference to an independent country. A colony such as Hong Kong or Martinique may also be referred to as a country but it is dependent and therefore not sovereign. The terms *area* and *region* are often interchanged. Area commonly refers both to actual territorial extent and to a particular space on the earth's surface. In this book the word region is used to refer to a part of the earth's surface that can be defined because for some reason it differs from other parts. For example one can refer to New England in the U.S.A. or to the Midlands of England meaning an accepted part of the earth's surface.

The term *geographical* has various uses but in non-technical language it usually refers either to the influence of the physical environment on man's activities or to location. The term *spatial* will be used to refer to aspects of the position, location or site of places and to relations involving transactions between them, such as flows along transportation links.

The terms *central* and *peripheral* are sometimes used in a spatial sense. They are usually relative terms. For example the French town of Strasbourg is peripheral in the land of France itself but central in the context of the whole European Economic Community (see Figure 1.1).

(ii) The term *development* has not so far been used in this book. It has come to be the most widely used term and concept referring to the gap between the rich and poor countries and it summarizes the situation. It is, however, a controversial and emotional term. People in poorer countries may not like their countries to be referred to as underdeveloped. Another drawback is that the term developed implies unfolding, stages, evolution, processes, and progress. Not everyone sees development as a straightforward process. To some material 'progress' is not even desirable.

Instead of attempting to define development through other words it was decided to use examples from the *United Nations Statistical Yearbook*. In United Nations publications three groups of country are distinguished in the world: developed market economies, developing market economies, and centrally planned economies. The centrally planned economies are implicitly subdivided into developed and developing as those of East Europe and the U.S.S.R. on the one hand and those of Asia on the other. The

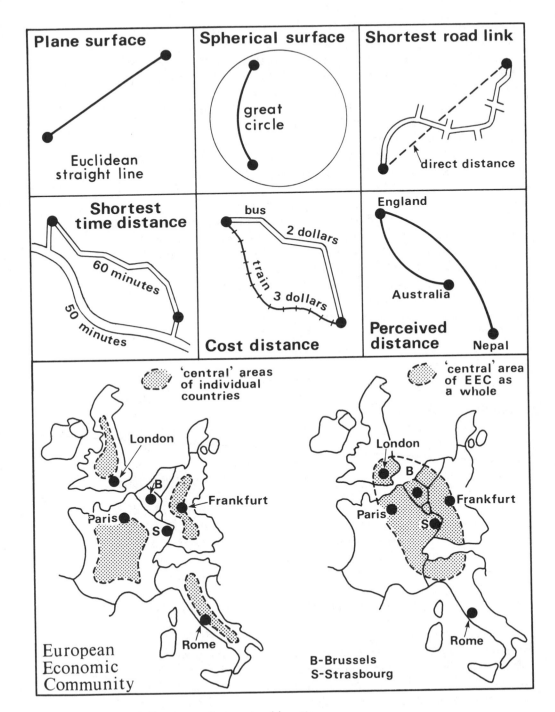

Figure 1.1 Types of distance and aspects of location

countries with centrally planned economies may also be referred to as communist or more correctly as socialist.

The developed market economies consist of Canada and the U.S.A., all of Europe not in the centrally planned economies, plus South Africa, Israel, Japan, Australia, and New Zealand. All countries not included with the 'developed' or 'centrally planned' economies are referred to as 'developing' market economies.

In the present book, *developing* and *developed* will be used as they are used in the above United Nations groupings. The term Third World will not be used, as it originally had political or ideological connotations rather than economic ones. The use of 'North-South' is also to be deplored and the use of northern hemisphere and southern hemisphere as applied to developed and developing regions is absurd. About three-quarters of the population of the developing world actually live in the northern hemisphere while the temperate zone of the southern hemisphere contains some very affluent regions. In the view of the author the terms *underdeveloped* and *less developed* are interchangeable with developing. The terms *undeveloped* and *overdeveloped* are reserved for describing the relationship between natural resources and population rather than the relationship between production and population.

(iii) To economists the terms *wealth* and *income* have difference meanings, though popularly they are often confused. For the purposes of this book wealth represents a source of unearned income while income measures the power to purchase goods and services. The two concepts can be distinguished by reference to the U.S.S.R. and most other socialist countries. Here the state owns virtually all means of production of goods and services. Individuals cannot therefore (theoretically at least) possess wealth and cannot receive unearned income. They do, however, receive earned income, and the purchasing power of individuals varies greatly within the U.S.S.R. between types of employment, between town and country, and from republic to republic.

In most market economy countries part of the means of production is in the public sector, as is the coal industry in the U.K. Theoretically everyone has an equal share in the ownership of such state concerns. The rest of the national wealth is owned by individuals or by groups and is often very unevenly shared out. Estimates published in *The Guardian* (12 July 1979) showed that around 1970 the wealthiest 1 percent of the population of the U.K. owned 30 percent of all the wealth while in the U.S.A. the concentration was 25 percent. Sweden (16 percent) and Australia (9 percent) had a much lower concentration of wealth. It is ironical that the media in rich countries often draw attention to the uneven distribution of wealth and/or income in poor countries.

The distinction between wealth and income has been discussed at some length because the two terms may be applied also to a broader context. Wealth might be thought of as the natural resources of a country plus the means of production while income corresponds to what is produced and consumed.

(iv) When economists use the term *money* they presumably know which use of it they mean and what money actually is. Unfortunately the term or rather the concept *money* is widely misused and misunderstood in popular discussion. To most people money is something concrete and something around which other things change value. It is really absurd to say that the dollar or the pound buys much less than it used to without considering whether or not one actually also has more money available. It is hardly desirable or realistic to avoid referring to money altogether in a book on development. An economist might avoid doing so, but not a geographer. The reader is asked to think carefully what money really does mean. It is hoped that the situation described below will bring home the meaning of money.

In 1976 I contributed £10 towards buying a £1000 knitting machine to send to a village in Tanzania. The point is that we were not really sending a cheque or banknotes worth £1000 to Tanzania, which would have been not only useless in itself but meaningless. I was forgoing the purchase of goods or services in England valued at £10 in order that I could send £10 worth of a machine to a developing country. The narrowing of the development gap requires the *transfer* of goods and services of one kind or another, and financial assistance or capital investment must be thought of in terms of actual objects to be moved about the world.

I tested out on several people the view that even if the rich countries suddenly became generous and were prepared to renounce a large proportion of their consumption of material goods and services it would be physically impossible to provide the means of transport to make the necessary transfers to reach the poor countries. The almost inevitable answer was 'but they could be sent money'.

1.4 The quality of life

The reader may feel that material standards are now unnecessarily high and life excessively complicated in developed countries. To anticipate such a view it is accepted that there are both advantages

Table 1.1 Quality of life expressed qualitatively

	Tasaday group, Philippines	Rural India	Argentina	U.S.A.
Food quantity	Adequate	Marginal	Good	Excessive
Food quality	Deficient	Deficient	Adequate	Good
Water	Satisfactory	Deficient	Satisfactory	Good
Clothing	Redundant	Adequate	Reasonable	Good
Dwelling itself	Cave	Hut	3 rooms	5 rooms
Dwelling amenities	None	Minimal	Reasonable	(Too) many
Energy consumed	None	Animal power	Considerable	Enormous
Consumer durables	None	Few	Reasonable	(Too) many
Education	None	A little	Moderate	Good
Health services	None	Too expensive	Good	Expensive
Transport	None	Animal	Quite good	Car or two
Mobility	Limited	Limited	Considerable	Fabulous
Vacation	None	Unlikely	Seaside	Continental or even world-wide
Gross national product ($U.S.) per inhabitant c.1980	0	200	2000	10,000

and disadvantages in the way of life in developed countries. One might measure development, living standards, and quality of life by other standards as well as those that are strictly material. It has been argued that too much attention is given to consumer items such as food and household gadgets, or to services which themselves depend on material construction and equipment, such as schools and hospitals. On the other hand, relations between individuals and between groups are not necessarily inferior in poor countries compared with relations in rich countries.

Regard for one's family, extended family, fellow citizens, and the community in general is not a monopoly of people in rich countries. Such aspects of life are rarely counted in assessments of the development gap. Norman (1975) argued that if one takes certain criteria, a citizen of Botswana, for all his 'poverty', may be *happier* than a citizen of Britain, although the quantity of material products consumed per inhabitant in Britain is indisputably much greater.

Table 1.2 Physical Quality of Life Index of selected countries

Highest scoring		Selected intermediate		Lowest scoring	
Sweden	97	U.S.S.R.	91	Somalia	19
Norway	97	Argentina	85	Mauritania	18
Iceland	97	Sri Lanka	82	C.African Rep.	18
Denmark	96	China	71	Chad	18
Netherlands	96	Brazil	66	Afghanistan	17
Japan	96	Turkey	56	Upper Volta	16
U.S.A.	95	Indonesia	48	Angola	16
Canada	95	India	41	Guinea-Bissau	14
France	95	Bangladesh	32	Mali	14
U.K.	94	Nigeria	27	Niger	14

When such a view is presented by someone from a rich country to someone in a poor one it can easily be seen as a recipe for keeping the poor materially poor. Quality and quantity may not, however, be as inseparable as many people think. Two examples illustrate the difficulty of giving an assessment of the quality of life.

An attempt by the author to provide a verbal description to some aspects of living conditions in four parts of the world is shown in Table 1.1. The Tasaday, to be referred to again in the next chapter, are a small group of people who were discovered in the early 1970s living in very simple conditions in the tropical forest of the Philippines. For the other three countries the descriptions refer to the average level for the regions concerned.

The second example is the Physical Quality of Life Index, devised by the Overseas Development Council, Washington D.C. It is intended to be a non-income measure that summarizes the many aspects of human well-being. In reality the index is a simple assessment of health and educational levels. Three indicators contribute to produce a single composite index: infant mortality, life expectancy at age one, and literacy. The end product is a numerical (or quantitative) index ranging from 0 to 100 and 'measuring' quality. Table 1.2 shows the scores of selected countries including the highest and lowest, the source being the Population Reference Bureau (1979).

1.5 The problem of aggregation and regionalization

Studies of inequality within countries are usually based on traditional regional subdivisions such as administrative units, in which people are grouped in an arbitrary fashion. Measures to modify regional contrasts are likely, for convenience, to be implemented on the basis of such systems of subdivisions. On a world scale, sovereign states themselves usually form the regional subdivisions of the earth's land surface on which development studies are based and through which aid is allocated. In this section it will be argued that the way regional inequality and contrasts in development are perceived depends to some extent on the framework of regional subdivisions used.

Two distinct effects of the regional aggregation of individuals may be noted. The first is that exactly the same proportions of 'rich' and 'poor' individuals can produce either 'rich' and 'poor' regions or 'uniform' regions depending on the spatial distribution of individuals and the system of regional units into which they are grouped. The second effect, most marked at world level, and particularly relevant in the present book, is that of having a system of political units that vary greatly in population size. This second effect will be discussed after the first has been considered.

Equalia and Irregula are fictitious countries each with the same proportion of rich people, medium income people, and poor people (see Figure 1.2). The same degree of inequality between the inhabitants of the two countries at one level may give quite different appearances spatially at a higher level according to the distribution of rich and poor within the national area. Equalia and Irregula are each divided into five provinces. Each country as a whole has 5000 rich people, 10,000 medium income people, and 20,000 poor people. For simplicity these are grouped in the maps into symbols each representing 1000 people. In Equalia there are 1000, 2000, and 4000 rich, medium income, and poor people respectively in each province. Viewed through the regional system provided at the province level there is no difference in average level between the five regions. On the other hand the south of Irregula is much richer than the north. The proportions of rich, medium, and poor in Irregula are the same as in Equalia but the spatial distribution is very different. In Irregula marked regional disparities are evident when the population is grouped into five provinces.

If the Equalia and Irregula situation is extended to the world as a whole then the present world situation is more like that in Irregula than that in Equalia. This discovery may not seem very profound but it is clear that one could still find rich and poor individuals in the world even if every country had the same average income per inhabitant. Irregula would represent the world situation more closely still if instead of having subdivisions (the provinces) that are equal in population size, it had subdivisions that differed greatly in population size. This is the second effect referred to above of the

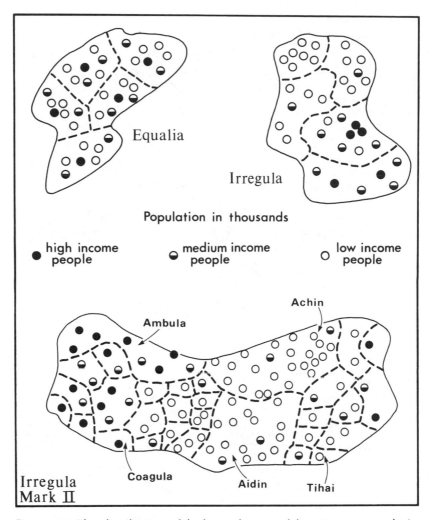

Figure 1.2 The distribution of high, medium, and low income people in three fictitious countries

influence of the system of regional subdivisions on the way inequality in the world is perceived. The world situation is therefore more like Irregula Mark II in Figure 1.2 than the original Irregula. It contains some very large countries that are rich (Ambula) or poor (Achin and Aidin) as well as many very small countries that are rich (Coagula) or poor (Tihai). The system of sovereign states of the world has formed the basis for most development studies at world level in which a regional breakdown has been used. Reference will be made in Chapter 4 to some of the development studies of the 1960s and 1970s.

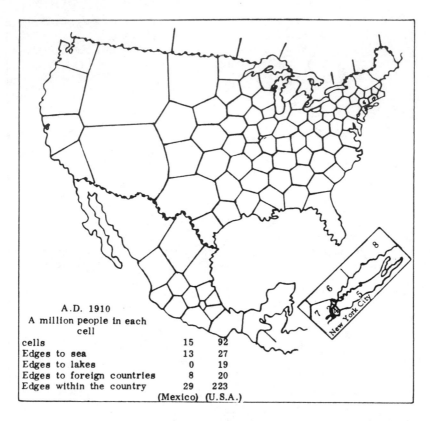

A.D. 1910
A million people in each
cell

cells	15	92
Edges to sea	13	27
Edges to lakes	0	19
Edges to foreign countries	8	20
Edges within the country	29	223
	(Mexico)	(U.S.A.)

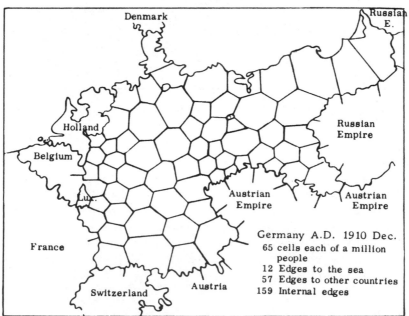

Germany A.D. 1910 Dec.
    65 cells each of a million
        people
    12 Edges to the sea
    57 Edges to other countries
    159 Internal edges

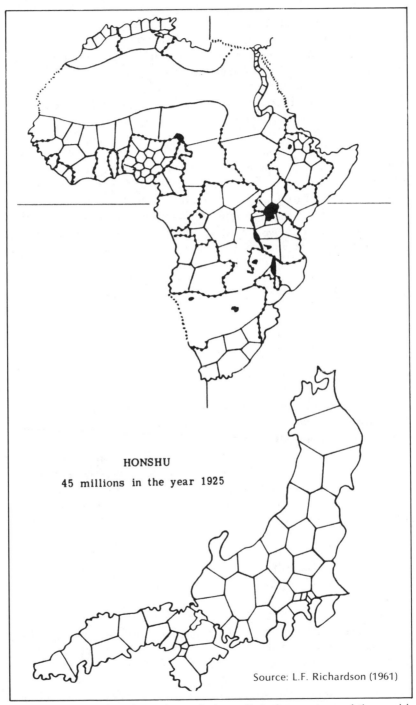

Figure 1.3 Examples of equal population cells in four regions of the world. source: L.F. Richardson (1961)

Early in the present century a physicist, L.F. Richardson (1961), experimented with the idea of dividing countries of the world into units, each with the same number of inhabitants. He referred to the units as *cells* and he used the networks of uniform population cells to work out the liability of countries to be involved in conflict with neighbours. Four of his systems of cells are shown in Figure 1.3.

The idea of Richardson will be used in the present book to produce a new regionalization of the world (see Chapter 6). The basis will be a system of 100 'cells', each containing approximately 1 percent of the population of the world in the mid-1970s, or 40 million out of the total of 4000 million. The regional distribution in relation to population of natural resources and of production can be measured and its features appreciated better in some respects on the basis of the uniform population regions or cells than on the basis of the present sovereign states of the world. The mismatching of natural resources and of production in relation to population can be expressed clearly and the situation appraised. The use of the 100 cells is a convenient device for studying inequality in the world. It is not being suggested that such a system is ever likely actually to come into being in place of the present system of political units of the world.

1.6   The plan of the book

In studies on the subject of development there has been a tendency to emphasize certain aspects and approaches and to neglect others. Three related themes have in the view of the author dominated the subject since the Second World War: the question of how long natural resources will last, the concept of stages of economic growth, and the features and problems of inequality in living standards in the world. Inadequate attention has been given to considering spatial aspects of the above three themes. When regional aspects of development have been considered the tendency has been to use the sovereign states of the world in order to examine the distribution of production and consumption of goods and services. Trade has been emphasized as the main form of transactions between countries and the framework for considering solutions to aspects of development such as inequality.

In the present book, three further aspects are added. Firstly, the new regionalization of the world described in the last section uses 100 regions each with about 1 percent of the world's population (see Figure 6.11, p. 202). Secondly, a greater emphasis than usual is placed on the assessment and distribution of natural resources in relation to population. Thirdly, net transfers of goods and population between regions are considered as well as exchange by trading. As a result, the topics in the present book are arranged in a rather more devious sequence than the usual one for such studies. In view of this different sequence it is opportune here to justify briefly the choice and order of topics as they come, chapter by chapter.

It was considered necessary to discuss the subject of poverty and to identify a number of ingredients that make up the total process of development. These are described in Chapter 2. Since the book is about inequality in the world, Chapters 3 and 4 have been written to provide examples of regional differences at local, regional, and international levels. Chapter 5 shows with the help of historical data for the last hundred to two hundred years how the present contrasts in the world have come about or at least have become accentuated.

Chapter 6 describes a new spatial framework devised by the author to make clearer the disparities or mismatchings in the distribution of key phenomena in the world. The distribution of natural resources, means of production, products, and the consumption of products in the world is studied in Chapters 7 and 8 on the basis of the above framework. Types of region are identified and compared in Chapter 9 and the transfers required to reduce or remove the development gap are then assessed in Chapter 10. In Chapter 11 the implications of what has been argued so far are applied back to the world as it is, the world of some 200 distinct political units of various shapes and sizes. In Chapter 12 some future prospects are discussed.

2

The nature of the
development gap

2.1 The idea of regional inequalities is not a new one

There are many references in Greek and Roman literature to fertile
and infertile areas. Sparta in Greece comes to mind as a region with
difficult environmental conditions and the volcanic soils round
Naples as particularly productive. The main argument in the
present book is that it is very difficult to reduce or remove regional
inequalities in the world. It is therefore worth providing examples in
this section to show that these have existed for a long time already.

There is an old saying about a yeoman of Kent going back at least
several hundred years:

> A Knight of Cales
> A Gentleman of Wales
>   And a Laird of the North Countree;
> A Yeoman of Kent,
> With his yearly Rent,
>   Will buy 'em out all three.

Arnold (1949) comments on this rhyme as follows:

> While the emphasis of this rhyme is on wealth, the opposition,
> on closer examination, is not very formidable. The so-called
> Knights of Cales were sixty men, some of them of humble
> origin and small fortune, whom Robert earl of Essex knighted in
> the course of his expedition to Cadiz — to the annoyance, it is
> believed, of his Sovereign. Gentlemen of Wales were not
> accounted wealthy. And Scottish lairds were notoriously poor.

r comforts and
the wants and
he gratification
ther. In highly
s of enjoyment
es to exertion,
consequence,
leness, and its
ear.

ven in Western
had more than
m to subsist.
production of
ssity and the
in a modern
early in the
for economic
as absolutely

ntury that the
below, which
e, does give
or. Ironically,
c of Ireland it
ld by the year
elsewhere in
be described

person who
ble. Shoes or
often not on
women are
rdly possible
e originally
r never take
t is, that not
if they once
et them on
rally falls to
ally cast-off
ho ever gets
s long been

But there was a good deal of truth in the suggestion that Kentish yeomen were richer than the general run of yeomen elsewhere in the country.

His explanation of why Kent was a prosperous region is also of interest because it touches on various themes in the present book. The Kentish yeoman thrived:

> thanks to the operation of a number of factors connected fairly directly with the special form of land tenure which once obtained in Kent; with the characteristic form that the common- or open-field system of farming took in that county; with the fertility of Kentish soil; with the presence in Kent of the Weald and of marsh-lands along great stretches of its coast-line; and with the geographical position of the county, easily accessible to London by water and astride the highway to the capital from the Channel Ports and the Continent.

Thus three distinct influences are proposed: economic organization (land tenure), natural resources (soil fertility), and position. Contrasts have long been noted between different towns or local areas within countries and between whole countries on a world scale. The differences have often been attributed either to the quality and quantity of natural resources or to the energy and inventiveness of the population.

Current contrasts in standards of living in the world are to some extent due to the uneven diffusion of innovations from Britain, the rest of Europe, and later the U.S.A. to the rest of the world since the start of the Industrial Revolution in the eighteenth century. It is therefore of interest to refer to Adam Smith (1776), who was writing towards the end of that century. He drew attention to contrasts within Britain itself, within Europe, and within the world as a whole. Adam Smith found 'the prices of bread and butcher's meat … generally the same or very nearly the same through the greater part of the United Kingdom' yet the wages of labour varying greatly between places only a few miles apart. In Europe, he noted that British and French agriculture were better organized than Polish agriculture. He considered British industry to be more sophisticated than French industry but Poland to be industrially far behind either.

Adam Smith's examples of contrasts in the world as a whole 200 years ago are of interest both in their own right and because in some respects they are even valid today. England was the richest country at the time, as he explained in *The Wealth of Nations*:

It is not the actual greatness of national wealth, bu
continual increase, which occasions a rise in the wage
labour. It is not, accordingly, in the richest countries, but i
most thriving, or in those which are growing rich the fa
that the wages of labour are highest. England is certainly,
present times, a much richer country than any part of
America. The wages of labour, however, are much hig
North America than in any part of England.

Elsewhere in *The Wealth of Nations* he wrote:

> But though North America is not yet so rich as Englar
> much more thriving, and advancing, with much greater i
> to the further acquisition of riches. The most decisive
> the prosperity of any country is the increase of the nu
> its inhabitants. In Great Britain, and most other E
> countries, they are not supposed to double in less t
> hundred years. In the British colonies in North Ameri
> been found that they double in twenty or five-ar
> years.

Adam Smith implied that although the population
America was growing fast, productive capacity and p
were growing even more quickly. In contrast:

> China has been long one of the richest, that is, one
> fertile, best cultivated, most industrious, and mos
> countries in the world. It seems, however, to have
> stationary. Marco Polo, who visited it more than f
> years ago, describes its cultivation, ind
> populousness, almost in the same terms in whi
> described by travellers in the present times. It l
> even long before his time, acquired that full cor
> riches which the nature of its laws and institutions
> acquire.

China to Adam Smith seemed to be stagnating, wit
population pressing against the limits of cultiv;
contrast, he found one area, now roughly th
Bangladesh, in which:

> The funds destined for the maintenance o
> sensibly decaying .... This perhaps is nearly the
> Bengal, and some other of the English settlem

gratifying them increase. Whenever a taste fc
conveniences has been generally diffused,
desires of man become altogether unlimited. 1
of one leads directly to the formation of an
civilised societies, new products and new mode
are constantly presenting themselves as motiv
and as means of rewarding it. Perseverance is, i
given to all the operations of industry; and ic
attendant train of evils, almost entirely disapp

At the time when the above passage was written, e
Europe only a small proportion of the population
what would now be regarded as a bare minimu
Material development was associated with the
'luxuries'. One man's luxury is another man's nec
basic material expectations of the ordinary citizer
industrial country are far greater than they were
nineteenth century. Nevertheless, one of the reasons
growth, the desire of people to acquire more than v
essential to exist, was clearly appreciated.

There is little evidence early in the nineteenth ce
rich were prepared to help the poor. The passage
illustrates the poverty in rural Ireland at that tin
evidence of a kind of aid, though from poor to very pc
if oil is discovered in or off the shores of the Republi
could be one of the most affluent countries in the wor
2000. At the same time, hundreds of millions of peopl
the world live now in conditions similar to those to
(source *Encyclopaedia Britannica*, 1816-24):

> The dress of the people is so wretched, that to
> has not visited the country, it is almost inconceiva
> stockings are seldom to be seen on children and
> grown persons. The rags in which both men and
> clothed are so worn and complicated, that it is ha
> to imagine to what article of dress they hav
> belonged. It has been observed that the Irish poc
> off their clothes when they go to bed; but the fac
> only are they in general destitute of blankets, but,
> took off their clothes, it would be difficult to
> again. Their dress is worn day and night till it lite
> pieces; and even when it is first put on, it is usu
> clothing; for there is not one cottager out of ten w
> a coat made for himself. A considerable trade ha

Plate 2.1 A less reverent approach to the matter of luxuries than that quoted in the text from an early *Encyclopaedia Britannica* was published in *Punch* in the late 1940s. Perhaps it reflects the failure at the time of the Tanganyikan groundnut scheme. (Reproduced by permission of *Punch*)

carried on from the west of Scotland to Ireland, consisting of
the old clothes of the former country, and to those who know
how long all ranks in Scotland wear their dress there is no more
convincing proof of the poverty of the latter country can be
given.

Long before the early nineteenth century contrasts had existed
between different regions of the world. European explorers noted
the civilization of China hundreds of years ago. The Spaniards
encountered differences in the New World in the sixteenth century
between the Inca and Aztec civilizations and the much simpler
societies elsewhere in the Americas. The contrast gradually
increased during the three centuries following the beginning of the
modern colonial period of world history when the Portuguese and
Spaniards were each allocated half of the tropical world by the
Pope of the time in the Treaty of Tordesillas in 1493-4.

The quotations in this section show that a development gap
already existed two centuries ago. The reason for stressing this
point at some length is that if it has taken so long for the
inequalities in the world to form, it seems reasonable to assume
that it will be difficult for them to disappear in only a few decades.

2.2 Conditions in poor countries now

Though big contrasts between different parts of the world were
recognized at least two centuries ago, the contrasts between
extremes are certainly much greater now than they were. Also the
proportion of the population of the world that is aware of them is
probably much higher now than it was then.

It is still possible to find small groups of people living in virtual
isolation and using very few implements to produce their food and
other needs. Such simple societies are found mainly in areas of
tropical rain forest in South America and Southeast Asia. In the
early 1970s a group of about twenty-five people were discovered in
the island of Mindanao, in the Philippines. This group, the Tasaday,
had been living in isolation at least for some decades, in a rugged
tropical rain forest environment. They lived in a communal cave,
had fire, but used no tools. Their only clothing was made of leaves.
They gathered their food from the dense forest in which their cave
was situated. The life of the Tasaday has now been described in
some depth by MacLeish (1972) and Nance (1975). The primitive
group forms a base against which the living standards of others can
be measured. Most of the consumer durables of the modern

affluent society would have no meaning in such a community and environment.

The future of simple societies like that of the Tasaday is very precarious. The threat from more 'developed' societies is strong. J. Nance is an American involved in the future of the Tasaday and cooperating with Panamin, the Philippine organization that is concerned with such communities. In his book published in 1975 he wrote:

> When I returned to Manila in mid-February, 1974, Elisalde reported that Panamin had received numerous requests to visit the Tasaday from journalists and others, notably Christian missionaries. 'Man, you ought to hear them' he said. 'The missionaries want to give the Tasaday a chance to be saved from eternal damnation.' Logging companies wrote a letter proposing cutting only the largest trees so smaller growths would thrive; the cut timber would be used to build a school and community center for the Tasaday, and, if there just happened to be any cut wood left, the loggers would be willing to remove it from the forest. The whole operation, said the letter writer, a former congressman, was to help the nation's tribal brothers. An American psychiatrist proposed bringing two Tasaday children out of the forest and raising them in the United States to demonstrate the universal qualities of man.

At least several million people in the forests of Amazonia, Central Africa, and Southeast Asia live in conditions in which material levels are not much higher than those among the Tasaday. Their existence is precarious in two senses. Firstly they depend very much on an unpredictable environment for food and other things consumed. Secondly they constantly face the danger of elimination by or integration with more sophisticated people.

In the late nineteenth century the simple Indian societies of the Amazon region of South America were exploited during the search for wild rubber in that region. In the 1970s the Brazilian Amazon Indians have again come under threat as roads have been built into previously inaccessible areas. Brazilians from the southeast of the country have sought natural resources and settlers from the crowded northeast have been moved into the area. The fate of the Amazon Indians could be elimination through diseases from outside, relegation to reservations or integration with population from other parts of Brazil. Brooks (1973) appropriately entitles an article in *The Geographical Magazine* 'Twilight of Brazilian Tribes'. The accompanying caption is 'People in the path of progress'.

If it is only a matter of decades before the simplest kinds of society disappear altogether, the prospect for the rural poor in the agricultural sector of the poor countries of the world seems different. About two-thirds of the total population of the developing countries is in the agricultural sector. A rural family usually has a dwelling with only one or two rooms. Diet is minimal, often inadequate, and often deficient in quality. Little energy is consumed. Educational and health facilities are limited. The opportunity to travel is very restricted. The following descriptions of conditions in Haiti in the late 1940s are now of some historical interest since they are from the first report ever produced by the United Nations on a developing country (United Nations, 1949). Rural poverty in developing countries varies in detail from country to country but the scene in Haiti is reasonably representative.

> Studies made of family income in the Plaisance region in the north of Haiti, in the Marbial Valley in the south, and elsewhere show that the cash income of the average peasant is next to negligible and the level of subsistence extremely low on the whole, the family income being barely sufficient to meet even rudimentary requirements of food, clothing and shelter.
>
> The majority of the rural population and a large part also of the people living in the towns show signs of under-nourishment and a poorly balanced diet. We observed some variations in the consumption of milk and proteins as between regions, but even in the areas where the food intake seemed higher than the average a substantial proportion of the people were apparently under-fed or ill-fed.
>
> Rural housing in particular is quite primitive and generally inadequate. The government has received technical advice from a United States expert who in October 1948 wrote:
>
>> The family has limited resources with which to rent a home, let alone buy a house. Consequently, it has been the tradition over more than 100 years for most Haitians of low income to build their own homes. The typical house consists of a single room, usually with less than 100 square feet, bare dirt floor, wood frame construction, woven clay mixed with grass (not unlike the adobe walls found in the southwestern United States and Mexico) and a thatched roof. The homes have no sanitary facilities or running water. The cooking is done on the ground outside over a metal brazier and charcoal fire. A handmade bed, chair, chest, counter and metal eating utensils are all one usually finds inside. The more fortunate families have a

community privy nearby. The land is frequently rented from a large land owner. Sometimes a plot of ground is handed down from father to son and is owned outright and sometimes the dwelling or shack is built on public property. Thousands upon thousands of Haitian families in urban as well as rural areas live in this fashion. Generations have lived in this same way.'

The plight of an increasing number of people living in very restricted material conditions in towns in the developing world has perhaps received more publicity in developed countries than the poor rural conditions described above. The urban poor live both in slum areas with low rents and in poor conditions, often in the central parts of towns, and in squatter settlements or shanty towns on unclaimed land, in housing they themselves build and gradually improve. Massive migration from rural to urban areas in many parts of Latin America, Africa, and Asia has put pressure on the housing and services of developing world towns in the last few decades.

Plates 2.2-2.5 show scenes in Peru. Living conditions in the rural settlements of the Andes can be very harsh and precarious. Steep slopes are widely cultivated, soil erosion is common, and rainfall unreliable. For some decades now, large numbers of people have moved from the rural areas of the country to seek employment in the larger towns, especially the national capital, Lima. Here a small, comparatively well-off middle and upper class minority has been increasingly swamped out by newcomers. The shanty towns of Lima are among the most studied in the world. The poor here live in close contact with the rich, many of them actually as domestic servants.

Peru is by no means near the lowest end of the world poverty scale. One of the poorest areas of the world is Bengal, as it apparently was in Adam Smith's day. Calcutta is both very large and very poor. The following lines by Chatterjee (1976) outline some aspects of conditions in Calcutta:

Any number of variables can be used to indicate the magnitude of the problem. For example, a density of 400 to 760 persons per acre (0.4 hectares) in the central part of the city implies an enormous overcrowding, expecially in the light of the low-rise housing found in Calcutta. Such densities place great demands on the provision of urban services such as water, sanitation, utilities, and transport. We consequently find that 79 per cent of the families live in a single room, 1.8 million people live in slums, 61 per cent have no bathrooms, 30-50 persons share a single latrine, and 62 per cent have no regular water supply. Much of this can be attributed to the fact that 66 per cent of

Plate 2.2 The village of Chacayan in the Central Andes of Peru. Virtually everyone is engaged full or part time in agriculture. Cultivation on partly terraced slopes is difficult and links with the rest of the country are on rough roads. The more affluent villagers replace their thatched roofs with corrugated iron

Plate 2.3 A mud-brick dwelling, typical of the Andes of South America, has no windows and few comforts. Behind are steep, partly terraced slopes. Ground sloping as much as 30° is cultivated

Plate 2.4 The home of a well-off family in Ica, a town in the coastal region of Peru. In most developing world countries a small portion of the population lives in comparative luxury, often with servants as well as gadgets associated with a life-style prevalent in developed countries

Plate 2.5 An increasing number of people live in squatters' settlements in and around the larger towns of the developing world. A temporary home in the desert outside Lima, capital of Peru, illustrates conditions

the families have less than $28.00 income (approximately Rs 200) per month. Poverty combines with poor management to create some of the worst living conditions anywhere in the world.

While the mass of the population in developing countries has a very low level of consumption of goods and services, in some a minority has living standards comparable with those of the average West European or American. In Latin American countries in particular the well-off 5-10 per cent, landowners, professional people, some skilled workers, form outposts of developed countries in the sense that they have many of the material benefits associated with industrial countries. The idea of 'two nations' is conveyed in the words of Ullman (1960):

> In some cases, as in India, one has an impression of two worlds — (1) the great cities with education, libraries, utilities, etc. connected with each other by strategic transport, but floating like islands in (2) a vast sea of rural villages without schools and facilities of any kind.

Plate 2.6 (Opposite) Ethiopia is among the lowest ranked countries on many scales of development. Conditions in rural Ethiopia are generally poorer than those in rural Peru, one of the more developed of the developing countries. A village in North-Central Ethiopia typifies minimum living standards. Food is generally short, wood for fuel comes from rapidly disappearing woodland and scrub. Pastures are overgrazed

Plate 2.7 An Ethiopian child in the Simian Mountains stands on a piece of land where rocks cover much of the surface and any attempt to mechanize agriculture would be futile. The child probably has no other clothing

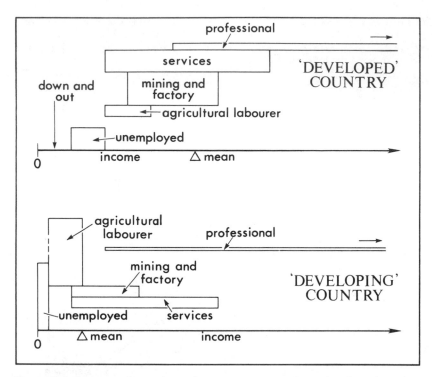

Figure 2.1 A comparison of employment structure in a 'developed' and a 'developing' country. Each rectangle is roughly proportional to the number of persons engaged in each economic activity. The horizontal scale measures their income

He does not refer here to the numerous urban poor, on whom the urban rich also 'float'.

   An imbalance between the numbers of rich and poor also exists in developed countries, but the people defined as poor are usually a small minority. It is hardly desirable to be poor in an affluent country, but the material levels of such people are nowhere as low as those of the poor in developing countries. The diagrams in Figure 2.1 help to describe and explain the difference between developed and developing countries. The horizontal axis represents level of income. Since one's income depends very much on the type of employment in any country, developed or developing, socialist or with a market economy, employment structure gives some indication of the distribution of income. A developing country tends to have a very large number of people engaged in agriculture or in the poorly remunerated end of the service sector. In a developed country it is difficult to exist at an excessively low level and the welfare net is likely to catch anyone who tries, though a number of people do slip through it. Poverty is defined at a much higher level than in developing countries, where indeed it may just be ignored.

Towards the end of the Second World War conditions were becoming desperate for large numbers of people in Europe as food supplies ran out locally. The inmates of Nazi concentration camps were kept at a level of consumption as low as any imaginable, with virtually no personal possessions or personal space. The shock of poverty for a person accustomed to European living standards of the twentieth century was enormous. With the bad times of the Industrial Revolution in the nineteenth century in mind, the economic depression of the interwar period, and the destruction of the World Wars, the developed countries have sought ways to prevent the return of poverty to any sectors of their communities.

Approximately 25 per cent of the population of the world lived in developed countries around 1980. Not everyone in the rest of the world was materially 'poor'. Nevertheless, one can say that while 1100-1200 million people experienced 'high' living standards in 1980, some 3200-3300 million lived in developing countries. Even if only half of these are defined as poor, there are more *poor* in the world in 1980 than the total population of the world in 1880. The relative proportion of poor has declined in the world but the absolute number continues to rise. It is necessary, then, to assess more exactly the ways in which the development gap can be measured.

2.3 Measuring the development gap

In order to assess the scale and nature of the development gap of the 1970s it is necessary to view the world situation in an objective way. Only when numerical values are placed on material production and consumption can the magnitude of the gap be appreciated. Even then, one cannot be entirely objective about the weight to give to different aspects of development.

The following introduction to the idea of the development gap is based on a comparison of four countries. The countries used here are taken out of the context of the study of 60 countries that follows in Chapter 4. Among the larger countries of the world the U.S.A. is the one with the highest average levels of material consumption while Bangladesh is one of the countries with very low levels. On a scale of development, Italy occupies a middle position among the developed group and Thailand a middle position among the developing group.

In Tables 2.1 and 2.2 the four countries are compared with regard to levels of production and consumption of each of 20 selected

Table 2.1 Production per inhabitant of 20 items in four selected countries around 1975. U.S.A. = 100

		U.S.A.	Italy	Thailand	Bangladesh
1	Rice yields	100	110	36	35
2	Maize yields	100	112	46	16
3	Physicians (services provided)	100	124	7	6
4	Nitrogenous fertilizers	100	41	(0)	4
5	Hospital beds (use made)	100	156	18	2
6	Phosphate fertilizers	100	21	0	1
7	Petroleum refining	100	107	6	1
8	Cement	100	212	33	1
9	All energy	100	5	(0)	(0)
10	Electricity generating capacity	100	32	2	(0)
11	Electricity production	100	28	2	(0)
12	Steel	100	78	(0)	(0)
13	Pig iron	100	60	(0)	0
14	Aluminium	100	36	0	0
15	Lead	100	34	0	0
16	Radio receivers	100	57	0	0
17	TV receivers	100	111	0	0
18	Merchant vessels	100	378	0	0
19	Passenger cars	100	77	0	0
20	Commercial vehicles	100	18	0	0

(0), under 0.50.
Main source: various tables in *United Nations Statistical Yearbook 1976*.

items. The original data have been transformed, where necessary, in two ways. Firstly, all values have been expressed in terms of the amount per inhabitant (or per so many inhabitants). Secondly, the value for the U.S.A., per inhabitant, whatever it was originally, has been transformed to 100 units. The three corresponding values for each of the other countries have then likewise been converted to maintain their correct relationship to the U.S. value. In each table the items are arranged in descending order of the ratio of production or consumption in Bangladesh to that in the U.S.A. Thus in Table 2.1, for example, rice yields in the U.S.A. are nearly three times as high as rice yields in Bangladesh (100:35) while the production of nitrogenous fertilizers per inhabitant is about 25 times as high (100:4). Many sectors of industry are not represented in Bangladesh at all.

The data in Tables 2.1 and 2.2 indicate a considerable spread of production and consumption levels among countries rather than two clearcut classes, developed and developing. Bangladesh

Table 2.2 Consumption per inhabitant of 20 items in four selected countries around 1975. U.S.A. = 100

		U.S.A.	Italy	Thailand	Bangladesh
1	Rail passenger/km	100	872	176	58
2	Food consumption	100	96	77	55
3	Protein	100	94	53	38
4	Cotton	100	46	28	6
5	Nitrogenous fertilizers	100	29	4	5
6	Phosphate fertilizers	100	40	7	3
7	Sugar	100	87	30	3
8	Shipping	100	28	6	3
9	Tourism	100	320	38	1
10	Gross domestic product	100	38	5	1
11	Potash fertilizers	100	22	4	1
12	Energy	100	27	3	(0)
13	Tractors	100	77	2	(0)
14	Newsprint	100	11	3	(0)
15	Goods carried by rail	100	5	1	(0)
16	Passenger cars in use	100	51	1	(0)
17	Commercial vehicles in use	100	24	5	(0)
18	Steel	100	58	4	(0)
19	Tin	100	55	3	(0)
20	Telephones	100	37	1	(0)

(0), under 0.50.
Main source: various tables in *United Nations Statistical Yearbook 1976*.

almost invariably lags far behind Thailand, and the gross domestic product 'gap' between the two countries is roughly 5 to 1. Similarly Italy falls a long way behind the U.S.A. in many respects, as would be expected from the gross domestic product gap of 5 to 2. In certain respects, however, Italy actually surpasses the U.S.A., especially with regard to production per inhabitant.

A more critical and striking contrast between an 'average' developed and an 'average' developing country is provided in Table 2.3, in which Italy and Thailand are again compared. Columns (1) and (2) show the respective production or consumption per inhabitant of selected items, in the form of the original data on which the calculations in Tables 2.1 and 2.2 were based. Columns (3) and (4) in Table 2.3 show by how many times consumption or production would have to be raised in Thailand in 1975 and again by 2005 to give that country a standard of living comparable to the 1975 level of Italy. The values in column (3) are the Italian value in column (1) divided by the Thailand value in column (2). Since it is

Table 2.3 Contrasts between Italy and Thailand

		Italy	Thailand	Increase needed to achieve equality with Italy by	
				1975	2005
		(1)	(2)	(3)	(4)
C	Food	3180	2560	1.24	2.5
C	Cotton	3.4	1.1	1.6	3.2
C	Protein	100	56	1.8	3.6
C	Newsprint	4.4	1.3	3.4	6.8
C	Commercial vehicles	28	6	4.7	9.4
C	Potash fertilizers	4.9	0.9	5.5	11.0
C	Phosphate fertilizers	8.8	1.5	5.9	11.8
P	Cement	614	95	6.5	13.0
C	Nitrogenous fertilizers	12.9	1.9	6.8	13.6
	Hospital beds	103	12	8.6	17.2
C	Energy	3010	284	11.6	23.2
P	Electricity	2610	190	13.7	27.4
C	Steel	319	20	16.0	32.0
	Physicians	196	11	17.8	35.6
C	Passenger cars	256	7	36.6	73.2
C	Telephones	259	7	41.5	83.0
P	Energy	480	11	43.6	87.2

C, consumption; P, production.
Main source: various tables in *United Nations Statistical Yearbook 1976*.

assumed that the population of Thailand will roughly double between 1975 and 2005, the value in column (4) is the value in column (3) also doubled, to allow for the expected increase in population. The population pyramids of Thailand and Italy are compared in Figure 2.2. Many of the potential mothers of the next three decades are already alive in Thailand.

The estimate of what Thailand would need to have done in 1975 to reach the level of Italy in 1975 is purely hypothetical. On the other hand the estimate of what Thailand would have to do to reach by 2005 the 1975 levels of an average developed country is of great interest. The magnitude of the task is vividly if only very approximately illustrated by some examples from Table 2.3. About two and a half times as much food would have to be consumed and presumably produced in Thailand in 2005 as in 1975, and three and a half times as much protein. About 25 times as much electricity would have to be generated and energy consumed. There would have to be more than 70 times as many cars in circulation in

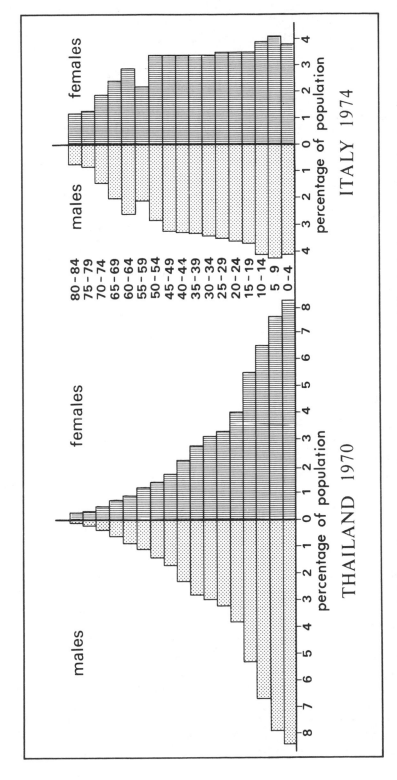

Figure 2.2 A comparison of the population age and sex structure of a typical 'developing' and a typical 'developed' country

Thailand in 30 years' time for the country to be as motorized as Italy was in 1975.

The method used to estimate what roughly Thailand would have to do to 'catch up' with Italy (if it wanted to do so) can be applied to the world as a whole. In 1975 the gross national product per inhabitant in Italy was very roughly $2000. In that year the average for the developing world as a whole was roughly $250. It is assumed for the sake of this exercise that between 1975 and 2005 the population of the developing world will increase by 50 percent. Then for the average gross national product of the developing countries to rise eight times (in constant dollars) and allowing for the increase in population, a twelvefold increase would have to be achieved in the production of goods and services in three decades. As was evident in the Italy-Thailand comparison, some sectors of production would have to be increased far more than 12 times, others, like food production, only about twice. To expect to increase productive capacity in developing countries by 12 times as much in 30 years as has been achieved in thousands of years is to say the least highly ambitious. In practice it is unlikely that the developed countries would be prepared to assist such a process. A major preoccupation of political leaders of developed countries in the 1970s has been how to sustain a high rate of economic growth for themselves. There could be competition for natural resources and capital investment.

2.4   Is the development gap widening?

During the nineteenth century, old empires collapsed and new ones emerged. During that century, however, the growing gap in levels of material production and consumption between the industrial countries of Europe and their colonies was not a matter of great concern to the former. There was more concern about inequality within the industrial countries themselves, the emergence of 'two nations'. Colonies remained underprivileged politically and their economic function was to be a source of food and raw materials. During 1914-1945 the industrial countries were preoccupied with the two World Wars, the Russian Revolution, and the economic depression.

Concern about the world development gap has been widely expressed only since 1945. Ironically, however, in an absolute sense the gap between rich and poor countries in the production and consumption per inhabitant of at least some goods and services has widened more quickly since 1945 than before. One example, the

Table 2.4 Relative and absolute differences in growth

		1945	1945-55	1955	1955-65	1965	1965-75	1975
(a)	Units per inhabitant							
	Country A	100		200		400		800
	Country B	40		100		250		625
	Country C	10		15		30		75
(b)	Relative growth							
	Country A		2.0		2.0		2.0	
	Country B		2.5		2.5		2.5	
	Country C		1.5		2.0		2.5	
(c)	Absolute growth							
	Country A		100		200		400	
	Country B		60		150		375	
	Country C		5		15		45	
(d)	Gap per inhabitant							
	Country A-B	60		100		150		175
	Country A-C	90		185		370		725
	Country B-C	30		85		220		550

consumption of energy, will be used to illustrate the situation. Energy is particularly useful as an indicator of development both because it forms a major part of the economy of all countries and because it remains constant and therefore retains comparability through time (a tonne of coal is a tonne of coal) whereas a dollar or a franc changes in real value.

Before the example of energy is discussed, some thought must be given to the contrasting meanings of relative and absolute growth. Data for three fictitious countries are given in Table 2.4. The data are represented diagrammatically in Figure 2.3.

(a) shows consumption of a given product in four different years for the three countries.

(b) shows the number of times the units consumed per inhabitant have increased each decade. The relative growth has been greater in country B than in country A.

(c) shows the absolute amount gained per inhabitant for each country during each 10-year period. The absolute gain has been greater in country A than in country B.

(d) shows that the *absolute* difference in consumption between countries A and B was greater in 1975 than it was in 1945. Country C lags behind countries A and B by an increasing amount as the years go by.

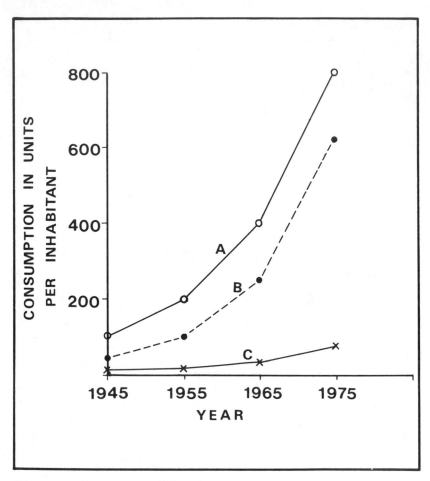

Figure 2.3 Comparative rates of economic growth. See text and Table 2.4 for explanation

The example has shown that while the rate of growth of consumption (or production) per inhabitant can be faster in a poor country than in a rich one, the absolute gap may still be widening. This is what has been happening with regard to world energy consumption. Table 2.5 shows the consumption of energy in kilogrammes of coal equivalent in six selected countries of the world and Figure 2.4 shows the data graphically.

In order to illustrate the situation, Venezuela and the U.S.A. may be compared. Between 1949 and 1976 the consumption of energy per inhabitant in Venezuela increased more than four times whereas in the U.S.A. it increased only by a little more than 50 percent. The absolute gain in Venezuela was, however, only from

640 to 2840, or by 2200 kg, while in the U.S.A. it was from 6920 to 11,560, or by more than 4500 kg. India and Peru both show very much smaller absolute gains than Japan or the U.S.A. From the examples given it can be seen that in absolute terms the energy gap has grown greatly since the Second World War. Further examples of the widening gap between rich and poor countries will be given later in the book.

The implications of the widening of the development gap have given rise, in the view of the author, to three successive appraisals of the world situation. The three views overlap in time. During the 1950s and much of the 1960s, it was widely assumed that eventually the development gap would somehow either close altogether or narrow to 'acceptable' proportions by the poor countries

Table 2.5 Consumption of energy per inhabitant in six selected countries in kilogrammes of coal equivalent

	India	Peru	Venezuela	Japan	U.K.	U.S.A.
1937	90	130	300	930	4280	5890
1949	100	210	640	720	4300	6920
1950	100	190	770	780	4420	7740
1951	100	250	1240	870	4650	7970
1952	110	300	1270	890	4570	7840
1953	110	300	1320	970	4530	7950
1954	110	330	1650	960	4760	7640
1955	120	300	2030	980	4870	7770
1956	130	320	2520	1080	4710	8580
1957	130	300	2590	930	4780	7770
1958	130	320	2520	870	4710	7640
1959	130	320	2500	970	4590	7820
1960	140	490	2620	1170	4910	8050
1961	150	510	2640	1300	4900	8050
1962	160	390	2920	1390	4950	8260
1963	110	580	2720	1530	5090	8510
1964	160	550	2290	1660	5100	8910
1965	170	550	2540	1780	5120	9200
1966	170	610	2460	1940	5090	9620
1967	180	610	2250	2250	4890	9830
1968	190	650	2600	2520	4960	10330
1969	190	620	2150	2830	5140	10770
1970	190	610	2500	3220	5360	11080
1971	190	620	2520	3480	5510	11150
1972	190	600	2480	3570	5350	11620
1973	190	640	2820	3870	5780	11960
1974	200	650	2920	3840	5460	11490
1975	220	680	2640	3620	5270	11000
1976	220	640	2840	3680	5270	11560

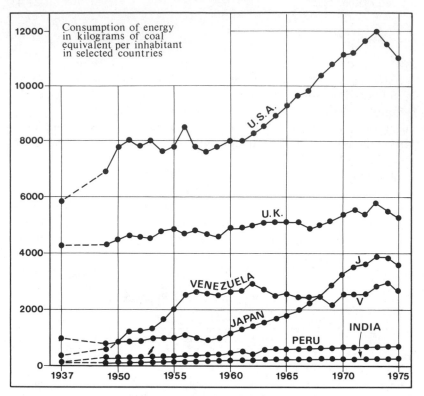

Figure 2.4 Changes in energy consumption per inhabitant between 1937 and 1975 in selected countries

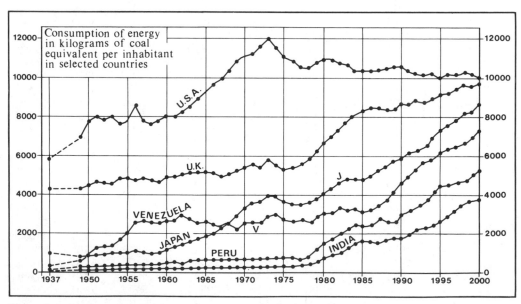

Figure 2.5 A future for energy consumption in which levels in selected countries converge towards the level of the U.S.A. as it was in the 1970s

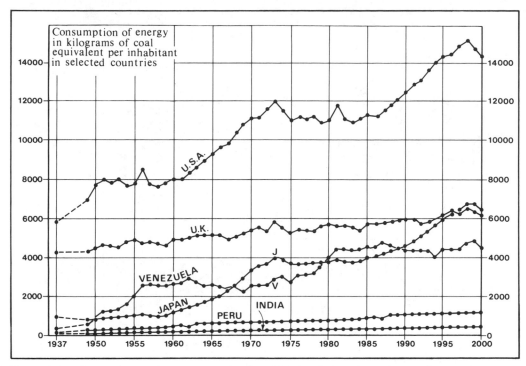

Figure 2.6 A future for energy consumption in which levels in selected countries continue to diverge as they did during the 1950s and 1960s

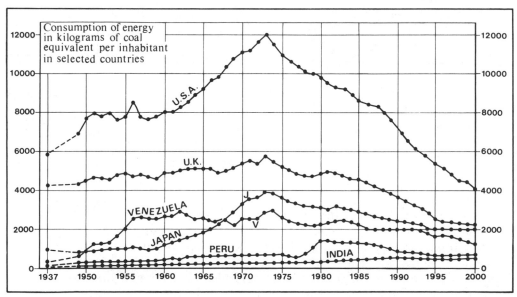

Figure 2.7 A future for energy consumption in which levels in selected countries converge towards the low level of India

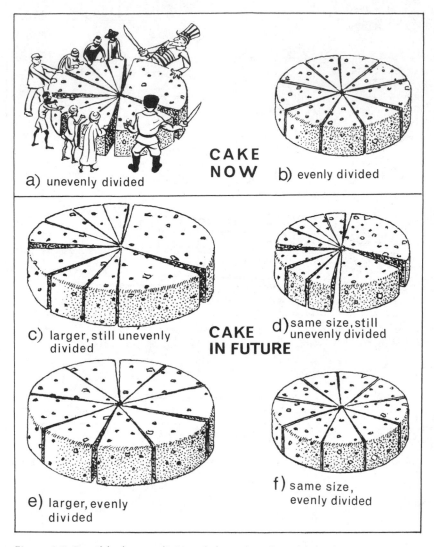

CAKE NOW

a) unevenly divided

b) evenly divided

CAKE IN FUTURE

c) larger, still unevenly divided

d) same size, still unevenly divided

e) larger, evenly divided

f) same size, evenly divided

Figure 2.8 Possible future slicing of the cake of world production

'developing' to the level of the rich. By the late 1960s, however, the magnitude of the gap was being emphasized and the difficulty even of narrowing it, let alone closing it, was stressed. More recently still, especially since the early 1970s, the limited nature of non-renewable natural resources has become widely appreciated, if perhaps overstated by some. The possibility that the development gap might therefore in fact be narrowed, but by a decline in the standards of the rich countries, began to be seriously considered.

The three appraisals of the prospects for the development gap are represented graphically in Figures 2.5-2.7, still using the energy example, as alternative mutually exclusive futures. In Figure 2.5, the country with the highest consumption per inhabitant stays roughly at its 1975 level while the remaining countries converge 'upwards'. In Figure 2.6, it is assumed that the rate of consumption of energy per inhabitant changes in the next 25 years in exactly the same way as it did in the last 25. In this future, divergence between rich and poor countries continues. In Figure 2.7, consumption per inhabitant drops sharply in the period 1975-2000 in the richest countries and convergence takes place 'downwards'.

The prospects for the future may be illustrated by the frequently referred to 'cake' (see Figure 2.8). The analogy may seem flippant but it helps to clarify the main alternatives. Three changes are possible. The world cake, representing the production and consumption of goods and services, may change in size. The way the cake is divided may change. The number of participants at the party may change.

2.5 Six ingredients of development

Social scientists often discuss the world in abstract terms rather than in terms of material objects. Labour resources, financial transactions, and input-output models are valuable terms and concepts. When it comes to actually assessing what material objects can be moved about the world, how far and in what quantities, then a down-to-earth classification of phenomena may also be worth consideration.

The ingredients of development, as perceived by the author, have for convenience been divided into six categories. In fact the classification greatly oversimplifies the real world situation and the categories, as described below, overlap and could also be subdivided. They are referred to throughout the rest of this chapter by the letters A-F; A-D appear also in some of the diagrams in this and the next section.

A. *Human population.*
B. *Natural resources:* parts of the earth's surface and crust from which plant, animal or mineral materials are derived.
C. *Means of production:* man-made instruments of various kinds such as agricultural implements, factories, hospitals from which goods and services are produced.
D. *Products:* goods and services produced.

E. *Links:* since things happen in various places, not just on one
   spot, the movement of goods, people, and information is
   necessary between places.
F. *Organization:* a more abstract aspect, one function of which is
   to ensure that items A-E are integrated.

Each ingredient will now be discussed briefly.

   A. *Population.* Usually one is dealing with subsets of the total
human population of the world when considering a particular
situation or problem. The subset may consist of members defined by
their structural or functional relationship to total population, as for
example male or female, old or young, economically active or
dependent. The subset may on the other hand be a spatial one, such
as all the citizens of California or all the people *in* California (on a
particular day), or the urban population of California. Subsets of
people based on physiological, psychological or cultural
characteristics such as 'race', intelligence or religion tend to be
more difficult to define to everyone's satisfaction than subsets
based on administrative regions.

   B. *Natural resources.* These include:

(i) Soil and water bodies from which plants and animals including
    marine products are derived, either from cultivated land or
    from natural sources such as natural pastures. These are
    sometimes referred to as bioclimatic resources.
(ii) Minerals, which may be subdivided into fossil fuels and non-
    fuel minerals.
(iii) Other items such as hydroelectric power, solar power, and wind
    power not obviously belonging to the first two types.

   The location and extent of the bioclimatic resources of the world
are now broadly known. In contrast, many parts of the world have
not yet been thoroughly explored for minerals and the location and
extent of mineral resources are therefore not fully known.

   The natural resources of type (ii) are non-renewable (or
exhaustible). The fossil fuels are either burnt or, like the non-fuel
minerals, end up as raw materials. In contrast, the items of type (iii)
do not (for practical purposes) run out. Soil and water are not
regarded as non-renewable. When plants are removed from the soil
they in fact take away nutrients from it. A soil to which nutrients are
not returned when plants are removed from it loses fertility. Soil
can also be lost through erosion. The implications of the obvious
but often overlooked fact that soil is exhaustible will be discussed
in more detail later in the book.

   C. *Means of production* are used here to refer to man-made or
man-controlled objects used to produce goods and services. These

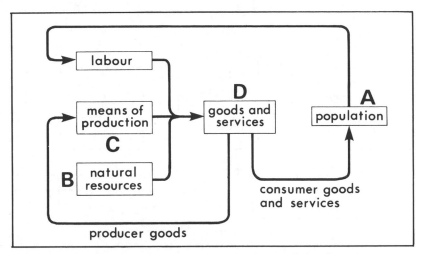

Figure 2.9 Basic relationships between ingredients of development

range from simple implements such as a digging stick or hunter's bow and arrows, to an oil refinery or an airliner. The category may conveniently be extended to include such less obvious means of production as domesticated animals used for draught purposes and buildings used for production purposes as well as the equipment in them. Many of the means of production in the sense defined above started as capital or producer goods, provided by existing means of production. The term means of production is used in the present book rather than the term capital resources.

Items defined as means of production in agriculture by the Food and Agriculture Organisation include agricultural tractors, harvester-threshers, milking machines, pesticides, fungicides, and nitrogen, phosphate and potash fertilizers. Some of the items are manufactured goods in the form of machines while others are simply raw materials that have been processed. Some are used for a long time while others go back into the ground and hopefully into the plants being cultivated. The soil itself is a natural resource.

In the electricity industry the contrast between means of production and products is clearly illustrated by the generating equipment of the power station, measured in capacity of kilowatts or megawatts, and output of electricity, measured in kilowatt hours. The coal or oil used to fire a thermal station is a product on its way to the station but a means of production as it is used up to generate energy.

D. *Products.* In the diagram in Figure 2.9, four 'ingredients' are shown. A subset of population A, the economically active population (or labour), uses natural resources B with the help of

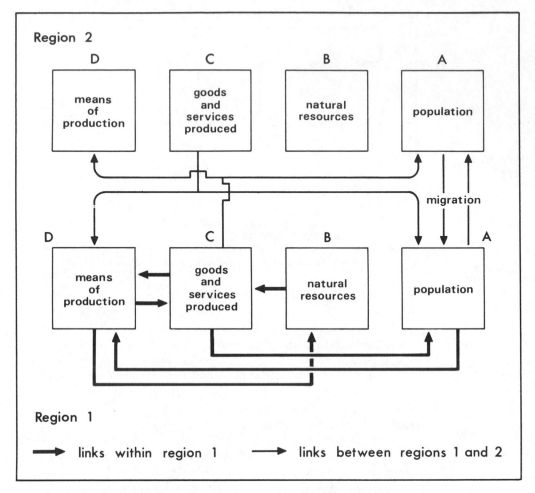

Figure 2.10 Basic relationships between ingredients of development within and between regions

means of production C and produces goods and services (or products). Products may be of two types. Some are capital or producer goods, which are destined to become means of production (category C), while some are consumer goods or services, which are destined to support population (category A). The diagram in Figure 2.9 implies, however, that everything happens in one place. As this is obviously not so, it is necessary to identify another basic category of features.

E. *Links.* Because different things are produced in different places, it is necessary to exchange goods between places. A category is therefore needed to take account of the means of linking places, the system of transportation and communications.

In considering links one should distinguish between channels that link places (railway track, pipeline), the conveyance (train, aircraft), and the things moved (goods, passengers, information). A transportation system may be thought of as a means of producing a service but in the present book it has been separated from category C. The distinction has been made because one of the main themes is the difficulty of redistributing people and products between different regions of the world.

The relationship among categories A-D was indicated diagrammatically in Figure 2.9. A spatial element may be added to the situation with the appearance in Figure 2.10 of two regions, each with ingredients of categories A-D. Various flows are possible between elements in the two regions.

F. *Organization,* the final category, is intended to cover such features as government, planning, and the international bodies that affect man's activities. Decisions made with regard to economic growth are affected both by the spatial layout of international boundaries between countries and by boundaries of internal political units within countries. These barriers may also be included here as part of organization.

2.6   Relationships between the six ingredients

In view of the importance of the six ingredients described in Section 2.5 to an understanding of the development gap it has been considered desirable to examine their relationship more closely. The four categories A-D already illustrated in Figures 2.9 and 2.10 can be further broken down. The result of so doing is seen in Figure 2.11. The picture is complex, but some key relationships can be picked out.

Means of production C are applied at 1 in the diagram in Figure 2.11 to use natural resources. The means of production C themselves are built up and maintained by producer goods 2d from 3a, manufactures. They are operated by the economically active population 2c. A variety of products D are derived from natural resources B, with the help of means of production C.

In the diagram in Figure 2.11, 3a and 3b are critical points. For the sake of simplicity it is assumed that all food, and all services from D, are consumed by population A, while all raw materials move along 2b to 'factories'. In contrast, energy at 3b and manufactures at 3a in D are of two kinds. Some go straight to population as consumer products (e.g. domestic coal and gas, clothing) while some go to means of production C as capital or producer goods

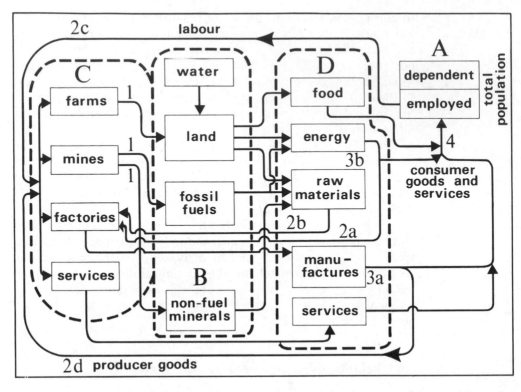

Figure 2.11 A more detailed view of basic ingredients of development, elaborated from the diagram in Figure 2.9. See text for explanation

along 2a and 2d. Part of the producer goods produced in D (manufactures) and flowing along 2d are needed simply to replace and maintain existing productive capacity in C while part will be used to expand capacity. From the situation represented in the diagram in Figure 2.11 two matters will next be briefly considered, the question of economic growth and the relationship of the four ingredients A-D to one another at different periods in history.

In Figure 2.11, the division of the products at 3a between destination A via 4, the consumer, and destination C via 2d, the producer, is critical. Since in the long run it is possible to change the ratio of capital to consumer goods produced, a country in which the inhabitants seem willing (e.g. Japan) or are forced (e.g. the U.S.S.R.) to forgo consumption can concentrate on expanding its means of production more rapidly than one (e.g. the U.K.) in which the expectations of the population are high and government influence on investment is weak. Ownership of the means of production of goods and services is largely in the private sector in

Western industrial countries and most developing countries but in state hands in socialist countries. Government influence on the rate of economic growth is therefore stronger in a socialist than in a non-socialist country.

One way in which the poorer countries might 'catch up' the richer countries would be for them to sustain for a long time a much faster rate of economic growth. Since the Second World War this has not usually happened. Even if it did, the success of the operation would depend on the *efficient* use of investment in the development of the poorer countries. The developing countries also carry the burden of a fast growing population, the existence of which itself requires some economic growth just to keep the level of production per inhabitant from declining.

The gap between developed and developing countries appears to have widened both over a very long period and, as shown in Section 2.4, also over the last few decades. Four levels of technology and society (I-IV), based on broad and not too controversial 'stages' of development, are shown in Table 2.6.

The complexity of our world situation late in the twentieth century arises from the fact that all the four levels identified in Table 2.6 can still be found somewhere in the world. Perhaps a few million people in the Amazon region and in parts of Africa and Southeast Asia still live in pre-agricultural conditions, though their simple ways of life are rapidly being affected by influence from more sophisticated levels. Again, much of the rural, agricultural population of the developing world countries lives in conditions outlined in column II, though again, increasingly, influences are coming from level III. The life style of the population of the developed world and of the affluent sector of urban dwellers of the developing world is outlined in column III.

The world trading system tends to maintain the affluence of the people living at level III, and the gap between developed and developing countries seems to be stable. Only a few developing countries are moving across it. Within the developed world, however, new technologies are being worked out. Pressure on non-renewable natural resources has no doubt been one reason why increasing attention is being given to research, for example, to develop non-exhaustible sources of energy. Competition between industrial countries has also been an incentive to achieve efficiency in various sectors of the economy, one way being by increasing productivity per worker. Automation, talked of at least since the 1950s, becomes increasingly a reality as cheap electronic equipment supplements and replaces the human brain in the same way that the steam engine and other kinds *of* power have

Table 2.6 The relationships through time of the ingredients of development (A-F)

Ingredients	I Pre-agricultural	II Agricultural since several thousand years B.C.	III Industrial (about 1770-)	IV Post-industrial (about 1970-)
A Population	Tens of millions	Hundreds of millions	Thousands of millions	?
	No education	Education largely by imitation	Formal education	
B Natural resources	Gathering plant and animal products from natural environment	Largely plant products from agriculture; some minerals	Land plus mineral resources	Some running out? Substitution, switch to renewable
C Means of production (technology)	Very simple	Some sophisticated but depending on limited help from animals, wind, falling water	Energy and machines help or replace human energy	Machines (electronics) help or replace human brain
D Products	Subsistence	Luxury for the few	Lavish use of materials in products and their use (e.g. car)	Sparing use of materials?
E Links	Not needed	Maintained by human porters, animals, sails, wagons	Capable of moving vast amounts of material over great distances	Regions becoming more self-sufficient?
F Organization	Local	Large areas at times under one control	Much of rest of world 'organized' by Europe until after Second World War	Further fragmentation or present system or increased size (e.g. EEC)

supplemented and replaced human muscle power since the eighteenth century. A fourth 'stage' is tentatively suggested in Table 2.6.

2.7   Different types of region

The model that has been described in Sections 2.5 and 2.6 does not take into account exchanges between different regions. To someone viewing the earth from a very great distance, the world would look like one place and the relationships outlined above might be appreciated while distances between places could reasonably be ignored or overlooked. On the ground, however, the distribution of the various ingedients of development on the earth's surface is, in the view of the author, one of the keys to the development gap.

In this section three actual countries will be used to examine in a preliminary way the implications of transferring the basic ingredients A-D in Figure 2.11, people, natural resources, means of production, and products, between different parts of the world. The quantities of ingredients in the example are expressed only very approximately. In order to illustrate the problem, three countries have been chosen to represent the world situation, the U.K., Bangladesh, and Australia. They are shown in Figure 2.12, not drawn on the same scale.

The U.K. produces enough food to feed about half of its population and expects for a time in the 1980s to produce almost all of its energy needs. It has few non-fuel minerals and the land produces few plant raw materials. About half of its food is imported, as are almost all of the raw materials it uses. In the mid-1970s about half of its energy needs were imported. These items are largely paid for with manufactured goods and services.

Bangladesh usually produces enough food to feed its population, but inadequately. The prospects for extending the area under cultivation are slight but yields could be increased. It has virtually no energy resources and no mineral raw materials. The capacity to produce manufactured goods is very limited.

In relation to its population Australia has a very large area of land that can be cultivated, used as pasture or forested. It has very large energy resources and very large quantities of mineral raw materials. Australia could import all the manufactured goods it needs but in fact it has its own growing manufacturing sector.

The U.K. and Australia both have a high level of technology and high productivity per person employed but in Bangladesh the level

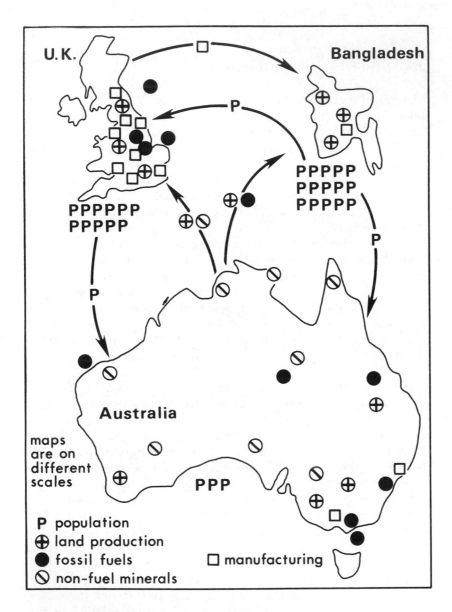

Figure 2.12 Possible transfers of population and of products between three countries, the U.K., Australia, and Bangladesh

is generally very low. Australia, however, has far larger quantities of natural resources per inhabitant than either the U.K. or Bangladesh. In the diagram in Figure 2.12 the symbol P is proportional roughly to five million people. The total natural resources divided by the total population gives the resource/population ratio or balance of a country or region. Each Australian has many times more natural resources to his name than each citizen of the U.K. (Japan, West Germany) or Bangladesh (India, China).

The population of Bangladesh is growing fast while that of Australia is growing fairly slowly and that of the U.K. is almost stationary. Conventional trade is unlikely to change greatly the present differences in living standards between Bangladesh on the one hand and Australia on the other. At the same time, as long as more and more countries like Australia (Argentina, Canada, Brazil) industrialize it will be increasingly difficult for countries like the U.K. (France, Italy, Japan) to obtain food, energy or raw materials to maintain their present standards.

If the present differences in living standards in the world between developing and developed countries cannot be quickly changed by trade, can they be changed by net transfers? If it is assumed that the three countries in the example in Figure 2.12 are under one strong central control and it is planned to achieve equal living standards throughout all three, then it would be possible to organize and enforce the transfer of some combination of the following: people, food, energy, raw materials, manufactured consumer goods, and capital (producer) goods. In Figure 2.12 some transfers are indicated. The U.K. and Bangladesh both send population to Australia. Australia sends energy and food to Bangladesh, food and raw materials to the U.K. The U.K. sends producer goods to Bangladesh. All transfers are net.

As a result of the above transfers living standards would drop in Australia, be maintained in the U.K., and rise in Bangladesh. One might justifiably ask the following questions: are such transfers ever likely to be acceptable to the 'losers' and, even if they were accepted as necessary, could they be implemented? How much of what could be transferred over how long a period? Probably not much. Even the argument that the productive capacity and production of the whole world should be greatly increased (enlarging the 'cake') as soon as possible to the benefit of the world in general ignores the fact that a large part of the population of the world is concentrated in a few very small areas, with few natural resources to hand, with a very low level of technology, or even with neither resources nor technology.

2.8   Why is there a development gap?

Many reasons have been proposed to explain why some parts of the world are more affluent than others. The idea that some populations are more energetic than others, while discredited in some respects, perhaps deserves consideration. The difficulty of settling in and using the resources of some regions on account of harsh climatic conditions will be referred to later. The location of a region in relation to land and sea, trade routes, and other more developed regions must be taken into account in measuring its economic position. This chapter concludes with a further reference to what in the view of the author are the two major influences on the development gap, the ratio of natural resources to population and the level of productivity per inhabitant.

In Table 2.7 selected countries of the world are placed in one of two classes according to the favourability of their resource/population ratio and in one of two classes according to the level of technology available for the production of goods and services. Estimates of the resource/population ratio have been made by the author and are discussed in Chapters 4 and 7. A rough estimate of the level of technology in a country may be obtained from the level of energy consumption per inhabitant and also from the proportion of the economically active population engaged in activities other than agriculture. The four types of country that emerge from the classification, numbered (1)–(4) in Table 2.7, are discussed in turn.

(1) Regions with small populations in relation to their natural resources but with a high productivity per inhabitant. They tend to provide a surplus of food, energy, and/or raw materials for regions in group (2). They have been inhabited until comparatively recently only by a small indigenous population, usually with very low levels of technology, as the aborigines of Australia and the Yakuts of parts of Siberia. Settlement by Europeans has largely been since about 1800.

(2) Regions with a high level of consumption of energy and raw materials per inhabitant but with few reserves of these themselves in relation to population. They obtain food, energy, and/or raw materials from the other three regions, especially from those in group (1) and in parts of group (3).

(3) Regions with a favourable resource/population ratio but with a low level of technology except in a few localities.

(4) Regions with a poor resource/population ratio and a low level of technology generally.

The regions in groups (1) and (2) conventionally form the developed world and the regions in groups (3) and (4) the developing

Table 2.7

| | | Resource/population ratio | |
		Favourable (1)	Unfavourable (2)
	High	Australia Canada Western U.S.A. Siberia (U.S.S.R.) Argentina	West Europe Japan Hong Kong Singapore New England (U.S.A.)
Technology and Productivity		(3)	(4)
	Low	Zaire Amazonia New Guinea	Bangladesh Haiti Ethiopia Northeast Brazil

world. The main criterion for this distinction is the level of technology and productivity per member of the economically active population. From a different viewpoint, however, the regions in groups (1) and (3) may be regarded as undeveloped because their natural resources have been little used, while the regions in groups (2) and (4) may be referred to as overdeveloped in the sense that there are many (too many?) people in relation to the natural resources available.

Differences in level of productivity vary enormously in the world. With tractors and other equipment, a North American or Australian farmer is able to farm fifty to a hundred times as much land as a farmer in parts of China using hand implements and perhaps some draught animals. Such disparities in productivity per worker can also be found in industry. In a comparison of a Japanese commercial motor vehicles plant with a Chinese one, it was estimated that in the late 1970s a given number of workers in the Japanese plant produced about fifty times as many vehicles in a given period as the same number of their Chinese counterparts.

As pointed out in Chapter 1, differences in productivity may be attributed to the quality or accessibility of natural resources rather than to the level of mechanization used in production. In the coalmining industry of the U.K., for the same hours and with similar equipment, a Nottinghamshire or Yorkshire miner gets out of the ground about twice as much coal per shift as a Welsh or Scottish miner. Such disparity is also found between coalmines in western and eastern U.S.A., and between Kuzbass and Donbass coalfields in the U.S.S.R. A high level of mechanization is used in all the

Plate 2.8 Chinese publications available in Western countries have frequently shown illustrations of labour-intensive activities. Cereals are being harvested by hand. The introduction of a few machines would put many people out of work. 'Many hands (or Hans) make light work' could be a Chinese proverb. Source: *China Pictorial*, 1970, No. 9, p. 9 (Peking). (Reproduced by permission of *China Pictorial*)

Plate 2.9 When it comes to extracting oil, any amount of hand labour is useless. China has high technology alongside simple technology. The productivity gap between workers is enormous. Source: *Chinese Pictorial,* 1974, No. 2, p. 6. (Reproduced by permission of *China Pictorial*)

coalfields mentioned so the difference in productivity per worker arises not for technological reasons but for geological ones. The coal reserves in some coalfields are found in thicker seams than in others, and in seams that are less folded, faulted or dipping. For the same labour and machine inputs, more coal can therefore be extracted in some coalfields of the world than in others.

3

Variations in development at local and regional levels

3.1 Introduction

The main aim of the present book is to examine differences in level of development in different parts of the world as a whole. It was felt, however, that some examples of inequality within countries should be included. Very marked regional differences in living standards are found in most countries of the world. When the magnitude of these internal differences is appreciated the world problem can be seen in better perspective.

In this chapter the term local refers to individual communities such as villages, or groups of villages, in low-level political units such as parishes or communes. The term regional refers to larger parts of a single country such as states in the U.S.A. Given the great differences in size of the countries of the world, local and regional scales refer to units of vastly different areal extent in different countries. For example some *municipios* in the Amazon region of Brazil, equivalent to local government areas in England, are larger in area than the *whole* of England itself. The political and administrative units into which the world is divided may be seen as a massive hierarchy, a minute portion of which is illustrated in Figure 3.1, with some Italian examples. Level III, that of sovereign states, is the key level because below that level international influence does not intrude.

In this chapter a number of examples of spatial differences in development and standard of living within sovereign states are mapped and discussed. No attempt is made to provide a full explanation of variations since each area studied is taken out of its regional or national context. Examples have been taken from three developing market economy countries, Peru, Brazil, and Mexico,

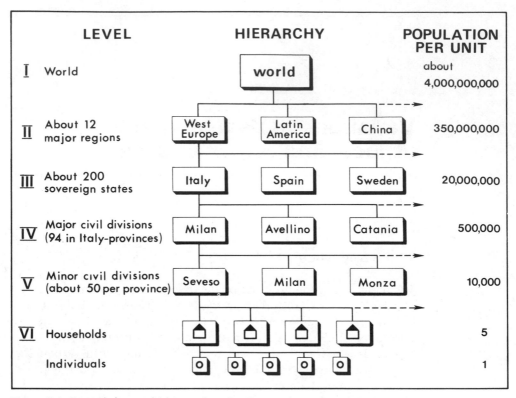

LEVEL		HIERARCHY		POPULATION PER UNIT
I	World	**world**		about 4,000,000,000
II	About 12 major regions	West Europe · Latin America · China		350,000,000
III	About 200 sovereign states	Italy · Spain · Sweden		20,000,000
IV	Major civil divisions (94 in Italy-provinces)	Milan · Avellino · Catania		500,000
V	Minor civil divisions (about 50 per province)	Seveso · Milan · Monza		10,000
VI	Households			5
	Individuals			1

Figure 3.1 Part of the world hierarchy of politico-administrative units

from two developed market economy countries, Italy and the U.S.A., and from one centrally planned or socialist economy, the U.S.S.R.

Since the Second World War much has been published on inequalities both within and between countries. These are to some extent different situations. There is no coordinating body with political power to redistribute population or income among countries. Within many countries, on the other hand, some effort is made by national governments to reduce regional inequalities that may have developed as result of market forces. Ullman (1960) points out:

> Some characteristics of political units also favor the equal spread of opportunity; this is one reason why national states have considerable validity as units of measurement. Common schools, roads, armies, markets, services of all kinds, relative freedom to migrate, and subsidy to the poorer regions, are all features of political area and work powerfully to even out the

differences, although many remain and are even accentuated
... in spite of this political uniformity.

One of the key studies of internal inequalities is by Williamson
(1968). His broad thesis, supported reasonably well by empirical
evidence, is that regional disparities in living standards are small in
very poor countries. As a country 'develops', some regions become
more affluent than others. Finally, when the overall production of
goods and services is very high, the poorer regions tend to catch up.
Coates *et al.* (1977) have gathered material on regional problems
and policies in many countries and Gilbert (1976) has edited a series
of studies on the subject. These may be consulted for a fuller
account of regional inequalities. Whether or not the world as a
whole will follow the expected path of an individual country
through the stages proposed by Williamson is a matter the reader
may like to speculate about.

3.2   Regional inequality at different scales

One of the principal methodological problems in the study of
spatial data is the possibility that the way a given distribution is
perceived and interpreted may be affected by the fineness of
regionalization at which it is represented. The finer the network of
units imposed on an area and the greater the detail used in studying
it, the greater the regional and local differences observed. This
problem was referred to in Chapter 1. It will be exemplified by two
cases from the real world in this section.

Very marked differences in educational standards are shown by
data from the 1940 census of Peru, mapped in Figure 3.2. The data
show the proportion of persons in central Peru over the age of 15
who had received at least some formal education. Each number is
placed in the district it represents. A remarkable feature of
development is revealed by the map. In 1940 there were some
districts in which virtually everyone had received some formal
education and others in which virtually no one had. Thus in part of
one developing country in 1940 it was possible to find almost as
great extremes in levels of elementary education as could occur in
the world as a whole.

The contrasts in central Peru shown to exist in 1940 can be
explained through the combination of a number of influences.
Towns tended to be better equipped than adjacent rural areas (the
big numbers are in the larger towns). The coastal zone was both
richer and more accessible to outside influences than the Andes

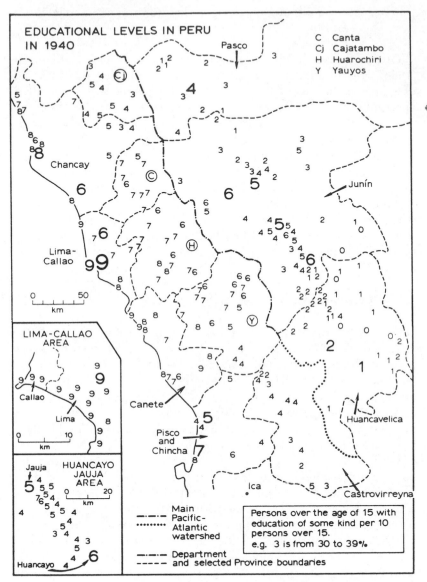

Figure 3.2 Variations in educational levels in Peru in 1940. Source: *Censo Nacional de Población y Ocupación de 1940,* various Department volumes, Dirección Nacional de Estadística, Lima, 1944

and interior lowlands. Innovations have tended to spread particularly from the capital, Lima, which is located on one side of the region studied. In parts of the Andes, Indian languages were still widely spoken and educational levels lagged there. Though such influences are still at work, by the 1970s, as a result of various

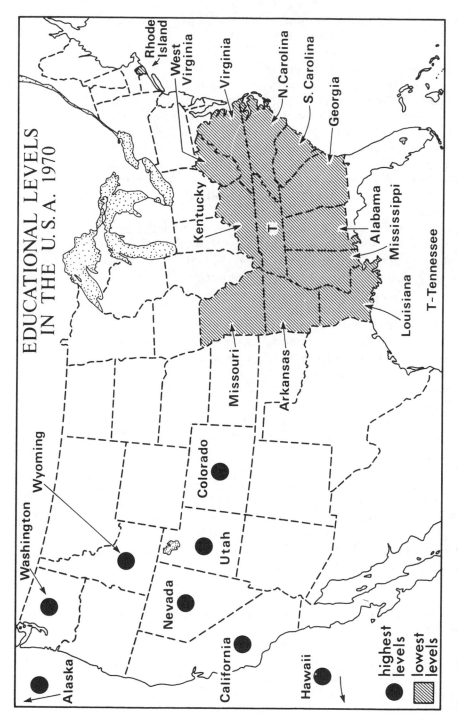

Figure 3.3 Variations in educational levels in the U.S.A. in 1970. The map shows the states with the highest and the lowest levels of high school attendance. Source: *Statistical Abstract of the United States*, Bureau of the Census, Washington, 1976, p. 126, Table 205

programmes to make elementary education more widely available, disparities between the coastal region and the Andes had been reduced, though not eliminated.

Some problems of spatial grouping or aggregation can be illustrated by the above example from Peru. At district (*distrito*) level one can find a range from over 90 percent of the population with some education in the Lima area to under 5 percent (expressed as 0) in parts of Junín and Huancavelica. When data for all the *distritos* in the provinces of Lima and of Huancavelica are aggregated, the province average for Lima is about 85 percent and that for the Department of Huancavelica about 15 percent. Some convergence has taken place, though the gap is still wide. When the seven provinces of Lima Department (Chancay to Canete) are further aggregated, the average for the Department of Lima drops to about 60 percent, since the Department as a whole contains district values ranging between over 90 percent and under 30 percent. Thus as aggregation proceeds, regional disparities appear to diminish.

The example from Peru in Figure 3.2 covers an area which in 1940 had about 2 million people. The U.S.A. had about 200 million people in 1970 and each state on average about 4 million people. The level of aggregation of information about education in the U.S. example in Figure 3.3 is therefore much greater than for central Peru. Even so, considerable regional disparities occur in the U.S. example. Educational levels tend to be lowest in southeastern U.S.A., the old 'Deep South', and highest in western U.S.A. The lowest scoring 13 and highest scoring eight states are named on the map.

The variable used in Figure 3.3 is high school graduates as a percentage of all school leavers. In 1970 the U.S. mean was 52 percent. South Carolina was the lowest scoring state with only 38 percent, Utah the highest scoring with 67 percent. At the more detailed level of counties there would be disparities within each state and a greater range would be observed between the extreme counties than between the extreme states.

3.3   Variations in literacy and employment in agriculture in three states of Brazil

Among the information published for Brazil at the local level of *município* in the 1970 census are data for the level of literacy and for the proportion of economically active population engaged in agriculture. The first variable reflects reasonably well the general

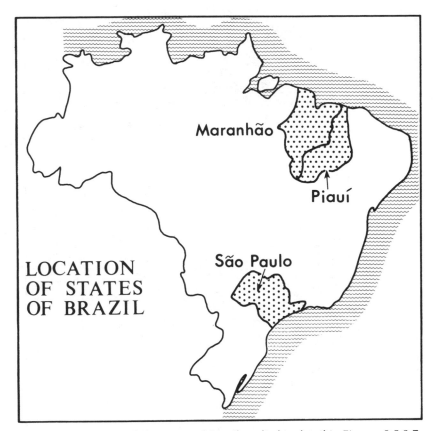

Figure 3.4 Location of the states of Brazil studied in detail in Figures 3.5-3.7

availability of schools in relation to population while the second gives an idea of the degree of change in Brazil from a predominantly rural economy to a predominantly industrial one.

Brazil is a large country in area, roughly comparable in territorial extent to the whole of Europe or to the U.S.A. It is not surprising, therefore, to find large regional variations in both level of literacy and employment in agriculture, as well as in other economic and social aspects of Brazilian life. Two areas of Brazil have been chosen for comparison, the state of São Paulo and the two states of Maranhão and Piauí. Their positions in Brazil are shown in Figure 3.4. São Paulo represents the Southeast region of Brazil, the most highly industrialized and most prosperous part of the country, while Maranhão and Piauí are the most deeply agricultural part of the country and in some respects the poorest. Since the number of local level units, the *municípios,* is very large, being over 500 in São Paulo state alone, groups of *municípios* in micro-regions (*micro-*

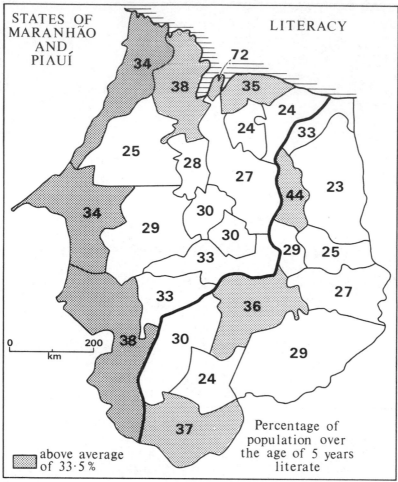

STATES OF MARANHÃO AND PIAUÍ

LITERACY

34
38
72
35
24
24
33
25
28
27
23
34
30
44
29
30
29
25
33
27
33
36
38
30
29
24
37

0   200
km

Percentage of
population over
the age of 5 years
literate

above average
of 33·5%

Figure 3.5 Literacy levels by micro-regions in the states of Maranhão and Piauí, Northeast Brazil. Source: *VIII Recenseamento Geral — 1970,* Serie Regional, volumes for relevant states, Fundaçao IBGE-Instituto Brasileiro de Estatística, Departamento de Censos

região) have been used instead as the base for the data from which the maps have been compiled.

Literate population is defined in the 1970 census of Brazil as population over the age of five able to read and write to a given standard. It seems a little exacting for the youngest age groups involved but is consistent throughout Brazil, so areas are comparable with regard to the literacy percentage. Figure 3.5 shows the percentage of eligible population actually defined as literate in each of the micro-regions of the states of Maranhão and Piauí. The lowest level is only 23 percent while the highest is 72 percent, actually the micro-region containing São Luis, the state capital of Maranhão; the second highest level, 44 percent, is in the capital of Piauí, Teresina. Thus on a local scale large variations are found within the poorest part of Brazil, though they are not so marked as those shown in Peru in 1940.

The average level of literacy is considerably higher in Southeast Brazil than in the Northeast and, as can be seen in Figure 3.6, upper map, only two micro-regions in the state of São Paulo fall below the level of 60 percent while four, including the micro-region with several million people of Greater São Paulo, have over 80 percent of the eligible population literate. Altogether in Brazil as a whole at the level of micro-region one can find extremes from about 20 percent to nearly 100 percent literate though there are small communities in the Amazon region where the level is presumably zero or near zero.

Non-agricultural employment, like literacy, varies greatly from one part of Brazil to another. In most micro-regions of Maranhão and Piauí in Figure 3.7 the percentage of economically active population not engaged in agriculture is between 10 and 20 percent, but the level is 84 percent in São Luis and 54 percent in Teresina. Figure 3.6, lower map, shows that very marked contrasts also occur at micro-region level in São Paulo, though in general the level is much higher than in the Northeast. Only a few percent of the economically active population is engaged in agriculture around São Paulo itself but in the mountainous micro-regions by the coast one still finds a very heavy dependence on it.

The Brazilian example has provided enough data to illustrate two basic features regarding development in developing countries. Firstly, very great regional differences in living standards exist within many developing countries, especially the larger ones. Secondly, it is possible to find within some developing countries, including Brazil, areas which, if separated from the whole country, might qualify as 'developed' countries. If São Paulo state were a separate country it would easily stand comparison with several countries of Europe with regard to level of industrialization and to productivity per worker in all sectors of the economy.

Brazil has been covered at some length in this section in order to illustrate a further point. The country differs so much from one major region to another that in a study of development in the world it hardly seems realistic to treat the country as one unit. In their own ways, other large developing countries such as China, India, Indonesia, Nigeria, and Mexico also vary greatly internally. This fact may not be widely appreciated by people in Europe or North America. Variations in literacy in Mexico will be described briefly in the next section to bear out this point.

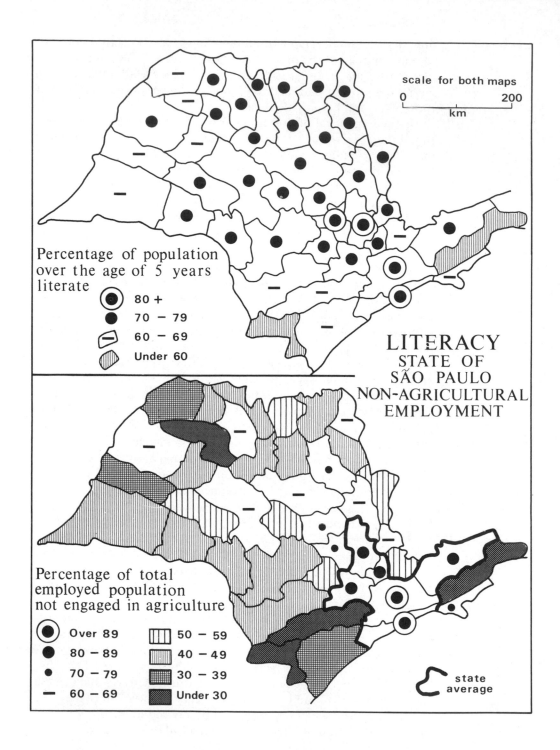

scale for both maps
0 200
km

Percentage of population
over the age of 5 years
literate

- 80 +
- 70 – 79
- 60 – 69
- Under 60

LITERACY
STATE OF
SÃO PAULO
NON-AGRICULTURAL
EMPLOYMENT

Percentage of total
employed population
not engaged in agriculture

- Over 89
- 80 – 89
- 70 – 79
- 60 – 69
- 50 – 59
- 40 – 49
- 30 – 39
- Under 30

state
average

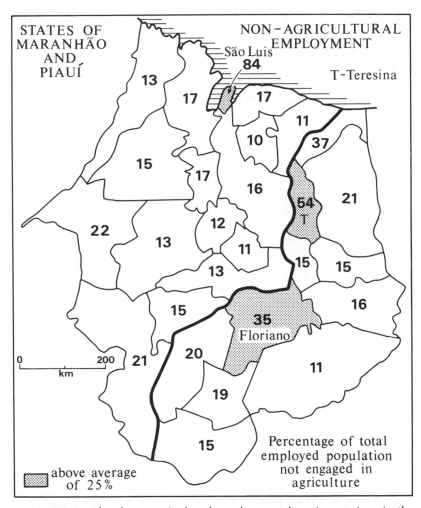

Figure 3.7 Levels of non-agricultural employment by micro-regions in the states of Maranhão and Piauí, Northeast Brazil. Source: *VIII Recenseamento Geral — 1970,* Serie Regional, volumes for relevant states, Fundação IBGE-Instituto Brasileiro de Estatística, Departmento de Censos

Figure 3.6 (Opposite) Literacy levels (upper map) and levels of non-agricultural employment (lower map) by micro-regions in the state of São Paulo, Southeast Brazil. Source: *VIII Recenseamento Geral — 1970,* Serie Regional, volume for state of São Paulo, Fundação IBGE-Instituto Brasileiro de Estatística, Departmento de Censos

3.4   Variations in literacy in two states of Mexico

Mexico consists of 32 *entidades,* of which 29 are states, two are
territories, and one is the Federal District. Two states have been
chosen for consideration, Sonora in the extreme north, adjoining
the U.S.A., and Chiapas in the extreme south, adjoining Guatemala.
The positions of the two states in Mexico are shown in Figure 3.8.
Levels of material development and living standards decline
generally across Mexico from northwest to southeast, though the
national capital, towards the south of the country, stands out above
the general trend.

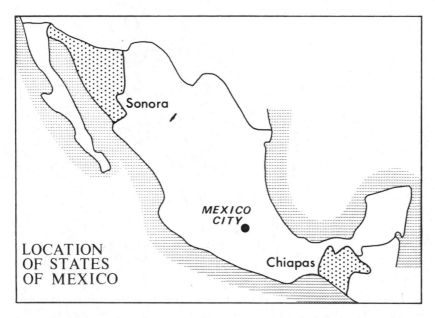

Figure 3.8 Location of the states of Mexico studied in detail in Figures 3.9
and 3.10

According to the 1970 census of Mexico, 76 percent of the
population of 10 years or over was literate in that year. In the state
of Sonora the percentage was 86.4 and in the state of Chiapas it was
only 56.8. Within both states, however, there are considerable
variations from one *municipio* to another. In 1970 Sonora had 69
municipios and Chiapas had 111. The extremes in level of literacy
among the *municipios* of Sonora were 95 percent (Tepache) and 68
percent (Trincheras). The extremes in level of literacy among the
municipios of Chiapas were 85 percent (Mazapa) and 12 percent
(Chalchihuitán).

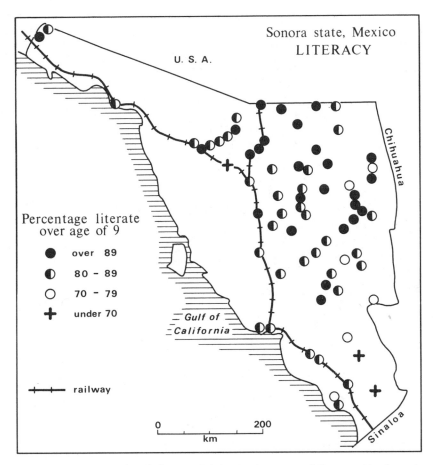

Figure 3.9 Literacy levels by *municipios* in the state of Sonora, Northwest Mexico. Source: *IX Censo General de Población, 1970,* 28 de enero de 1970, Estado de Sonora and Estado de Chiapas, Dirección General de Estadística, Mexico D.F., 1971

Levels of literacy by *municipios* are shown for Sonora and Chiapas in Figures 3.9 and 3.10. The symbols on the two maps form a continuum ranging from over 89 percent literate (solid black circle) to under 30 percent literate ('equals' sign). There is little evidence of concentration of *municipios* with high or low levels of literacy in Sonora though the level does seem to decline somewhat towards the southeast of the state. In Chiapas, on the other hand, the *municipios* with the highest levels of literacy tend to be along the railways or the main road through the state.

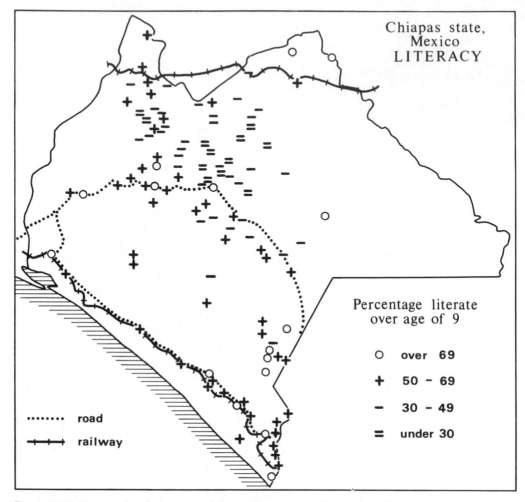

Figure 3.10 Literacy levels by *municipios* in the state of Chiapas, Southern Mexico. Source as for Figure 3.9

It is clear from the Mexican, as from the Brazilian, example that levels of development as measured by literacy can vary greatly within developing countries. In Mexico as a whole one can find *municipios* in which nearly all the population of 10 years or more is literate and *municipios* in which as few at 10-15 percent are literate. To bring the level of literacy all over Mexico to the 90 percent found in the most 'literate' states in a generation (say three decades), the number of primary schools would have to be increased roughly threefold to accomplish the dual task of catering for double the population of schoolchildren and of raising levels in the states with below 90 percent literate.

3.5 Variations in automobile ownership and money income in California and Mississippi, U.S.A.

Disparities in the level of automobile ownership and in money income are examined at county level in two states of the U.S.A., California which is one of the richest states and Mississippi which is the poorest, according to various criteria. The positions of the two states are shown in Figure 3.11.

The ownership of an automobile is considered a necessity by most Americans. Data for the early 1970s show that in some counties of the U.S.A. automobile ownership (*at least* one automobile) was an attribute of well over 90 percent of all households. In other counties the level was as low as 60-65 percent. Such a disparity looks more marked when it is expressed the other way round: in some counties only around 10 percent were without an automobile while in others the proportion without was around 40 percent.

An examination of automobile ownership at county level in the comparatively rich state of California and in the poor state of Mississippi shows considerable variations within each state. The data are mapped in Figure 3.12. The range in Mississippi is from 62.4 percent in Coahoma to 91 percent in Jackson (extreme southeast,

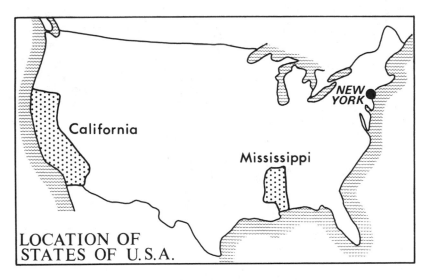

Figure 3.11 Location of the states of the U.S.A. studied in detail in Figures 3.12 and 3.13

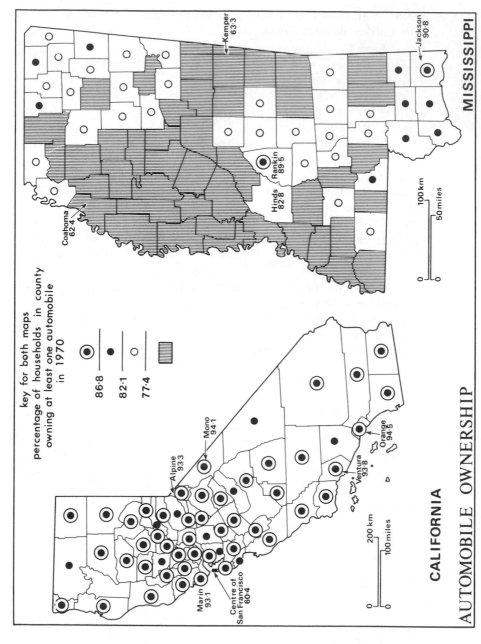

Figure 3.12 Levels of automobile ownership by counties in the states of California and Mississippi, U.S.A., in 1970.
Source: City and County Data Book, 1972, Bureau of the Census, U.S. Department of Commerce, Washington D.C.

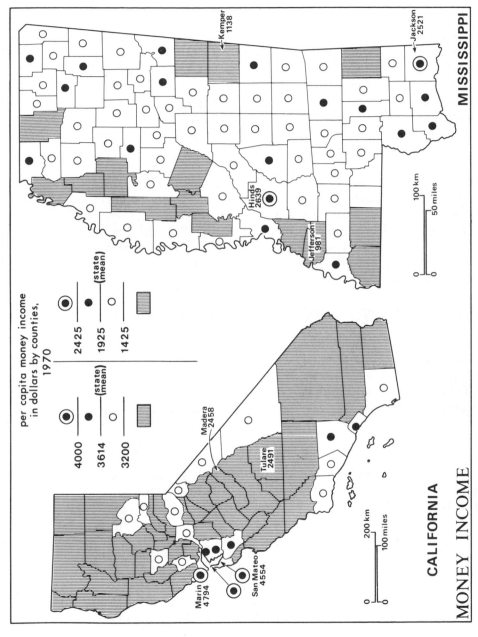

Figure 3.13 Levels of money income by counties in the states of California and Mississippi, U.S.A., in 1970. Source: *City and County Data Book, 1972*, Bureau of the Census, U.S. Department of Commerce, Washington D.C.

but not the state capital, Jackson, which is in Hinds county). In California, all the counties but one (San Francisco Centre itself) had very high levels of automobile ownership.

One might expect the ownership of automobiles in the U.S.A. to be related to income. Figure 3.13 shows the average money income in dollars per inhabitant in California and in Mississippi in 1970. The state means were $3614 and $1925 respectively. The shading scales are therefore different on the two maps. In each state there is a great spread of incomes at county level. In California the extremes are Marin, a suburb of San Francisco, at $4794, and Madera at $2458. In Mississippi the extremes are Hinds at $2639 and Jefferson at $981. The ratio between the richest and poorest counties in California is less than 2 to 1, whereas in the generally much poorer state of Mississippi it is about 2.6 to 1. Relatively speaking, then, the contrast is greater in Mississippi than in California. In absolute terms, however, the difference of about $2340 between Marin and Madera in California is greater than that of about $1660 between Hinds and Jefferson.

3.6   Variations in employment in agriculture in Italy

In 1971, 17.3 percent of the total economically active population of Italy was engaged in agriculture. Data in the 1971 census of Italy for the communes show very large contrasts at this local level. The level of employment in agriculture rises from the northwest of Italy to the southeast. Locally the level is low in and around the large towns.

Three provinces have been chosen to illustrate the great contrasts in employment structure in Italy, Varese in the extreme north of the country and Benevento and Brindisi in the south (see Figure 3.14). The proportions of the economically active population in agriculture in 1971 in the three provinces were: Varese 1.3 percent, Benevento 49.4 percent, Brindisi 50.4 percent. These were the lowest and the two highest for the whole of Italy. When the three provinces are broken down into communes considerable differences can be observed at this local level.

Figure 3.15 shows employment in agriculture in Varese on a commune basis. The province is situated largely in the foothills of the Alps but some areas in the north are very rugged indeed while the southern part extends into the North Italian Lowland. Most of the province is either of little use for cultivation or of poor quality agriculturally. It has never supported a large agricultural population. In the last hundred years, many of the settlements in the southern part of the province have become industrialized. The

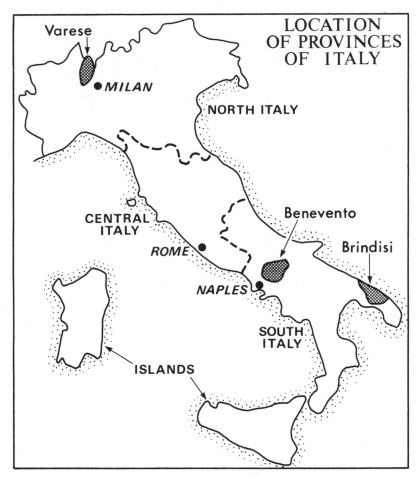

Figure 3.14 Location of the provinces of Italy studied in detail in Figures 3.15 and 3.16

largest concentration of industry in Italy occurs in and to the north of Milan, which is only about 20 km from the southern extremity of Varese province. Thus employment in agriculture has become overshadowed by employment in industry and in services, including tourism. Busto Arsizio and Gallarate are industrial towns. The province of Varese has a smaller percentage of its employed population in agriculture than the least agricultural country in the world, the U.K., and is only about 1/13 the Italian average.

In contrast, about half of the employed population of the provinces of Brindisi and Benevento was still engaged in agriculture in 1971. The communes are mapped in Figure 3.16. In one commune in Benevento the proportion was over 80 percent. Even in the

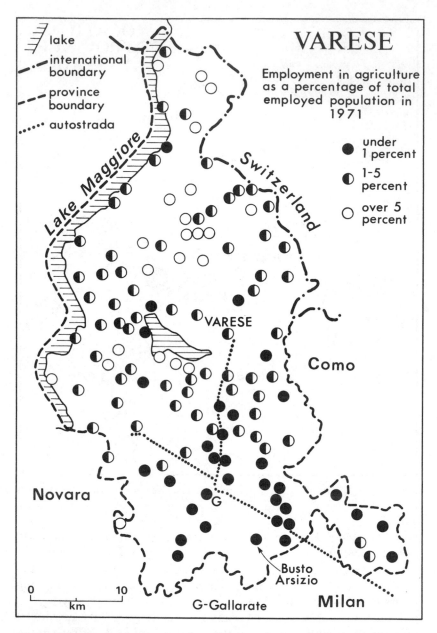

Figure 3.15 Levels of agricultural employment by commune in the province of Varese, North Italy, in 1971. Source: *Il Censimento Generale della Popolazione*, 24 Ottobre 1971, Volume I, *Primi risultati provinciali e comunali sulla popolazione e sulle abitazione*, Istituto Centrale di Statistica, Rome, 1972, p. 65

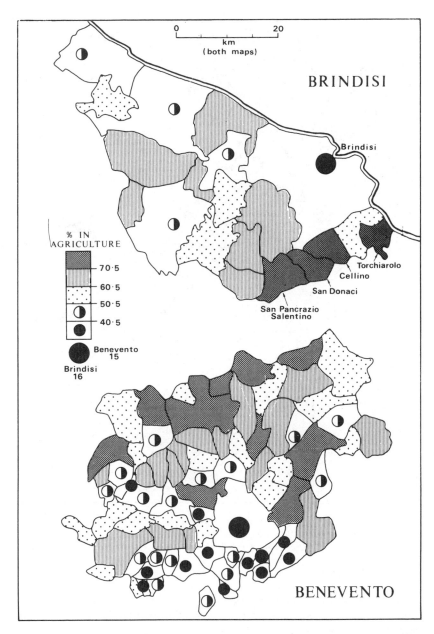

Figure 3.16 Levels of agricultural employment by commune in the provinces of Benevento and Brindisi, South Italy, in 1971. Source: *Il Censimento Generale della Popolazione,* 24 Ottobre 1971, Volume 1, *Primi risultati provinciali e communali sulla popolazione e sulle abitazioni,* Istituto Centrale di Statistica, Rome, 1972, pp. 127, 134-5

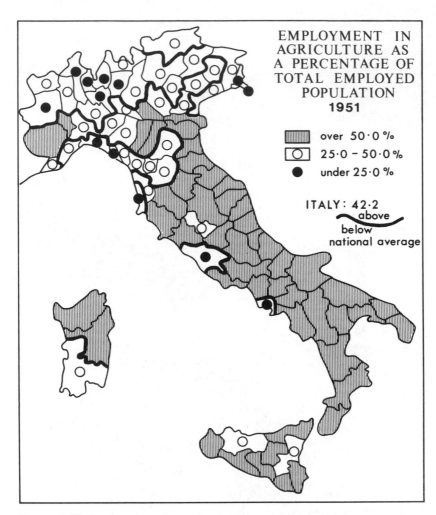

EMPLOYMENT IN
AGRICULTURE AS
A PERCENTAGE OF
TOTAL EMPLOYED
POPULATION
1951

over 50·0 %
25·0 – 50·0%
under 25·0 %

ITALY: 42·2
above
below
national average

Figure 3.17 Percentage of economically active population engaged in agriculture in Italy in 1951 by provinces. Source: *IX Censimento Generale della Popolazione,* 4 Novembre 1951, Volume I, *Date sommari per commune,* Appendice A, 'Dati riassuntivi provinciali', ISTAT, Rome, 1956

communes containing the largest towns, the province capitals of Benevento and Brindisi, a considerable proportion, 15 and 16 percent respectively of the employed population, were in agriculture. In both provinces conditions of soil, slope, and climate are far from ideal for agriculture but some of the crops grown, especially the tree crops in Brindisi, require a large labour force.

The brief review of contrasts in agricultural employment in Italy again shows great differences within a country. The level of employment in agriculture in the most agricultural provinces of Southern Italy is similar to that in many of the 'more developed' developing countries of the world. The gap between extremes in Italy is enormous, one that could hardly be expected to change very quickly, even if a further drastic reduction in agricultural employment is still expected in Italy as a whole.

Italian employment data do in fact permit a comparison of the distributions of agricultural employment in the country in 1951, 1961, and 1971. The proportion of economically active population in agriculture in these years was 42 percent, 29 percent, and 17 percent respectively.

Figure 3.17 shows the large number of provinces still with over half of their employed population in agriculture in 1951. Only 11 remained in 1961 and none in 1971 (see Figures 3.18 and 3.19). By 1971 about half of the provinces had less than a quarter of their employed population in agriculture. The spread of industrialization from the north can be seen clearly with the help of the three maps. The service sector has also absorbed many people during the 20 years under consideration. The data mapped also show that contrasts between north and south appear throughout. Some provinces in the north had, however, fallen behind some in the south and islands by 1971.

3.7 Regional inequality in the U.S.S.R. and in other socialist countries

The doctor gap in part of the U.S.S.R. will be described at some length in this section because the country is defined as socialist. Concern has frequently been expressed over regional disparities in living standards dating from colonial times before the Revolution of 1917. With its centrally planned economy the U.S.S.R. theoretically has the means to reduce regional inequalities. Cole and Harrison (1978) have shown with the help of Soviet data that in practice regional contrasts still occur in the U.S.S.R. in retail sales per inhabitant and in places available in higher educational establishments in relation to potential student population, as well as in the availability of doctors.

The U.S.S.R. is divided into 15 Soviet Socialist Republics. Each corresponds approximately in its territorial extent to one of the main nationalities of the country. By far the largest Republic in the U.S.S.R. is the Russian Soviet Federal Socialist Republic (R.S.F.S.R.). This extends from Leningrad in the west and the Caucasus in the south to the Pacific Ocean in the Soviet Far East. It is populated mainly though not entirely by Russians. In this section, variations in

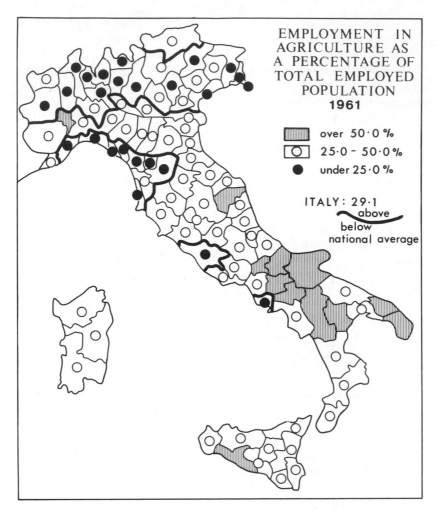

Figure 3.18 Percentage of economically active population engaged in agriculture in Italy in 1961 by provinces. Source: *Annuario di Statistiche Provinciali,* Vol. V — 1963, Istituto Centrale di Statistica, Rome, 1964, pp. 26-7

the availability of doctors in part of the R.S.F.S.R. have been taken to illustrate spatial inequality in a developed socialist country.

The number of doctors per 100,000 inhabitants in each of 53 administrative units of the European part of the R.S.F.S.R. is given in Table 3.1 for 1940, 1960, and 1976. The administrative units consist of 13 Autonomous Soviet Socialist Republics and 40 oblasts, two of them the special city areas of Moscow and Leningrad. The location of the units listed in Table 3.1 is shown in Figure 3.20.

Figure 3.19 Percentage of economically active population engaged in agriculture in Italy in 1971 by provinces. Source: *Annuario di Statistiche Provinciali,* Vol. XIII — 1974, Istituto Centrale di Statistica, Rome, 1974, pp. 30-1

The definition of doctor (*vrach*) in the Soviet Union is a very broad and generous one, and includes persons not fully enough trained to qualify as physicians in many developed Western countries. Thus in 1976 the actual number of doctors per 100,000 inhabitants was much higher in the U.S.S.R. than in West European countries or North America.

The last row of the data in Table 3.1 shows the number of doctors per 100,000 inhabitants in the R.S.F.S.R. as a whole in three years.

Figure 3.20 Location of the oblasts and A.S.S.R.s of the U.S.S.R. studied in detail in Figures 3.21-3.23. See Table 3.1 for key to numbering

Table 3.1 Doctors per 100,000 inhabitants in 1940, 1960, and 1976 in 53 administrative units of the R.S.F.S.R.

	Oblast	1940	1960	1976		Oblast	1940	1960	1976
1	Archangel	67	154	324	28	Belgorod	20	73	231
2	Vologda	34	94	248	29	Voronezh	78	151	312
3	Leningrad City	328	555	754	30	Kursk	49	103	260
4	Leningrad oblast	75	180	286	31	Lipetsk	28	103	243
5	Murmansk	143	295	446	32	Tambov	42	101	216
6	Novgorod	33	120	294	33	Astrakhan	128	294	578
7	Pskov	27	111	278	34	Volgograd	71	199	336
8	Karelian (A)	74	159	397	35	Kuybyshev	81	224	354
9	Komi (A)	81	148	333	36	Penza	35	99	209
10	Bryansk	29	92	227	37	Saratov	104	237	374
11	Vladimir	47	118	274	38	Ulyanovsk	29	102	245
12	Ivanovo	78	192	364	39	Bashkir (A)	32	110	240
13	Kalinin	47	121	299	40	Kalmyk (A)	32	99	287
14	Kaluga	34	108	272	41	Tatar (A)	62	169	286
15	Kostroma	33	101	276	42	Krasnodar	75	172	329
16	Moscow City	417	567	883	43	Stavropol	89	205	357
17	Moscow oblast	84	185	352	44	Rostov	113	190	307
18	Orel	48	82	256	45	Dagestan (A)	57	134	277
19	Ryazan	39	117	342	46	Kabardino-B. (A)	67	147	349
20	Smolensk	58	146	352	47	Severo-Os. (A)	98	288	516
21	Tula	51	117	279	48	Checheno-Ing. (A)	57	149	233
22	Yaroslavl	61	166	371	49	Orenburg	37	127	268
23	Gorky	61	160	322	50	Perm	68	156	303
24	Kirov	32	93	248	51	Sverdlovsk	82	177	309
25	Mariysk (A)	40	102	258	52	Chelyabinsk	59	161	292
26	Mordov (A)	26	77	250	53	Udmurt (A)	44	146	311
27	Chuvash (A)	33	83	226		R.S.F.S.R.	82	186	358

Source for 1960: *Narodnoye khozyaystvo RSFSR v 1962 godu*, pp. 554-5.
Source for 1940 and 1976: *Narodnoye khozyaystvo RSFSR za 60 let*, pp. 279-80.
(A) Autonomous Soviet Socialist Republic.

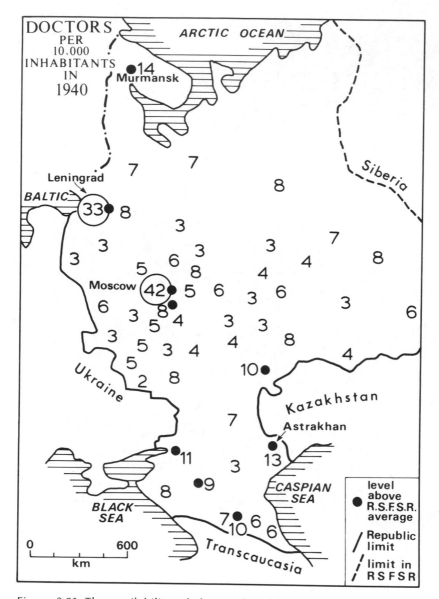

Figure 3.21 The availability of doctors by oblasts and A.S.S.R.s of the European part of the R.S.F.S.R. in 1940. Source: Cole and Harrison (1978) and *Narodnoye khozyaystvo RSFSR,* Moscow, various volumes

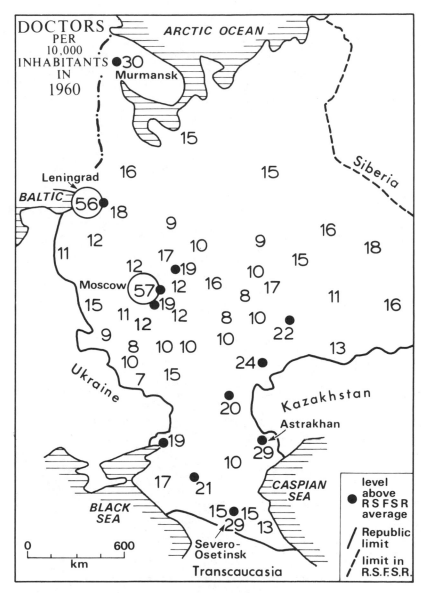

Figure 3.22 The availability of doctors by oblasts and A.S.S.R.s of the European part of the R.S.F.S.R. in 1960. Source: Cole and Harrison (1978) and *Narodnoye khozyaystvo RSFSR*, Moscow, various volumes

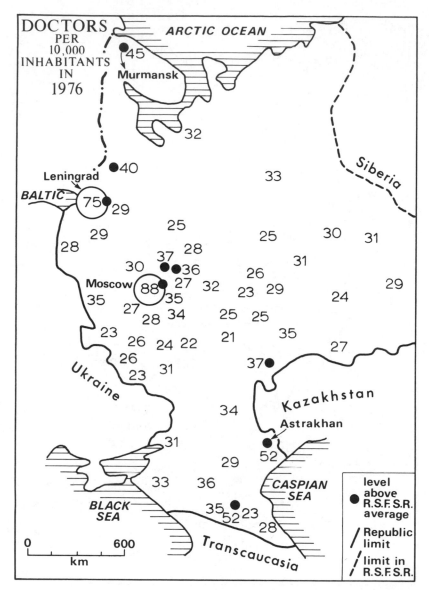

Figure 3.23 The availability of doctors by oblasts and A.S.S.R.s of the European part of the R.S.F.S.R. in 1976. Source: Cole and Harrison (1978) and *Narodnoye khozyaystvo RSFSR,* Moscow, various volumes

The figure is the average for the whole of the Republic, which includes 20 additional units to the east, in the Asiatic part of the R.S.F.S.R. Between 1940 and 1976 the number of doctors per 100,000 inhabitants in the R.S.F.S.R. has increased nearly four and a half times. The absolute number has actually increased by more than this amount because the total population of the R.S.F.S.R. has itself grown. The maps in Figures 3.21-3.23 show regional variations in the availability of doctors in 1940, 1960, and 1976. The number of doctors is given per 10,000 inhabitants, not per 100,000 as in the table.

The maps show that there were large variations in the availability of doctors in European R.S.F.S.R. in all three years. For example in 1976 Moscow City (unit 16) had 883 doctors per 100,000 inhabitants while Tambov (unit 32) only had 216. The inequality cannot be explained or justified entirely through variations in local conditions. On the whole it is the deeply rural oblasts that are most poorly provided with doctors. In theory such areas would need higher indices of doctors to population than urban areas on account of the difficulties of providing services for more scattered populations.

The relative gap between the extremes among the 53 units was narrower in 1976 than in 1940 but the absolute gap was wider. An example will show the arithmetic of the calculation. The number of doctors per 100,000 inhabitants in Moscow City oblast in 1940 was 417 while that in Tambov oblast was 42. There were 10 times as many doctors per population in Moscow as in Tambov in 1940 and the absolute gap was 375. In 1976 the corresponding figures were 883 and 216. There were therefore only about four times as many doctors per population in Moscow as in Tambov in 1976 but an absolute gap of 667.

On the whole the oblasts with the lowest numbers of doctors per population in 1940 had faster rates of increase between 1940 and 1976 than oblasts with the highest numbers in 1940, but this was not sufficient in most cases to narrow the absolute gap, as illustrated by the example of Moscow and Tambov. Thus although detailed study of changes in the ratio of doctors to population shows that the distribution is more even in 1976 than in 1940 the fact remains that the absolute gap is greater.

A comparison of Figures 3.21-3.23 shows that the spatial distribution of the more and the less favoured oblasts has not changed greatly. There are marked concentrations of doctors in Leningrad and Moscow, the two largest urban agglomerations in the whole of the U.S.S.R. Indices are also high in some other oblasts, including Murmansk in the extreme north, where conditions are

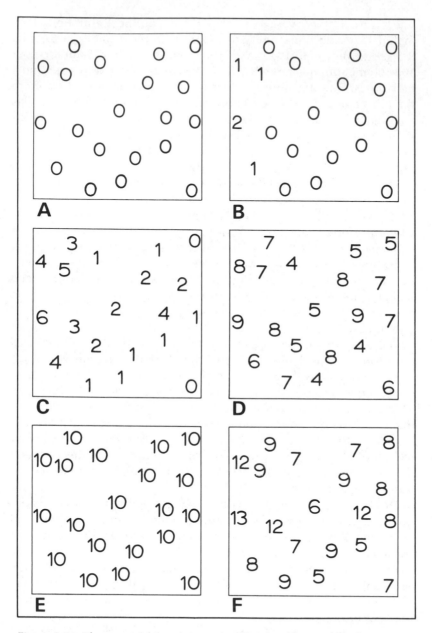

Figure 3.24 The spread of an innovation. See text for explanation

particularly harsh, and the Severo-Osetinsk A.S.S.R. in North Caucasus, an area with many resort towns. Throughout the period 1940-1976 many deeply rural, heavily agricultural oblasts to the south and east of Moscow remained well below the R.S.F.S.R. average for doctors per 100,000 inhabitants. Examples are oblasts 18 (Orel), 28 (Belgorod), and 32 (Tambov).

Regional variations in living standards appear to occur in other socialist countries as well as in the U.S.S.R., though data to illustrate them are not usually readily available. Romania became a socialist country at the end of the Second World War. Previously there were marked regional differences in living standards, the reason being related both to natural conditions and to cultural contrasts. An area in the northwest, for a time part of the Austro-Hungarian Empire, became industrialized and modernized to some extent in the nineteenth and early twentieth centuries. The south and east, long held by Turkey, remained rural and backward. Recent Romanian data show that considerable differences in living standards still exist between different parts of Romania and contrasts can easily be seen between the countryside and towns.

Though China is widely described in the Western press and through other media as being a country where near-equality has been achieved, behind the scenes marked differences in conditions have been noted. The idea that no-one owns a private car and everyone has a bicycle is naïve. Certainly cars are not available for private use, but there are many areas of China in which a bicycle would be useless too. From a serious consideration of regional variations in China it can be deduced that living standards must be much higher for some members of society than for others. Sophisticated factories, coalmines, and oilfields employ highly skilled personnel, especially in the northeast of the country and in ports such as Shanghai. In most rural communes large numbers of people depend almost exclusively on limited land resources to scrape a living. Even here some areas are more favoured than others with regard to such features as fertility of soil, availability of water for irrigation, and ruggedness of terrain.

3.8   Some aspects of regional inequality

A number of situations have been described in this chapter to exemplify regional contrasts in the availability of goods and services and in employment structure. The examples of agricultural employment in Italy and of doctors in part of European U.S.S.R. showed how distributions in a given region may change substantially in a short time. In this section a simple model will be used to summarize some of the features of the distributions discussed in this chapter and others that occur in later chapters.

In a paper that subsequently influenced much further geographical investigation the Swedish geographer Hagerstrand (1952) broke new ground by showing the way innovations had spread over an area of southern Sweden through time. One innovation studied was the spread of the private passenger car from the time early in the twentieth century when only a few were in circulation to a time several decades later when cars were widely used.

The general idea of the process of diffusion shown to occur in southern Sweden has been used in Figure 3.24 to produce a fictitious region with 20 settlements and six situations (A-F). The situations may be regarded as six distinct distributions or they may be taken broadly to represent the spread of an innovation through time from A to E or from A to D and then to F.

Each of the 20 settlements in the region has (for simplicity) 10 households. The values on each of the maps may represent two distinct types of distribution. They may indicate simply the presence or absence of an attribute which each household may or may not possess. Thus, for example, 3 or 8 means that three or eight households out of the total of 10 in a given settlement has a certain possession such as a car or a television set. Maps A-E in Figure 3.24 thus indicate a range between A where no household has the attribute to E where every household has the attribute. On the other hand a rather more complicated situation may be illustrated with maps A-D and map F. Some households may actually have more than one of a certain possession. In North America and Western Europe, for example, many households have one car, many also have no car, but some have two or more cars. Thus in Figure F, where some settlements have more of a given attribute than they have of households, some households must have more than one car. Here 'saturation' has been exceeded. The situations in the model in Figure 3.24 will now be briefly discussed with regard to real world situations that they represent. The letters refer to the six maps A-F in Figure 3.24.

Hagerstrand's diffusion of the car in southern Sweden is represented through time by situations A-D. At time A the car had not been invented. At time B a few families had got the idea of buying a car through contacts in Denmark and Germany to the west. At time C more families in the west had cars than in the east. By time D differences in car ownership from one settlement to another were to be explained in terms of differences in income rather than by the bias of the western side where the innovation first came in. By the 1960s car ownership in southern Sweden was roughly like that in situation F.

The distributions in the three Latin American countries used as examples in this chapter are represented by situations B, C, and D. The availability of education in central Peru in 1940 (Figure 3.2) resembles situation C. Literacy and non-agricultural employment in Brazil (Figures 3.5-3.7) extend from B (without actually any zeros) to D. Literacy in the two states of Mexico (Figures 3.9 and 3.10) is represented in C by the southern state of Chiapas and in D by the northern state of Sonora.

Car ownership by counties in Mississippi (Figure 3.12) is equivalent to situation D, but that in California (Figure 3.13) is closer to E or to F. Situation E is unlikely to be reached anywhere exactly, but with most counties of California having over 90 percent car ownership saturation has been reached over much of the state. On the other hand, if two and three car families are taken into account (as opposed to families with *at least one* car) the situation F may also be said to represent California. If two cars for every family were regarded as saturation, then the scores on E should all be raised from 10 to 20.

The study of agricultural employment in Italy in Figures 3.15-3.19 may be matched with situations in Figure 3.24. The percentage of economically active population in agriculture in Varese (Figure 3.15) is somewhere between C and B while the two southern provinces (Figure 3.16) are equivalent to D. Italy as a whole has been changing in recent decades from D to C.

The distribution of doctors in part of European U.S.S.R. (Figures 3.21-3.23) is similar in 1940 to that in situation D. By 1976 there appears to be an excess of doctors at least in Leningrad and Moscow, even allowing for many to be in special positions such as research, teaching hospitals, and administration. Another, rather dubious, explanation is that people are more prone to illness in the two large cities. The situation therefore has reached that in F, because some regions still appear to be inadequately provided with doctors, at least by Soviet standards.

Many other distributions can be matched approximately to the situations in maps A-F. If situation A represents car ownership in China, where virtually no-one owns a car, then situation E represents literacy in Japan, where, it is claimed, virtually everyone (over a minimum age) is literate. Situation B might represent the availability of colour television in the world around 1970. The world development gap is not in general, however, closely represented by any of the situations A-F in Figure 3.24. In some respects it

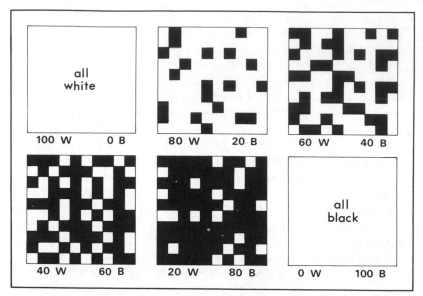

Figure 3.25 The spread of an innovation. See text for explanation

resembles situation C, but mostly with values 0-2 and 8-10 and few intermediate ones. In other respects it resembles situation F, where some places have a superabundance of a given attribute while others do not have enough of it.

This whole chapter has been devoted to illustrating the way in which the inhabitants of some regions have more of a given object or attribute than the inhabitants of other regions. The situations in Figure 3.24 are represented again in a more formal way in Figure 3.25. In the series of diagrams in this figure there are 100 small squares (or areas). If a small square is white it lacks a given attribute. If it is black it possesses that attribute. The spatial aspect of development seems to be about how a region that starts with white (or zeros) all over it ends up with black (or tens) all over it. With 80 white areas and 20 black areas the region looks white with black patches. With 80 black areas and 20 white areas the region looks black with white patches.

While various 'stages' of distribution from all white to all black have been identified in this chapter the situation in many countries is towards one extreme or another. Developing countries are basically white (poor) with a few black (rich) areas. Developed countries are basically black (rich) with a few white (*relatively* poor) areas. Intermediate or 'transition' situations are difficult to find.

When the above analogy is applied to the world as a whole and each country is a single unit then the world is basically white (poor)

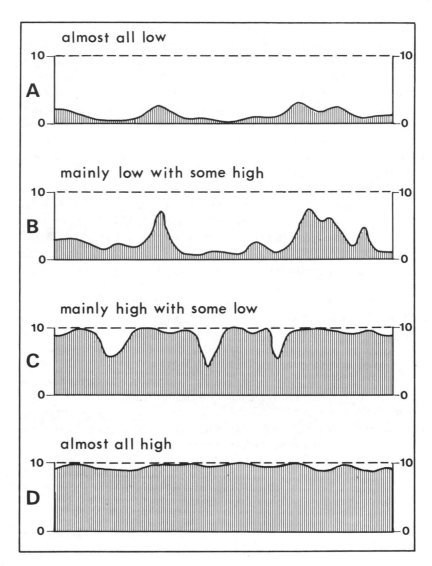

Figure 3.26 The transition from all poor to all rich. Sections across a fictitious region. The vertical scale measures the level of income. See text for further explanation

but with black (rich) patches. It is important that this situation should be appreciated, even if the analogy is a little laboured, heading towards the controversy as to whether a zebra is a white animal with black stripes or a black animal with white stripes.

The matter under consideration in this section may be represented graphically. Figure 3.26 shows four cross sections across fictitious regions. The scales on each section are from 0 (zero) for nothing to 10 for saturation. Situation A is like a country that is poor all over. One finds such countries mainly in Africa and Asia. Situation B is like a country in which there are 'outposts' of development, as in the larger towns of many Latin American countries. Situation C is a generally prosperous country in which, however, 'sinks' of poverty are perceived, perhaps the U.S.A. with its run-down urban centres and rural hillbillies. Situation D is like a Scandinavian country or Australia, in which virtually everywhere is prosperous. The question may again be asked: how can a country or the world as a whole change from being B to being C? Perhaps a sudden change occurs over a short period. The concepts of catastrophe theory (see for example Zeeman (1976)) have not been seriously applied to changes in regional distributions. The rest of the present book is devoted to an examination of the world development gap and the problem of moving from B to C in Figure 3.26.

It seems reasonable to observe at this stage that even on the limited evidence given in this chapter, great regional disparities in living standards exist *within* countries. Government policy in many countries in recent decades has been to reduce existing regional disparities and to prevent further disparities from emerging. Even so, positive results have been limited. It may be inferred that the possibility of reducing inequalities in living standards in the world as a whole is very much more difficult still, both on account of the much greater scale of the world as a single entity and because there is no strong force whose task it is to do so.

4

Variations in development
at international level

4.1 World data based on sovereign states

Since the Second World War a considerable number of studies have
compared countries according to level of development and have
correlated variables considered to cause or reflect development. In
their *Atlas of Economic Development* Ginsburg (1961) and Berry
used multivariate analysis to study a large number of countries on
the basis of various criteria. Russett (1965) and Cole (1979) have
made similar studies.

To some extent the study in this chapter continues the
multivariate approach to regional development data. It was
considered necessary to include such a study here for two reasons.
Through the familiar system of countries it introduces aspects of
development that further on are to be looked at in a completely
new regional framework. In addition it contains information on the
ratio of natural resources to population on a country basis. Such
material is not taken into account in development studies so often
or so fully as levels of production and consumption of goods and
services, though Eyre (1978) has produced his own comprehensive
assessment of natural resources on a country by country basis.

A study of spatial aspects of development on the basis of
sovereign states has advantages and disadvantages. Sovereign
states are a realistic basis for study at a macro-level because the
world economy is largely organized on this basis. Political and
ideological influences are felt through the sovereign state system
and boundaries separate discrete spatial units.

A disadvantage of looking at the development gap through data
based on sovereign states is that these units vary greatly in size,
whether measured according to area, to population, or to total

The development gap

Table 4.1 World data matrix

	(1) Total area	(2) popn.	(3) Area/ popn.	(4) Land use/ popn.	(5) Fossil fuels/ popn.	(6) Minl. matls/ popn.	(7) Employ. % not agri.	(8) % urban	(9) Demographic Popn. grow.	(10) % under 15	(11) Production Energy (kg/ inh.)	(12) Steel (kg/ inh.)	(13) Food intake (cal/ day)	(14) Energy cons. (kg)	(15) Teleph. per 1000	(16) Infant mort.	(17) Life expect. (yr)	(18) GNP($/ inh.)
1 China	9561	838.8	11	4	37	40	37	23	1.7	33	710	35	2170	690	0	55	62	350
2 India	3046	598.1	5	6	5	13	34	20	2.1	40	190	13	2070	220	3	122	50	150
3 U.S.S.R.	22,402	254.4	88	15	473	591	80	60	0.9	28	6490	556	3280	5550	66	16	69	2620
4 U.S.A.	9363	213.6	44	20	340	579	97	74	0.8	27	9360	495	3330	11,000	695	16	72	7060
5 Indonesia	1492	136.0	11	3	22	44	38	18	2.6	44	760	0	1790	180	2	137	48	180
6 Japan	370	111.0	3	1	3	27	86	72	1.2	24	340	922	2510	3620	405	10	74	4460
7 Brazil	8512	107.1	80	5	3	173	59	58	3.0	42	240	78	2620	670	31	82	61	1010
8 Bangladesh	143	76.8	2	2	0	0	15	9	2.4	46	10	1	1840	30	1	132	47	110
9 Pakistan	804	70.3	3	6	1	0	44	26	3.0	46	120	0	2160	180	3	121	51	140
10 Nigeria	924	62.9	15	4	69	24	43	16	2.7	45	2080	0	2270	90	2	180	38	310
11 W. Germany	248	61.8	4	2	137	65	95	88	0.4	23	2680	654	3220	5350	317	20	71	6610
12 Mexico	1973	60.1	33	10	30	150	60	61	3.5	46	1400	86	2580	1220	28	66	63	1190
13 U.K.	244	56.0	4	3	126	54	98	76	0.2	24	3290	361	3190	5270	379	16	72	3840
14 Italy	301	55.8	5	4	6	54	86	53	0.8	24	480	387	3180	3010	259	21	72	2940
15 France	547	52.8	10	8	7	85	89	70	0.8	24	900	408	3210	3940	262	12	72	5760
16 Vietnam	333	45.2	7	3	0	11	27	16	2.9	41	100	0	2340	190	3	100	50	160
17 Philippines	300	42.5	7	5	0	140	51	32	2.9	43	10	0	1940	330	12	74	63	370
18 Thailand	514	41.9	12	7	0	167	23	13	2.9	45	10	0	2560	280	7	89	58	350
19 Turkey	781	39.2	20	13	0	51	40	39	2.4	42	320	37	3250	630	25	93	57	860
20 Egypt	1000	37.2	27	3	14	0	52	43	2.2	41	360	9	2500	410	14	116	52	310
21 Spain	505	35.5	14	10	6	167	79	61	1.0	28	580	313	2600	2150	220	14	72	2700
22 S. Korea	98	34.7	3	3	6	29	57	41	2.1	40	510	58	2520	1040	40	47	65	550
23 Poland	312	34.0	9	7	103	59	66	55	0.9	25	5660	429	3280	5010	75	25	70	2910
24 Iran	1648	33.0	50	5	837	0	58	43	2.9	47	12,930	0	2300	1350	20	139	51	1440
25 Burma	678	31.2	22	9	0	16	45	19	2.5	41	0	0	2210	50	1	126	50	110
26 Ethiopia	1184	27.9	42	7	0	0	19	11	2.6	44	0	0	2160	30	3	181	42	100
27 S. Africa	1223	25.5	48	11	86	1981	71	48	2.5	41	2740	258	2740	2950	78	117	52	1320
28 Argentina	2777	25.4	111	26	33	0	86	81	1.3	29	1640	58	3060	1750	78	59	68	1590
29 Zaire	2345	24.9	94	4	8	1280	24	25	2.8	44	30	0	2060	80	2	160	44	150
30 Colombia	1138	23.5	48	3	12	42	69	64	2.8	46	810	11	2200	670	55	97	61	550

31 Canada	9976	22.8	438	21	161	2783	94	76	1.4	29	11,770	571	3180	9880	572	15	73	6650
32 Yugoslavia	256	21.3	12	7	9	429	58	39	0.9	27	1320	137	3190	1930	61	40	68	1480
33 Romania	238	21.2	11	11	23	0	49	42	1.0	25	3810	450	3140	3800	51	35	69	1300
34 Afghanistan	658	19.3	34	5	0	0	21	15	2.4	44	220	0	1970	50	2	182	40	130
35 Sudan	2506	17.8	141	7	0	0	21	13	2.5	45	0	0	2160	140	3	141	51	290
36 Morocco	444	17.3	26	5	0	529	47	37	2.9	44	50	0	2220	270	10	130	53	470
37 E. Germany	108	16.9	6	5	79	88	89	75	-0.2	23	4800	383	3290	6840	152	16	71	4230
38 Algeria	2382	16.8	142	6	371	29	46	50	3.2	48	4960	11	1730	750	14	142	53	780
39 Peru	1285	15.6	82	6	13	1750	60	60	3.0	44	440	28	2320	680	21	110	56	810
40 Tanzania	937	15.3	61	7	0	0	17	7	2.9	47	0	0	2260	70	4	162	44	170
41 Czechoslo-vakia	128	14.8	9	6	68	0	87	56	0.6	23	5530	968	3180	7150	176	21	71	3710
42 Sri Lanka	66	14.0	5	3	0	0	46	22	2.2	39	10	0	2170	130	5	45	68	150
43 Netherlands	34	13.7	2	3	170	0	94	77	0.8	27	8160	352	3320	5780	368	11	74	5590
44 Australia	7695	13.5	570	67	441	6214	93	86	1.5	29	8230	597	3280	6490	390	16	71	5640
45 Kenya	583	13.4	44	2	0	0	20	10	3.6	46	10	0	2360	170	9	119	50	220
46 Nepal	141	12.6	11	2	0	0	7	4	2.3	40	0	0	2080	10	1	169	44	110
47 Venezuela	912	12.0	76	7	467	417	79	75	2.9	44	16,760	90	2430	2640	53	49	65	2220
48 Malaysia	333	11.9	28	4	60	417	49	27	2.8	44	590	0	2460	560	25	75	63	720
49 Uganda	236	11.5	21	5	0	42	17	8	3.3	44	10	0	2130	60	4	160	50	250
50 Iraq	435	11.1	39	9	736	0	57	61	3.3	48	14,920	0	2050	710	17	99	53	1280
51 Hungary	93	10.5	9	10	35	455	81	49	0.4	20	2260	350	3280	3620	99	33	70	2480
52 Chile	757	10.3	73	7	8	4100	79	76	1.8	39	460	44	2670	770	45	77	63	760
53 Ghana	239	9.9	24	5	0	900	46	29	2.7	47	50	0	2320	180	6	156	48	460
54 Belgium	31	9.8	3	4	0	0	96	87	0.2	23	860	1182	3380	5580	285	16	71	6070
55 Cuba	115	9.5	12	6	0	900	74	50	2.0	37	30	31	2700	1160	32	29	70	800
56 Mozam-bique	783	9.2	85	9	0	0	32	10	2.3	43	50	0	2050	190	6	165	44	310
57 Greece	132	9.0	15	6	13	333	59	53	0.6	25	690	68	3190	2090	221	24	72	2360
58 Saudi Arabia	2149	9.0	258	7	2752	0	37	18	3.0	45	58,900	0	2270	1400	10	152	45	3010
59 Portugal	92	8.8	10	7	0	0	71	26	0.2	28	110	44	2900	980	113	38	69	1610
60 Bulgaria	111	8.7	13	8	45	0	62	59	0.5	22	1720	260	3290	4780	89	23	71	2040

Table 4.2 Sources and definition of variables in Table 4.1

Sources

S1	*United Nations Statistical Yearbook 1976,* New York, 1977.
S2a	*Food and Agriculture Production Yearbook 1974,* Vol.28, Rome, 1975.
S2b	*Food and Agriculture Production Yearbook 1976,* Vol.30, Rome, 1977.
S3	*Mineral Facts and Problems,* Bureau of Mines Bulletin 650, U.S. Department of the Interior, Washington, 1970.
S4a	*1976 World Population Data Sheet,* Population Reference Bureau, Inc., Washington, 1976.
S4b	*1977 World Population Data Sheet,* Popluation Reference Bureau, Inc., Washington, 1977.
S4c	*1975 World Population Data Sheet,* Population Reference Bureau, Inc., Washington, 1975.

Variables

(1)	Area in thousands of square kilometres (S1, Table 18).
(2)	Population in millions (S1, Table 18).
(3)	Square kilometres per 1000 inhabitants (variable (1) divided by variable (2)).
(4)	Potential for producing plant and animal products, i.e. productive land and water, in units per inhabitant (derived from data in S2a, Table 1).
(5)	Fossil fuel (coal, lignite, oil, natural gas) reserves in units per inhabitant (from S1, Tables 50-3). The world average is 100.
(6)	Mineral raw materials (39 items) reserves in units per inhabitant (derived from data in S3). The world average is 100.
(7)	Economically active population in activities other than agriculture as a percentage of total economically active population in 1975 (S2b, Table 3).
(8)	Urban population as a percentage of total population (S4a).
(9)	Annual rate of population growth as a percentage of total population (S1, Table 18).
(10)	Persons under the age of 15 years as a percentage of total population (S4a).
(11)	Production of energy in kilogrammes of coal equivalent per inhabitant in 1975 (S1, table 142).
(12)	Production of steel in kilogrammes per inhabitant in 1975 (S1, Table 172).
(13)	Dietary energy supply in kilocalories per person per day, mid-1970s.
(14)	Consumption of energy in kilogrammes of coal equivalent per inhabitant in 1975 (S1, Table 142).
(15)	Telephones in use per 1000 inhabitants in 1975 (S1, Table 165).
(16)	Infant mortality rate, deaths of infants under the age of one year per 1000 live births, 1975 or near year (S4b).
(17)	Life expectancy at birth in years, mid-1970s (S4b).
(18)	Gross national product in U.S. dollars per inhabitant around 1975 (S4b).

production of goods and services. In development studies and possibly in decisions arising from them, greater attention may therefore be devoted to smaller countries than their population size merits while large ones are given less weight than they deserve. This is because each country tends to be thought of as one unit, regardless of its size.

Table 4.1 is referred to throughout this chapter. It consists of 18 sets of data for the 60 largest countries of the world in population in 1975 excluding Taiwan and North Korea, for which information was considered inadequate. The countries are ranked in the table in descending order of population size. Each variable is defined fully in Table 4.2.

Columns (1) and (2) of data in Table 4.1 show the absolute area and population of the 60 countries. Columns (3)-(18) show data in a form that removes the direct influence of area or population size. Columns (3)-(6) are rough assessments of natural resources per inhabitant. Columns (7)-(18) are selected from demographic and economic variables widely used to measure development.

The methods used to calculate the data in columns (4)-(6) are described in Section 4.3 and more fully in Section 7.1. These three variables, together with variable (3), are used to assess approximately the availability of different kinds of natural resource in each country. Variable (3) simply shows the amount of territory per 1000 inhabitants. It is included on the grounds that, in spite of the concentration of natural resources in small areas of the earth's surface, some credit must be given for sheer areal extent per inhabitant since, all other things being equal, more water, undiscovered minerals, solar and wind power may be expected in a large area than in a small one.

Variable (4) gives productive land units (weighted arable, grazing, and forest land) per population. Fossil fuels and mineral raw materials in columns (5) and (6) are estimates of how much each country has per inhabitant compared with a world average of 100. A score of 0 (zero) indicates that reserves of fossil fuels and/or mineral raw materials appear to be negligible, though in reality there must be some economic minerals in any country.

The remaining sections of this chapter contain a discussion of various sets of variables in Table 4.1 and a final multivariate study in which all are considered together. This section concludes with a brief discussion of the degree of concentration of a number of items of production and consumption in the world as a whole.

Various examples of inequality at local and regional level were given in Chapter 3. As an introduction to inequality at world level a number of gini coefficients of inequality have been calculated for

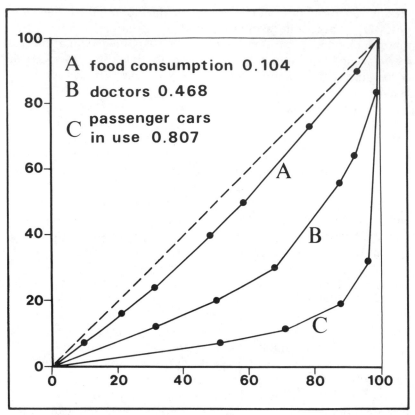

Figure 4.1 Distributions of food consumption, doctors, and passenger cars by selected countries of the world. Note that in this and in other Lorenz curve diagrams the vertical scale measures population

the world as a whole. The gini coefficient is explained in detail in Appendix 1. The basis of the calculation here is to compare the proportion of total world population in a country with the proportion that country produces or consumes of a given item. If every country produced or consumed exactly the same percentage of the world total of a given item as its percentage of total world population then the gini coefficient of concentration would be 0.0. If only one country accounted for all the production or consumption the coefficient would approach 1.00, the index for complete concentration.

Seventeen gini coefficients of concentration have been calculated on the basis of data for countries of the world for selected items of production and consumption. The items are listed in Table 4.3 in ascending order of concentration. The Lorenz curves for three of the variables are shown diagrammatically in Figure 4.1.

Table 4.3 Concentration of production and consumption in the world in 1974, ranked in order of increasing concentration

	Distribution (all are per population)	Gini coefficient
1	Food consumption	0.104
2	Doctors	0.468
3	Hospital beds	0.558
4	Cement production	0.613
5	Gross national product	0.651
6	Steel consumption	0.653
7	Energy consumption	0.665
8	Energy production	0.701
9	Electricity production	0.708
10	Steel production	0.709
11	Television sets in use	0.747
12	Commercial vehicles in use	0.753
13	Newsprint consumption	0.758
14	Telephones in use	0.789
15	Commercial vehicles production	0.806
16	Passenger cars in use	0.807
17	Passenger cars produced	0.811

The data from which the coefficients are calculated are for the 50 largest countries of the world in 1974 (excluding Taiwan and North Korea) and are for that year. The coefficients in the table should be interpreted in a relative rather than an absolute sense since the items studied are not strictly comparable numerically.

From the coefficients in Table 4.3 some tentative conclusions can be drawn. All other things being equal, it may be assumed that the higher the present degree of concentration of something produced or consumed the greater the effort needed to disperse the concentration, if such an effort were ever contemplated. The data show a high degree of concentration of everything except food consumption. Food consumption has to be fairly even throughout the world for obvious biological reasons. The average consumption per inhabitant is only about twice as high in the countries with the highest levels of intake of calories as in those with the lowest (see column (13) in Table 4.1).

The consumption of several items in Table 4.3 is a little less concentrated than production. For example steel production shows a concentration of 0.709 while steel consumption has one of 0.653.

This is the result of the net outflow (export) of steel from countries with a high output per inhabitant (e.g. Japan, Sweden) to countries with a low output per inhabitant or no production at all (e.g. Turkey, Indonesia, virtually all African countries).

The gini coefficient will be used again in Chapters 7 and 8 to show the concentration of natural resources, production, and consumption on the basis of 100 regions each with 1 percent of the total population of the world. In Chapter 11 it will be used to compare the concentration of production and consumption in the world now with concentration over the last 40 years. It will be seen that there have not been marked changes between the 1930s and the 1970s.

4.2   Demographic aspects of development

Table 4.1 in the previous section contains data for 1975, the latest year at the time of writing for which a reasonably complete set could be obtained. In this section use has been made in columns (2)-(4) of Table 4.4 of somewhat more recent data than those in Table 4.1. Four variables related to population have been selected for brief consideration: employment in non-agricultural activities as a percentage of total employed population, annual rate of population increase, proportion of population under the age of 15, and infant mortality. From the larger countries of the world, five have been selected for inclusion in the table to represent the extremes of each variable and five from near the world average. The columns referred to in the rest of this section concern data in Table 4.4.

Column (1). Between Nepal and the U.K. there is an enormous range in the proportion of the economically active population *not* engaged in agriculture. With only 7 percent of its economically active population estimated to be engaged in sectors outside agriculture, Nepal has an employment structure similar to that in Europe at least several centuries ago. In contrast, many industrial countries have over 90 percent of their economically active population in sectors other than agriculture. Even as far back as the early part of the nineteenth century, 75 percent of the economically active population of Britain was outside the agricultural sector.

Column (2). It would take about 40 years from 1978 for the population of the world of 4220 million to double at an annual rate of increase of 1.7 percent per year. Countries such as Mexico and Algeria, with an increase of 3.4 percent per year in the 1970s, can expect their populations to double in about two decades if the trend continues. In contrast, the population of Europe as a whole had an

Plate 4.1 Almost two-thirds of the economically active population of China were still engaged in agriculture in the 1970s. Such a large labour force provides enough people not only to work the land mainly without mechanization but also to be deployed in construction projects like the one above, a water conservancy project. Source: *China Pictorial,* 1974, No. 3, p. 29 (Peking). (Reproduced by permission of *China Pictorial*)

annual rate of increase of about 0.4 percent around 1978 and a doubling rate of near 200 years. Some countries of Europe in the late 1970s had a population that was virtually stable.

Column (3). The proportion of population under the age of 15 is a quick measure of population age structure. A population with a high proportion of its members in young age groups is one that is unstable and likely to go on growing for some time. Many countries of Southwest Asia and Middle America have populations with a large proportion of young people. European countries tend to have the smallest proportion of young people in their populations.

Column (4). Infant mortality measures only the deaths of infants before their first birthday and is therefore only a small part of total mortality. Nevertheless the level closely represents mortality in general and it also reflects the availability or lack of medical services. There is a very great gap between the high level of infant mortality in many African and Asian countries and the low level in Europe, Japan, North America, and Australia.

Table 4.4 The position of extreme and near average countries on four selected demographic variables

(1) Percentage of population not in agriculture		(2) Annual rate of natural increase as percentage		(3) Percentage of population under 15 years		(4) Infant mortality rate per 1000 live births	
U.K.	98	Mexico	3.4	Mali	49	Angola	203
U.S.A.	97	Algeria	3.4	Algeria	48	Niger	200
Belgium	96	Iraq	3.4	Nicaragua	48	Afghanistan	190
W. Germany	94	Kenya	3.3	Jordan	48	Mali	188
Canada	94	Ecuador	3.2	Iran	47	Somalia	177
Yugoslavia	58	Chile	1.8	S. Korea	39	Brazil	109
Iraq	57	S. Korea	1.7	Dominican Rep.	37	Iran	104
S. Korea	57	Sri Lanka	1.7	Cuba	37	Madagascar	102
WORLD	57	WORLD	1.7	WORLD	36	WORLD	99
Egypt	52	Cuba	1.5	Taiwan	35	Dominican Rep.	96
Philippines	51	China	1.4	Puerto Rico	35	Colombia	90
Ethiopia	19	Sweden	0.1	Finland	22	Netherlands	11
Uganda	17	U.K.	0.0	Bulgaria	22	Spain	11
Tanzania	17	Austria	−0.1	Sweden	21	Denmark	10
Bangladesh	15	E. Germany	−0.2	W. Germany	21	Japan	9
Nepal	7	W. Germany	−0.2	Hungary	20	Sweden	9

4.3 Natural resources per population

Columns (3)-(6) in Table 4.1 show the comparative amount of space and natural resources per inhabitant in the 60 largest countries of the world in population. Table 4.5 shows the 10 best and 10 most poorly endowed countries from the lists. The units per inhabitant cannot be compared *across* the table but they may be compared down the columns. The columns referred to in the rest of this section are in Table 4.5.

Column (1). The familiar relationship of population divided by area to give density of population has been expressed here the other way round to give the amount of area, in square kilometres, per 1000 inhabitants. It can be seen that the average Australian or Canadian has two to three hundred times as much space at his disposal as the average Dutchman or Bangladeshi. Much of the area of Australia and Canada is waste, whether hot or cold desert,

Table 4.5 Area and natural resources per population

	(1) Area per population		(2) Usable land per population		(3) Fossil fuels per population		(4) Non-fuel minerals per population	
1	Australia	570	Australia	67	Saudi Arabia	2752	Australia	6214
2	Canada	438	Argentina	26	Iran	837	Chile	4100
3	Saudi Arabia	238	Canada	21	Iraq	736	Canada	2783
4	Algeria	142	U.S.A.	20	U.S.S.R.	473	S. Africa	1981
5	Sudan	141	U.S.S.R.	15	Venezuela	467	Peru	1750
6	Argentina	111	Turkey	13	Australia	441	Zaire	1280
7	Zaire	94	Romania	11	Algeria	371	Cuba	900
8	U.S.S.R.	88	S. Africa	11	U.S.A.	340	Ghana	900
9	Mozambique	85	Spain	10	Netherlands	170	U.S.S.R.	591
10	Brazil	80	Mexico	10	Canada	161	U.S.A.	579
51	Italy	5	S. Korea	3	Bangladesh	0	Bangladesh	0
52	India	5	Egypt	3	Vietnam	0	Pakistan	0
53	W. Germany	4	Vietnam	3	Philippines	0	Egypt	0
54	U.K.	4	U.K.	3	Thailand	0	Iran	0
55	Japan	3	Indonesia	3	Turkey	0	Ethiopia	0
56	Pakistan	3	Kenya	2	Burma	0	Argentina	0
57	S. Korea	3	Nepal	2	Ethiopia	0	Romania	0
58	Belgium	3	W. Germany	2	Afghanistan	0	Afghanistan	0
59	Bangladesh	2	Bangladesh	2	Sudan	0	Sudan	0
60	Netherlands	2	Japan	1	Morocco	0	Tanzania	0

mountain or swamp. Even so, the difference is so great that area in its own right must be counted as an asset. It is interesting to note that the very 'crowded' countries are all in Europe or in South and East Asia.

Column (2). It certainly cannot be argued that large area alone assures a country of large natural resources. The values in column (2) have therefore been calculated to assess productive land area per inhabitant. The units are square kilometres per 1000 inhabitants, but land surface has been weighted according to its use and quality. For example some cultivated land is very fertile (alluvial plains, blackearth soils) or is double or even triple cropped. Other cultivated land is of very poor quality and may only be used periodically. In general the natural pastures of the world provide comparatively little fodder per unit of area compared with good arable land. Forests vary greatly in quality. In assessing the area of land used in each country to produce plants or animals for human use, weight has therefore been given to different types of land. The result of the calculation shows that Australia has at least thirty times as many productive land units per inhabitant as the countries with the smallest amounts. This scale gives a better idea of the availability of useful land per inhabitant than the more extreme scale of total area used in column (1). It shows, nevertheless, that even after the usefulness of the land has been taken into account there are still very marked differences in the world in the quantity per inhabitant.

Column (3). Estimates of the reserves of fossil fuels in each country of the world are published in the *United Nations Statistical Yearbook* under four headings, coal, lignite, oil, and natural gas. Coal and lignite are subdivided according to whether they are commercially accessible. Very roughly, when the four fossil fuels are compared in terms of coal equivalent, it emerges that the proved reserves of coal and lignite in the world are about ten times as great as the proved reserves of oil and natural gas. Oil in shales and in tar sands is not included in this calculation since estimates are very approximate and oil is not yet obtainable commercially from them. In the *long* term the coal and lignite of the world would last very much longer than the oil and natural gas.

In assessing the reserves of fossil fuels per inhabitant for the purpose of the present study, a compromise was arrived at. The same weight was given to coal plus lignite as to oil plus natural gas. By the 1970s world oil and natural gas production actually exceeded world coal and lignite production (in coal equivalent) since oil and natural gas are generally much cheaper to extract than the solid fuels. It was considered reasonable to assume that in the

Table 4.6 Countries of the world with the largest reserves of fossil fuels and years of production at mid-1970s rate

	Total	% of world	Years life		Total	% of world	Years life
Coal (tonnes × 10⁹)				Brown coal and lignite (tonnes × 10⁹)			
1 U.S.S.R.	483	38.2	1000	1 U.S.S.R.	110	61.1	1380
2 U.S.A.	388	30.7	680	2 U.S.A.	29	16.0	4830
3 China	195	15.4	420	3 Yugoslavia	9	5.0	490
4 W. Germany	52	4.1	540	4 E. Germany	8	4.4	100
5 U.K.	29	2.3	230	5 Australia	7	3.9	790
6 Australia	25	2.0	400	6 W. Germany	5	2.8	110
7 Poland	22	1.7	130	7 Bulgaria	3	1.7	180
8 India	19	1.5	200	8 Czechoslo-vakia	3	1.7	60
9 S. Africa	16	1.3	230	9 Poland	2	1.1	150
10 Canada	15	1.2	680	10 Hungary	1	0.6	90
Rest of world	21	1.6		Rest of world	3	1.7	
World total	1265	100.0	530	World total	180	100.0	490
Oil (tonnes × 10⁹)				Natural gas (m³ × 10¹²)			
1 Saudi Arabia	15.1	19.1	43	1 U.S.S.R.	20.1	33.1	76
2 Kuwait	10.2	12.9	97	2 Iran	10.6	17.5	480
3 Iran	9.1	11.5	34	3 U.S.A.	6.4	10.6	11
4 U.S.S.R.	8.1	10.3	17	4 Algeria	3.3	5.4	510
5 U.A. Emirates	5.6	7.0	70	5 Netherlands	1.8	3.0	26
6 Iraq	4.7	5.9	42	6 Saudi Arabia	1.8	3.0	540
7 U.S.A.	4.4	5.6	11	7 Canada	1.6	2.7	22
8 Libya	3.8	4.8	53	8 Nigeria	1.4	2.3	2480
9 Venezuela	2.6	3.3	22	9 Qatar	1.4	2.2	1350
10 China	2.4	3.0	29	10 Venezuela	1.2	2.0	105
Rest of world	13.2	16.6		Rest of world	11.0	18.2	
World total	79.3	100.0	30	World total	60.8	100.0	47

next few decades very roughly the same quantity (in coal equivalent) of coal and lignite will be extracted as of oil and natural gas.

The units of fossil fuel per inhabitant in Table 4.5 are of notional value and only for comparative purposes. The world average is 100 units. The units include only commercial or proved reserves of oil and gas but some weight is given to 'possible' coal and lignite reserves in addition to those regarded as commercially extractable. The score of a zero for many countries implies that the reserves of fossil fuels in these countries are so small that they come out at less than 0.5 on the scale used. From column (3) in Table 4.5 it is therefore clear that the countries of the world differ enormously with regard to the availability of fossil fuels per inhabitant. Table 4.6 is a supplement to this column and shows actual quantities of fossil fuels for the 10 countries with the largest reserves of each of the four considered. The third column in each part of the table shows how long the fuels would last at rates of production in the mid-1970s. In the following two sections (4.4 and 4.5) production and consumption of fuel will be reviewed and the reader will be asked to remember or refer back to the main features of the distribution of reserves described here.

Column (4) in Table 4.5 shows estimates of reserves of non-fuel minerals in each country of the world. These have been calculated by the author from various sources, but *Mineral Facts and Problems,* U.S. Bureau of Mines (1970), was an essential reference. As with fossil fuels, the value in units per inhabitant is a notional score showing the relative position of each country. The world average is 100 units per inhabitant. Again no allowance is made for 'possible' reserves not yet properly explored and the zero against many countries does not imply that they have no non-fuel mineral resources at all but that those known to exist are very small in quantity. The make-up of the mineral points varies greatly from country to country. For example most of the reserves in Chile are accounted for by copper, while Australia has deposits of world significance of several minerals. The data in column (4) show that, as with fossil fuels, there is a very uneven distribution of non-fuel mineral reserves among the countries of the world.

4.4   Production

This section contains a brief review of three aspects of production, energy, steel, and gross national product. The data for 60 countries are shown in columns (11), (12), and (18) of Table 4.1. The highest and lowest scoring 10 countries are shown in Table 4.7. Energy and steel are assessed in units that can be measured in a straightforward way and compared over time. The two industries represent key sectors of the world economy in which the gap between the production per inhabitant in the developed and the developing

Table 4.7 Production of energy, steel, and gross national product

(1) Energy production 1975 (kg/inhabitant)		(2) Steel production 1975 (kg/inhabitant)		(3) GNP 1975 ($/inhabitant	
1 Saudi Arabia	58,900	Belgium	1182	U.S.A.	7060
2 Venezuela	16,760	Czechoslovakia	968	Canada	6650
3 Iraq	14,920	Japan	922	W. Germany	6610
4 Iran	12,930	W. Germany	654	Belgium	6070
5 Canada	11,770	Australia	597	France	5760
6 U.S.A.	9360	Canada	571	Australia	5640
7 Australia	8230	U.S.S.R.	556	Netherlands	5590
8 Netherlands	8160	U.S.A.	495	Japan、	4460
9 U.S.S.R.	6490	Romania	450	E. Germany	4230
10 Poland	5660	Poland	429	U.K.	3840
51 Uganda	10	Zaire	0	Vietnam	160
52 Kenya	10	Ethiopia	0	Sri Lanka	150
53 Sri Lanka	10	Burma	0	Zaire	150
54 Thailand	10	Iran	0	India	150
55 Philippines	10	Thailand	0	Pakistan	140
56 Bangladesh	10	Philippines	0	Afghanistan	130
57 Nepal	0	Vietnam	0	Nepal	110
58 Tanzania	0	Nigeria	0	Burma	110
59 Sudan	0	Pakistan	0	Bangladesh	110
60 Ethiopia	0	Indonesia	0	Ethiopia	100

countries is very great. The columns referred to in the rest of this section are in Table 4.7.

Column (1). Energy in Table 4.7 includes hydroelectric power, oil from oil shales, wood, and other sources not included in the estimates of fossil fuels in the previous section. The four main fossil fuels account, however, for well over 90 percent of all the energy produced in the world. Firewood and dung are wastefully used for such purposes as domestic heating and cooking fuel in many developing countries but are very limited in terms of coal equivalent. As a result of rounding to 10kg, the value of 0 (zero) in column (1) implies less than 5kg per inhabitant.

The top producers of energy in terms of kilogrammes per inhabitant are of two broad types. The first four produce oil and export most of this output. The next six produce various fuels and either, like Australia and the U.S.S.R., use a substantial part while exporting some, or, like the U.S.A., actually have a deficit.

Column (2). Steel production shows a different picture from energy production. In the last few decades it has been easy for industrialized countries of the developed world to organize the production of oil and natural gas in such countries as Venezuela, Saudi Arabia, and Nigeria in order to extract these fuels largely for their own use. There has been little incentive for the older industrial countries to establish iron and steel mills in countries that were little industrialized. Thus while energy production per inhabitant reflects very closely energy reserves per inhabitant, the production of steel per inhabitant reflects much more the gap in level of industrialization, or the development gap.

All the 10 top steel producers in terms of quantity per inhabitant are highly industrialized countries. Several of them, however, depend heavily on the importation of the most bulky ingredients of iron and steel making, iron ore and coking coal. A score of zero in the 10 'lowest' producers means that these countries have no iron and steel industry at all. Of the 60 largest countries of the world in population, 23 produced no steel at all and several more only produced negligible quantities per inhabitant. Some developing countries have, however, made efforts to build up heavy industrial capacity, including iron and steel making, among them Mexico, Brazil and Venezuela in Latin America, and also India. The establishment of an iron and steel industry appears to be a high priority in several oil-exporting countries.

Column (3). The use of gross national product (GNP) as a measure of development has been criticized for various reasons. There are problems of interpretation when national currencies are converted to one currency, in this case the U.S. dollar. Gross national product does not include all aspects of the national production and does not necessarily assess the quality of life. Again, it is argued that the aim of governments in most countries to expand continuously the production of goods and services is not necessarily a desirable or a realistic one. In spite of the drawbacks mentioned, gross national product does indicate broadly the magnitude of the development gap. It has the advantage of covering the production of most goods and services in an economy. Data in Table 4.7, column (3), show that in the mid-1970s the ratio between the richest and poorest countries was about 70 to 1. It is difficult to see how such a disparity could be greatly reduced, let alone eliminated, over a short period.

4.5   Consumption

This section contains a brief review of three aspects of consumption, food, energy, and telephones in use. These variables are shown in full for 60 countries in table 4.1, columns (13), (14), and (15) respectively. The countries with the highest and the lowest levels of consumption are shown in Table 4.8, in which will be found the columns referred to in the first part of this section.

Column (1). The average consumption of food per inhabitant is about twice as great in the countries with the highest levels of intake as in the countries with the lowest levels. Two main aspects of food intake are often distinguished in a comparison of diet in different parts of the world. These are the total intake of food over a given period, usually measured in kilocalories per day, and the composition of the diet, the intake of protein per inhabitant over a given period often being used as an indicator of quality of diet. Total calorie intake affects weight and general health while deficiencies and excesses of certain elements such as lack of protein or vitamins and excess of sugar lead to more specific problems and ailments.

It is to be expected that people in different parts of the world have different food requirements, whether on account of their own

Table 4.8 Food, energy, and telephones

Food intake (kcal)		Energy consumption (kg/inhabitant		Telephones in use/1000 population	
1 Belgium	3380	U.S.A.	11,000	U.S.A.	695
2 U.S.A.	3330	Canada	9880	Canada	572
3 Netherlands	3320	Czechoslovakia	7150	Japan	405
4 E. Germany	3290	E. Germany	6840	Australia	390
5 Bulgaria	3290	Australia	6490	U.K.	379
6 U.S.S.R.	3280	Netherlands	5780	Netherlands	368
7 Poland	3280	Belgium	5580	W. Germany	317
8 Australia	3280	U.S.S.R.	5550	Belgium	285
9 Hungary	3280	W. Germany	5350	France	262
10 Turkey	3250	U.K.	5270	Italy	259
51 Nepal	2080	Sri Lanka	130	Vietnam	3
52 India	2070	Nigeria	90	Pakistan	3
53 Zaire	2060	Zaire	80	India	3
54 Mozambique	2060	Tanzania	70	Afghanistan	2
55 Iraq	2050	Uganda	60	Zaire	2
56 Afghanistan	1970	Afghanistan	50	Nigeria	2
57 Philippines	1940	Burma	50	Nepal	1
58 Bangladesh	1840	Ethiopia	30	Burma	1
59 Indonesia	1790	Bangladesh	30	Bangladesh	1
60 Algeria	1730	Nepal	10	China	0

Table 4.9 Energy surplus and deficit. 1.00 = balance

Countries with greatest energy surplus			Countries with greatest energy deficit			
1 Saudi Arabia	42.4	41 Bangladesh	0.32	51 Japan	0.09
2 Nigeria	23.4	42 Mozambique	0.29	52 Nepal	0.08
3 Iraq	21.0	43 Ghana	0.28	53 Sri Lanka	0.08
4 Iran	9.5	44 Spain	0.27	54 Ethiopia	0.05
5 Algeria	6.6	45 France	0.23	55 Kenya	0.04
6 Venezuela	6.3	46 Morocco	0.19	56 Tanzania	0.04
7 Indonesia	4.3	47 Uganda	0.17	57 Thailand	0.04
8 Afghanistan	4.2	48 Italy	0.16	58 Philippines	0.04
9 Netherlands	1.4	49 Belgium	0.15	59 Cuba	0.03
10 Australia	1.3	50 Portugal	0.12	60 Sudan	0.01

physical make-up such as body size, or on account of features of their environment such as climatic conditions. Even so the food intake gap in the world is a considerable one. In theory the unnecessarily large intake in the rich countries could be transferred to poor countries, but even if such a transfer were feasible and acceptable it would only go some way to bringing diet throughout the poor countries to a satisfactory level.

Column (2). The consumption of energy per inhabitant in a country is widely accepted as being closely related to the level of development of that country. The correlation between the variables energy consumption and gross national product in Table 4.1, columns (14) and (18), is a coefficient of + 0.90, a high one. Column (2) in Table 4.8 shows that the gap in energy consumption per inhabitant between extremes in the world is over 1000 to 1, between the U.S.A. with 11,000kg and Nepal with 10kg. Energy production per inhabitant is not closely correlated with energy consumption per inhabitant. Countries such as France, Italy, and Japan produce comparatively little energy themselves but have high levels of consumption. Oil producers such as Saudi Arabia, Algeria, and Venezuela produce large amounts of energy per inhabitant but consume only a small part of their production, and have levels of consumption of energy per inhabitant well below those in highly industrialized countries. The world trade in oil and to a lesser extent coal and natural gas represents a massive international flow of fuel. Something like a quarter of all the fuel produced in the world crosses international boundaries. The spatial pattern of this trade will be described in Chapter 6.

The relationship between production and consumption of energy is measured in Table 4.9. In each country total production is divided by total consumption. For example the U.K. in 1975 produced 184 million tonnes of coal equivalent of energy but consumed 295 million tonnes. Its coefficient was therefore 0.62. In contrast, Australia produced 111 million tonnes but consumed 88 million tonnes. Its coefficient was 1.27. Saudi Arabia produced more than forty (42.4) times as much energy as it consumed. The

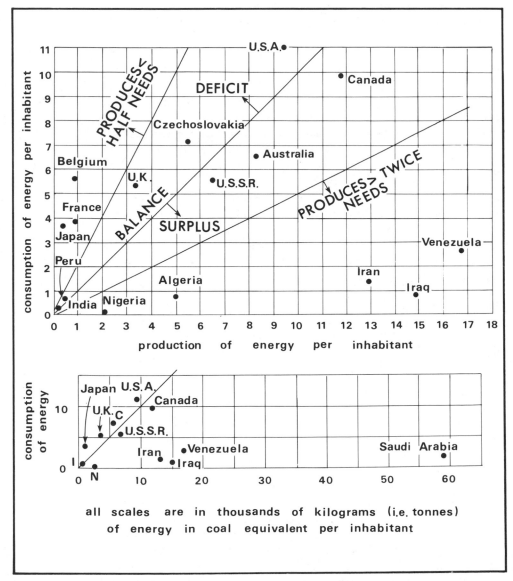

Figure 4.2 A comparison of energy production and energy consumption per inhabitant in selected countries of the world. See Table 4.1, columns (11) and (14), for data used

data in Table 4.9 bring out some aspects of the very complex world energy situation.

Among the countries in the left-hand column of Table 4.9 are several of the poorest in the world, in particular Nigeria and Indonesia. These countries have a very low consumption of energy per inhabitant yet they export very large quantities of oil. Here there is clearly a big disparity between 'demand', which keeps consumption low, and 'need', a consumption that would raise the standard of living from its current dismally low level.

Among the countries in Table 4.9 in which consumption greatly exceeds production there are also many very poor countries. The plight of such countries as the Philippines and Kenya is that they have to import highly priced oil even to maintain very low levels of energy consumption because they have virtually no fossil fuels themselves. They are, however, competing with industrialized countries that are also deficient in fossil fuels but which consume enormous amounts of imported oil, among them Japan and most West European countries. Figure 4.2 represents the situation in 1975 graphically. Selected countries are plotted on the graph according to the consumption of energy per inhabitant (vertical axis) and production of energy per inhabitant (horizontal axis). The balance is a line running across the graph from lower left to upper right. The lower graph is an extension of the upper graph to show the special position of Saudi Arabia.

4.6   Relationships between variables

The technique of principal components analysis has been used in many development studies since the early 1960s. Probably the first to be published was that by Ginsburg and Berry (Ginsburg, 1961) in their *Atlas of Economic Development*. The findings of the application of principal components analysis to the data in Table 4.1 will be discussed in this section but the procedure itself will not be described. The technique is used here descriptively rather than inferentially.

A drawback to be considered when principal components analysis is used on data for countries of the world is that each county is an aggregate made up of many places, people, and units of production, not an individual. Another problem is that the 60 largest countries of the world, while meaningful, vital entities in the study of spatial variations in development in the world as a whole, are not an unbiased sample of a large number of cases. The total set of 'population' (in a statistical sense) of countries in the world is 150 to 200 depending on definition.

Table 4.10 Correlation matrix

	(1)	(2)	(3)	(4)	(5)	(6)	(7)	(8)	(9)	(10)	(11)	(12)	(13)	(14)	(15)	(16)	(17)	(18)
(1) Total area	1.00																	
(2) Total population	0.47	1.00																
(3) Area/person	0.44	−0.11	1.00															
(4) Land resources/population	0.41	−0.04	0.79	1.00														
(5) Fossil fuels/population	0.18	−0.04	0.37	0.14	1.00													
(6) Mineral materials/population	0.28	−0.10	0.73	0.72	0.04	1.00												
(7) Not in agriculture	0.19	−0.08	0.16	0.31	0.04	0.30	1.00											
(8) Urban	0.19	−0.10	0.23	0.35	0.04	0.35	0.92	1.00										
(9) Population change	−0.08	−0.06	0.08	−0.14	0.14	−0.03	−0.69	−0.56	1.00									
(10) Percent under 15	−0.11	−0.06	0.03	−0.20	0.13	−0.06	−0.72	−0.61	0.96	1.00								
(11) Energy production/population	0.15	−0.07	0.40	0.15	0.97	0.05	0.12	0.11	0.07	0.04	1.00							
(12) Steel production/population	0.18	−0.03	0.14	0.23	−0.04	0.30	0.72	0.68	−0.68	−0.73	0.04	1.00						
(13) Food consumption/population	0.18	−0.12	0.10	0.34	−0.05	0.20	0.75	0.68	−0.81	−0.85	0.04	0.67	1.00					
(14) Energy consumption/population	0.36	−0.01	0.30	0.39	0.11	0.27	0.77	0.71	−0.71	−0.75	0.22	0.76	0.78	1.00				
(15) Telephones/population	0.24	−0.01	0.31	0.37	0.02	0.29	0.73	0.67	−0.62	−0.67	0.11	0.67	0.64	0.86	1.00			
(16) Infant mortality	−0.16	−0.05	−0.03	−0.24	0.10	−0.15	−0.82	−0.75	0.76	0.83	0.01	−0.66	−0.80	−0.72	−0.66	1.00		
(17) Life expectancy	0.15	−0.00	0.04	0.24	−0.12	0.16	0.83	0.77	−0.75	−0.82	−0.03	0.64	0.79	0.70	0.65	−0.98	1.00	
(18) GNP/population	0.23	−0.06	0.31	0.35	0.20	0.24	0.80	0.76	−0.68	−0.73	0.29	0.77	0.74	0.90	0.90	−0.71	0.69	1.00
	(1)	(2)	(3)	(4)	(5)	(6)	(7)	(8)	(9)	(10)	(11)	(12)	(13)	(14)	(15)	(16)	(17)	(18)

Table 4.11 Loadings of variables on components. Note that only loadings more than 0.5 above or below 0.0 are shown. For technical reasons all signs have been reversed except those on component IV

		I	II	III	IV
(1)	Total area				+0.67
(2)	Total population				+0.91
(3)	Area/person		+0.87		
(4)	Land resources/population		+0.65		
(5)	Fossil fuels/population		+0.66	+0.72	
(6)	Mineral materials/population		+0.60	−0.54	
(7)	Not in agriculture	+0.91			
(8)	Percent urban	+0.84			
(9)	Population change	−0.82			
(10)	Percent under 15	−0.87			
(11)	Energy production/population		+0.64	+0.74	
(12)	Steel production/population	+0.82			
(13)	Food consumption/population	+0.88			
(14)	Energy consumption/population	+0.91			
(15)	Telephones/population	+0.85			
(16)	Infant mortality	−0.88			
(17)	Life expectancy	+0.88			
(18)	GNP/population	+0.91			

The advantage of using principal components to analyse development data is that it gives concise and precise numerical values to relationships between sets of correlated variables. In addition the scores of the countries on the components that are formed may be processed by a linkage procedure to produce a classification of the countries studied, based on a large part of the information contained in the many variables used, in this case 18. The results of classification are described in Section 4.7.

For convenience, the findings of the application of principal components analysis to the world data matrix are described in a number of stages.

(1) The correlation matrix in Table 4.10 shows the Pearson product moment coefficient of correlation (r) between each pair of variables in Table 4.1. The correlation ranges between the extremes of -1.00 for a perfect negative correlation and $+1.00$ for a perfect positive correlation. The perfect correlation of 1.00 between each variable and itself is shown on the principal diagonal of the matrix. All the other coefficients are between different pairs of the variables. Only half the matrix needs to be shown.

An example will help to clarify what is being shown in Table 4.10. The correlation between variable (8) Urban and (7) Not in agriculture is shown where row (8) crosses column (7), and is + 0.92. This indicates a strong positive correlation between the two variables and shows that the more urbanized a country the smaller the proportion of its employed population engaged in agriculture. This high positive correlation results from the fact, which the reader may check by comparing columns (7) and (8) in the data matrix in Table 4.1, that when a country has a high score on the urban

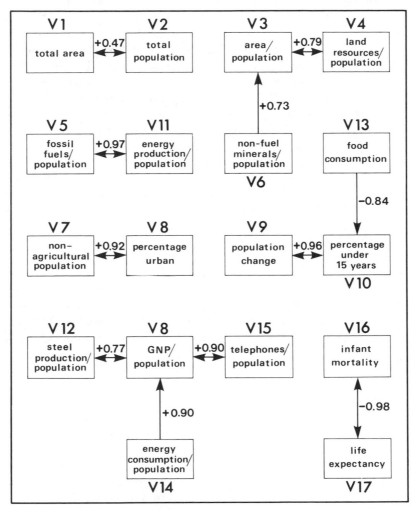

Figure 4.3 'Families' of highly correlated variables from the correlation matrix in Table 4.10. Each variable is linked by arrow to the variable with which it correlates most highly

variable it tends to have a high score on the non-agricultural one, while when a country has a low value on urban it tends to have a low value on non-agricultural. For example in the U.K. 76 percent of the population is defined as urban while 98 percent of the economically active population is not engaged in agriculture. In Bangladesh only 9 percent of the population is urban and only 15 percent is not in agriculture.

Although a large number of the variables in Table 4.1 are highly correlated with each other, as can be seen by the many high coefficients in Table 4.10, one cannot infer that the relationship is causal simply from the coefficients. What the correlation matrix does show is broad associations of variables. In the diagram in Figure 4.3 each variable in Table 4.10 is linked by an arrow to the variable with which it is most highly correlated. The correlation coefficient is shown on the arrow. It should be noted that with three of the variables, (9), (10), and (16), high values mean 'unfavourable' or adverse. Thus the higher the rate of population increase (9), the percentage of population under 15 years of age (10), and the infant mortality rate (16), the less developed the country. These three variables correlate negatively with all the other development variables, (7)-(18). The linkages in Figure 4.3 show that there are several sets of interrelated variables. In fact most variables have strong links with more than just one other variable and more arrows could be added to indicate strong correlations between other pairs of variables in Figure 4.3.

(2) Principal components analysis takes the grouping of associated variables further than is done in Figure 4.3. The 60 countries are viewed not through the 18 original variables but through a new set of complex variables, the components. While each variable is regarded as being of one unit in 'length' (geometrically speaking), the components will differ considerably in 'length' or 'weight' if there is much correlation between the original variables, as in the present study. The coefficients in Table 4.10 show that all the economic and demographic variables from (7) to (18) except (11) Energy production correlate *highly* with one another, some negatively. A new 'super variable' or component representing development in general emerges from the study. It is a consensus of all the variables from (7) to (18) except (11). These 'tell (roughly) the same story' about the countries. Development may be thought of as 'indivisible' because a country with a high level of development in one sphere (e.g. education) tends to have a high level of development in another (e.g. health or industrial production). The first component (I) in Table 4.11 has nearly half of all the total amount of variance in the original data matrix. Actually

Table 4.12 Scores of the 60 countries on component I

1	Australia	19.9	31	China	−3.2
2	Canada	18.8	32	Colombia	−3.6
3	U.S.A.	18.7	33	Peru	−3.6
4	Belgium	15.4	34	Sri Lanka	−4.3
5	W. Germany	13.7	35	Malaysia	−4.5
6	Netherlands	12.3	36	Egypt	−5.0
7	U.K.	11.8	37	Iraq	−5.1
8	Czechoslovakia	11.7	38	Iran	−5.4
9	E. Germany	11.6	39	Saudi Arabia	−5.4
10	France	11.0	40	Philippines	−5.6
11	Japan	10.8	41	Morocco	−6.6
12	U.S.S.R.	10.5	42	Thailand	−6.9
13	Italy	8.2	43	Algeria	−7.1
14	Hungary	7.8	44	Burma	−7.2
15	Poland	7.3	45	India	−7.3
16	Bulgaria	7.1	46	Ghana	−7.7
17	Spain	6.3	47	Vietnam	−7.9
18	Greece	5.7	48	Pakistan	−8.0
19	Argentina	5.7	49	Sudan	−8.4
20	Romania	4.6	50	Zaire	−9.0
21	Chile	3.7	51	Mozambique	−9.0
22	Yugoslavia	3.1	52	Indonesia	−9.1
23	Portugal	2.8	53	Kenya	−9.5
24	Venezuela	1.1	54	Nigeria	−9.7
25	Cuba	0.8	55	Uganda	−10.3
26	S. Africa	−0.4	56	Ethiopia	−10.4
27	Brazil	−1.9	57	Tanzania	−10.4
28	S. Korea	−2.0	58	Bangladesh	−10.4
29	Mexico	−2.8	59	Nepal	−10.6
30	Turkey	−2.8	60	Afghanistan	−10.6

it has an eigenvalue of 8.8, containing about 49 percent of the variance.

Table 4.11 also shows that a second, less prominent component (with an eigenvalue of 3.0 and a percentage of total variance of about 17) picks out an association among the four variables (3)-(6) representing space and natural resources and between these and variable (11) Energy production. A third component (III) is more difficult to interpret, but the fourth highlights the broad though far from perfect correlation between area and population size. This fourth component is relatively small because only two variables were included to assess size of country, compared with 12 measuring aspects of development. Altogether the first four components (I-IV) account for 83 percent of all the variance on the 18 original variables.

(3) Each of the 60 countries in the original data matrix in Table 4.1 has a position on each of the four components. The first component expresses level of development in a very broad sense and is therefore particularly useful in the present study as a scale on which the 60 countries may be placed for comparative purposes. The 60 countries are ranked in Table 4.12 according to their scores on the overall development scale. The values are meaningless in themselves but they show the relative position of each country on the new scale. One feature of development emerges at once. There is no sharp division of the countries of the world into two obvious classes, developed and developing, Some, like Australia and West Germany, are clearly 'developed' and others, like Afghanistan and Ethiopia, are clearly 'developing'. It is interesting, however, to find that there are only three fairly small countries between Portugal at + 2.8 and Brazil at − 1.9. This perhaps is the part of the scale where a cut-off between developed and developing might be made if one was thought to be at all meaningful.

On component II, not tabulated in full, Australia (13.3), Saudi Arabia (11.8), and Canada (7.1) emerge as the countries most highly endowed with natural resources in relation to population; those of Saudi Arabia are largely limited to oil. Belgium (− 3.2), Italy (− 3.0), and Japan (− 3.0) come out as the countries least endowed with natural resources per inhabitant, but many others in Europe, including the U.K., come close behind the trailing three.

4.7   Types of country

It is popularly assumed that there are two broad types of country, developed and developing. Level of development is, however, only one feature of a country. Other aspects such as total size (measured by area, population, production), physical environment, political or ideological system, and ratio of natural resources to population are not necessarily related to level of development. Even when a single 'development' variable is used, such as energy consumption per inhabitant, the countries of the world do not fall immediately into two clear-cut classes, high and low level consumers. When various development criteria are taken into account, as in component I in the previous section, the countries of the world are spread out fairly evenly on a continuum.

What has been said about development is true also for resources. There are not just two types of country with regard to the availability of natural resources per inhabitant, 'resource rich' and 'resource poor'. Again, in the 1970s if not in the 1950s, various shades of political system and ideology are found. The world can no longer be divided into capitalist and communist, as it tended to be in the 1950s. Nevertheless one feels that there are close similarities between pairs of countries and among groups of countries. The U.K. and West Germany are similar to one another in many respects and very different from Bangladesh or Australia.

The purpose of the final section of this chapter is to discuss a classification of the 60 countries studied in it. The method used depends on the positions or scores of the 60 countries on each of the four components (I-IV) described in the previous section. Together the four components account for 83 percent of the variance on the 18 variables in Table 4.1. They cover three aspects of the 60 countries: size of country, resource/population ratio, and development level. Greater weight is given to the third aspect than to the other two since more variables are included in the original data on the subject of development than on the other two aspects.

Each of the four components contains information about each of the 60 countries. Since the components are not correlated with each other at all they are orthogonal (at right angles to one another) and may therefore be thought of as four distinct dimensions. Although the situation cannot be represented geometrically, each country, mathematically, has a position in such four-dimensional space according to where it ends up after being located according to its scores on each of the four components. Each country is in a position at a measurable distance from every other one. The distance is equivalent to similarity. The closer two countries are to one another, the more similar they are to one another.

With the help of a computer program the classification procedure finds which pair of countries are closest, and therefore most similar. These are joined into a 'group'. The next closest are then joined. The process continues, with each successive country joining another country or an existing group of countries. Eventually large groups join. Thus the original 60 countries are progressively reduced in number until eventually they are all joined. The process can be shown in a linkage tree or dendogram. The dendogram for the present study is shown in Figure 4.4.

The calculations (not included here) from which the linkage tree was constructed show that the most similar pair of countries among all 60 are Ethiopia (country 26) and Tanzania (country 40). These join early near the top of the linkage tree in Figure 4.4. It is possible

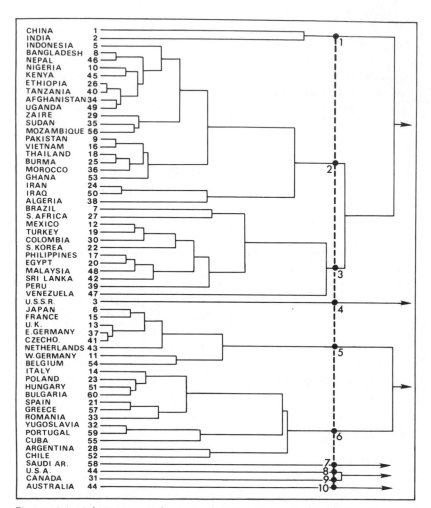

Figure 4.4 Linkage 'tree' diagram showing the sequence of pairing and grouping of similar countries according to the information loading on the four principal components in Table 4.11. The 'tree' has been cut to produce 10 comparatively homogeneous regions. These are mapped in Figure 4.5. The data used in the study are in Table 4.1

to verify their similarity by comparing them in the data matrix in Table 4.1 by looking across the table. The next most similar pair are East Germany (country 37) and Czechoslovakia (country 41). Table 4.13(a) shows how the joining continues. The next step, surprisingly perhaps, is the joining of the U.K. to the existing 'group' of East Germany and Czechoslovakia. Then Thailand and Burma join.

It must be remembered that only certain criteria are being taken into account in the classification. The 18 original variables contain

Table 4.13 First stages in the joining sequence

Joining sequence	Name and rank number (in Table 4.1) of most similar countries	
(a) *In the present study*		
1	26 Ethiopia	40 Tanzania
2	37 E. Germany	41 Czechoslovakia
3	13 U.K.	37 E. Germany
4	18 Thailand	25 Burma
5	34 Afghanistan	49 Uganda
6	8 Bangladesh	46 Nepal
7	9 Pakistan	16 Vietnam
8	26 Ethiopia	34 Afghanistan
9	24 Iran	50 Iraq
10	17 Philippines	20 Egypt
11	10 Nigeria	45 Kenya
12	32 Yugoslavia	59 Portugal
(b) *In a different study*		
1	67 Ivory Coast	85 Senegal
2	55 Mozambique	113 C. African Republic
3	110 Jamaica	111 Costa Rica
4	34 Afghanistan	49 Uganda
5	16 Vietnam	25 Burma
6	74 Mali	88 Rwanda
7	20 Egypt	105 Paraguay
8	46 Nepal	92 Burundi
9	84 Haiti	94 Laos
10	98 Benin	117 Mauritania
11	53 Ghana	103 Papua-New Guinea
12	68 Yemen	96 Somalia

nothing that would directly separate countries on a political or ideological dimension. If they did, the U.K. would not join East Germany and Czechoslovakia so early as it does. Similarly, if physical conditions were included, particularly altitude and climate, then Bangladesh and Nepal would not join so early as stage 6. One is mainly on a low-lying delta area while the other is mainly very mountainous. It is essential to appreciate that in the classification of countries (or any other cases studied) the results obtained from the procedure used depend on the information about the countries included in the original data matrix. The classification has been included to emphasize some ideas that are important in the rest of the book rather than to provide 'the'

definitive classification of the countries of the world or to reach
any outstanding conclusions.

One result of the classification is to show which pairs of
countries are similar and which are different. Whether one is a
geographer or not, it is satisfying to find that two countries in the
same part of the world are very similar. The early pairing of East
Germany and Czechoslovakia and of Thailand and Burma appeals
to one's sense of spatial tidiness and perhaps to one's expectations.
It is more difficult to adjust to the idea that such spatially separate
countries as Afghanistan and Uganda or the Philippines and Egypt
can also be very similar.

One of the values of the linkage exercise therefore is to draw
attention to the spatial complexity of development. It shows the
danger of automatically grouping individual countries in the same
part of the world into regions of contiguous countries thought to be
very similar to each other, or of accepting the traditional continents
as being comparatively homogeneous regions. Table 4.13(b) gives
other examples of the 'unexpected' pairing of countries on different
sides of the world. The pairing is from another study made by the
author, in which 118 countries were included and 23 variables used,
virtually all of them measuring conventional aspects of
development. Interestingly, Afghanistan and Uganda remain loyal
to one another. Further down, Haiti in the Caribbean and Laos in
Southeast Asia join. Haiti has a very different historical background
from that of other Latin American countries but one might have
expected it to associate with an African country rather than with an
Asian one.

A second result of the classification to be noted is the fact that
by the time most of the joining of similar countries has taken place,
some countries remain unattached while others have already
congregated into large groups. The linkage tree in Figure 4.4 has
been cut where there are 10 groups left. The groups are mapped in
Figure 4.5 on a world map of the 60 countries in which the area of
each is drawn proportional to the population of the country, not its
territorial extent. Five of the 10 are single countries, the U.S.S.R.,
Saudi Arabia, the U.S.A., Canada, and Australia. These countries are
so different from any of the other 55, Saudi Arabia, for example, on
account of its high position on the resource/population dimension,
that they have not picked up partners yet. Groups 2 (21 members)
and 3 (12 members), which may be interpreted as containing the less
and the more developed of the *developing* countries, are about to
join to give a group with more than half of all the countries. Groups
5 (8 members) and 6 (12 members) may be interpreted as the more
and the less developed of the *developed* countries.

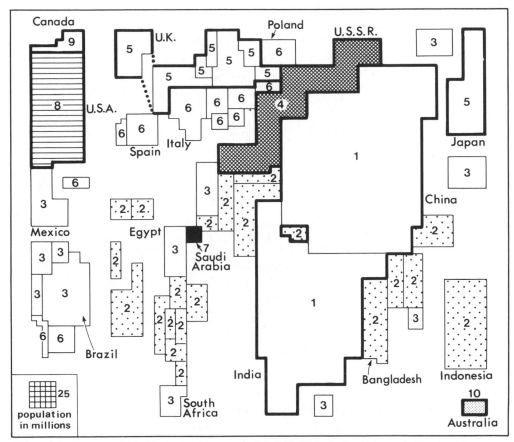

Figure 4.5 Groups of 'similar' countries as defined in the linkage diagram in Figure 4.4

　　　　Attention may be drawn at this point to the inadequacy of the present system of sovereign states as a set of regions for giving a balanced coverage of the world in a study of development. As comes out clearly in the population based map in Figure 4.5, about half of the population of all the 60 countries is concentrated in just four, China, India, the U.S.S.R., and the U.S.A. Thus about half of the population of the world is broken down into only four units while the other half is broken down into about 200 units, of which the largest 56 are included in this study. To appreciate the world development situation in a more balanced way it would be helpful to group the smaller countries and subdivide the larger ones. This methodological question will be reconsidered in Chapter 6.

　　　　In conclusion, it is suggested that the development gap cannot be seen simply as a one-dimensional problem. From the data in this chapter it is possible to distinguish two different major aspects of

Table 4.14 Two dimensions of development

GNP per inhabitant	Very low	Low	Medium	High	Very high
Very high	Switzerland	Sweden	U.S.A.	Canada	Australia
High	Japan	U.K.	U.S.S.R.		
Moderate	Portugal	Romania	Argentina	Venezuela	
Low		China	Peru		Saudi Arabia
Very low	Bangladesh Haiti	Ethiopia Tanzania		Zaire	
	Very low	Low	Medium	High	Very high

Natural resources per inhabitant

development, one reflecting the technological level of a country, the other the availability of natural resources in relation to population. Table 4.14 shows the relationship between the two dimensions. It is an amplification of Table 2.7 in Chapter 2. Neither scale is exactly linear or arithmetical. Four extremes of country can be seen, having the following per inhabitant (with examples):

High GNP, low resources: Switzerland, Japan
High GNP, high resources: Australia, Canada
Low GNP, low resources: Bangladesh
Low GNP, high resources: Saudi Arabia, Zaire

Through time each country changes its position in the table. For example Saudi Arabia (lower right) would move to the right if new natural resources were found. It would move to the left as natural resources were used up, or if population grew, or both. It would move up the vertical scale if GNP grew faster than population.

The position of Australia at the upper right of the table is at first sight the most desirable place to be because a high material standard of living is experienced by the population yet natural resources are abundant. Whether the upper left or lower left position is the least desirable is left to the reader to think about. The relationship between the two vital development dimensions noted here will be discussed again later when natural resources have been appraised more thoroughly. A distinction between development terms made in Chapter 1 may be recalled here. *Developing* and *developed* refer to technology and are roughly measured by gross national product per inhabitant. *Undeveloped* (or *underdeveloped*) and *overdeveloped* refer to the availability or lack of natural resources per inhabitant.

5

Development trends to the present

5.1 Change over a long period

In Chapters 3 and 4 spatial variations in development were described within regions, within whole countries, and in the world as a whole in the immediate past. Changes through time in Italy and the U.S.S.R. were referred to briefly. Before considering the problems and prospects of narrowing the development gap in the chapters that follow, it is helpful to trace changes over a long period leading up to the present. By noting which spatial inequalities have existed for a long time in the world and which have appeared more recently an idea may be obtained of how long changes may be expected to take to come about in the future and what changes are possible.

Change is studied in this chapter under five headings. These have been chosen to cover a broad range of economic and social aspects of development. The choice of the actual sectors and countries used has been determined partly by the availability of data.

(1) Demographic change will be illustrated by data for birthrate and deathrate.
(2) Changes in the economic structure of countries will be traced through data for employment in agriculture.
(3) Steel production and consumption will be used to show changes in production and consumption levels.
(4) Efficiency will be exemplified by yields of major crops.
(5) The quality of life will be represented by infant mortality data.

How far back can and should one trace changes? It was shown in Chapter 2 that a development gap was recognized by Adam Smith in the eighteenth century, though the word 'development' was not itself used. In *How it all Began,* Rostow (1975) ranges over a time

Plate 5.1 (Above) The first iron-smelting furnace in the world to use coke, now in the industrial museum at Coalbrookdale, Shropshire (Ironbridge Gorge Museum)

Plate 5.2 (Opposite) A blast furnace in Tanzania. The one in the illustration is in a museum in Dar es Salaam but such charcoal-burning furnaces are still in use in the interior of the country

span of several centuries in an effort to tie down critical events that led to the Industrial Revolution. More locally, the citizens of Coalbrookdale in the Midlands of England may point to 1755 or 1781 as examples of critical dates. In 1755 the first coke-using blast furnace to be fully competitive with furnaces employing charcoal was brought into use, while in the same area the world's first iron bridge was opened in 1781. Nef (1977) shows, however, that coal was being used for various industrial purposes in England even in the seventeenth century. According to his estimate of the consumption of energy per inhabitant in England in the 1670s, this was already about 10 times as high then as it is in the least developed African and Asian countries in the 1970s.

One might argue that the development gap began to appear when the technology of Europe became notably more sophisticated or at least more widely applied in practical terms than that of China. Unfortunately few data for the world as a whole are available until the nineteenth century. What is more, even now many data for developing countries are only very approximate. P. Bairoch (1975) provides a great deal of useful material on changes in the developing world during the twentieth century.

As shown by the linkage exercise in the last chapter, two or more countries may be very similar. To be similar now they may have followed similar paths of change through time. Thus, for example, data for Norway and Sweden since the 1750s that demographically the two countries have been very similar right to the present. The countries chosen for consideration in the following sections are intended to be broadly representative of types of country.

5.2   Demographic change

In this section attention is focused on changes in birthrate and in deathrate over a long period. These measure respectively the number of live births and of deaths per 1000 total population of a region in a year. The difference between birthrate and deathrate gives the rate of change of population of a given region, unless net

Plate 5.3 (Opposite top) Small beginnings! The first iron bridge in the world, across the River Severn at Coalbrookdale, Shropshire

Plate 5.4 (Opposite bottom) Population explosions in the past were kept in check by very high mortality among the young. The sixteenth century Culpepper Monument, Goudhurst Church, Kent, shows that the lady of the family was kept busy producing children. In 1969 the author saw a television show in Brazil in which the cities of São Paulo and Rio de Janeiro were competing to find the largest family. São Paulo produced one with 22 live children but Rio won with 23

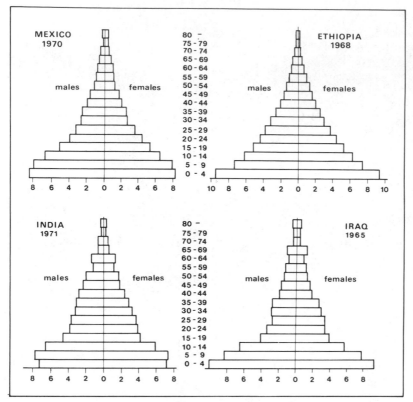

Figure 5.1 The population age and sex structure of developing countries from three different continents. Source: *United Nations Demographic Yearbook,* various numbers. The horizontal scales are percentages

migration in or out occurs.

Very broadly, three types of demographic structure can be found in the world, though they are on a continuum rather than being discrete situations.

(1) Birthrate and deathrate are both high. Such a situation must have been common throughout history and it is found among simple societies today. The average age and life expectancy are both low.

(2) Birthrate is high but deathrate low. As mortality is lowered, births exceed deaths and a growing population is the result with large numbers of children and young adults and few older people. Such a structure is found in many developing countries today. Four examples are given in Figure 5.1: Mexico, Ethiopia, India, and Iraq.

(3) Birthrate and deathrate are both low. Such a structure is characteristic of developed countries today. The average age

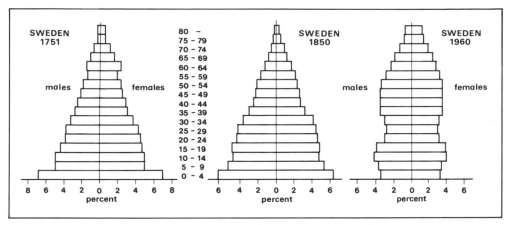

Figure 5.2 The population age and sex structure of Sweden in 1751, 1850, and 1960. Source: Mitchell (1975)

Table 5.1 Live births (B), deaths (D), and natural increase (N) per 1000 population in selected countries, 1977 or nearest year

	B	D	N		B	D	N
Africa				*Latin America*			
Algeria	48	15	32	Mexico	42	7	35
Egypt	36	12	23	Cuba	22	6	16
Nigeria	49	23	27	Brazil	37	9	28
Ivory Coast	46	21	25	Venezuela	37	6	31
Kenya	49	16	33	Argentina	23	9	13
Ethiopia	43	18	25				
Zaire	45	20	25				
S. Africa	40	15	25				
				Europe and North America			
				Sweden	13	11	2
Asia				U.K.	12	12	1
Iraq	44	11	32	France	14	11	4
Saudi Arabia	50	20	29	W. Germany	10	12	−2
Turkey	39	12	27	E. Germany	11	14	−4
Afghanistan	43	21	22	Poland	19	9	10
India	34	13	21	Italy	15	10	5
Burma	40	16	24	Spain	18	8	10
Indonesia	38	14	24	U.S.S.R.	18	9	9
China	27	10	17	U.S.A.	15	9	6
Japan	17	6	11	Canada	16	7	8

Source: *World Population Data Sheet,* 1977, Population Reference Bureau.

and life expectancy are both high. Figure 5.2 shows Sweden in 1960 and also as it was in 1850 and 1751.

Data for birthrate and deathrate in the late 1970s are given for selected countries in Table 5.1. The contrast in birthrate between developed and developing countries is very marked but even within the developing group there is a large range (Nigeria and Kenya with 49 per 1000 to Argentina and Cuba with 23 and 22 respectively). The contrast in deathrate is much less marked.

Long-term trends in birthrate and deathrate are shown for selected developed countries in Table 5.2. The fall in birthrate in Sweden, the U.S.A., and England and Wales is shown graphically in Figure 5.3. The rise and decline of the birthrate in Japan is also indicated, together with the trend in Sri Lanka and the current position of selected African and Latin American countries.

During the second half of the eighteenth century the birthrate in Finland fluctuated between 35 and 45 per 1000, a level comparable to that in many Latin American countries in the second half of the twentieth century. In contrast, the deathrate in Finland, which fluctuated in the second half of the eighteenth century between 20 and 40 per 1000, was much higher than it is now in Latin American countries. Thus the rate of natural increase of the population of Finland was much lower than it has been for the current developing countries in recent decades.

The birthrate in Sweden and Norway was appreciably lower than that in Finland, being mostly between 30 and 35 per 1000 in the period 1750-1850. The deathrate then was usually between 20 and 30 per 1000. The birthrate in Sweden from 1800 to the present can be followed in Figure 5.3. A gradual decline started around 1860 and continued until recently, falling from around 35 per 1000 to 15 per 1000. A broadly similar trend occurred in England and Wales and also in the United States (white population); the latter, however, had a very different demographic background. On the other hand, the birthrate in Japan has taken only roughly half as long as it took in Sweden to fall from 35 per 1000 (1910-20) to around 15-20 per 1000 (1970s).

Figure 5.4 shows birthrate and deathrate together in selected countries at different periods. At no time in its history since 1750 (see top diagrams in Figure 5.4) did Sweden have a gap between birthrate and deathrate anywhere near that found in most developing countries now. The gap between birthrate and deathrate for each country is shaded in the figure. Again, the rate of natural increase (birthrate minus deathrate) in Japan was never more than 15 per 1000 (1.5 percent) per year for any length of time during the

Table 5.2 Long term trends in live births (B) and deaths (D) per 1000 population in selected countries

	Sweden		U.S.A.	England and Wales		Japan		
	B	D	B	B	D		B	D
1800	29	31	55					
1810	33	32	54					
1820	33	25	53					
1830	33	24	51					
1840	31	20	48	32	23			
1850	32	20	43	33	21			
1860	35	18	41	34	21			
1870	29	20	38	35	23	1873	22	17
1880	29	18	35	34	21	1883	28	18
1890	28	17	32	30	20	1893	31	22
1900	26	18	30	29	18	1903	34	21
1910	25	14	29	25	14	1913	36	21
1920	24	13	27	26	12	1923	36	23
1930	15	12	21	16	11	1933	32	18
1940	15	11	19	14	14	1943	31	16
1950	17	10	23	16	12	1953	22	9
1960	14	10		17	12	1963	17	7
1970	13	10		16	12	1973	19	6
1975	13	11	15	12	12 (U.K.)	1975	17	6
1976	12	11	15	12	12 (U.K.)	1976	15	6

Sources: Mitchell (1975) and *World Population Data Sheets,* Population Reference Bureau

period of growth of the Japanese population and the modernization of its economy.

Birthrate and deathrate have virtually converged in some West European countries and it appears that they will both stabilize somewhere between 12 and 15 per 1000 in most developed countries in a decade or two. Most developed countries have a population structure similar to that of Sweden in 1960 (see Figure 5.2), though Australia, Canada, the U.S.S.R., and U.S.A. have proportionally rather more young people.

With regard to the developing countries, nothing very precise can be said either about their demographic history or about their future prospects. Data are lacking in most to show clearly when deathrate began to drop substantially below birthrate. Again, a comparison of past trends in now developed countries with future prospects for developing countries only shows what *could* happen. Even, however, if the birthrate in developing countries which currently have a level around 40-50 per 1000 drops in the future as fast as it

dropped in Japan from 35 to 15-20 per 1000 this century, some 50-70
years would still be needed for birthrate and deathrate to converge.
The population of the developing countries would grow
enormously between now and that future convergence.

5.3   The move out of agriculture

According to the Food and Agriculture Organisation (FAO), in the
early 1970s about half of the total economically active population
of the world was in agriculture and half in all other activities. The
percentage in agriculture in 1977 was estimated to be 47. Crossing
the 50 percent mark is itself no more than symbolic but the trend
from a predominantly agricultural economy is one of the major
transformations in the world and a key indicator of development.
Historical data for employment in various countries have been
gathered by Bairoch *et al.* (1968). Recent data are available from
FAO publications. The general heading of agriculture usually
includes forestry and fishing as well as all sectors of farming such as
crop farming and pastoralism. It is customary to study the change
from agriculture in terms of the declining share of employment
accounted for by that sector. In the present discussion, the
percentage *not* employed in agriculture is used. Agriculture will be
discussed again in Chapter 11.

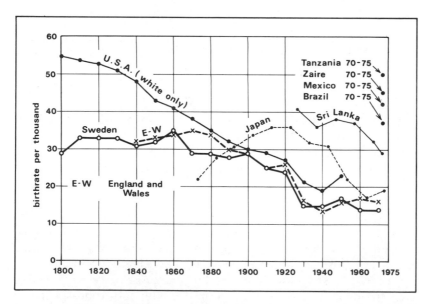

Figure 5.3 Birthrate (births per 1000 total population per year) in selected
countries from 1800 to 1974. Main sources: Mitchell (1975), *Nippon* (1975),
and U.S. Bureau of the Census (1975)

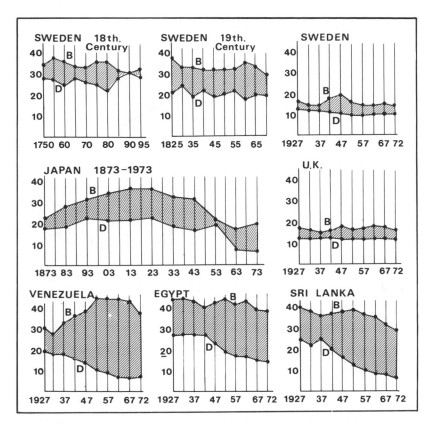

Figure 5.4 Birthrate and deathrate (births and deaths per 1000 total population per year) in countries during selected periods. Main sources: Mitchell (1975) and *United Nations Demographic Yearbook,* various years

Countries of the world with more than 85 percent or with less than 20 percent of their economically active population in employment other than agriculture are listed in Table 5.3. The percentage of total economically active population not employed in agriculture in 10 selected countries is shown in Table 5.4 for the whole period during which employment data have been available.

The U.K. has consistently been the least 'agricultural' country in the world. Already early in the nineteenth century over 75 percent of the economically active population were no longer in agriculture and in 1900 the share was over 90 percent. The long-term shift of employment out of agriculture for five countries that are now industrialized is shown in Figure 5.5. The graph shows a remarkable convergence throughout the period under consideration. In just over a century the share of non-agricultural employment in Japan rose from 15 percent to 85 percent, a 70 percent shift during 1872-1975. During this period the shift in the U.K. was from about 85

Table 5.3 Employment in activities other than agriculture

Over 85 percent not in agriculture	in 1977	Around 1900	Under 20 percent not in agriculture	in 1977
U.K.	98	91	Bhutan	6
Kuwait	98		Nepal	7
U.S.A.	97	62	Rwanda	9
Singapore	97		Niger	10
Hong Kong	97		C. African Republic	11
Belgium	96	73	Mali	12
W. Germany	95	62*	Chad	14
Puerto Rico	95		Lesotho	14
Canada	94	60	Madagascar	14
Luxembourg	94		Malawi	14
Malta	94		Bangladash	15
Netherlands	94	69	Mauritania	16
Sweden	94	46	Burundi	16
Switzerland	94	65	Upper Volta	17
Australia	94	68	Tanzania	17
Israel	92		Uganda	17
Denmark	92	53	Botswana	18
Norway	91	59	Cameroon	18
New Zealand	90	67	Guinea	18
France	90	58	Somalia	18
E. Germany	89	62*	Ivory Coast	19
Uruguay	88		Ethiopia	19
Czechoslovakia	88		*World regions*	
Lebanon	88		North America	97
Iceland	87		Europe	83
Italy	87		Oceania	78
Japan	87	41	South America	66
Argentina	86	30	Africa	33
			World	53

* All Germany
Sources: *Food and Agriculture Organisation Production Yearbook* 1977, and Bairoch *et al.* (1968)

percent to 98 percent, or by 13 percent, but it would obviously have been impossible to change by much more than this amount.

In Chapter 2 a comparison was made between the U.S.A., Italy, Thailand, and Bangladesh. The employment structure of these four countries in the 1970s may be compared (see Figure 5.6) with that of Japan now and Japan a century ago. The U.S.A. and Italy roughly resemble Japan now while Thailand and Bangladesh roughly resemble Japan as it was a century ago. It is tempting to assume

Table 5.4 The movement out of agriculture in 10 selected countries. Percentage not in agriculture

U.K.		U.S.A.		France		Italy		Japan	
1841	78			1842	48				
1851	78	1850	36	1856	48				
1861	81	1860	41	1866	50				
1871	85	1870	50			1871	39	1872	15
1881	87	1880	50	1886	53	(1881	49)	1880	18
1891	89	1890	57	1896	55			1890	26
1901	91	1900	62	1906	57	1901	41	1900	30
1911	91	1910	68	1911	59	1911	45	1910	37
1921	93	1920	73	1921	58	1921	44	1920	46
1931	94	1930	78	1931	64	1931	55	1930	51
		1940	84	1946	64			1940	56
1951	95	1950	88	1954	73	1951	58	1950	52
1961	96	1960	93	1962	80	1961	71	1960	67
1976	98	1976	97	1976	89	1976	86	1976	86
1977	98	1977	97	1977	90	1977	87	1977	87

India		Egypt		Mexico		Venezuela		Australia	
1901	33							1901	68
1911	28	1907	31	1910	36			1911	76
1921	27	1917	31	1921	37			1921	78
1931	33	1927	40	1930	32			1933	79
		1937	29	1940	35	1941	49	1947	85
1951	26	1947	36	1950	42	1950	56	1954	86
1961	27	1960	42	1960	46	1961	68	1961	89
1976	34	1976	48	1976	60	1976	79	1976	93
1977	35	1977	48	1977	61	1977	80	1977	94

Sources: *Food and Agriculture Organisation Production Yearbook* (various years) and Bairoch *et al.* (1968)

that such developing countries might follow the path of Japan, perhaps at an even faster rate.

Changes in employment structure during the twentieth century in both developed and developing countries are shown in Figure 5.7. One finding that emerges from a study of employment trends is that Latin American countries, though conventionally classed as developing, in most cases have more than half of their economically active population in non-agricultural sectors (Puerto Rico 95 percent, Argentina 86, Venezuela 79, Mexico 60). The overall average for South America is 66 percent. In contrast, about two-thirds of the economically active population of Africa is still in agriculture.

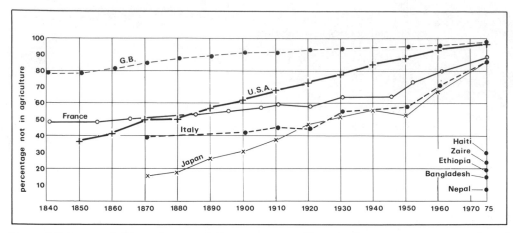

Figure 5.5 Economically active population not engaged in agriculture as a percentage of total economically active population in selected countries during 1840-1975. Source: Bairoch *et al.* (1968)

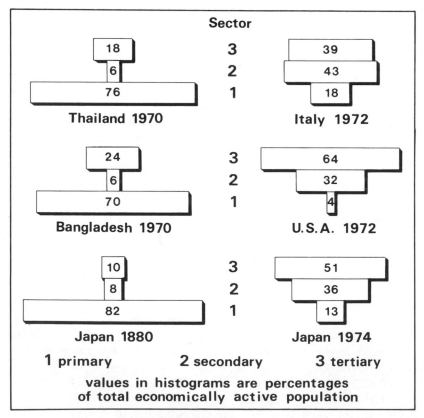

Figure 5.6 The comparative employment structure of selected countries. See text for explanation

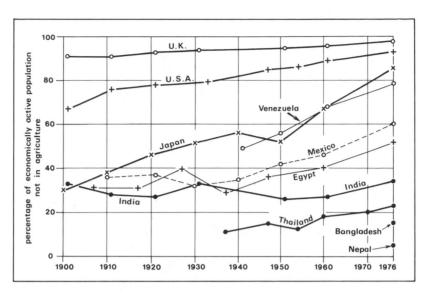

Figure 5.7 Economically active population not engaged in agriculture as a percentage of total economically active population in selected countries during 1900-1976. Main source: Bairoch *et al.* (1968)

If the U.K. trend in Figure 5.5 is projected back in time, it seems reasonable to estimate that by 1700 at least 25 percent of the economically active population was no longer in agriculture, by 1750 at least a third, and by 1800 at least half. The U.K. took from about 1700 to 1870, or about 170 years, to move from 25 percent not in agriculture to 85 percent not in agriculture, a process which Japan achieved in half the time, during 1890-1975, or in 85 years. The implications of such a comparison and of others that can be shown from the data are far from clear. Nevertheless it seems reasonable to assume that the other currently industrialized countries in Figure 5.5 were able to learn something from the slowly gained experience of the U.K. Even, however, if the developing countries plotted in Figure 5.5 on their 1975 positions were to follow the path of Japan, they would take around 100 years to reach the 85 percent level of employment not in agriculture achieved by Japan.

5.4 Changes in the production and consumption of steel

The gap between developed and developing countries with regard to the output and consumption of products from heavy industry is very marked. The iron and steel industry has been chosen to illustrate the gap, since its great size and key position in a modern

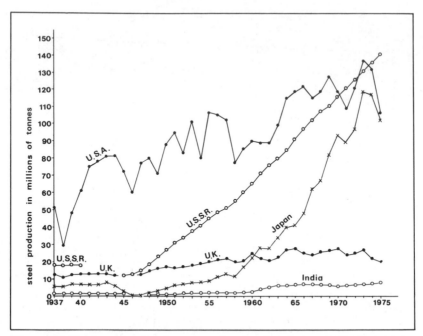

Figure 5.8 Steel production in selected countries during 1937-1975. Main source: *United Nations Statistical Yearbook,* various numbers

economy give it a prominent place. This section is subdivided into a consideration first of steel production and then of steel consumption.

Steel production in the last four decades is shown in Table 5.5 for the 10 countries of the world with the largest production in 1975 and also for seven selected developing countries. Year by year production data are shown graphically in Figure 5.8 for four leading producers and for India from 1937 to 1975. As total production is considered in Table 5.5 and in Figure 5.8, the population size of the countries should be taken into account. The U.S.S.R. is somewhat larger in population than the U.S.A. but more than twice as large as Japan. India, however, has about three times as many inhabitants as the U.S.A. The British iron and steel industry has stagnated since the mid-1950s while production in the U.S.S.R. has risen steadily since the Second World War and production in Japan very fast since the late 1950s.

Although only the major producers of steel are shown in Table 5.5 there are enough data to demonstrate again the commonly found paradox of a faster relative increase in production in developing countries than in developed ones but a growing absolute gap between them. In 1937 virtually all the world's steel

Table 5.5 Steel production in selected countries, 1937-76, in millions of tonnes

	1937	1940	1945	1950	1955	1960	1965	1970	1975	1976
U.S.S.R.	18	18	12	27	45	65	91	116	141	145
U.S.A.	51	61	72	88	106	90	119	119	106	116
Japan	6	7	2	5	9	22	41	93	102	107
W. Germany	20*	22*	—	12	21	34	37	45	40	42
France	8	4	2	9	13	17	20	24	22	23
Italy	2	2	—	2	5	8	13	17	22	23
U.K.	13	13	12	17	20	25	27	28	20	22
Poland	1	—	—	3	4	7	9	12	15	15
Czechoslovakia	2	2	1	3	4	7	9	11	14	15
Canada	1	2	3	3	4	5	9	11	13	13
China	—	1	—	—	3	18	15	18	29	27
Brazil	—	—	—	1	1	2	3	5	8	9
India	1	1	1	1	2	3	6	6	8	9
Mexico	—	—	—	—	1	2	2	4	5	5
Turkey	—	—	—	—	—	—	1	1	1	1
N. Korea	—	—	—	—	—	1	1	2	3	3
Venezuela	—	—	—	—	—	—	1	1	1	1
World	135	142	113	189	266	328	443	594	643	673

* All Germany.
— Under 0.5 million tonnes or data not available (but production small).
Source: *United Nations Statistical Yearbook 1957, 1966, 1976.*

came from the developed countries. In 1975 about 10 percent came from developing countries, including China. The rate of growth of steel production was faster in several developing countries than in developed ones during the period but the gap in the quantity actually produced rose from about 130 million in 1937 to about 550 million in 1975. In addition, the population of the developing countries has roughly doubled during 1937-75 whereas that of the developed ones has not changed greatly.

The steel gap has long been in evidence. Eighteenth century Europe produced considerable quantities of iron using charcoal for smelting ore, but Britain began to achieve a dominant position by replacing charcoal with coke from coal. France, Belgium, and other countries gradually adopted the process. It was about 120 years after the first commercial smelting of iron with coke at Coalbrookdale that steel production per inhabitant began to rise very fast in the U.K., as is shown in Table 5.6. By 1890, however, the U.S.A. was producing more per inhabitant than the U.K. In a historical perspective it can be seen that in 1975 India produced about 10kg of steel per inhabitant, the amount produced per inhabitant in the U.K. in 1870. By 1890 the U.K. and U.S.A. were each producing more than ten times as much steel per inhabitant as India does now and about four times as much as China does now.

Table 5.6 Total and *per capita* steel *production* in four countries

	Total in thousands of tonnes				Kg per inhabitant			
	U.K.	France	Sweden	U.S.A.	U.K.	France	Sweden	U.S.A.
1870	300	80	10		12	2	2	
1880	1380	380	40		47	10	9	
1890	3490	680	160	7700	110	18	35	120
1900	4970	1500	280	19,400	140	40	50	250
1910	6340	3430	420	39,600	160	90	80	430
1920	7000	2650	380	60,400	160	70	60	570
1930	7510	8990	610	71,900	170	220	100	580
1940	13,040	5560	1150	82,800	280	140	180	630
1950	16,080	9210	1440	100,100	330	220	210	660
1960	22,550	16,690	3180	90,070	440	370	420	500
1970	26,450	23,050	5370	119,310	490	460	660	590
1975	20,200	21,530	5610	105,820	360	410	680	490
1976	22,270	23,220	5170	116,120	400	440	630	540

Sources: Mitchell (1975), *United Nations Statistical Yearbooks,* and U.S. Bureau of the Census (1975).

Table 5.7 Steel consumption in kilogrammes per inhabitant in selected countries, 1930s-1970s

	1936-38	1950	1955	1960	1965	1970	1975	1976
U.K.	230	280	370	430	420	460	390	410
U.S.A.	320	570	620	500	660	620	550	600
France	130	160	240	310	330	460	350	430
Japan	80	50	80	210	290	680	580	530
Sweden	220	290	400	550	680	730	770	730
Australia	180	270	330	400	510	490	470	350
U.S.S.R.	100	140	240*	300	380	460	550	570
Italy	50	60	120	190	240	390	320	390
India	4	5	7	11	16	12	14	13
Indonesia	3	2	3	3	3	4	10	10
Venezuela	40	50	120	80	140	160	190	230
Peru	10	10	20	20	30	30	60	30
China	3	2	6	27	14	29	42	32

* 1956.
Source: *United Nations Statistical Yearbook* (various years).

Table 5.8 Steel consumption in kilogrammes per inhabitant in 1970 and 1976 in countries with a very low level of consumption

	1970	1976		1970	1976
Afghanistan	1	1	Mozambique	8	3
Bangladesh	1	1	Rwanda	2	2
Burma	3	3	Sierra Leone	4	4
Ethiopia	3	1	Sri Lanka	8	5
Guinea	15	2	Sudan	7	6
Haiti	5	7	Tanzania	6	6
Kampuchea	2	1	Uganda	3	0
Laos	3	0	Vietnam	10	6
Madagascar	10	4	Zaire	9	2
Malawi	2	3			

Source: *United Nations Statistical Yearbook* (various years).

In view of the economies of scale achieved by producing iron and steel in comparatively large plants and the high cost of establishing an iron and steel works, few developing countries produce steel, though all import and consume some. It is possible to view the steel gap in terms of consumption as well as of production. Table 5.7 shows the enormous gap in consumption per inhabitant between the developed and the developing countries. Of the five developing countries included, only Venezuela is showing signs of crossing from one league to the other. The countries of the world with a consumption of 5kg of steel per inhabitant or less are shown in Table 5.8, arranged alphabetically by continent. In most of these very poor countries a reduction can be seen in the amount consumed during the first half of the 1970s.

Apart from a slight decline in steel production in Western industrial countries since 1973 there is little about world steel production and consumption in the last few decades or even longer to suggest that the gap between developed and developing countries has done anything but widen. To reach the level of consumption of steel achieved in France or the U.K. in the 1970s, Brazil would have to achieve a fivefold increase, India a thirtyfold increase, and many African countries a hundredfold increase.

5.5   Changes in efficiency illustrated by yields per hectare of selected crops

Changes in yields of major crops have been chosen to represent differences in productive efficiency between developed and

Table 5.9 Yields of maize, wheat, and rice in hundreds of kilogrammes per hectare in selected countries and in selected years or periods. Countries ranked according to 1972-76 averages

	1934-38	1948/49-52/53	1961-65	1972-76	1972	1973	1974	1975	1976	1977
Maize										
1 U.S.A.	14	25	42	54	61	57	45	54	55	57
2 Italy	21	18	33	50	40	40	57	59	56	66
3 France	16	14	30	45	44	54	47	42	38	53
4 U.S.S.R.	11	13	22	29	25	33	31	28	31	33
World	13	16	22	28	28	28	25	29	28	30
5 Brazil	14	12	13	15	14	14	16	16	16	17
6 S. Africa	n.a.	8	13	15	17	10	18	16	13	17
7 Mexico	6	8	11	13	13	11	13	13	13	12
8 Kenya	n.a.	13	11	12	13	13	13	13	11	14
9 Venezuela	14	10	11	12	11	10	12	13	11	15
10 Nigeria	n.a.	9	6	7	8	6	8	7	7	8
Wheat										
1 U.K.	23	27	41	44	42	44	50	43	39	49
2 France	16	18	29	43	46	45	46	39	38	42
3 Switzerland	23	27	33	42	42	38	46	40	44	37
4 Mexico	8	9	19	35	27	35	36	36	42	34
5 U.S.A.	9	11	17	21	22	22	18	21	20	21
6 Canada	7	13	14	18	17	17	15	18	21	19
World	13	10	12	17	16	17	16	16	18	17
7 U.S.S.R.	9	8	10	15	15	17	14	11	16	15
8 India	7	7	8	13	14	13	12	13	14	14
9 Ethiopia	n.a.	4	7	8	8	8	7	8	10	11

Rice

1 Japan	36	40	50	59	58	60	58	62	55	62
2 Italy	53	49	51	54	41	55	52	58	54	39
3 U.S.A.	25	26	44	51	53	48	50	51	52	50
4 China	25	22	28	32	32	32	33	33	33	35
World	18	16	21	24	23	24	24	25	24	26
5 Pakistan	15*	14*	14	23	24	24	22	23	23	24
6 Thailand	13	13	18	18	18	19	17	18	18	18
7 Bangladesh	15*	14*	17	18	16	20	17	19	19	19
8 India	14	11	15	17	16	17	16	19	18	19
9 Philippines	11	12	13	17	15	16	16	17	18	20
10 Brazil	14	16	16	15	14	15	16	14	15	17

* Both parts of Pakistan
n.a. Not available
Source: *Food and Agriculture Organisation Production Yearbook* 1953, Vol. 7, Pt 1; 1962, Vol. 16; 1974, Vol. 28.1; 1976, Vol. 30; 1977, Vol. 31.

developing countries. Yields tend to vary considerably from year to year in a given country. Averages over several years are therefore a more reliable guide to general features and trends.

Data for yields of three cereals are shown in Table 5.9 during three periods since the end of the Second World War and yearly from 1972-1977. Wheat is grown mainly in developed countries, rice in developing countries, but maize widely in both types of country.

Table 5.10 Yields of selected crops in Peru and other countries, 1930s-1970s. All yields are in hundreds of kilogrammes per hectare

	1934-38	1946-49	1961-65	1972-3	1975-76	1977
Potatoes						
1 Switzerland	158	163	248	405	404	378
2 Canada	88	113	177	201	244	224
3 U.K.	169	173	228	286	214	285
4 Colombia	46	47	108	121	120	126
5 PERU	29	51	58	66	66	64
Barley						
1 Switzerland	19	23	33	42	40	39
2 U.K.	21	23	36	39	36	45
3 Canada	11	12	17	22	23	25
4 Argentina	9	12	12	14	14	11
5 PERU	10	12	10	9	9	9
Maize						
1 Italy	21	17	33	53	58	66
2 Canada	25	28	48	57	56	59
3 France	16	10	30	52	40	53
4 PERU	16	18	15	18	17	17
5 Mexico	6	7	11	13	13	12
Cotton seed						
1 Mexico	5	5	17	22	23	n.a.
2 Turkey	4	5	11	19	20	n.a.
3 PERU	8	9	16	15	17	n.a.
4 U.S.A.	4	5	15	14	13	n.a.
5 India	2	2	4	5	5	n.a.
Sugar cane						
1 PERU	n.a.	1330	1450	1610	1580	1560
2 Australia	n.a.	600	730	820	830	800
3 India	n.a.	450	450	490	510	540
4 Argentina	n.a.	330	500	530	500	460
5 Cuba	n.a.	380	380	440	440	440

n.a. Not available.
Source: *Food and Agriculture Organisation Production Yearbook,* 1976, 1977.

In each section of Table 5.9 the countries chosen are ranked in descending order of the average yield for 1972-76.

The data for all three cereals show clearly that on the whole the yield gap between developed and developing countries was greater in the 1970s than the 1930s. For example the yield of maize in France rose between the mid-1930s and mid-1970s from 1600 to 4500kg per hectare while that in Mexico, Kenya, Venezuela, and Nigeria stayed roughly the same or only rose slightly. In one respect the current low cereal yields in most developing countries may be regarded as advantageous. If increases in yields could be achieved comparable to those in such countries as France and the U.S.A., then there is much potential for increasing cereal output. The 'Green Revolution' of the 1960s produced increases in cereal yields in parts of some developing countries but not enough to make much overall impression on the yield gap.

Yields in selected periods for four crops not shown in Table 5.9 are given in Table 5.10 and the trends are shown graphically in Figure 5.9. The familiar yield gap between developed and developing countries is evident in some trends, as for example in yields per hectare of potatoes and barley between Switzerland and Peru. The latter country is included under all the five crops in Table 5.10 and, although thought of as a developing country, achieves higher yields of some crops than developed countries. Mexico and Peru both have higher yields per hectare of cotton seed than the U.S.A. and Peru outstrips Australia in sugar cane yields. The explanation of the changing position of Peru in the table is that potatoes, barley, and maize are grown mainly in the Andean mountain region of Peru, where bioclimatic conditions are harsh and techniques primitive, while cotton and sugar cane are grown in fertile coastal oases easily supplied with fishmeal fertilizer. This example shows that one must not assume that levels of productivity and efficiency are always higher in developed than in developing countries.

5.6 Changes in infant mortality

Infant mortality has been taken as an index to trace changes in the quality of life in developed and developing countries. It has the advantage of having been recorded as far back as the eighteenth century for Sweden. By the 1970s some developed countries had reached the very low level of about 10 deaths of infants under the age of one year per 1000 live births. For both technical and economic reasons it seems unlikely that levels much below 10 per 1000 could be widely achieved.

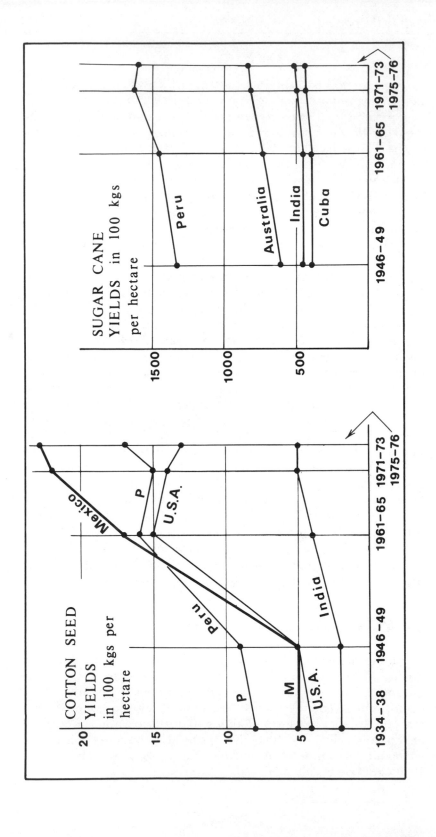

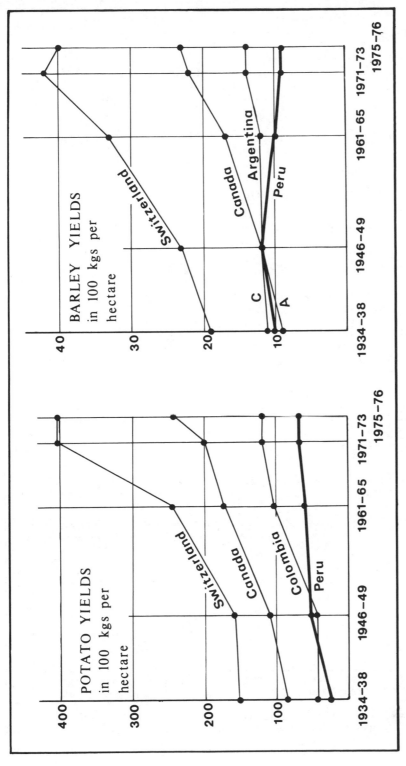

Figure 5.9 Yields of potatoes, barley, cotton seed, and sugar cane in selected countries from 1934-38 to 1975-76. Peru is included in all four diagrams for comparative purposes

Table 5.11 Infant deaths per 1000 live births in selected countries, 1977

Sweden	8	Guinea-Bissau	208
Japan	10	Angola	203
Finland	10	Niger	200
Netherlands	11	C. African Republic	190
Norway	11	Mali	188
France	12	Mauritania	187
Denmark	12	Benin	185
Switzerland	12	Afghanistan	182
Spain	14	Upper Volta	182
Canada	15	Kenya	181
Australia	16	Nigeria	180
New Zealand	16	Congo (P.R.)	180
E. Germany	16	Gabon	178
Belgium	16	Somalia	177
U.K.	16	Namibia	177
U.S.A.	16	Guinea	175

Source: *1977 World Population Data Sheet,* Population Reference Bureau.

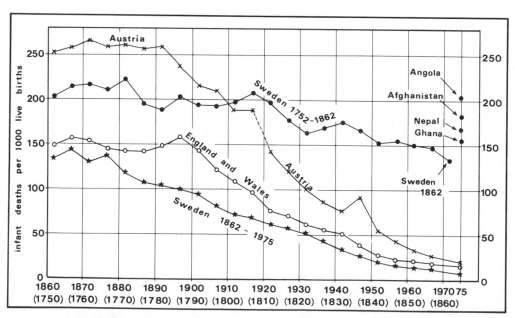

Figure 5.10 Deaths of infants under the age of one year per 1000 live births in selected countries during 1860-1975 and also during 1750-1860 for Sweden. Main source: Mitchell (1975)

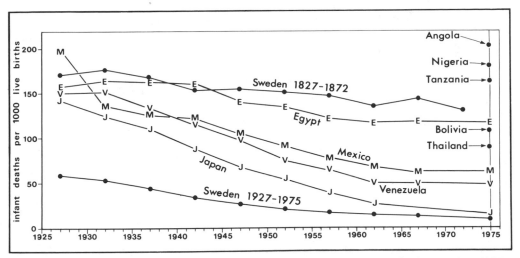

Figure 5.11 Deaths of infants under the age of one year per 1000 live births during 1925-1975. Main source: Mitchell (1975)

The countries of the world with the lowest and the highest infant mortality rates are given in Table 5.11. Eleven of the 16 countries with the lowest indices are in Europe. All but one of the 16 countries with the highest indices are in Africa. The gap revealed in Table 5.11 is massive. The rates in the worst African countries are similar to those recorded in Sweden during 1750-1810. Many Asian countries currently have infant mortality rates similar to those recorded in Sweden during 1840-1890.

Infant mortality rates in Sweden since 1750 and in Austria and England and Wales since 1860 are shown graphically in Figure 5.10. The values for the three countries are averages for five-year periods (e.g. 1862 for 1860-64). A steady decline in infant mortality rates can be observed in Sweden since about 1875 and in England and Wales since about 1895. Before Austria took its present territorial form after the First World War it had very high infant mortality rates during 1860-1890, about twice as high as those in Sweden during the same period. Austria at that time included some very backward areas in the Balkans. The Austrian data do suggest, however, that infant mortality was significantly higher in some of the present developed countries during their past than in the present developing countries today according to official estimates. On the other hand, mortality rates are probably undercounted or underestimated in many developing countries because not all births and deaths are registered.

Infant mortality trends in 17 selected countries are given in Table 5.12. In Figure 5.11 the experiences of Egypt, Mexico, Venezuela,

Table 5.12 Average yearly deaths of infants per 1000 live births in selected countries during the twentieth century

	Egypt	Canada	Mexico	Puerto Rico	Peru	Venezuela	India	France	Australia
1920-24	141	94	226			155		97	61
25-29	153	94	194			150		91	53
30-34	163	80	135	128		152		80	43
35-39	163	69	128	123	113	135		71	39
40-44	158	57	119	106	117	117	183	82	37
45-49	139	47	105	79	109	98		72	28
50-54	134	37	92	64	100	75	139	46	24
55-59	122	31	78	52	99	64		34	21
60-64	117	27	69	45	88	50		26	20
1975	116	15	66	24	110	49	122	12	16

	Sierra Leone	Chile	Japan	Philippines	Bulgaria	Portugal	U.S.S.R.	U.S.A.
1920-24		241	165	157	157	153		77
25-29		224	141	155	150	142	178	69
30-34		206	124	153	144	145		60
35-39		213	110	142	146	139	166	53
40-44		176	87	136	128	132	182	42
45-49	185	150	67	115	127	111		33
50-54	143	128	53	102	94	92	75	28
55-59	139	117	38	83	66	88	47	26
60-64	119	115	26	71	38	77	32	25
1975	136	77	10	74	23	38	28	16

Main sources: *United Nations Demographic Yearbook 1966*, Table 14, and *1977 World Population Data Sheet*, Population Reference Bureau.

and Japan during 1925-1975 are compared with those of Sweden during the same period and of Sweden exactly 100 years earlier. In all the developing countries represented in Table 5.12 there has been a decline in the infant mortality rate since the 1920s, but evidence for the 1970s suggests little change in the last 10-15 years. It is possible that an actual continuation of the decline is hidden by a more thorough counting and recording of infant deaths now than some decades ago.

5.7   The concept of stages of growth

The purpose of this chapter has been to give some examples of the way the development gap has grown in recent decades and to show longer-term trends. There are both advantages and disadvantages in comparing the present developed countries as they were in the past with the present developing countries now.

The developing countries of the late twentieth century have already been considerably affected by the technology of developed countries. For example, even limited improvements in health and hygiene introduced to many developing countries from developed ones in recent decades appear to have been a major cause in reducing mortality. 'Technology' to reduce fertility has been slower to diffuse in developing countries. As a result the rate of natural increase of population has risen sharply and reached higher levels in developing countries in the latter part of the twentieth century than the levels experienced in the nineteenth century by the present developed countries.

Sophisticated means of production and transportation not available in the developed countries have been imposed on developing countries in the twentieth century. Thus oil can be extracted as easily in Saudi Arabia or Gabon as in the U.S.A. or the U.S.S.R. Until late in the nineteenth century it was available only in very small quantities in the present developed countries, when they were 'developing'.

It was considered necessary in this chapter to trace briefly the paths of the present developed countries to their present high levels of production and consumption and their stable demographic structure. Much that has been written on development contains assumptions or hopes about stages of economic growth to be followed by each country. It has been assumed that very broadly the developing countries of now will follow the path already taken by the present developed countries. Some ideas on the matter will now be briefly reviewed.

The concept of stages of development as applied to political units is not a new one. In the eighteenth century, for example, Vico (1744) proposed three types of state. The credit seems to go to Karl Marx for the first serious attempt to identify stages of social and economic development.

A recent official version of the Soviet line on the state of Marxism-Leninism is explained in a light, popular publication by B. Datsiouk (1976) and will serve for the purposes of the present book. The following stages are identified:

(1) A very *simple society* (perhaps the Tasaday of the Philippines). There is collective ownership of resources and means of production. Everyone consumes about the same (very little).
(2) The *slave stage*.
(3) The *feudal stage*.
(4) *Capitalism,* in which ownership of means of production is concentrated in a few hands and a market economy (*laissez-faire*) prevails. Regional inequalities are marked. *Imperialism* follows, a stage Marx did not predict but which was inserted by Lenin. An 'unfair' international division of labour prevails, with colonial (or former colonial) powers highly developed and industrialized and their colonies (or ex-colonies) producing raw materials and having few industries.
(5) *Socialism* (Soviet style 1970s) or 'advanced' socialism. No unemployment, reduction of regional contrasts, no private ownership of means of production but classes still in existence (intelligentsia, workers, and collective farm peasants), and big differences still in income (according to type of employment), but not in wealth.
(6) *Communism,* with no social classes, the state disappearing, abundance for all, and no unpleasant work.

The stages described are summarized in the two diagrams in Figure 5.12. Since they have been 'scientifically' worked out by Marx, and 'proved' to be inevitable, they presumably take place 'naturally' and do not therefore need to be fostered. They do not, however, fit into a clearcut time scale so there is no way of saying where they will happen or when. The Soviet Union itself has in practice taken a pragmatic view towards Marxist-type stages of development. It has, however, criticized the Chinese Communist Party for attempting to miss out stages and leap into a communist stage prematurely.

The Soviet Union has itself contributed to the introduction of communist parties in several developing countries including Cuba, Vietnam, and possibly Angola and Ethiopia, the last three very

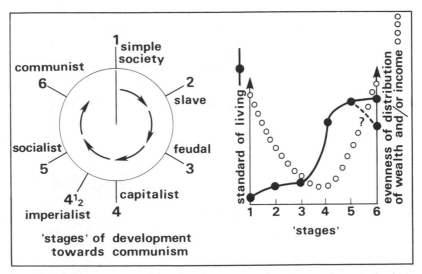

Figure 5.12 'Stages' of development towards communism and their implications in terms of living standards and evenness of distribution of wealth or income. See text for explanation

backward technologically and, in the case of Ethiopia, still feudal, in the early 1970s. It remains to be seen to what extent Soviet influence can alter material conditions in the three very poor countries. Even to keep the economy of Cuba at a reasonable level the U.S.S.R. according to Soviet data has been contributing about a million dollars a day to Cuba, or $30-40 per year to each Cuban citizen. Without or even with Soviet aid it seems unlikely that the launching of developing countries into a socialist 'stage' of economic and social development will make much immediate difference to living standards there.

The American economic historian W.W. Rostow was not prepared to accept the Marxist-Leninist interpretation of history as of universal validity. In 1960 *The Stages of Economic Growth* was published. Its subtitle is *A non-Communist manifesto*. In his preface to the above book, Rostow wrote of his time as an undergraduate in the mid-1930s: 'Specifically, I found Marx's solution to the problem of linking economic and non-economic behaviour — and the solutions of others who had grappled with it — unsatisfactory, without then feeling prepared to offer an alternative'. Elsewhere in the same book he stated: 'I have gradually come to the view that it is possible and, for certain limited purposes, it is useful to break down the story of each national economy — and sometimes the story of regions — according to this set of stages'. The five stages (see Figure 5.13) are:

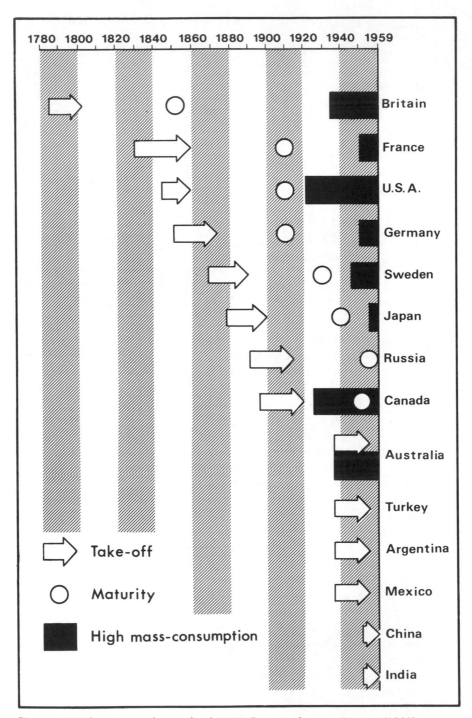

Figure 5.13 The stages of growth of W.W. Rostow. Source: Rostow (1960)

   (i) The traditional society
  (ii) The preconditions for take-off
 (iii) The take-off
 (iv) The drive to maturity
  (v) The age of high mass-consumption.

Among other rather rigid features of the scheme is the idea that it takes about 40 years for a country to pass from the end of stage (iii) to the beginning of stage (v), as though at a certain point in its development it gets on a conveyor belt moving along at a fixed speed.

In *The Stages of Economic Growth,* Rostow stresses: 'I cannot emphasize too strongly at the outset, that the stages-of-growth are an arbitrary and limited way of looking at the sequence of modern history: and they are, in no absolute sense, a correct way. They are designed, in fact, to dramatize not merely the uniformities of modernization but also — and equally — the uniqueness of each nation's experience.' Rostow's stages are shown with reference to selected countries on a time scale from 1780 to 1959 in Figure 5.13. Unfortunately the apparently easy or inevitable stages of growth seem to have been taken very literally by various people since 1960 though less enthusiastically perhaps by economists and economic historians.

In later writings, Rostow has been less emphatic about stages of growth of countries or regions. In *How it all Began,* Rostow (1975) is concerned with the beginnings and causes of industrialization. For example he considers that a 'commercial revolution' in Europe in the eighteenth century contributed to an expansion of income and to Europe's ability to support an enlarged population. In addition to this a regular flow of new technology was needed. He regards the expansion of income and population, the process of urbanization, and aspects of foreign trade as stimulating the development of certain technologies:

> Third, there was some oblique linkage of foreign trade to the new technologies that were at the heart of the phase of the industrial revolution. These technologies arose in Britain from three problems: how to produce good pig and wrought iron cheaply with coke as the fuel; how to make a reasonably efficient steam engine; and how to spin cotton with machinery.

The uniqueness of the British experience, rather than the universal occurrence of take-off for every country at some instant of time, is now stressed by Rostow.

The ideas of Marx and his disciples and of Rostow have been referred to here because in the view of the author they have had a great influence on the way people who are not economists or economic historians have viewed development. The Marxist 'stages' have more often been brought about by 'revolutionary' events or by being imposed on countries from outside than in smooth transitions from one state to another. Rostow's stages ignore basic features of countries such as their spatial layout, size, and natural resources. One finds it hard to think of Haiti or Chad or Nepal going through the five stages of economic growth.

Any stages of development in history seem too close to the analogy of the organism, programmed for a once-for-all young, adult and old-age life process. A particular region might set out on some process of growth but through lack of natural resources or technology grow crippled during its stages of growth. Does it have another chance later on?

Like Rostow, the Swedish economist Myrdal (1957) has influenced Western thought on development since the late 1950s. In *Economic Theory and Under-Developed Regions* he was not greatly concerned about stages of development but more than Rostow about the actual plight of the underdeveloped regions of the world of the 1950s. He was particularly concerned about the large gap between rich and poor countries, and stressed that the gap was growing. The passage that follows applies to differences within countries but could with reservations be about the world as a whole:

> The main idea I want to convey is that the play of forces in the market normally tends to increase, rather than to decrease, the inequalities between regions.

> If things were left to market forces unhampered by any policy interferences, industrial production, commerce, banking, insurance, shipping and, indeed, almost all those economic activities which in a developing economy tend to give a bigger than average return — and, in addition, science, art, literature, education and higher culture generally — would cluster in certain localities and regions, leaving the rest of the country more or less in a backwater.

> Occasionally these favoured localities and regions offer particularly good natural conditions for the economic activities concentrated there; in rather more cases they did so at the time when they started to gain a competitive advantage.

For naturally economic geography sets the stage. Commercial centres are, of course usually located in places where there are reasonably good natural conditions for the construction of a port, and centres for heavy industry are most often located not too far away from coal and iron resources.

Myrdal also felt that in market economy countries 'market forces tend to increase rather than decrease inequalities between regions'. He stressed the enormous effort and sacrifices that would have to be made by underdeveloped countries to change their economies and raise living standards. Countries already industrialized by the 1950s had made such sacrifices in the past:

> ... the one-century-delayed industrial revolution which has been taking place in the Soviet Union under very different political and institutional conditions has closely followed, in this one respect, the pattern of earliest capitalist development, in that the levels of real income and consumption of the working masses were kept exceedingly low to allow for sustained rapid capital formation.

> There is no other road to economic development than a compulsory rise in the share of the national income which is withheld from consumption and devoted to investment. This implies a policy of the utmost austerity — quite independently of whether the increased savings are engendered by high levels of profit to be ploughed back in industrial expansion or by increased taxation.

Things would have to get worse in the developed countries before they could be made better.

An examination in this chapter of past trends casts doubt on the prospects that the present developing countries can meaningfully follow the earlier path of the currently developed ones. As noted, they must be profoundly affected by scientific and technological developments that exist now and are available to them but which were still being invented or slowly applied 100-200 years ago. Brookfield (1973) warns: 'underdevelopment is a discrete historical experience that cannot be identified in the earlier experience of the present developed countries'.

If natural resources are really restricted, and are very unevenly distributed according to population, as will be clearly shown in Chapter 7, then the prospect of rapid economic growth is dim for most developing countries of today. The 'growing season' for nations to take off and reach maturity could be nearly over. A few developing countries like Venezuela, Saudi Arabia, and South Korea may just make it. It may even be that *because* the present developed countries have increased material production so massively in the last 100 years they have made it impossible for the developing countries to close the gap in the fashion that theoretically they should according to ideas of stages of growth and the achievement of maturity. To pursue the 'take-off' analogy of Rostow, it could be that so many countries have already 'taken-off' that there is not room in the sky for others to join them.

The present framework for studying world development

6.1 The present system of sovereign states

Almost all the land surface of the earth and an increasing proportion of the sea is subdivided into the territory of some 200 sovereign states. The governments of these states are committed to guarding and furthering the interests of their citizens. The acquisition of new territory, either hitherto unoccupied or at the expense of another state, has been a frequent theme in history. European powers in the period 1500-1900 were engaged for long periods in acquiring colonies, together with their natural resources and people. Although virtually no land areas now remain unclaimed, vast areas of the world's seas are being annexed as water in which states have prior claim to natural resources.

The present countries of the world rarely fit exactly into the underlying cultural features of human society, reflected in language, religion, and other forms. The U.S.S.R., for example, contains over 100 national groups, most with distinctive languages. Speakers of German, on the other hand, are found in both Germanies, in Austria, and in much of Switzerland.

Although it does not conform precisely to cultural distributions, the basic system of world sovereign states is very resilient. Figure 6.1 shows names on a world map published in 1771. Nearly all the major countries of the world of the 1970s can be distinguished, though Africa had not yet been carved up into the arbitrary European colonies that have subsequently emerged as about 50 new countries in that continent.

In the view of the author, without the occurrence of a major world conflict comparable in extent to those of the First and Second World Wars, drastic changes in the present system of

169

sovereign states seem very unlikely. Regional movements, such as those of the Basques and Catalans in Spain and the Kurds in four countries of Southwest Asia, may be strong in many countries. Complete sovereignty has rarely been given easily by a central government to one of its regions. In the opposite direction, moves towards greater unity and unification in such supranational groups as the European Economic Community and the Latin American Free Trade Association have been slower than might have been expected or hoped for in the 1960s. It seems reasonable to forecast that there will be comparatively few changes in the number or territorial extent of the countries of the world for at least a few decades.

International trade is a balanced exchange between countries, at least globally, of various goods, even if the flow between particular pairs of trading partners is not exactly equal in each direction. The prices of certain types of commodities may be regarded as unfairly high (or low) by different countries. Thus in countries exporting raw materials it is argued that they have to export too much for the manufactured goods they receive in return. On the other hand, in the Western industrial countries it was felt in 1973-74 that the sudden increases in the price of oil were unfair to them and also to the many non-industrialized countries without oil reserves.

International boundaries tend to discourage trade. Total trade *between* countries is therefore probably considerably less than it would be between the same areas in a world organized as a single state. Some very large countries like China, India, and the U.S.S.R., which trade comparatively little, might manage to carry on without great changes if forced to exist in complete isolation. Most countries depend to a considerable extent on foreign trade. Even so, trading takes place for the most part only where necessary, either because a country cannot or does not itself produce a particular raw material or manufactured item or because that product can be obtained more cheaply elsewhere. The yearly value of the exports (or imports) of many countries is between 15 and 25 percent of the value of their total gross national product. In some very large countries the proportion is much smaller. In 1976 exports were equal in value to 6.6 percent of total gross national product in both the U.S.A. and U.S.S.R., for example, compared with 22 percent for the U.K. (1973). In some countries, like the Netherlands and Hong Kong, the proportion is much higher.

International trade does not mean the net transfer of goods from richer to poorer countries. Political leaders are not in power to give away goods and services that have been produced by and for their own citizens. When the government of a rich country does give aid, it tends to justify the transfer on grounds that reflect self-interest rather than philanthropy and altruism. If the *exchange* of products

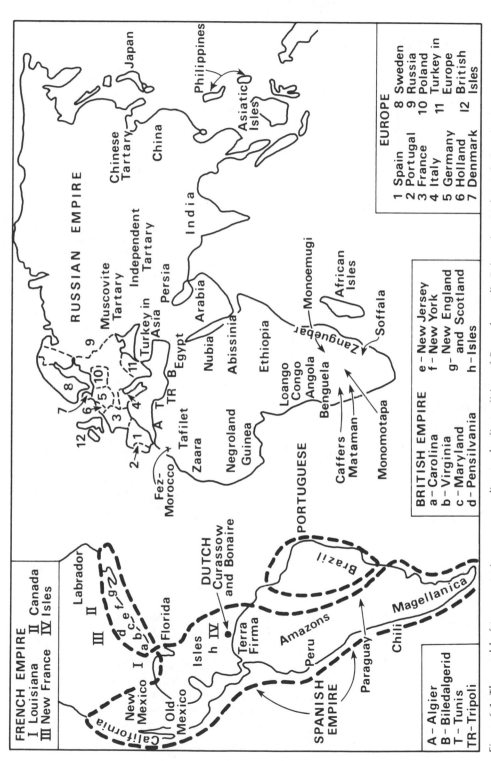

Figure 6.1 The world of two centuries ago according to the first edition of *Encyclopaedia Britannica*, Vol. 2, Edinburgh, 1771, pp. 682-4. The names of Japan and Philippines have been added by the author to the names on the original map

Table 6.1 The 40 largest countries of the world in population in 1978

		(1) Population (millions)	(2) Area (thous. km²)	(3) GNP (thous. millions of $U.S.)	(4) GNP ($U.S. per inhabitant)
	World	4219	135,783	6961	1650
1	China	930.0	9561	381	410
2	India	634.7	3046	95	150
3	U.S.S.R.	261.0	22,402	720	2760
4	U.S.A.	218.4	9363	1723	7890
5	Indonesia	140.2	1492	34	240
6	Brazil	115.4	8512	132	1140
7	Japan	114.4	370	562	4910
8	Bangladesh	85.0	143	9	110
9	Pakistan	76.8	804	13	170
10	Nigeria	68.4	924	26	380
11	Mexico	66.9	1973	73	1090
12	W. Germany	61.3	248	452	7380
13	Italy	56.7	301	173	3050
14	U.K.	56.0	244	225	4020
15	France	53.4	547	350	6550
16	Vietnam	49.2	333	8	160*
17	Philippines	46.3	300	19	410
18	Thailand	45.1	514	17	380
19	Turkey	42.2	781	42	990
20	Egypt	39.6	1000	11	280

* Vietnam estimated by the author.

between different parts of the world is discouraged by the existence of separate states then the actual *net transfer* of products is even more likely to be impeded.

Foreign aid given by richer countries since the Second World War has rarely reached 1 percent of the total gross national product of the donor countries and has usually been well below this modest proportion. Just as countries keep their doors closed to the outflow of gifts of goods and services, so some tend to keep their own citizens from migrating (e.g. U.S.S.R.) while others keep out migrants entirely or restrict the numbers entering to small quotas (e.g. U.S.A., increasingly Australia).

Table 6.1 (continued)

		(1) Population (millions)	(2) Area (thous. km²)	(3) GNP (thous. millions of $U.S.)	(4) GNP ($U.S. per inhabitant)
	World	4219	135,783	6961	1650
21	S. Korea	37.1	98	25	670
22	Spain	36.8	505	107	2920
23	Iran	35.5	1648	69	1930
24	Poland	35.1	312	100	2860
25	Burma	32.2	678	4	120
26	Ethiopia	30.2	1184	3	100
27	Zaire	26.7	2345	4	140
28	S. Africa	27.5	1223	37	1340
29	Argentina	26.4	2777	41	1550
30	Colombia	25.8	1138	16	630
31	Canada	23.6	9976	177	7510
32	Yugoslavia	22.0	256	37	1680
33	Romania	21.9	238	32	1450
34	Morocco	18.9	444	10	540
35	Algeria	18.4	2382	18	990
36	Afghanistan	17.8	238	3	160
37	E. Germany	17.1	108	72	4220
38	Peru	17.1	1285	14	800
39	Taiwan	16.9	36	18	1070
40	N. Korea	16.7	121	8	470

Source: *1978 World Population Data Sheet,* Population Reference Bureau.

The freedom of movement of goods, services, and people *within* countries may for particular reasons also be restricted. In general, however, internal trade is free and people can move freely from region to region. The world as it is currently organized may therefore be thought of as a large number of discrete compartments of greatly varying size, each internally without serious barriers to flows of goods or people between different parts but separated from all other compartments by barriers of varying strength. Formal trade between compartments is roughly balanced overall, while the net international transfer of goods, services, and people is very limited.

Table 6.2 The 15 largest countries of the world according to population in 1978

		Population (millions)	Percentage of world Individual	Percentage of world Cumulative
1	China	930.0	22.0	22.0
2	India	634.7	15.0	37.0
3	U.S.S.R.	261.0	6.2	43.2
4	U.S.A.	218.4	5.2	48.4
5	Indonesia	140.2	3.3	51.7
6	Brazil	115.4	2.7	54.4
7	Japan	114.4	2.7	57.1
8	Bangladesh	85.0	2.0	59.1
9	Pakistan	76.8	1.8	60.9
10	Nigeria	68.4	1.6	62.5
11	Mexico	66.9	1.6	64.1
12	W. Germany	61.3	1.5	65.6
13	Italy	56.7	1.3	66.9
14	U.K.	56.0	1.3	68.2
15	France	53.4	1.3	69.5
	World	4219.0	100.0	100.0

As indicated in Chapter 3, great internal contrasts in wealth and income occur within many countries. Thus *even when* barriers to the movement of goods and people within a country are weak, regional contrasts in living standards still occur. Government policy in many countries, especially since the Second World War, has been to reduce disparities in income, in employment levels, and in other aspects of material and cultural conditions. Even so, in many, such as Italy, Yugoslavia, Brazil, and Mexico, not much progress has been made towards changing basic distributions. Even in the U.S.S.R., with strong central control and state ownership of means of production, Soviet figures show that considerable regional differences occur. An example of internal inequalities in the Soviet Union was given in Chapter 3.

The two following points may be made about what has been said so far. Firstly, even under theoretically ideal conditions for reducing and eliminating regional disparities in living standards within a country the task has proved difficult and a reduction in regional differences has been slow. Secondly, the world as a whole is organized in such a way that there are enormous barriers to the net transfer of goods and people between countries while the will

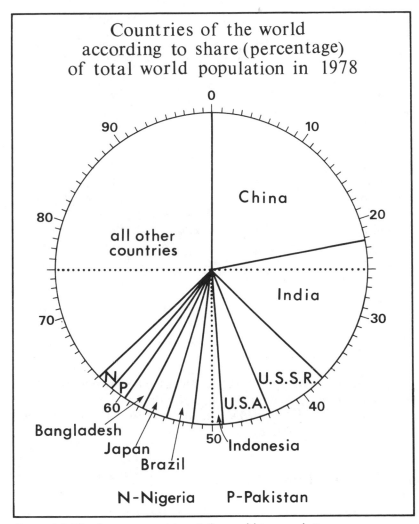

Figure 6.2 The largest countries of the world in population

to make transfers is on the whole also very weak and there is no central control to compel countries to make transfers.

In the politics of the real world, great economic and military power is concentrated in the hands of a few countries that are large in productive capacity (Japan, West Germany), population size (China) or both (the U.S.A., U.S.S.R.). The economic and ideological rivalry between the great powers distracts attention from the development gap and leaves most of the developing world with little prospect of being seriously assisted. Just as the governments

Table 6.3 The 15 largest countries of the world according to area

Area rank	Population rank (1977)	Area (thous. km²)	Percentage of area Individual	Cumulative
1 U.S.S.R.	(3)	22,402	16.5	16.5
2 Canada	(31)	9976	7.3	23.8
3 China	(1)	9561	7.0	30.8
4 U.S.A.	(4)	9363	6.9	37.7
5 Brazil	(7)	8512	6.3	44.0
6 Australia	(46)	7695	5.7	49.7
7 India	(2)	3046	2.2	51.9
8 Argentina	(28)	2777	2.0	53.9
9 Sudan	(41)	2506	1.8	55.7
10 Algeria	(36)	2382	1.8	57.5
11 Zaire	(27)	2345	1.7	59.2
12 Saudi Arabia	(66)	2150	1.6	60.8
13 Mexico	(11)	1973	1.5	62.3
14 Libya	(109)	1760	1.3	63.6
15 Iran	(23)	1648	1.2	64.8
World		135,783	100.0	100.0

of individual countries put the interests of their own citizens first, so richer countries, even if ideologically opposed to one another like the U.S.A. and U.S.S.R., tend to respect each other's membership of the club of rich countries.

6.2   The size of sovereign states

One of the difficulties in appreciating the nature of the world development gap is the fact that almost half of the population of the world is concentrated in four countries (China, India, the U.S.S.R., and the U.S.A.) while six countries (the U.S.S.R., Canada, China, the U.S.A., Brazil, and Australia) contain about half the world's land area. The other half of the population and of the area of the world are distributed, still very unevenly, among some 200 smaller units. Table 6.1 gives the population size of the 40 largest countries of the world in population in 1978. It also shows their area, estimated total gross national product in U.S. dollars, and gross national product per inhabitant.

One would hardly expect to find that every country in the world had exactly the same number of inhabitants, was of the same

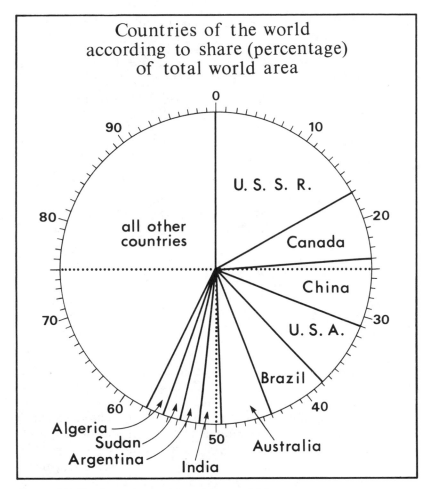

Figure 6.3 The largest countries of the world in area

territorial extent or produced the same quantity of goods and services. Figures 6.2-6.4 show diagrammatically how great the contrasts are among countries in population, area, and production size respectively. Tables 6.2-6.4 show the data from which the diagrams were drawn. It will be noted that the three sets of the top 15 contain some members in common while other countries appear only in two lists or just one.

Although countries vary greatly in size, there is a tendency for people to think of each as an individual player in the world affairs game. The great difference in size between them is not fully appreciated. Internal major civil divisions of large countries are in some cases larger than most single countries. In China the province

Table 6.4 The 15 largest countries of the world according to gross national
product, late 1970s

		GNP ($U.S. $\times$ 10^9)	Percentage Individual	Percentage Cumulative
1	U.S.A.	1723	24.8	24.8
2	U.S.S.R.	720	10.3	35.1
3	Japan	562	8.1	43.2
4	W. Germany	452	6.5	49.7
5	China	381	5.5	55.2
6	France	350	5.0	60.2
7	U.K.	225	3.2	63.4
8	Canada	177	2.5	65.9
9	Italy	173	2.5	68.4
10	Brazil	132	1.9	70.3
11	Spain	107	1.5	71.8
12	Poland	100	1.4	73.2
13	India	95	1.4	74.6
14	Australia	87	1.2	75.8
15	Netherlands	86	1.2	77.0
	World	6961	100.0	100.0

of Szechwan has about 80 million people and in India the state of
Uttar Pradesh has nearly 100 million. Only seven whole countries in
the world have more inhabitants than Uttar Pradesh.

The effect on development studies of the great disparities in size
among the countries of the world is not immediately obvious. What
may, however, happen is that small countries tend to attract greater
attention in relation to their population size than large ones. As will
be shown in Section 6.5, countries with a few million or a few
hundred thousand inhabitants may attract far more aid per
inhabitant than very large countries. For example the French
Caribbean islands of Guadeloupe and Martinique receive about
one hundred times as much overseas aid per inhabitant as India or
Indonesia. Together the two islands have less than one million
inhabitants. The industrial countries may show great concern over
small countries and provide large amounts of aid of various kinds
for them. Examples of such recipients have been Bolivia, Taiwan,
the Mongolian People's Republic, and Cuba. What goes on in
individual regions in India, Indonesia or China attracts much less
interest and attention.

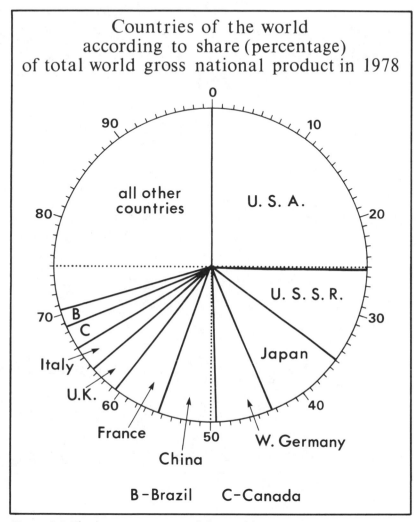

Figure 6.4 The largest countries of the world in gross national product

6.3 Hypothetical transfers of gross national product

The last column of data in Table 6.1 shows clearly the development gap as expressed in terms of gross national product per inhabitant in the mid-1970s. The 'richest' country was the U.S.A. with nearly 8000 U.S. dollars per inhabitant. Ethiopia, with 100 U.S. dollars per inhabitant, was at the other extreme. The gap was actually even greater between smaller countries not in the table (Kuwait with 15,480 and Bhutan with 70, both in Asia).

Table 6.5 Hypothetical transfers of GNP

		(1) Population (millions)	(2) Cum. population	(3) GNP per inh. ($)	(4) Total GNP	(5) GNP per inh. in relation to mean	(6) GNP that gives mean	(7) Transfer (i.e. difference between (4) and (6))
1	U.S.A.	218.4	218.4	7890	1723	4.93	348	−1375
2	W. Germany	61.3	279.7	7380	452	4.61	98	− 354
3	France	53.4	333.1	6550	350	4.09	86	− 264
4	Japan	114.4	447.5	4910	562	3.06	184	− 378
5	U.K.	56.0	503.5	4020	225	2.51	90	− 135
6	Italy	56.7	560.2	3050	173	1.90	91	− 82
7	U.S.S.R.	261.0	821.2	2760	720	1.72	418	− 302
8	Brazil	115.4	936.6	1140	132	0.71	186	+ 54
9	Mexico	66.9	1003.5	1090	73	0.68	107	+ 34
10	Turkey	42.2	1045.7	990	42	0.62	68	+ 26
11	China	930.0	1975.7	410	381	0.26	1463	+1082
12	Philippines	46.3	2022.0	410	19	0.26	73	+ 54
13	Nigeria	68.4	2090.4	380	26	0.24	108	+ 82
14	Thailand	45.1	2135.5	380	17	0.24	71	+ 54
15	Egypt	39.6	2175.1	280	11	0.17	65	+ 54
16	Indonesia	140.2	2315.3	240	34	0.15	227	+ 193
17	Pakistan	76.8	2392.1	170	13	0.11	118	+ 105
18	Vietnam	49.2	2441.3	160	8	1.10	80	+ 72
19	India	634.7	3076.0	150	95	0.09	1055	+ 960
20	Bangladesh	85.0	3161.0	110	9	0.07	129	+ 120
			3161.0	1602	5065		5065	

(4) Total GNP is in thousands of millions of dollars.
(5) Number of times the GNP per inhabitant of the country exceeds world mean GNP per inhabitant.
(6) Is equal to population times world mean GNP per inhabitant.

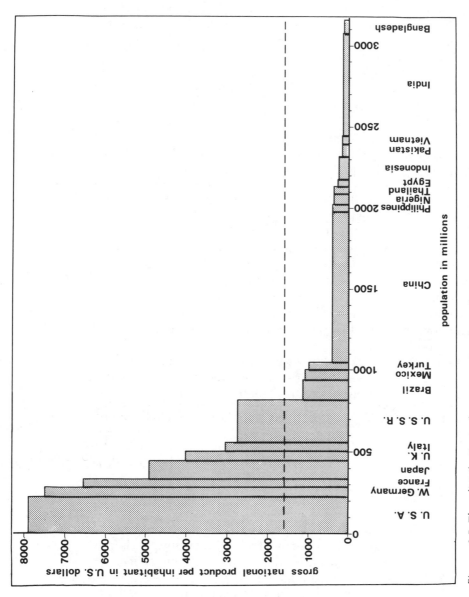

Figure 6.5 The distribution of gross national product among the largest countries of the world in population. The countries are arranged from left to right in descending order of GNP per inhabitant. The data are for the mid-1970s

Since the sovereign states of the world are familiar and are actual units of organization they have been used here to describe what would need to be done to eliminate international differences in gross national product per inhabitant. The transfer to be calculated is purely hypothetical and no attempt is made here to estimate what quantities and what kinds of goods (or people) might be moved. Only the 20 largest countries of the world in population have been used in the calculation that follows but the inclusion of all countries would have little effect on the results. Together the 20 largest countries have nearly 75 percent of the total population of the world.

The 20 countries in Table 6.5 are ranked in descending order of gross national product per inhabitant, shown in column (3). The data in the table are used to calculate how much gross national product would have to be transferred from countries with a level per inhabitant above the world average ($1602) to the countries with a level below the world average. The calculation can be appreciated with the help of Figure 6.5. Two groups of country may be seen, those with GNP per inhabitant above the broken horizontal line in the diagram, which is the weighted average for the 20 countries, and those with GNP per inhabitant below it. The transfer contemplated involves cutting off all columns of the 'rich' countries at the broken line and transferring this GNP to the white space between the tops of the columns of the poor countries and the same broken line.

The calculations required to arrive at an estimate of the size of transfers needed to even out gross national product in the above way may now be followed step by step in Table 6.5.

Columns (1) and (2) show respectively population for each country and cumulative population (for working out the horizontal scale in Figure 6.5).

Columns (3) and (4) show respectively GNP per inhabitant and total GNP.

Column (5) shows how many times above or below the world average of $1602 the GNP per inhabitant of each country is.

Column (6) shows how much total GNP each country would have if it had the average of $1602 per inhabitant. The values in column (6) are calculated by dividing the score for each country in column (4) by its score in column (5).

Column (7) shows the transfer from or to each country needed to produce the average of $1602 per inhabitant in each.

The final result of the calculation is as follows. Of the total GNP of $5065 thousand million produced by all the 20 countries combined, the richer seven (with above average GNP per inhabitant) produce $4205 thousand million. Of this latter quantity, $2888 thousand million, or nearly 70 percent (68.7), would have to be transferred to the other 13 countries. When a much larger number of countries are taken into account the proportion falls very slightly.

The magnitude of the income transfer needed to achieve equality in the world between all the countries is very great. The gap has been calculated to compare what would have to be done with what is being done. It is not being argued that the rich countries would want to, should or even could make such massive sacrifices. It is, however, thought-provoking to compare the 70 percent transfer calculated above with the transfer of 0.7 percent proposed for the rich countries to aim at but itself not actually achieved.

6.4 World trade

In a study of development the movement of goods between places on the earth's surface is a vital aspect. Trade is usually divided into two types, international and internal. Foreign trade crosses international boundaries while internal does not. There are two basic differences between international trade and internal trade. Firstly, international trade can be influenced and even prevented by the application of tariff barriers or regulations along national boundaries while internal trade is not usually hindered in this way by tolls on major civil division boundaries, though it was in previous centuries. Secondly, goods are usually carried over greater distances on international transactions than on internal ones. There are, however, notable exceptions to this tendency, as a comparison of distances between selected pairs of places in Figure 6.6 shows with the help of examples in Europe of five internal journeys that are longer than five international ones.

In the previous section it was noted that foreign aid, to be discussed in the following section, transfers from rich to poor countries less than 1 percent of the amount of gross national product of the world. Trade is of a different nature since it is an exchange. The aim of this section is to describe the flows of the main types of commodity in world trade in the 1970s and to assess this in relation to total production in the world.

For the purposes of this section it has been necessary to use 11 regions of the world, some such as Africa including a large number of countries, some such as Japan and the U.S.S.R. consisting of single countries. The membership of the groups in the trade tables below is as follows (*United Nations Statistical Yearbook 1976*):

1   West Europe includes Yugoslavia
2   Japan
3   U.S.A.
4   Canada/Australia includes New Zealand
5   East Europe excludes Yugoslavia and the U.S.S.R.
6   U.S.S.R.
7   Latin America, all countries of the Americas south of the
    U.S.A.
8   Africa excludes the Republic of South Africa
9   The Middle East extends from Turkey in the west to Yemen and
    Iran in the south and east
10 Southeast Asia extends from India to Indonesia and the
    Philippines but excludes China, the Mongolian People's
    Republic, North Korea, Vietnam, and Japan ('group' 2)
11 China includes the Mongolian People's Republic, North Korea,
    and Vietnam

   The commodities in world trade are subdivided into four classes:
food, mineral fuels, crude materials, and manufactures. The four

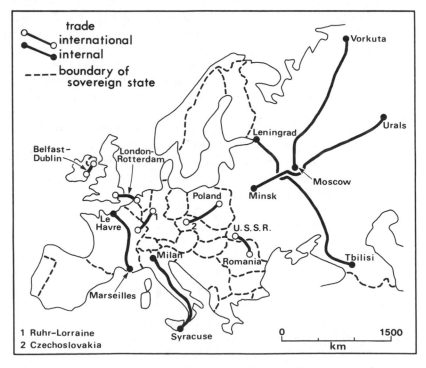

Figure 6.6 Examples of flows of internal and international trade of varying
lengths

Table 6.6(a) World trade in food in hundreds of millions of U.S. dollars, 1975

						To						
	1	2	3	4	5	6	7	8	9	10	11	
From	WEU	JAP	USA	CAU	EEU	USR	LAM	AFR	MEA	SEA	CHI	World
1 W. Europe	282	5	19	5	7	4	9	24	9	9	0	374
2 Japan	2	—	2	1	0	0	0	1	1	2	0	8
3 U.S.A.	51	21	—	11	5	11	20	9	8	24	0	168
4 Canada/Australia	15	14	17	4	2	6	4	5	5	14	5	91
5 E. Europe	15	0	2	0	9	18	1	2	2	0	0	52
6 U.S.S.R.	1	0	0	0	5	—	3	1	0	2	1	12
7 Latin America	50	7	34	2	6	26	16	5	4	1	2	155
8 Africa	28	1	6	1	2	4	0	4	2	1	0	51
9 Middle East	4	0	2	0	1	1	0	0	4	0	0	12
10 Southeast Asia	14	18	9	2	1	3	0	3	8	18	1	77
11 China	2	2	0	0	1	2	0	1	1	10	—	21
World	479	73	91	28	38	74	54	55	44	82	9	1042

Table 6.6(b) Food trade surplus and deficit in hundreds of millions of U.S. dollars

1	Latin America	+101
2	U.S.A.	+ 77
3	Canada/Australia	+ 63
4	E. Europe	+ 14
5	China	+ 12
6	Africa	− 4
7	Southeast Asia	− 5
8	Middle East	− 32
9	U.S.S.R.	− 62
10	Japan	− 65
11	W. Europe	−105

Table 6.6(c) World trade in food in hundreds of millions of U.S. dollars, 1975

			To		
From	1	2	3	4	5
1 Developed market	473	145	34	5	663
2 Developed central	180	67	43	3	295
3 Developing market	5	11	31	1	64
4 Developing central	20	13	3	0	21
5 World	678	236	112	9	1042

classes of trade are very convenient for the present book because they match closely four types of product discussed in Chapter 2. Apart from minimal experimental quantities of food made synthetically from hydrocarbons, food is of plant or animal origin. Some plant and animal products (e.g. cotton, hides) enter the crude materials category, while some plants are used as fuel (though these hardly enter international trade). Mineral fuels can be used as raw materials (e.g. for synthetic fibres) rather than for combustion but only a small proportion are actually so used. The class of manufactures is very broad indeed and includes both producer (capital) and consumer goods.

In spite of complications such as those raised above, the four classes of commodity appeal to common sense and common knowledge. They are discussed in turn. For each of the four classes a table shows the trade between every possible pair of the 11 regions while a diagram shows the direction of the main flows on a world 'map'. All values are in hundreds of millions of U.S. dollars. A dash in the tables indicates the non-existent trade between single countries ('regions' 1, 3, and 6) and also between China and other centrally planned countries of Asia in group 11, for which information is not available. The Republic of South Africa is excluded altogether as data for it are not adequate. As a result of various deliberate omissions and of rounding errors, the row and column totals for each region are greater than the sums of the 11 regional totals which they include. The presence of a 0 (zero) in a table usually indicates a very small amount of trade (rounded down to 0), rather than no trade at all.

(1) Table 6.6. *Food* accounted for about 12 percent of the value of all foreign trade in the world in 1975. Table 6.6(a) shows trade in food between the regions of the world while Table 6.6(b) shows net exporting and net importing regions, the differences between the row and column totals in Table 6.6(a). The regions are ranked in order according to size of surplus or deficit. The main flows are mapped in Figure 6.7.

Table 6.6(a) shows that over a quarter of all world trade in food is between countries of West Europe. Table 6.6(b) shows that West Europe, Japan, and the U.S.S.R. were the regions with the largest net imports of food while the Americas and Australia (with New Zealand) were the regions with the largest net exports of food. The summary data in Table 6.6(c) show that about two-thirds of world food exports came from developed market economy countries (regions 1-4) and less than one-third from developing market economy countries (regions 7-10). Gone are the days when the tropical, colonial, primary product countries supplied the

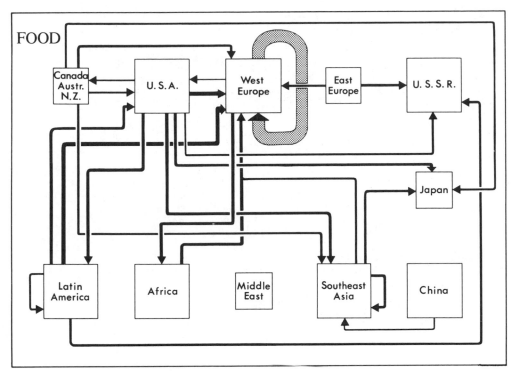

Figure 6.7 International trade in foodstuffs between major regions of the world. See Table 6.6(a) for numerical data used

industrialized countries with food surplus. In 1975 the flow of food from developing countries to developed ones barely exceeded the flow from developed countries to developing ones. The data in both tables indicate clearly that Asia and Africa are broadly 'self-sufficient' in food, even if the amount available is inadequate.

(2) Table 6.7. *Mineral fuels* accounted for about 20 percent of the total value of world trade in 1975. Table 6.7(a) shows trade in mineral fuels between the regions of the world while Table 6.7(b) shows net exporting and net importing regions, the differences between the row and column totals in Table 6.7(a). The countries are ranked in order of size of surplus or deficit. The main flows are mapped in Figure 6.8.

Table 6.7(a) shows that nearly half of the mineral fuels entering world trade are accounted for by the Middle East, while nearly half the imports are taken by West Europe and most of the rest by the U.S.A. and Japan. Developing market economy countries (regions 7-10) provide about three-quarters of all mineral fuel exports.

Table 6.7(a) World trade in mineral fuels in hundreds of millions of U.S. dollars, 1975

From	To											
	1 WEU	2 JAP	3 USA	4 CAU	5 EEU	6 USR	7 LAM	8 AFR	9 MEA	10 SEA	11 CHI	World
1 W. Europe	142	1	5	0	1	0	1	6	2	0	0	177
2 Japan	0	—	0	0	0	0	0	0	0	1	0	2
3 U.S.A.	13	16	—	9	0	0	5	0	1	1	0	45
4 Canada/Australia	15	25	48	2	0	0	0	0	0	0	0	59
5 E. Europe	18	1	1	0	7	6	1	0	0	0	1	36
6 U.S.S.R.	104	2	0	0	44	—	1	2	0	2	1	104
7 Latin America	15	0	103	13	0	0	47	6	3	1	0	190
8 Africa	128	7	50	2	1	0	14	5	0	1	0	208
9 Middle East	332	152	52	26	9	6	43	14	23	81	0	758
10 Southeast Asia	2	41	19	2	0	1	7	1	1	17	0	90
11 China	0	8	0	0	0	0	0	0	0	1	0	8
World	702	241	277	52	62	13	123	34	30	105	2	1686

Table 6.7(b) Mineral fuels trade surplus and deficit in hundreds of millions of U.S. dollars

1	Middle East	+728
2	Africa	+174
3	U.S.S.R.	+ 91
4	Latin America	+ 67
5	Canada/Australia	+ 7
6	China	+ 6
7	Southeast Asia	− 15
8	E. Europe	− 26
9	U.S.A.	−232
10	Japan	−239
11	W. Europe	−525

(3) Table 6.8. *Crude materials* accounted for about 8 percent of the total value of world trade in 1975. Table 6.8(a) shows trade in crude materials between the regions of the world while Table 6.8(b) shows net exporting and net importing regions, the differences between the row and column totals in Table 6.8(a). The countries are ranked in order according to size of surplus or deficit. The main flows are mapped in Figure 6.9.

Table 6.8(a) shows that West Europe takes about half of the imports of crude materials in the world. Developed countries surprisingly provide nearly two-thirds of all the exports of crude materials. They take over five-sixths of all the imports.

Table 6.8(a) World trade in crude materials in hundreds of millions of U.S. dollars, 1975

From	To											
	1 WEU	2 JAP	3 USA	4 CAU	5 EEU	6 USR	7 LAM	8 AFR	9 MEA	10 SEA	11 CHI	World
1 W. Europe	136	1	4	1	7	2	2	5	4	1	0	166
2 Japan	2	—	0	0	0	0	0	0	1	4	1	9
3 U.S.A.	41	24	—	11	2	0	9	3	2	13	1	107
4 Canada/Australia	31	38	29	1	2	2	1	3	1	3	1	99
5 E. Europe	10	0	0	0	3	3	0	0	1	0	1	19
6 U.S.S.R.	15	6	0	0	24	—	1	1	1	0	0	49
7 Latin America	24	8	11	1	2	3	6	1	1	1	0	58
8 Africa	32	2	2	0	5	3	1	2	1	1	2	51
9 Middle East	4	0	0	0	1	1	0	0	1	1	0	10
10 Southeast Asia	17	20	10	3	2	2	1	1	2	17	2	77
11 China	3	3	0	0	1	1	0	0	0	1	—	10
World	323	83	58	18	48	17	22	15	15	43	8	667

Table 6.8(b) Crude materials trade surplus and deficit in hundreds of millions of U.S. dollars

1	Canada/Australia	+ 81
2	U.S.A.	+ 49
3	Latin America	+ 36
4	Africa	+ 36
5	Southeast Asia	+ 34
6	U.S.S.R.	+ 32
7	China	+ 2
8	Middle East	− 5
9	E. Europe	− 29
10	Japan	− 74
11	W. Europe	−157

(4) Table 6.9. *Manufactures* accounted in 1975 for about 60 percent of total world trade. Table 6.9(a) shows trade in manufactures between 11 regions of the world. Table 6.9(b) gives the net surplus or deficit of each region. The main flows are mapped in Figure 6.10.

West Europe accounts for over half of the exports of manufactured goods in the world, but nearly one-third of all trade in this sector is within West Europe itself. The value of Japanese exports is about two-thirds as high as the value of West European exports actually leaving West Europe. A very considerable part of the trade in manufactured goods is therefore between developed

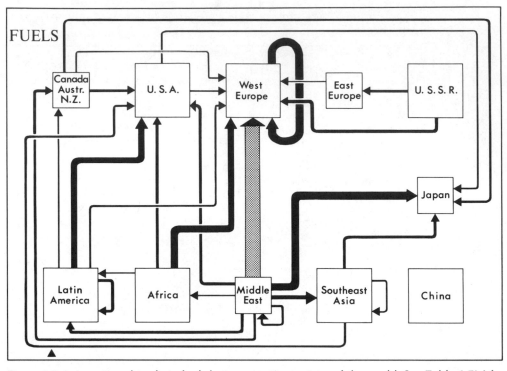

Figure 6.8 International trade in fuels between major regions of the world. See Table 6.7(a) for numerical data used

countries. The data in Table 6.9(a) and the map in Figure 6.10 show that trade in manufactured goods between developing countries is negligible in relation to their population sizes. With only about 30 percent of the population of the world, the six developed regions (1-6 in table 6.9(a)) account for over 90 percent of the exports of manufactured goods.

Table 6.10 shows the degree to which each of the 11 regions has a surplus of or is deficient in each of the four main classes of commodities in world trade. West Europe and Japan depend very heavily on fuel and materials from other regions and add value to these to produce manufactured goods, a part of which is exported. They also need to import some food. The U.S.A. only has a net deficiency in mineral fuels, Canada and Australia in manufactures, and the U.S.S.R. in food and manufactures.

All five developing regions import large quantities of manufactured goods. Southeast Asia and China, which together have nearly half of the population of the world, only account for a few percent of all world trade. Latin America, Africa, and the

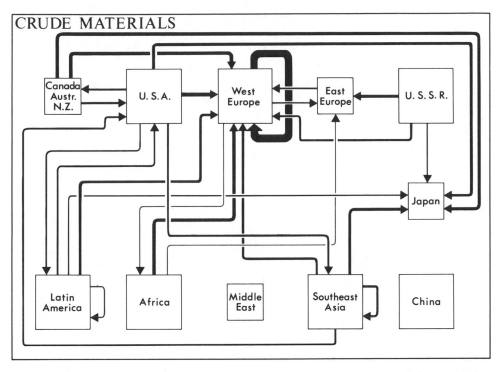

Figure 6.9 International trade in crude materials between major regions of the world. See Table 6.8(a) for numerical data used

Middle East export large quantities of mineral fuels and Latin America also exports food.

It may have been an advantage in the 1970s to be a net importer of fuel and materials and net exporter of manufactures. If the prices of food and materials were to rise as dramatically as the price of oil did in 1973-74, however, the values in the table would change substantially. Another potential threat to the manufacturing countries is the prospect that the developing countries, as they grow in population and also industrialize, are likely to use more and more of their shrinking surpluses of food and crude materials and, eventually, their energy output.

International trade as assessed either by exports or by imports (but not by the two combined) is equal in value to about 15-20 percent of total world gross national product. As pointed out earlier in this chapter, at national level this proportion varies greatly from one country to another. Although world trade does not in theory achieve any net transfer of goods from rich to poor countries, it is of interest to compare the proportion of 15-20 percent of world

Table 6.9(a) World trade in all manufactures in hundreds of millions of U.S. dollars, 1975

From	1 WEU	2 JAP	3 USA	4 CAU	5 EEU	6 USR	7 LAM	8 AFR	9 MEA	10 SEA	11 CHI	World
1 W. Europe	1749	29	173	71	104	85	127	193	167	82	21	2867
2 Japan	76	—	107	31	6	16	45	45	54	119	24	532
3 U.S.A.	175	32	—	199	2	7	128	23	52	57	3	710
4 Canada/Australia	21	5	130	7	0	0	12	2	3	11	1	200
5 E. Europe	53	0	1	1	105	128	6	8	13	5	7	333
6 U.S.S.R.	16	1	1	0	74	—	8	3	7	4	8	120
7 Latin America	20	2	22	2	1	1	26	1	0	0	2	79
8 Africa	17	2	0	0	1	3	0	4	0	0	1	30
9 Middle East	6	2	0	0	0	0	1	1	11	1	0	23
10 Southeast Asia	53	19	60	14	2	3	3	9	12	41	0	219
11 China	5	3	1	1	3	2	1	3	2	8	—	31
World	2208	98	507	329	305	246	357	298	324	333	63	5068 (down 5144)

Note: Columns headed "To".

Table 6.9(b) Manufactures trade surplus and deficit in hundreds of millions of U.S. dollars

1	W. Europe	+659
2	Japan	+434
3	U.S.A.	+203
4	E. Europe	+ 28
5	China	− 32
6	Southeast Asia	−114
7	U.S.S.R.	−126
8	Canada/Australia	−129
9	Africa	−268
10	Latin America	−278
11	Middle East	−301

gross national product 'on the move' per year between countries with the much higher figure of 70 percent transfer of gross national product needed from rich to poor countries to achieve equality in the world.

6.5   Development assistance

Aid, or assistance as it is termed in United Nations statistical publications, takes various forms. To illustrate the limited scope of

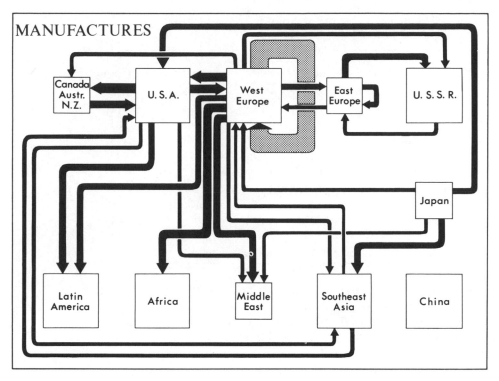

Figure 6.10 International trade in manufactures between major regions of the world. See Table 6.9(a) for numerical data used

true assistance provided by developed countries to developing ones, only certain types have been considered. It is felt that they are adequate to make the point. The data are from the *United Nations Statistical Yearbook 1976*.

Development assistance in the mid-1970s originated in three types of country: the developed market economies, the centrally planned economies of Comecon, and China, which though centrally planned, has a very much lower gross national product per inhabitant than Comecon. Assistance goes either bilaterally from an 'assisting' country direct to a particular developing one or first to a multilateral institution, such as the World Bank, from which it is then distributed. The assistance provided by the developed market economies may be: official development assistance, other official flows, or private capital flows. Development assistance provided by centrally planned economies is referred to as 'bilateral commitments of capital'.

In this section the amounts provided by the developed countries are examined on a country to country basis for 1975. The amounts

Table 6.10 Summary table of surpluses and deficits in four categories of trade, 1975, in hundreds of millions of U.S. dollars

		Food	Mineral fuels	Crude materials	Manufactures
1	W. Europe	−105	−525	−157	+659
2	Japan	− 65	−239	− 74	+434
3	U.S.A.	+ 77	−232	+ 49	+203
4	Canada/Australia	+ 63	+ 7	+ 81	−129
5	E. Europe	+ 14	− 26	− 29	+ 28
6	U.S.S.R.	− 62	+ 91	+ 32	−126
7	Latin America	+101	+ 67	+ 36	−278
8	Africa	− 4	+174	+ 36	−268
9	Middle East	− 32	+728	− 5	−301
10	Southeast Asia	− 5	− 15	+ 34	−114
11	China	+ 12	+ 6	+ 2	− 32

received by the developing countries are then considered for the same year. Finally recent views on aid are discussed.

In 1975 the total net outflow of resources from developed market economies was some $36,800 million, an amount very nearly equivalent to 1 percent of their total combined gross national product. Of this amount, some $20,000 million was private capital, roughly three-fifths of the total. The rest, the official development assistance flows, is shown in Table 6.11. If official development assistance is regarded as assistance in an undisputed sense, then in 1975 the developed market economy countries were giving only about 0.4 percent of their gross national product to poor countries.

The amounts given varied greatly from donor to donor (see Table 6.11). The amount given by a developed country would be expected to relate first of all to total population size of the country and secondly to total gross national product. Column (4) in Table 6.11 shows that the average amount given per inhabitant of the developed market economies was $21. This average, however, fell between extremes of $8 for Austria and $68 for Sweden. One might have expected the countries with a higher gross national product per inhabitant to provide more than those with a lower one. A comparison of columns (4), (5), and (6) shows that there is no immediately obvious correlation between high GNP per inhabitant in column (6) and amount given per inhabitant in column (4) or assistance as percentage of gross national product in column (5). For example, Austria, Japan, Switzerland, and the U.S.A. appear much less forthcoming than Sweden, the Netherlands, France or Australia.

Table 6.11 Official development assistance from developed market economy countries to developing countries and multilateral institutions

	(1) Assistance	(2) Population	(3) Total GNP	(4) Assistance Per popn.	(5) Assistance As % of GNP	(6) GNP per popn.
Australia	507	13.8	78,000	37	0.65	5640
Austria	63	7.5	35,000	8	0.18	4720
Belgium	373	9.8	59,000	38	0.63	6070
Canada	875	22.8	152,000	38	0.58	6650
Denmark	205	5.0	35,000	41	0.59	6920
Finland	48	4.7	24,000	10	0.50	5100
France	2098	52.9	305,000	40	0.69	5760
W.Germany	1598	61.9	409,000	26	0.39	6610
Italy	186	55.0	162,000	34	0.11	2940
Japan	1143	111.1	496,000	10	0.23	4460
Netherlands	601	13.6	76,000	44	0.79	5590
New Zealand	66	3.0	14,000	22	0.47	4680
Norway	184	4.0	26,000	46	0.71	6540
Sweden	565	8.3	65,000	68	0.87	7880
Switzerland	104	6.5	52,000	16	0.20	8050
U.K.	854	56.4	217,000	15	0.39	3840
U.S.A.	4034	213.9	1,510,000	19	0.27	7060
Total	13,578	650.2	3,715,000	21	0.37	

(1) Official development assistance in millions of U.S. dollars. Source: *United Nations Statistical Yearbook 1976*, Table 201.
(2) Population in millions. Source: *1975 World Population Data Sheet*, Population Reference Bureau.
(3) Gross national product in millions of U.S. dollars. Source: *1977 World Population Data Sheet* quoting 1975 data, Population Reference Bureau.
(4) Assistance given in dollars per inhabitant (column (1) divided by column (2)).
(5) Assistance as a percentage of gross national product (column (1) divided by column (3) $\times$ 100).
(6) Gross national product per inhabitant in U.S. dollars, 1975.

In 1975, total bilateral commitments of capital by socialist or centrally planned economies were just over $3000 million, less than one-tenth of the total flow of resources from market economies. Amounts are given in Table 6.12. When China is excluded, the remaining countries, all members of Comecon, provided less than $2800 million. The combined population of the Comecon countries was, however, little over half the combined population of the developed market economy countries. The data in Table 6.12 show that the centrally planned countries, like the developed market economy ones, differed greatly among themselves with regard to

Table 6.12 Bilateral commitments of capital by centrally planned economies to developing countries

	(1) Assistance	(2) Population	(3) Total GNP	(4) Assistance Per popn.	(5) As % of GNP	(6) GNP per popn.
Bulgaria	17	8.8	20,000	2	0.09	2040
Czechoslo-vakia	168	14.8	57,000	11	0.29	3710
E. Germany	277	17.2	73,000	16	0.38	4230
Hungary	151	10.5	24,000	14	0.63	2480
Poland	54	33.8	97,000	2	0.06	2910
Romania	465	21.2	31,000	22	1.50	1300
U.S.S.R.	1642	255.0	704,000	6	0.23	2620
Total	2774	361.3	1,006,000	6	0.28	
China	272	822.8	337,000	0.3	0.08	350

Sources and definitions as for Table 6.11.

the amount of assistance given per inhabitant and with regard to the proportion of their total gross national product committed. The gross national product data for the socialist countries are a Western estimate of their equivalent since they measure production in a different way from that used in the West.

The way assistance is allocated will now be examined. Table 6.13 shows 20 developing countries that in 1975 each had a gross national product per inhabitant of less than one-tenth of the world average of $1530. The amount shown per inhabitant is the annual average amount of official assistance received bilaterally during 1973-75 from developed market economy countries or from multilateral institutions. The average per inhabitant received for Africa as a whole was about $8, as was the average for Latin America. Table 6.13 shows clearly that the poorest developing countries do not appear to be benefiting particularly from assistance. It could perhaps be argued that they are too 'underdeveloped' to be able to make use of it.

A selection of developing countries that in 1975 received comparatively large amounts of assistance per inhabitant is given in Table 6.14. They are all small in population and all have gross national products per inhabitant considerably or very much *higher* than those of the 'poorest' developing countries, shown in Table 6.13. The largest recipients of assistance from the centrally planned economies are shown in Table 6.15. Commitments from these

Table 6.13 Disbursements received by developing countries, annual averages 1973-75

	Population 1975 (millions)	GNP in dollars per popn. 1975	Assistance per inh. ($)
West Africa			
Benin	3.1	130	12
Guinea	4.4	150	2
Guinea-Bissau	0.5	140	9
Mali	5.7	100	17
Upper Volta	6.0	110	14
East Africa			
Burundi	3.8	120	10
Ethiopia	28.0	100	4
Malawi	4.9	140	9
Rwanda	4.2	110	13
Somalia	3.2	110	15
Middle Africa			
Chad	4.0	120	14
Zaire	24.5	140	7
Asia			
Bangladesh	73.7	110	8
Bhutan	1.2	70	1
India	613.2	150	2
Maldives	0.1	110	10
Nepal	12.6	120	3
Burma	31.2	120	3
Laos	3.3	90	18

Source: *United Nations Statistical Yearbook 1976,* Table 204.

countries are distributed very irregularly both over area and over time. In 1975, for example, both Turkey and Afghanistan received large amounts of capital from socialist countries whereas in previous years neither had received very much. India received considerable quantities in the 1960s but none at all in 1972 and 1974 and very little in 1975.

When the total picture of assistance over the postwar period is considered, several features come out clearly. No rich country has given away so much that its own standard of living would be noticeably affected. Some countries, however, have been more

Table 6.14 Selected developing countries receiving a high level of assistance per inhabitant

	Population 1975 (millions)	GNP in dollars per popn. 1975	Assistance per inh. ($)
Africa			
Botswana	0.7	410	61
Congo	1.3	520	129
Gabon	0.5	2590	63
Latin America			
Guadeloupe	0.4	1500	320
Martinique	0.4	2350	347
Surinam	0.4	1370	106
Asia			
Jordan	2.7	610	39
Oceania			
French Polynesia	Very small		429
New Caledonia	Very small		505
Papua-New Guinea	2.7	490	96
Solomon Islands	0.2	250	82
Western Samoa	0.2	350	48

Table 6.15 Developing countries receiving more than $50 million commitments in 1975 from centrally planned countries

	Population (millions)	GNP per inh. ($)	Aid received $ million	Per inh. ($)
Turkey	39.9	860	706	18
Afghanistan	19.3	130	670	35
Algeria	16.8	780	295	18
Syria	7.3	660	248	34
Brazil	109.7	1010	180	2
Egypt	37.5	310	125	3
Indonesia	136.0	180	100	1
Iraq	11.1	1280	88	8
Nepal	12.6	110	80	6
Somalia	3.2	100	62	19
Sudan	18.3	290	62	3
Mozambique	9.2	310	59	6
Sri Lanka	14.0	150	59	4
Jordan	2.7	460	58	21

Source: *United Nations Statistical Yearbook 1976,* Table 202.

'generous' than others. Priority often seems to have been given to helping developing countries with special assets strategically or in terms of natural resources rather than to helping very poor countries. The considerable Soviet aid to Afghanistan and Turkey in the 1970s could have been related to a new strategic interest in the Middle East. Massive French aid to Gabon no doubt has to do with the minerals, especially the uranium, of that former French colony. Some small countries end up with very large amounts of assistance per inhabitant. If the amount of assistance given for each inhabitant of Guadeloupe or New Caledonia were given for each inhabitant of India, then a massive transfer of capital (or consumer goods) would indeed be required in the world.

Foreign aid is constantly under criticism. Much evidence is produced and publicized to show that it is misused, misplaced, and often does more harm than good. At a less emotional level it is pointed out that it is only a drop in the ocean. Westlake (1978) writes about the need for much faster economic growth in the poorest countries:

> For these countries it is not what happens to world trade that is important, but the level of aid on *concessional terms* that really matters.
>
> Unfortunately, aid seems very likely to increase less fast than it has in the past This trend has been allowed for by World Bank economists who see a 5 percent annual increase in net disbursements of overseas aid, in real terms, as the minimum necessary for achieving the economic growth targets postulated in their medium-term strategy.
>
> At the value of money today, this would raise concessional aid from the rich countries from \$19,100m in 1975, \$56,800m in 1985. But the annual increase in such aid would still be below the 7 percent seen in the previous decade. Moreover, it would only mean that the rich countries were allocating a mere 0.39 percent of their aggregate national incomes to this purpose. This would still be a long way short of the recommendation by United Nations that 0.7 percent of rich country's incomes be ear-marked for aid to the poor. Yet, even sums now proposed will not be forthcoming unless there are large increases in the .aid commitments of the three largest donors — the United States, Japan and West Germany.

No two people are exactly equal. It can easily be argued that some people need more than others. Even so, the gap between rich and poor in the world is far too great to be justified on such grounds.

6.6 One hundred equal population units

To obtain a regional breakdown of the earth's land surface and its unevenly distributed population suitable for the study of development on a regional basis it was considered desirable to divide the world into units roughly equal in population size. In this way, people in different parts of the world would be seen to have equal weight and significance. Electoral divisions of a certain type have such an aim. The recent districting of the European Economic Community for the purposes of electing members for the newly formed European Parliament is an example. Each constituency has several hundred thousand inhabitants. On a world scale, it was proposed at one time to make provisional constituencies for a future World Parliament. Each constituency was to have several million people.

A suitable existing division of the world into regions with equal population was sought by the author. In the end it was found necessary to devise a system for the special purposes of the present book. The world has been divided into 100 units, each with approximately 1 percent of the estimated 1975 population of the world of 3,960,000,000. The units will henceforth be referred to as cells. The choice of this term adopted from Richardson (1961) has no biological or political connotations. His 'cells' were shown in Figure 1.3. It is simply a short, easily remembered word. The choice of 100 was one of convenience.

For reasons that will become clear below, it was impracticable to get exactly 1 percent of the population of the world into each cell. In fact 77 out of the 100 cells each have between 35 and 45 million inhabitants. Two exceed 50 million, while at the other extreme a special case was made for Australia and New Zealand, which formed a cell with only about 15 million inhabitants.

There is no benefit in devising a new and complicated framework for looking at an old problem unless the advantage gained from using the new framework outweighs the time spent and the frustration felt by the reader in learning how it works. It is hoped that the effort will prove worthwhile. It is necessary, therefore, to clarify what the system does and does not do.

The 100 cells idea does not pretend to be a new regional division of the world for some future world state nor even, less ambitiously, a new framework for the study of regional geography. In fact it is a very transitory system since even in a matter of a decade or two, as a result of differential rates of population growth in different parts of the world, some cells will have grown substantially in population while others will hardly have changed. Moreover it violates hopelessly the present framework of sovereign states which, as hardly needs to be pointed out again, is the framework for the organization of the world economy at present.

The 100 cells provide a new way of working out the arithmetic of development. Most importantly, they allow appropriate weight and attention to be given to each part of the world. Any group of cells can immediately be counted and seen to form a given proportion of the world's population. Differences in the population size of countries do not have to be taken into account.

In composition the cells are of several different kinds. In a few instances the population of a single country was near enough to 40 million for that country to form a single cell. Such countries, with the population in millions, are Egypt (38), Turkey (40), Burma (31), Thailand (42), and the Philippines (44). Many cells were formed by amalgamating two or more existing sovereign state units, as for example Spain and Portugal (44 million combined) and Argentina, Chile, and Uruguay (39). Countries with more than about 45 million inhabitants had to be subdivided. In some cases it was sufficient to divide a single large country into regions each with around 40 million inhabitants, as with Japan. In other cases it was found convenient to amalgamate part of a large country with an adjoining country that was small in population. Thus for example Canada was joined with the northwestern part of the U.S.A.

The cells for large countries were based as far as possible on the major civil divisions of those countries. Thus the six cells that represent parts of the U.S.S.R. used the 19 economic planning regions as a basis to form the units. In the U.S.A., India, and China, states or provinces were used. The advantage of using within-country administrative divisions is that demographic and other data are more readily available at this level and easier to handle quickly than at more detailed local levels. The 100 cells finally worked out after considerable thought and not a little estimating and guesswork are listed in Table 6.16. Further details regarding the composition of the cells are given in Appendix 2.

The distribution of the 100 cells is shown in Figure 6.11. The map used has two advantages. It shows the land areas of the world in a familiar way and it is an equal area projection. Thus though there is distortion of shape, especially along the northern edge, area is correctly to scale. Each dot is placed roughly on the 'centre of gravity' of the population of the cell it represents. The numbering of the cells is that used throughout the rest of the book and may be checked with the list of cells in Table 6.16. Some cells such as 1 (England), 7 (Spain and Portugal), and 21-23 (Japan) are not difficult to identify. Others are unfamiliar.

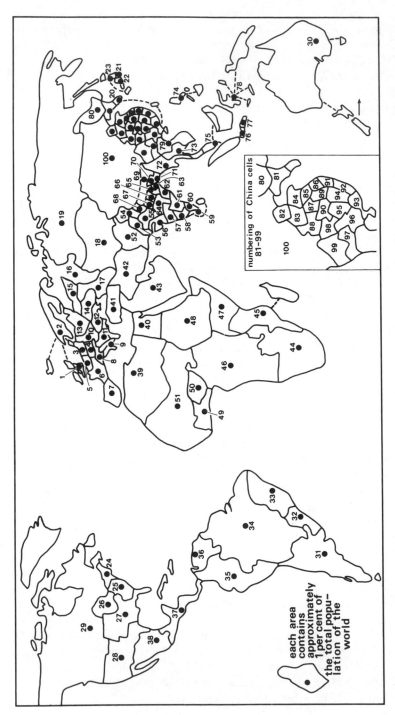

Figure 6.11 A system of 100 'equal population' cells. See text for explanation and Table 6.16 for key to numbering

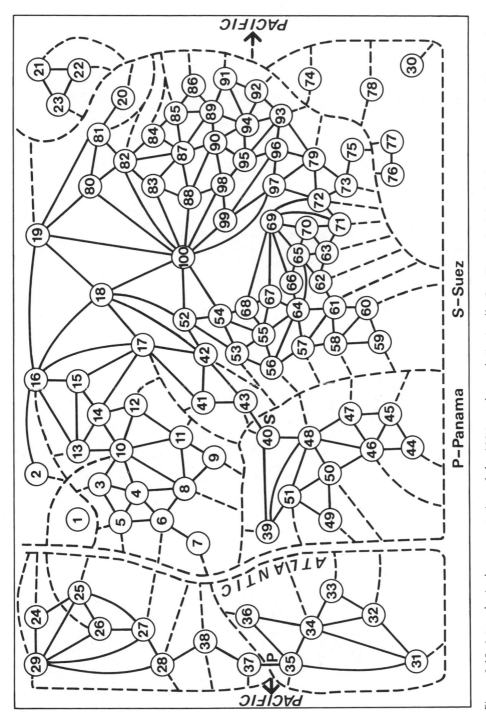

Figure 6.12 A topological representation of the 100 'equal population' cells. See Figure 6.11 for the base map and Table 6.16 for key to numbering

Table 6.16 The 100 cells — (detailed statement of each cell make-up provided where necessary)

Cell definition	Share of world population (per 10,000s)	Population (millions)	Area (thous. km²)	Density (persons/km²)
1 England	118.6	47	130	362
2 North Europe	88.4	35	1441	24
3 Netherlands, N. Germany	108.6	43	139	309
4 S. Germany	83.3	33	149	221
5 Belgium, N. France	83.3	33	147	224
6 Rest of France	75.8	30	431	70
7 Spain, Portugal	111.1	44	597	74
8 Switzerland, Austria, N.Italy	98.5	39	244	160
9 Rest of Italy, Greece	98.5	39	314	124
10 E.Germany, Czechoslovakia, Hungary	108.6	43	329	131
11 Yugoslavia, Bulgaria, Albania	80.8	32	396	81
12 Romania, Moldavia, S. Ukraine (U.S.S.R.)	80.8	32	385	83
13 Poland, Baltic (U.S.S.R.)	106.1	42	502	84
14 U.S.S.R.: Rest of Ukraine	106.1	42	490	86
15 U.S.S.R.: Belorussia, Centre	88.4	35	693	51
16 U.S.S.R.: Northwest, Volga-Vyatka, Volga	101.0	40	2606	15
17 U.S.S.R.: Blackearth C., Caucasuses	90.9	36	709	51
18 U.S.S.R.: Kazakhstan, C. Asia	93.4	37	3994	9
19 U.S.S.R.: Ural, Siberias, Far East	103.5	41	13,446	3
20 S. Korea, Hong Kong, Taiwan	136.4	54	135	400
21 Japan: Tokyo area	98.5	39	58	672
22 Japan: Osaka area	93.4	37	67	552
23 Rest of Japan	88.4	35	247	142
24 U.S.A.: N. Eng., N.Y., N.J.	96.0	38	322	118

25	U.S.A.: Penna. to Georgia	93.4	37	687	54
26	U.S.A.: East North Central	103.5	41	643	64
27	U.S.A.: Nebraska to Florida	106.1	42	1808	23
28	U.S.A.: Texas to California	106.1	42	2507	17
29	Canada, N.W. U.S.A., Alaska	90.9	36	13,375	3
30	Australia, New Zealand	40.4	16	7974	2
31	Argentina, Chile, Uruguay	98.5	39	3702	11
32	Brazil: Sul, São Paulo	103.5	41	809	51
33	Brazil: Rio to Pernambuco	111.1	44	1380	32
34	Rest of Brazil, Bolivia, Paraguay	88.4	35	8243	4
35	Colombia, Ecuador, Peru	121.2	48	2708	18
36	Venezuela, Caribbean	101.0	40	1145	35
37	C. America, S. Mexico	96.0	38	1054	36
38	C. Mexico and N. Mexico	103.5	41	1436	29
39	N. Africa	108.6	43	4753	16
40	Egypt	96.0	38	1001	38
41	Turkey	101.0	40	781	51
42	Iran, Iraq	111.1	44	2083	21
43	Rest of S.W. Asia	96.0	38	3309	11
44	Southern Africa	98.5	39	3836	10
45	Southeast Africa	101.0	40	2440	16
46	Central Africa	103.5	41	5300	8
47	East Africa	90.9	36	1533	23
48	Northeast Africa	116.2	46	3728	12
49	S. Nigeria, Benin to Ivory C.	113.6	45	924	49
50	N. Nigeria	96.0	38	758	50
51	Northwest Africa	90.9	36	6038	6
52	Afghanistan, N.W. Pakistan	103.5	41	1154	36
53	Rest of Pakistan	126.3	50	297	168
54	India: Kashmir to Delhi	98.5	39	373	105
55	India: Rajasthan and N.W.M.P.	90.9	36	392	92
56	India: Gujarat and N.W. Mah.	101.0	40	257	156

Table 6.16 (continued)

	Cell definition	Share of world population (per 10,000s)	Population (millions)	Area (thous. km²)	Density (persons/km²)
57	India: Maharashtra less N.W.	113.6	45	247	182
58	India: Karnataka	85.9	34	195	174
59	India: Kerala and Sri Lanka	96.0	38	105	362
60	India: Tamil Nadu	118.6	47	130	362
61	India: Andhra Pradesh	123.6	49	277	177
62	India: Orissa and S.W. of W. Bengal	88.4	35	176	199
63	India: W. Bengal less S.W.	98.5	39	68	574
64	India: Madhya Pradesh less N.W.	101.0	40	393	102
65	India: E. Bihar	101.0	40	110	364
66	India: W. Bihar, E. Uttar Pradesh	108.6	43	124	347
67	India: Mid-Uttar Pradesh	101.0	40	120	333
68	India: W. Uttar Pradesh	98.5	39	114	342
69	India: N.E., Nepal, Bhutan	90.9	36	461	78
70	North Bangladesh	101.0	40	66	606
71	South Bangladesh	85.9	34	78	436
72	Burma	78.3	31	677	46
73	Thailand	106.1	42	514	82
74	Philippines	111.1	44	300	147
75	Malaysia, Singapore, Sumatra	90.9	36	805	45
76	West Java	111.1	44	66	667
77	East Java	111.1	44	66	667
78	Rest of Indonesia, Papua-New Guinea	80.8	32	1270	25
79	Indo-China	128.7	51	751	68
80	China: Heilungkiang, Kirin	128.8	51	651	78

81	Liaoning (China), N. Korea	121.2	48	271	177
82	China: N. Hopei, Peking, Tientsin	111.1	44	144	306
83	China: S. Hopei, Shansi	98.5	39	227	172
84	China: N. Shantung	106.1	42	103	408
85	China: S. Shantung, N. Kiangsu	111.1	44	90	489
86	China: S. Kiangsu, Shanghai	108.6	43	66	652
87	China: E. Honan	101.0	40	115	348
88	China: W. Honan, Shensi	101.0	40	248	161
89	China: Anhwei	101.0	40	140	286
90	China: Hupei	106.1	42	188	223
91	China: Chekiang	88.4	35	102	343
92	China: Fukien, E. Kwangtung	85.9	34	193	176
93	China: W. Kwangtung	88.4	35	161	217
94	China: Kiangsi, S.E. Hunan	90.9	36	205	176
95	China: W. Hunan	88.4	35	171	205
96	China: Kwangsi-Chuang, E. Kweichow	98.5	39	310	126
97	China: Yunnan, W. Kweichow	93.4	37	520	71
98	China: E. Szechwan	101.0	40	169	237
99	China: W. Szechwan	98.5	39	400	98
100	Rest of China, Mongolian P.R.	96.0	38	6766	6
	World	10,000.0	3960	132,752	30

Table 6.17 Most and least densely populated cells in the world

Rank size of area	Cell No.	Name	Area (thous. km²)	Population (millions)	Density (persons /km²)
1	19	U.S.S.R.: Ural, Siberias, Far East	13,446	41	3
2	29	Canada, N.W. U.S.A., Alaska	13,375	36	3
3	34	Rest of Brazil, Bolivia, Paraguay	8243	35	4
4	30	Australia, New Zealand	7974	16	2
5	100	Rest of China, Mongolian P.R.	6766	38	6
6	51	Northwest Africa	6038	36	6
7	46	Central Africa	5300	41	8
8	39	North Africa	4753	43	16
9	18	U.S.S.R.: Kazakhstan, C. Asia	3994	37	9
10	44	Southern Africa	3836	39	10
91	84	China: N. Shantung	103	42	408
92	85	China: S. Shantung, N. Kiangsu	90	44	489
93	71	South Bangladesh	78	34	436
94	63	India: W. Bengal less S.W.	68	39	574
95	22	Japan: Osaka area	67	37	552
96	70	North Bangladesh	66	40	606
97	86	China: S. Kiangsu, Shanghai	66	43	652
98	77	Indonesia: East Java	66	44	667
99	76	Indonesia: West Java	66	44	667
100	21	Japan: Tokyo area	58	39	672

The great differences in the amount of land and adjacent sea available to people in different cells are brought out in Figure 6.11. Table 6.17 shows the 10 most and the 10 least densely populated cells in the world. The most densely populated ones have about 300 times as many people per square kilometre as the least densely populated cell, Australia. The 14 most densely populated cells in the world are in Asia, while England, which forms one cell, comes fifteenth.

It is not intended to imply by the brief discussion above of Figure 6.11 that population should or could be redistributed over the earth's land surface evenly according to area. Much of the land area in cells such as 29 (Canada, Northwest U.S.A., and Alaska), 19 (Siberia), and 20 (Australia) is useless waste. The densely populated cells of India, Java, and China consist largely of fertile farmlands with rich alluvial or volcanic soils, irrigation, and the possibility of growing two crops a year. The fact remains that, all other things being equal, a very thinly populated cell has a better chance than a very densely populated one of having a much more favourable ratio of natural resources to people. As was shown in Chapter 4 the same is true of the countries of the world, but the system of cells shown in Figure 6.11 has the advantage of including in each area not only roughly the same number of people but also places with broadly similar physical environments, cultural features, and levels of technological development and application.

The disadvantage of representing information about the world on a world map such as the one used in Figure 6.11 (Molleweide's Interrupted Homolographic) is that the true relationships of places to one another are not necessarily shown. Such relationships can only be shown on a globe. Another cartographical problem that arises from the above projection is that to be true to scale many cells are so small that they cannot be shaded or easily identified by symbols to distinguish them on distribution maps. To overcome such problems a diagram has been produced in which each cell stands out clearly and its relationship to those that touch it and to the world's seas and oceans is shown.

In Figure 6.12 each circle represents one cell. The cells are numbered as in Figure 6.11 and in Table 6.16. The continuous lines join cells that share a boundary on land. The broken lines run through the world's seas and oceans and also show which cells have a coastline. Some cells (e.g. 29, which includes Canada) have coastlines on three different oceans and therefore more than one link to the sea (the Arctic Ocean is not indicated). The Suez (S) and Panama (P) Canals are indicated. The cells in densely populated regions of the world like China, India, and West Europe have been spread out. Those in thinly populated regions have been brought closer together. From this transformation a base map has been produced for use in Chapters 7 and 8. The equal population cells will be useful for assessing the uneven distribution of natural resources and of production. They will also be useful in showing in Chapter 10 the kinds of transfer that will be needed in the world if some approximation to an equalization of living standards is to be achieved.

7

The distribution of natural resources in the 100 cells

7.1 Definitions of natural resources

The meaning of the term natural resources as understood in the present book was discussed briefly in Chapter 4. An estimate of the quantity of four types of natural resource per inhabitant was given for each of the 60 largest countries of the world in population. The four headings were: area of national territory, land capable of producing plants and raising animals, fossil fuel reserves, and non-fuel mineral reserves. It was clear from Table 4.1, columns (3)-(6), that very great disparities exist between countries with regard to the quantity of natural resources they possess per inhabitant.

The terms human resources, capital resources, and natural resources are commonly used. The first two types of resource are population, or the economically active part thereof, and means of production. The definition of natural resources is not so straightforward. Some views of the composition of natural resources are narrower than others. In the present book natural resources include anything in the natural environment used by man in the past, used at present, or likely to be used in the future. Three examples follow to illustrate the reason why the assessment of natural resources is very difficult.

(1) Materials in nature may be useless to man with one kind of technology but indispensable in another. Aluminium, for example, was virtually ignored as a useful metal until the twentieth century yet has always been in the ground. An eighteenth century inventory of natural resources would not have included bauxite.

(2) Even natural resources known currently to be useful, such as oil and copper, have not all been discovered yet. In assessing the quantity of natural resources in different regions of the world it seems desirable at least to try to allow for undiscovered resources.

England, for example, has been much more thoroughly explored for ·minerals than the centre of Australia or Amazonia yet even in England late in the twentieth century new mineral deposits are being discovered.

(3) Even if a particular natural resource becomes short or runs out it is often possible to make a satisfactory substitute material from another resource. Natural resources become increasingly interchangeable as technology advances.

In the view of the author it is a useful exercise to attempt a quantitative assessment of the distribution of natural resources by regions of the world. The problems referred to above and others, such as lack of readily available data, mean that the assessment can give only very approximate quantitative values to natural resources.

It is necessary to recognize a difference between what are commonly referred to as non-renewable and renewable natural resources. The terms exhaustible and non-exhaustible might be more appropriate. Conventionally, minerals tend to be regarded as exhaustible while land resources, water, and the sun's energy tend to be regarded as non-exhaustible. A consideration of some examples will show that the above view is an oversimplified one.

Over 90 percent of all energy used in the world in the 1970s was derived from fossil fuels. When used as combustible material these are entirely dissipated. Small quantities of coal, oil (petroleum), and natural gas are forming in places in the world at present but in the 100 years of the twentieth century oil and gas that took perhaps 100 million years to form will have been used up. The natural replacement or renewal rate of fossil fuels is so slow compared with their current use that it is negligible. Mineral raw materials are also eventually non-renewable. With appropriate means of recovery and recycling, materials such as steel, aluminium, and glass can be used more than once, being 'recoverable' from products no longer needed. Many mineral materials, however, defy recovery, like the steel and concrete in a demolished building or the tin in cans deposited on a rubbish dump.

At first sight, soil may be thought of as a natural resource that is not used up. It is, however, common knowledge and common sense that whenever plants are removed from a piece of land a certain proportion of the nutrients from that land are removed. When tropical forest is cut and the vegetation removed entirely a large proportion of the nutrients go with it. Soil may also disappear from a given area through erosion by water or by wind, especially if the land is ploughed excessively and left without plant cover. The land resources of the world are being reduced in some regions both through the loss of soil or a deterioration in its quality and through the spread of urban uses into cultivated areas.

Other features of the natural environment less widely thought of as natural resources should also be taken into consideration in a study of development. Water and the atmosphere may be thought of as 'renewable' natural resources, not used up or destroyed. Both the direct heat of the sun and its indirect effect in producing energy that can be used from the force of wind, waves, and tides may also be regarded as natural resources, potential rather than currently of major use. For the practical purposes of a human time scale, the sun's energy may be regarded as inexhaustible.

In this chapter natural resources have been classified into four groups.

(1) Land from which plants and animals are derived. For convenience such resources will be referred to as land resources. They are also referred to as bioclimatic resources. The products from these resources feed human beings, feed animals either for work purposes or as a source of food and raw materials, serve as raw materials themselves (e.g. cotton) or are used as fuel.

(2) Fossil fuels. The main forms used at present are coal, lignite, oil, and natural gas. Although nuclear fuels are not hydrocarbons they may conveniently be thought of in the category of non-renewable energy resources. In contrast, hydroelectric (falling water), wind and tidal power are 'renewable' (or repetitive). Fossil fuels are mainly used for heating or to drive machines, as food 'drives' humans, but they are increasingly used also as raw materials.

(3) Non-fuel minerals used commercially in the world economy are very numerous indeed and vary greatly in the extent of their application. Some, such as copper and asbestos, go into manufactured products while others, such as fertilizer minerals and lead in petrol (gasoline), go back into the ground or are burned.

(4) Total space has been calculated in the present study as a back-up resource, to some degree double-counting the items in categories (1)-(3). It was felt that the three widely recognized categories of natural resource outlined above did not cover all the resources of a given region for two main reasons. Firstly, they do not explicitly include features such as fishing grounds, water itself, and the potential energy from the sun, and secondly, they make no allowance for undiscovered minerals, especially those in shallow sea areas.

Before the distribution of each of the four types of natural resource is described in the sections that follow it is of interest to refer briefly to the categories used in two different Soviet studies of the subject. Runova (1973) used the following in a study of Soviet natural resources:

(1) Bioclimatic resources:
    (a) Reindeer pasture (in tundra and coniferous forest zones)
    (b) Timber (in coniferous and mixed forest zones)
    (c) Forage (of two types, range land in semi-desert and desert zones and pastures and hayfields in cultivated areas)
    (d) Arable (mainly in broadleaf forest, forest steppe, and steppe zones)
(2) Mineral resources:
    (a) Fuels, in the form of oil and gas, or of coal (and lignite), or of these in combination
    (b) Metals, either ferrous or non-ferrous or in combination

Bioclimatic resources tend to be distributed continuously over the surface of the land but precise regional limits to different types are difficult to establish. Mineral resources tend to be concentrated in 'cores', with large intervening areas in which few economic minerals occur. The method used by Runova to work out resource regions was to superimpose the distribution of mineral resource concentrations on the distribution of bioclimatic resource zones. The result of the first attempt to do this was a map of the U.S.S.R. with 86 regions.

In making a quantitative evaluation of the natural resource potential of the U.S.S.R., Mints and Kakhanovskaya (1974) ran into a number of problems. When a numerical value is given to a natural resource it is necessary to consider how long that resource will last if it is being used up at a given rate. It is claimed that the U.S.S.R. has about 9 million million tonnes of coal, enough at rates of production in the 1970s to last 18,000 years. Such a piece of information is hardly of immediate value even to long-term planners thinking as much as several decades ahead. The authors of the paper limited their assessment of natural resources very strictly, as will be shown.

The following items were chosen for the natural resource assessment of the U.S.S.R.: coal, oil and natural gas, iron ore, hydro-power, timber, arable, forage, and 'other', including other types of mineral. Mineral resources were only assessed if they were likely to be accessible in the next 10-15 years. The quantity that could be extracted each year was then estimated. The productive potential land was calculated according to the quality of the land. The quantity of plant and animal products that could be derived from the land could thus be estimated. The total resource potential was then expressed in monetary form. With the resources valued in terms of a set of unit prices, different types of resource could be compared, though problems arise in such a method. It is difficult, for example, to compare non-exhaustible natural resources, such as land, with exhaustible ones, such as coal and copper.

The value of the natural resource potential was calculated by Mints and Kakhanovskaya for 137 administrative territories in the U.S.S.R. The area and number of inhabitants of each territory was also known. It was therefore possible to calculate the size of resource potential per unit of area and per inhabitant.

The two Soviet papers have been referred to here for three reasons. Firstly, it is helpful to know how natural resources are perceived and defined in a socialist economy. Secondly, the U.S.S.R. is so large and so varied in its natural environments and resources that it can be regarded as a world in miniature. Thirdly, in the rest of this chapter a quantitative value is placed on the world's natural resources, though no monetary value is worked out.

7.2   The distribution of natural resources

In the previous section natural resources were divided by the author into four categories. It is not possible to assess precisely the relative importance of each of these four categories in the total inventory of resources and therefore it is not easy to put even an approximate weight to them. In the assessment of total natural resources of the world and in their assignment to 100 regions, equal weight has arbitrarily been given to land resources, fossil fuels, mineral raw materials, and territory. In reality these have changed in relative importance through time.

Land resources were by far the most heavily used and indispensable of the four types in the world until the Industrial Revolution in the eighteenth century. Since then, both fossil fuels and non-fuel minerals have come to assume major roles in the world economy. The decline during the nineteenth and twentieth centuries in employment in agriculture as a percentage of total employed population was described in Chapter 5. The contribution of the agricultural sector to total gross national product is now valued at only a modest few percent in many highly industrialized countries and at less than half even in many developing countries. In the 1970s the search for and exploitation of fossil fuels attracted more attention, if not more actual investment, than attempts to increase the productive capacity of the soil. Research into mining, manufacturing and military developments often seems to have higher priority than research in the agricultural sector. Should the present heavily industrialized world economy collapse for some

Table 7.1 Example of calculation used to achieve natural resource scores in Table 7.2

Cell No. and name	(1) Population Millions	(2) Per 10,000 of world	(3) Land resources Units	(4) Per 10,000 of world	(5) Col.(4)/ col.(2) × 100	(6) Fossil fuels Units	(7) Per 10,000 of world	(8) Col.(7)/ col.(2)
1 England	47	119	13	40	34	115	116	98
2 North Europe	35	88	27	84	95	110	111	126
3 Netherlands, N. Germany	43	109	12	37	34	260	262	241
4 S. Germany	33	83	10	31	37	13	13	15
5 Belgium, N. France	33	83	22	68	82	3	3	4
27 U.S.A.: Nebraska to Florida	42	106	120	373	352	400	403	380
28 U.S.A.: Texas to California	42	106	125	388	366	367	370	349
29 Canada, N.W. U.S.A., Alaska	36	91	190	589	648	506	510	561
30 Australia, New Zealand	16	40	103	320	792	150	151	374
31 Argentina, Chile, Uruguay	39	99	96	297	302	23	23	2
51 Northwest Africa	36	91	28	87	96	0	0	0
52 Afghanistan, N.W. Pakistan	41	104	21	65	63	0	0	0
53 Rest of Pakistan	50	126	28	87	69	1	1	1
54 India: Kashmir to Delhi	39	99	20	62	63	0	0	0
55 India: Rajasthan and N.W.M.P.	36	91	25	77	85	5	5	6
World	3960	10,000	3230	10,000		9918	10,000	

reason, the resources of the land would no doubt increase in relative importance once again.

The world as a whole is a subsistence economy since no food or other products come to or leave the planet. Once the world is subdivided, whether into the existing system of sovereign states or into synthetic 'geographical' regions, great regional disparities appear in the ratio of natural resources to population. It is the purpose of the rest of this chapter to describe the disparities.

The background material used in the chapter is given in Table 7.2 and will be referred to frequently. It is first necessary to describe the way the data were calculated. Table 7.1 shows the calculations that had to be carried out on natural resources to arrive at their relationship to population for the 100 cells. Fifteen cells have been chosen as examples from the 100 in Table 7.2. They are numbered in Table 7.1 according to their positions in Table 7.2. The columns referred to below are those in Table 7.1.

Column (1) gives the population of the cells in millions to the nearest million.

Column (2) gives the proportion in per 10,000s that the population of the given cell has of total world population. Most cells have approximately 1 percent of the population of the world but, as explained in Chapter 6, for practical reasons it was not desirable to have *exactly* 1 percent in each cell. Thus, for example, 119 means 1.19 percent, 83 means 0.83 percent, and 100 would be exactly 1 percent.

Column (3). Land resource units were calculated for each cell by a method to be explained in Section 7.3. Thus cell 1, England, has 13 units out of a world total of 3230 units.

Column (4). The land resource units of each cell are expressed as proportions of the world total in per 10,000s.

Column (5). It is possible to compare columns (2) and (4) directly because they express respectively population and land resources in per 10,000s. Thus England has 119 per 10,000 of the total population of the world but only 40 per 10,000 of the land resources. If a region had the same index in columns (2) and (4) it would have the same quantity of land resources per inhabitant as is found in the world as a whole. If the land resource per 10,000 of each cell is divided by the population per 10,000 of each cell it is possible to work out a value to show how favourably or unfavourably a cell is endowed compared with the world average. In column (5) each value is the value in column (4) divided by the value in column (2) multiplied by 100. A cell with a score of 100 in column (5) would have a ratio equivalent to that in the world as a whole. In the example, cell 1, England, has a score of only 34, which means that its land resources

Table 7.2 Natural resources by cells. (1) Land resources; (2) Fossil fuel reserves; (3) Non-fuel minerals; (4) Territory

Cell No. and name	(1)	(2)	(3)	(4)	Average (1)-(4)
1 England	34	98	19	12	41
2 North Europe	95	126	121	140	120
3 Netherlands, N. Germany	34	241	10	10	74
4 S. Germany	37	15	41	13	27
5 Belgium, N. France	82	4	34	13	33
6 Rest of France	123	8	30	46	52
7 Spain, Portugal	117	5	61	42	56
8 Switzerland, Austria, N. Italy	47	7	11	19	21
9 Rest of Italy, Greece	54	6	57	30	37
10 E. Germany, Czechoslovakia, Hungary	86	64	67	22	60
11 Yugoslavia, Bulgaria, Albania	95	19	126	37	69
12 Romania, Moldavia, S. Ukraine (U.S.S.R.)	181	15	0	37	58
13 Poland, Baltic (U.S.S.R.)	131	86	22	36	69
14 U.S.S.R.: Rest of Ukraine	125	157	64	33	63
15 U.S.S.R.: Belorussia, Centre	169	6	19	54	62
16 U.S.S.R.: Northwest, Volga-Vyatka, Volga	200	340	84	192	204
17 U.S.S.R.: Blackearth C., Caucasuses	184	84	186	57	127
18 U.S.S.R.: Kazakhstan, C. Asia	262	653	453	294	416
19 U.S.S.R.: Ural, Siberias, Far East	385	1892	898	904	1019
20 S. Korea, Hong Kong, Taiwan	27	4	0	10	10
21 Japan: Tokyo area	22	0	0	5	7
22 Japan: Osaka area	24	0	0	9	8
23 Rest of Japan	42	8	38	26	29
24 U.S.A.: N. Eng., N.Y., N.J.	71	0	29	27	32
25 U.S.A.: Penna. to Georgia	166	470	45	57	184
26 U.S.A.: East North Central	240	205	69	44	139
27 U.S.A.: Nebraska to Florida	352	380	266	129	282
28 U.S.A.: Texas to California	366	349	466	172	338
29 Canada, N.W. U.S.A., Alaska	648	561	1336	1039	823
30 Australia, New Zealand	792	374	2735	1520	1355
31 Argentina, Chile, Uruguay	302	2	470	288	271
32 Brazil. Sul, São Paulo	101	2	0	63	42
33 Brazil: Rio to Pernambuco	78	5	102	96	70
34 Rest of Brazil, Bolivia, Paraguay	207	2	319	740	317
35 Colombia, Ecuador, Peru	120	15	270	172	144
36 Venezuela, Caribbean	61	145	374	95	169
37 C. America, S. Mexico	113	32	35	100	70
38 C. Mexico and N. Mexico	120	14	66	107	80
39 N. Africa	74	316	107	317	203
40 Egypt	39	14	0	75	32

Table 7.2 (Continued)

Cell No. and name	(1)	(2)	(3)	(4)	Average (1)-(4)
41 Turkey	159	0	23	59	60
42 Iran, Iraq	84	818	0	135	260
43 Rest of S.W. Asia	58	1453	5	257	443
44 Southern Africa	148	57	898	281	346
45 Southeast Africa	101	0	18	187	76
46 Central Africa	150	5	387	394	234
47 East Africa	55	0	7	130	48
48 Northeast Africa	114	0	0	238	88
49 S. Nigeria, Benin to Ivory C.	68	98	94	66	81
50 N. Nigeria	65	0	11	60	34
51 Northwest Africa	96	0	491	492	270
52 Afghanistan, N.W. Pakistan	63	0	0	78	35
53 Rest of Pakistan	69	1	0	18	22
54 India: Kashmir to Delhi	63	0	6	28	24
55 India: Rajasthan and N.W.M.P.	85	6	7	31	32
56 India: Gujarat and N.W. Mah.	61	0	6	21	22
57 India: Maharashtra less N.W.	68	0	5	18	23
58 India: Karnataka	72	0	7	19	23
59 India: Kerala and Sri Lanka	55	0	6	11	18
60 India: Tamil Nadu	52	0	5	9	17
61 India: Andhra Pradesh	62	4	5	18	22
62 India: Orissa and S.W. of W. Bengal	87	0	7	16	27
63 India: W. Bengal less S.W.	47	25	6	5	21
64 India: Madhya Pradesh less N.W.	76	5	6	30	29
65 India: E. Bihar	61	25	6	8	25
66 India: W. Bihar, E. Uttar Pradesh	57	0	6	8	18
67 India: Mid-Uttar Pradesh	61	0	6	9	19
68 India: W. Uttar Pradesh	63	0	6	9	20
69 India: N.E., Nepal, Bhutan	102	9	7	39	39
70 North Bangladesh	44	0	0	6	11
71 South Bangladesh	50	0	0	8	15
72 Burma	151	1	8	73	58
73 Thailand	96	0	74	42	53
74 Philippines	67	0	61	25	38
75 Malaysia, Singapore, Sumatra	96	105	136	90	107
76 West Java	41	0	0	7	12
77 East Java	41	0	0	7	12
78 Rest of Indonesia, Papua New Guinea	99	0	0	152	63
79 Indo-China	62	0	5	51	30
80 China: Heilungkiang, Kirin	60	67	0	35	40

Table 7.2 (Continued)

Cell No. and name	(1)	(2)	(3)	(4)	Average (1)-(4)
81 Liaoning (China), N. Korea	51	37	74	19	45
82 China: N. Hopei, Peking, Tientsin	41	9	0	10	15
83 China: S. Hopei, Shansi	47	153	0	16	54
84 China: N. Shantung	43	33	8	9	23
85 China: S. Shantung, N. Kiangsu	41	5	7	6	15
86 China: S. Kiangsu, Shanghai	42	0	7	6	14
87 China: E. Honan	46	5	0	8	15
88 China: W. Honan, Shensi	55	150	0	18	56
89 China: Anhwei	55	5	8	10	20
90 China: Hupei	53	9	8	13	21
91 China: Chekiang	52	6	9	10	19
92 China: Fukien, E. Kwangtung	54	6	44	19	31
93 China: W. Kwangtung	63	0	43	19	31
94 China: Kiangsi, S.E. Hunan	62	6	42	18	32
95 China: W. Hunan	63	6	21	15	26
96 China: Kwangsi-Chuang, E. Kweichow	47	5	19	24	24
97 China: Yunnan, W. Kweichow	49	11	12	42	28
98 China: E. Szechwan	46	150	11	13	55
99 China: W. Szechwan	47	51	11	30	35
100 Rest of China, Mongolian P.R.	97	47	99	482	181

(as assessed by the author) in relation to population are only about one-third of the world average. Cell 30, Australia and New Zealand, has in contrast a score of 792, which means that it has nearly eight times the world average of land resources per inhabitant, and thus appears to be about 24 times as well endowed in this respect as England. As with all natural resource assessments in this book the estimate is only rough, and if different criteria were used the England-Australia gap might turn out narrower or wider, but it would always be there and would always be very large.

Columns (6)-(8). A similar calculation to that for land resources has been made for fossil fuels per inhabitant. In the case of fossil fuels, some cells have virtually no reserves at all while others have very large amounts, as can be seen from a comparison of cells 5 and 51-54 with cell 29.

The reader may now refer again to Table 7.2, in which each of the four sets of natural resources has been compared with the population of each cell in the way explained above for land resources. Each of the four resources will be discussed separately in the next four sections. First, some features of the table may be

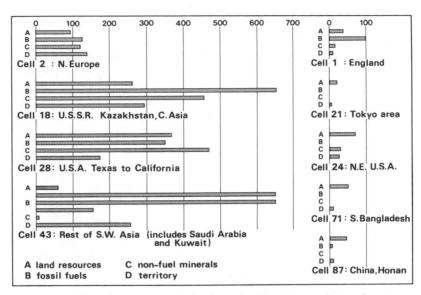

Figure 7.1 The resource scores of selected cells. See text for explanation

noted. In a cell with a score of 100, each inhabitant has a share equal to the world average. The zeros in the columns for fossil fuel reserves and mineral raw material reserves indicate a negligible amount rather than none at all. The disparities in population size of the cells have been eliminated in the calculations explained above, so the data now represent pure units per inhabitant.

When the data are read down the columns it can be seen that land resources are less concentrated in a few cells than the other three resources. When the data are read across the rows, and individual cells are compared, remarkable contrasts emerge. Some cells have very favourable resource/population ratios and some very unfavourable ones. In some cells, the 'profile' is very irregular because only one resource is strongly represented, as fossil fuels in cells 42 (Iran, Iraq) and 43 (Rest of Southwest Asia).

In Figure 7.1 nine selected cells are represented diagrammatically according to their resource units per inhabitant. Cell 2 (upper left in diagram) shows that North Europe (Scandinavia and British Isles except England) has balanced natural resources fairly near to the world average. Much of the land resource category is however accounted for by forest, while the fossil fuel sector is essentially North Sea Oil. Cell 1, England, has fewer resources per inhabitant than cell 2 and is less well balanced, with coal and North Sea gas bringing the fossil fuel reserves per inhabitant to near the world average but with land and non-fuel mineral resources limited.

Three very well endowed cells are shown on the left of the diagram in Figure 7.1. The Soviet and U.S. cells selected for illustration here are quite well balanced but the Rest of Southwest Asia cell has limited land resources and very few non-fuel minerals. Its main natural resource is oil. All the four remaining cells on the right of the diagram, 21, 24, 71, and 87, are very poorly provided with natural resources in relation to population. Two, however, cells 21 and 24, are highly industrialized and urbanized and are large importers of food, fossil fuels, and raw materials, the Tokyo area largely from cells in other countries, Northeast U.S.A. largely from other cells in the U.S.A. itself.

7.3   Land resources

The productive capacity of the land with regard to the growth of plants can be assessed in various ways. Two fundamentally different approaches may be distinguished. Eyre (1978) calculated the mass of vegetation produced under natural conditions in different environmental regions, which he terms natural vegetation regions. Another method of assessment is to give a rating to different parts of the earth's surface according to the kinds of plant that actually are or theoretically could be grown there by man. The second method is used here. Some drawbacks in Eyre's method of assessing the potential of the land from the mass of vegetation expected under theoretical climax conditions will first be noted.

Eyre discusses the problems of measuring the annual production of the earth's vegetation. He considers the net primary productivity of the original wild vegetation to be a satisfactory measure of potential productivity of land resources. In this way, tropical forest in particular and forest in general has a high net primary productivity per unit of area, desert obviously a low one. After refining the measure, Eyre compares the theoretical production of vegetation from the wild state with production (yields) achieved by farming, which, though taking place on improved land, yields less actual plant matter (though in a more digestible form, a point not emphasized sufficiently perhaps). When each country of the world is considered in relation to its land resources (as defined above) divided by its population, its 'potential *per capita* net primary productivity' (PPCNPP) can be calculated.

Countries that are very poorly endowed are those with less than 10 tonnes per inhabitant net primary productivity. Among those in the list are Egypt, the Netherlands, Belgium, South Korea, Japan,

West Germany, Switzerland, the U.K., Bangladesh, and India (China just escapes). The best endowed countries include a lunatic fringe like French Guiana, Gabon, and Surinam as well as Australia, Bolivia, Zaire, and Canada, all with over 200 tonnes per inhabitant. Eyre's assessment of land resources arrived at broadly the same ranking of countries as that arrived at by the present author with country data in Chapter 4. The extremes are much further apart in Eyre's definition, broadly by wild vegetation, compared with that of the present author, using actual cropland, pasture, and forest, weighted according to estimated value of production per unit of area.

The natural vegetation of the earth's surface has been greatly modified by man through clearance and 'improvement' for cultivation, by the use of grasslands for grazing, and by the cutting of forests for timber. Even if it were desirable, it would be very difficult and certainly time-consuming to restore 'natural' vegetation to areas now modified by man. A large part of the plant mass that still grows naturally, such as the tropical rain forest, is not in a form that can immediately be consumed by man as food or even processed suitably for this purpose. For the purposes of the present study, therefore, it was considered that a more realistic and practical assessment of land resources would be one based on what the land produces as currently farmed or what it might be expected to produce if developed for agriculture.

The quantity or weight of plants produced on any given piece of land is determined by a very wide range of influences, both environmental (weather, inherent soil fertility) and man-made (ploughing, weeding, use of fertilizer). Even so it is possible to say that for practical purposes some parts of the earth's land surface are more productive than others. In assessing the land resources in each of the countries of the world and in each of the 100 cells, a rough measure of productivity of the land was made by the author.

In publications of the Food and Agriculture Organisation (FAO) four main categories of land use are identified, cultivated land (arable plus permanent crops such as orchards), permanent meadows and pastures, forest land, and other land. Estimates of the proportion of the total area of each country of the world used for each of the four categories are given each year in the *Food and Agriculture Production Yearbook*. The category 'other uses' was not considered in the present study since it consists of urban and other non-agricultural uses or of waste land with a vegetation, if any, of no commercial use.

The areas of cropland, pasture, and forest were obtained for each country of the world. Some initial adjustments were made to areas where it was considered that the method of calculation used in the country was unsatisfactory. In many African countries land that is only tilled from time to time is classed as cultivated. In Tanzania, for example, the cultivated area seems to be greatly overstated.

After the final estimate of area for each of the three categories of land use in each country had been worked out it was modified according to its quality, as assessed by the author. Some examples of modifications made to each of the three categories are indicated below. The basic land use unit is 1 unit per million hectares of 'standard' cultivated land.

(1) Cultivated area was left unchanged in most countries but was multiplied up to four times in special instances. Thus for example Iran's cultivated area of 16 million hectares was left at 16 units while the 3 million hectares for Egypt, virtually all irrigated, was multiplied by four to give 12 units. In general, areas that are irrigated, double cropped or situated in regions of particularly fertile soil, such as the blackearth lands of the U.S.S.R., were upgraded.

(2) The areas of natural pasture in the world produce on average much less per unit of area than the cultivated areas. Thus to make the basic, poorest, natural pasture comparable with basic cultivated land, the area of pasture was everywhere arbitrarily reduced to one-tenth. After reduction, better quality natural pasture land was then upgraded. A wide range of productivity of pasture land occurs for example between valuable Alpine pastures in Europe and very poor grazing lands in the outback in Australia or the fringes of the Sahara desert in Africa.

(3) Forest areas include an increasing proportion of land actually planted or replanted by man, even in areas that might be used for cultivation, such as poplar plantations in the fertile North Italian lowlands, but usually where forest has been cut and replanted. The natural forest itself varies greatly from region to region in type of tree and timber and in rate of growth. Altogether, however, over a long period of time a given area of forest produces much less in terms of value (in economic terms), though not in terms of plant weight, than a comparable area of cultivated land. The area of 'basic' forest has therefore been reduced to one-tenth the rating given to basic cultivated land. Areas of better quality forest, such as that in Japan and parts of Europe, specially planted and tended, have then been upgraded above the basic score of 1/10 unit per million hectares.

The total land surface of the world is about 13,400 million hectares. Around 1970, 1425 million hectares, or between 10 and 11 percent of the earth's surface, was defined as being under cultivation. The areas for natural pasture and forest were 3000 million (22-23 percent) and 4000 million (30-31 percent) respectively. The effect of derating pasture and forest to a tenth the 'value' of cultivated land has been to make them equivalent respectively to about a fifth and a third the total weight of cultivated land rather than a tenth, on account of their larger extent.

The effect of the procedures outlined above on the assessment of land resource units for individual countries can be exemplified by two countries that form exact cells, Egypt (cell 40) and Turkey (cell 41). Egypt has a mere 3 million hectares of cultivated land and virtually no pasture or forest. Its total land resource score is 3 million cultivated, multiplied by four, or 12 points. Turkey has 28 million hectares of cultivated land, 26 million hectares of pasture, and 18 million hectares of forest. The cultivated area was multiplied by 1.5, the pasture area by 0.3, and the forest by 0.1 to give 42 plus 8 plus 2 units, a total land resource assessment of 52 units. Had different weightings been given to the various types of land use in the two countries, Turkey might have been credited with for example five or three times the land resources per inhabitant of Egypt rather than about four. Even so, the broad disparity would remain.

Altogether, according to the system of units used by the author, there were 3230 land resource units for the world as a whole. The units were calculated for each country and amounts divided by populations given in Table 4.1 for the 60 largest countries of the world. The number of land resource units was also calculated for each of the 100 'equal' population cells. There was an average of about 32 units per cell. The next step was to express the units in terms of per 10,000s (3230 equivalent to 10,000). Since in practice cells differ in population size it was necessary, then, to make the further adjustments described in the previous section of dividing the land resource points of each cell (in per 10,000s of the world total) by the population of each cell (also in per 10,000s of the world total).

Column (1) in Table 7.2 shows the final land resource units per population in each of the 100 cells. A cell that scores 100 has exactly the same share of land resource units as it has of population. In fact some cells have far more land resources per inhabitant than others. The extremes are shown in Table 7.3, which contains the 10 cells with the largest amounts of land resources per inhabitant and the 11 with the smallest amounts. Australia and New Zealand have about 40 times as many land resources per inhabitant as the Tokyo area and about 20 times as many as predominantly

Table 7.3 Cells with highest and lowest scores on land resources

Rank	Cell No.	Countries or regions in cell	Score
1	30	Australia, New Zealand	792
2	29	Canada, N.W. U.S.A., Alaska	648
3	19	U.S.S.R.: Ural, Siberias, Far East	385
4	28	U.S.A.: Texas to California	366
5	27	U.S.A.: Nebraska to Florida	352
6	31	Argentina, Chile, Uruguay	302
7	18	U.S.S.R.: Kazakhstan, C. Asia	262
8	26	U.S.A.: E.N. Central	240
9	34	Rest of Brazil, Bolivia, Paraguay	207
10	16	U.S.S.R.: N.W., Volga-Vyatka, Volga	200
World Average			100
90	85	China: S. Shantung, N. Kiangsu	41
91	82	China: N. Hopei, Peking, Tientsin	41
92	77	E. Java	41
93	76	W. Java	41
94	40	Egypt	39
95	4	S. Germany	37
96	3	Netherlands, N. Germany	34
97	1	England	34
98	20	S. Korea, Hong Kong, Taiwan	27
99	22	Japan: Osaka area	24
100	21	Japan: Tokyo area	22

agricultural cells such as the two in Java (Indonesia) and some cells in the plains and hills of North China. The best and most poorly endowed cells are mapped in Figure 7.2.

Nine cells have scores of over 200, or twice the world average amount of land resources per inhabitant. The best endowed cells coincide broadly with those areas of the world that were comparatively thinly populated until Europeans settled them, mainly in the nineteenth century.

Twenty-four cells have scores of 50 or less, that is less than half the world average. Some of the most poorly endowed cells are situated in highly urbanized countries or parts of countries, such as Japan, West Germany, the Netherlands, and England. Land resources per inhabitant are also very limited in many parts of China, India, and other parts of Southeast Asia.

The amount of plant and animal products actually derived from the land in each cell per year per inhabitant is not exactly related to the land resource scores of the cell. The last six cells in Table 7.3 are

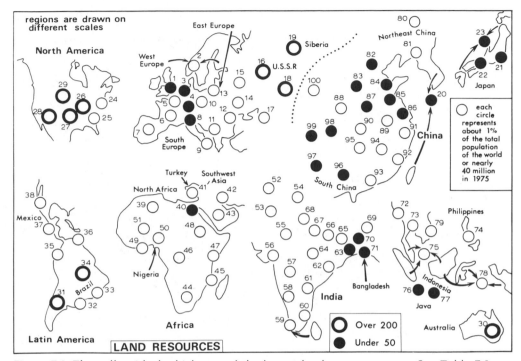

Figure 7.2 The cells with the highest and the lowest land resource scores. See Table 7.3

highly industrialized. They therefore have levels of technology that allow very high yields to be achieved in the limited areas cultivated. Further, they are able to buy agricultural produce from elsewhere. Thus the land resources as assessed in this section show potential rather than actual production.

When the share of the world's land resources in each cell is matched against the share each cell has of world population it is possible to calculate data to draw a Lorenz curve of inequality of distribution and to derive the gini coefficient (see Appendix 1 for explanation of method). Figure 7.3 shows the curve and the gini coefficient (0.397) for land resources. It is customary in diagrams of this kind to have the population proportion along the horizontal scale. Here and in the other Lorenz curve diagrams in this chapter and Chapter 8 population is placed on the vertical scale. The 'curve' has been fitted to data for every tenth cell. It is possible to read off on the graph for example that the 10 best endowed cells, that is, the 10 with the highest scores in Table 7.3, have 34 percent of the world's land resources between them.

This study of land resources has shown that population and land resources are mismatched. It will be seen in the next two sections

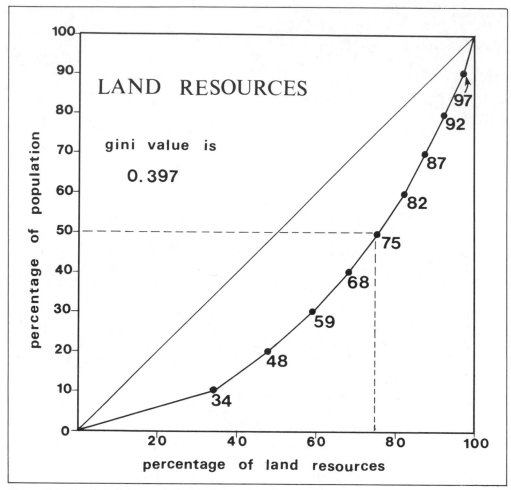

Figure 7.3 The distribution of the land resources of the world according to population

that fossil fuels and non-fuel minerals are still less evenly matched with population. Though far from close to that of land resources, the distribution of world population still reflects its great dependence on these.

7.4 Fossil fuel resources

Non-renewable fuels provided a very large part of the energy used in the world in the 1970s. Unless some major change takes place in the world economy, they are likely to continue to do so for some decades. Four types of fossil fuel have been used here to assess resources: coal, lignite (and brown coal), oil, and natural gas.

Table 7.4 World fossil fuel reserves and resources in the mid-1970s measured before conversion to coal equivalent

Coal:		
	Known recoverable reserves	430,000 million tonnes
	Other known economic reserves in place 644,000	'' ''
	Additional resources	7,063,000 '' ''
Lignite:		
	Known recoverable reserves	160,000 '' ''
	Other known economic reserves in place 180,000	'' ''
	Additional resources	2,290,000 '' ''
Crude petroleum (oil)		75,500 '' ''
Natural gas		59,000 thousand million cubic metres

Estimates of commercial reserves are available in *United Nations Statistical Yearbooks* on a country by country basis.

Comparability of fossil fuels can be achieved by expressing other fuels in terms of coal equivalent. One tonne of crude oil is equivalent to about 1.47 tonnes of coal according to the United Nations 1976 version (it was only rated at 1.33 in 1970). A tonne of lignite and brown coal varies from one country to another from 0.3 to 0.67 tonne of coal. Natural gas when measured in cubic metres gives an equivalent of 1.33 tonnes of coal per 1000 m^3 of gas. Estimates of world fossil fuel resources for around 1975 or for the latest available year are shown in Table 7.4.

Known recoverable reserves of coal and lignite, after the conversion of lignite to coal equivalent, are estimated to be about 500,000 million tonnes. Oil and natural gas reserves are estimated to be about 200,000 million tonnes of coal equivalent. Although it is reasonable to assume that additional oil and natural gas will be discovered, no allowance is made for these. On the other hand, it is already known that very large quantities of coal and lignite additional to the 500,000 million tonnes of known recoverable reserves are actually in the ground. They are not all easy to extract under present technological conditions and they have not been measured accurately.

In order to achieve a realistic value for total fossil fuel reserves for each of the 100 cells it was decided that the estimate should be one for several decades of use rather than several centuries. Whatever the size of reserves and resources, therefore, it was decided to give equal weight to coal and lignite on the one hand and oil and natural gas on the other. Total fossil fuel reserves are therefore divided roughly into coal 4/10, oil 3/10, natural gas 2/10, lignite 1/10. The reasoning behind these ratios is that although eventual usable coal and lignite resources combined may be 20 times as great as oil and natural gas resources combined, at present and in the next few decades about equal amounts of each are likely to be produced and consumed.

To assess fossil fuel reserves in the world the following calculations were made.

(1) Coal. Each tonne of *known recoverable reserves* (type 1) was rated as 1 tonne. Other *known economic reserves in place* (type 2) were reduced to one-fifth of their estimated value and each tonne of *additional resources* (type 3) to one-tenth. The three quantities were added to give a coal total. The calculations for the U.K. will serve as an example. In thousands of millions of tonnes, there were 4×1 (type 1) $+ 95 \times 0.2$ (type 2) $+ 64 \times 0.1$ (type 3), or $4 + 19 + 6 = 29 \times 10^9$ tonnes of coal 'reserves', actually about 2.3 percent of the world total.

(2) Lignite was treated in the same way as coal. The final total was then reduced according to the accepted conversion of lignite to coal equivalent of each country. Thus for example Australia's lignite in thousands of millions of tonnes was 10×1 (type 1) $+ 39 \times 0.2$ (type 2) $+ 38 \times 0.1$ (type 3), or $10 + 8 + 4 = 22$. The 22 was then multiplied by 0.33 to give about 7×10^9 tonnes of lignite reserves, actually about 4 percent of the world's lignite.

(3) Oil and natural gas reserves could both be used directly as no allowance was needed for different levels of probability of occurrence. Conversion to coal equivalent could be made immediately. Tar sands and oil shales are not taken into account.

When the four types of fuel reserves were weighted as noted above and combined, a single value was obtained for each country of the world. On the basis of the criteria used, it became evident that five countries alone have nearly two-thirds of all fossil fuel reserves in the world: the U.S.S.R. 30 percent, the U.S.A. 18 percent, Iran 7 percent, Saudi Arabia 6 percent, and Kuwait 4 percent. Table 4.1 in Chapter 4 shows estimates of fossil fuel reserves per inhabitant in the 60 largest countries of the world.

The fossil fuel reserves of the world were then distributed according to their occurrence among the 100 cells. Small countries such as Iran and Iraq were grouped into single cells while large countries such as China and the U.S.S.R. were subdivided and reserves allocated by cells. Lack of precise information made it particularly difficult to estimate how fossil fuel reserves are distributed among the cells of China and India.

Table 7.5 The highest scoring cells in fossil fuel reserves

Rank	Cell No.	Cell name	Score
1	19	U.S.S.R.: Ural, Siberias, Far East	1892
2	43	Rest of S.W. Asia	1453
3	42	Iran. Iraq	818
4	18	U.S.S.R.: Kazakhstan, C. Asia	653
5	29	Canada, N.W. U.S.A., Alaska	561
6	25	U.S.A.: Penna. to Georgia	470
7	27	U.S.A.: Nebraska to Florida	380
8	30	Australia, New Zealand	374
9	28	U.S.A.: Texas to California	349
10	16	U.S.S.R.: N.W., Volga-Vyatka, Volga	340
11	39	N. Africa	316
12	3	Netherlands, N. Germany	241
13	26	U.S.A.: E.N. Central	205
World average			100

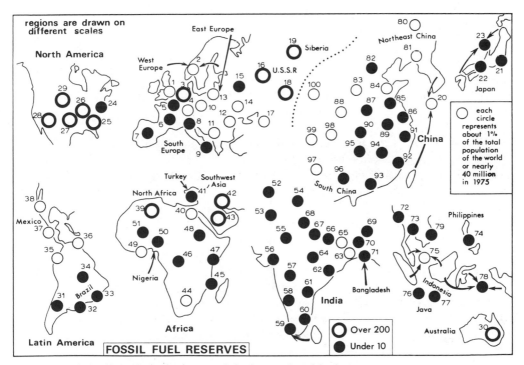

Figure 7.4 The cells with the highest and the lowest fossil fuel reserve scores.
See Tables 7.2 (column [2]) and 7.5

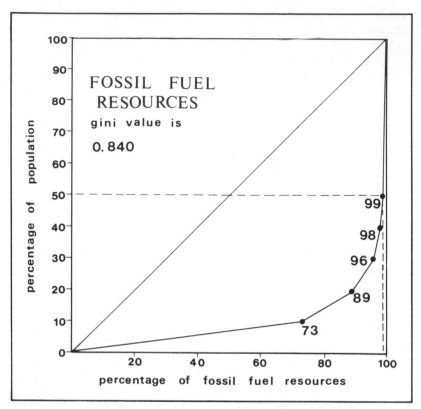

Figure 7.5 The distribution of the fossil fuel reserves of the world according to population

The proportion of the total fossil fuel reserves of each cell (in per 10,000s) was divided by the proportion of total world population in that cell. The resulting calculations, giving the quantity of fossil fuel reserves per inhabitant in each cell, are given in column (2) of Table 7.2 (Section 7.2). The 13 cells in which the quantity of fossil fuels per inhabitant is more than twice the world average (score over 200) are listed in Table 7.5. At the other extreme, 59 cells scored less than 10 (i.e. they had less than one-tenth of the world average per inhabitant) and 30 of them actually scored 0 (zero), having no known or only negligible fossil fuel reserves.

The best and the most poorly provided cells in the world with regard to fossil fuels are mapped in Figure 7.4. Even the thirteenth in rank, cell 26, East North Central U.S.A., has more than 20 times the quantity of fossil fuel reserves per inhabitant that each of some 60 cells with a score of less than 10 have. Fossil fuel reserves are very unevenly distributed in the world in relation to population.

Figure 7.5 shows the Lorenz curve constructed from data for fossil fuel reserves and population. The gini coefficient of 0.840 indicates a very uneven distribution. The 10 highest scoring cells (about 10 percent of the world's population) have 73 percent of the world's fossil fuel reserves according to the estimates made in this section. The highest scoring 50 cells have about 99 percent of the reserves.

7.5   Non-fuel minerals

This section is concerned with the distribution among the 100 cells of all minerals that are used as raw materials rather than as combustible material. The fossil fuel minerals dealt with in the previous section can also be used as a raw material in the chemicals industry and increasingly in the last few decades have been used as such. It is argued with good reason that they should be used to provide the basis for synthetic materials and other such products and that energy should be derived from 'renewable' sources. The small proportion of fossil fuels used as raw materials has not been separated from the combustible part and fossil fuels are therefore ignored in this section.

The main sources of information on non-fuel minerals used have been *Mineral Facts and Problems* (U.S. Bureau of Mines, 1970) and Kesler (1976). The former provides many of the quantitative data regarding estimated reserves, while the latter contains a thought-provoking account of geographical aspects and problems of mineral production. In *Mineral Facts and Problems*, four main types of mineral are identified: energy resources, ferrous minerals, non-ferrous minerals, and non-metallic minerals. Altogether some 90 minerals are discussed under the four headings, about 10 under energy resources and nearly 80 under the other three categories. As explained, the energy minerals are not considered in this section as they have already been covered in the last section. Estimates of the reserves of many of the non-fuel minerals are given only for the countries known to have or thought to have the largest reserves.

For the present study it was necessary to arrive at a single estimate of the reserves of each country and a regional breakdown of reserves within the larger countries. One of the problems in calculating a single figure for all mineral reserves was the question of relative importance of different minerals. It was decided to give a weighting to each mineral according to its value of production in a given year. To compare minerals according to the weight extracted or refined, while having some bearing on the cost of production and transportation, would be absurd, given the enormous differences in value per weight between for example salt, limestone, and iron on the one hand and gold and diamonds on the other.

From *Mineral Facts and Problems* it was possible to calculate the approximate total value of production around 1970 of each mineral considered. This could be regarded as a broad measure of the relative importance of the mineral in the world economy at the time, though not necessarily as it might be in the future. Twenty-three minerals were selected to form the main basis for the assessment of the mineral reserves of the world. They are listed in Table 7.6 in order of the value of their production, and grouped according to the nearest million dollars value. About 15 others were also taken into consideration, though given little weight. Some of very wide occurrence such as limestone, sand, and gravel were not taken into account at all.

The data in Table 7.6 shows that there are big differences in the total world value of production of different minerals. Thus the value of copper and iron production is about 10 times the value of silver and tin production and about 100 times the value of cobalt and antimony production. All six minerals are vital in one way or another to the economy of the industrial countries of the world but in assessing world mineral reserves it was not considered realistic to consider all minerals as equal. The most valuable mineral (copper) was arbitrarily given a weighting 20 times that of the least valuable shown in Table 7.6 (antimony and cobalt).

Table 7.6 Yearly value of production of selected minerals around 1970 in millions of U.S. dollars

7000-8000	1	Copper	Under 1000	9	Lead
6000-7000	2	Iron		10	Tin
5000-6000	3	Aluminium		11	Silver
1000-2000	4	Gold		12	Phosphorus
	5	Sulphur		13	Manganese
	6	Zinc		14	Potassium
	7	Sodium		15	Industrial diamonds
	8	Nickel		16	Asbestos
				17	Platinum
				18	Molybdenum
				19	Tungsten
				20	Mercury
				21	Chromium
				22	Cobalt
				23	Antimony

A score for all non-fuel mineral reserves on a country by country basis was calculated from the available data. The distribution of reserves of each mineral was expressed as a percentage for each country possessing the reserves. These were then weighted according to relative value of production as shown in Table 7.6. Thus the score given to each country is not concerned with the expected life of each mineral but with the share a country has of the estimated reserves. For example the U.S.A. is estimated to have 28 percent of the world's copper reserves, Chile 17 percent. Copper was given a weighting of 200, so the U.S. copper reserve score is 5600 points, that of Chile 2400 points. China is credited with 50 percent of the antimony reserves of the world, the U.S.A. with 3 percent. This mineral was given a weighting of 10. Thus China scores 500 points for antimony and the U.S.A. 30 points.

Once each country was credited with its non-fuel mineral points it was possible to compare countries with regard to their total mineral reserves and also to the amount per inhabitant and per area. The amounts per inhabitant are given in Table 4.1 (Chapter 4) for the 60 largest countries of the world. The value of 0 (zero) against some countries does not mean that they have no non-fuel minerals at all but that either they were not listed as countries with significant reserves or their reserves were only very small. Zero therefore indicates negligible or very small rather than non-existent.

The non-fuel mineral situation is shown in detail for 12 selected countries in Table 7.7. The first four countries are the largest in

Table 7.7 Non-fuel mineral reserves of selected countries

	(1) Total area (thous. km²)	(2) Total population (thousands)	(3) Minerals: total points	(4) Minerals/ area	(5) Minerals/ population
1 China	9561	839	3350	0.35	4.0
2 India	3046	598	800	0.26	1.3
3 U.S.S.R.	22,402	254	15,000	0.66	59.1
4 U.S.A.	9363	214	12,400	1.32	57.9
5 Australia	7695	14	8700	1.13	621.4
6 Chile	757	10	4100	5.42	410.0
7 Canada	9976	23	6400	0.64	278.3
8 South Africa	1223	26	5150	4.21	198.1
9 Cuba	115	10	900	7.80	90.0
10 Hungary	93	11	500	5.38	45.5
11 Bangladesh	143	77	0	0	0
12 Netherlands	34	14	0	0	0

population in the world. China, the U.S.S.R., and the U.S.A. all have large mineral reserves in an absolute sense, but when the reserves are measured in relation to area or to population they are not the highest scoring countries. Countries 5-8 in the table, Australia, Chile, Canada, and South Africa, have considerable total non-fuel mineral reserves but very large reserves in relation to their comparatively small populations. Thus the U.S.A. and Canada are roughly comparable in area but the U.S.A. has about twice the size of mineral reserves that Canada has. When, however, the U.S.A. and Canada are compared on a population basis, the former has about 10 times as many inhabitants as the latter so the Canadian score per inhabitant is about five times the U.S. score. Cuba and Hungary are examples of countries that are small in area but have considerable mineral reserves and therefore high scores in relation to their areas. Bangladesh and the Netherlands are among many countries not credited with reserves at all.

From the discussion of the method used to calculate mineral reserves it can be seen that there are various ways of interpreting the availability and distribution of minerals. Before the mineral reserves are expressed in relation to the 100 cells, the following should be noted:

(1) The mineral points do not themselves have a value or weight in terms of specific minerals.

(2) The make-up of mineral points differs greatly from country to country. Virtually all the 39 minerals considered in this study are found in commercial quantities in the U.S.S.R. On the other hand the high score for Chile comes largely from copper reserves, that for Cuba largely from nickel reserves.

(3) Some minerals are much more highly concentrated in certain areas than others. South Africa, for example, is credited with about half of the gold deposits of the world, Canada with nearly half of the asbestos, and Thailand and Malaysia together with about half of the world's tin.

(4) The mineral reserves of a given region can be expressed in various ways. The assessment can be of total reserves per unit of area or of reserves per inhabitant. The assessments can be very different. For example the island of New Caledonia has considerable deposits of nickel and cobalt but, with a very small area and population, its 1000 mineral points give an astronomical amount of mineral reserves both per area and per inhabitant. In the same way Kuwait and the United Arab Emirates have very high scores for fossil fuel reserves per area and per inhabitant.

As with land resources in Section 7.3 and fossil fuels in Section 7.4, non-fuel reserves have been estimated on a cell by cell basis.

Table 7.8 Cells with highest scores for non-fuel minerals

Rank	Cell No.	Cell Name	Score
1	30	Australia, New Zealand	2735
2	29	Canada, N.W. U.S.A., Alaska	1336
3	44	Southern Africa	898
4	19	U.S.S.R.: Ural, Siberias, Far East	898
5	51	Northwest Africa	491
6	31	Argentina, Chile, Uruguay	470
7	28	U.S.A.: Texas to California	466
8	18	U.S.S.R.: Kazakhstan, C. Asia	453
9	46	Central Africa	387
10	36	Venezuela, Caribbean	374
11	34	Rest of Brazil, Bolivia, Paraguay	319
12	35	Colombia, Ecuador, Peru	270
13	27	U.S.A.: Nebraska to Florida	266
World average			100

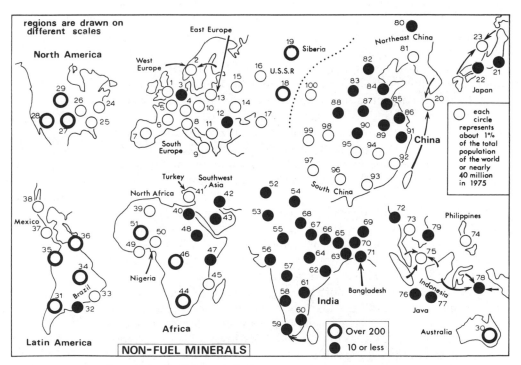

Figure 7.6 The cells with the highest and the lowest non-fuel mineral reserve scores.
See Tables 7.2 (column [3]) and 7.8

Scores for smaller countries could be added where two or more countries form a cell, but scores for the larger countries had to be broken down. It was possible to arrive at a reasonable estimate of mineral reserves in each of the North American and Soviet cells but it was very difficult to obtain a breakdown for China or for India, which, however, does not have large mineral reserves. Thus the within country cell by cell data in this section are only very approximate. Even so, the difference between the cells that are well endowed with non-fuel minerals and those that are poorly endowed or virtually lacking is so great that however the estimates are made enormous differences would be observed.

Each of the 100 cells was credited with a given number of non-fuel mineral points, though some ended up with zero scores. The points were expressed in per 10,000s of the world total for each cell. The share of minerals in each cell was then divided by the share of world population in that cell. The resulting calculations are shown in column (3) of Table 7.2. A score of 100 indicates that a cell has the same proportion of world non-fuel mineral reserves as it has of population. Out of the 100 cells, no less than 47 scored 10 or less, while 20 scored zero. Table 7.8 shows the 13 cells that scored over 200 and therefore had more than twice their 'share' of non-fuel minerals. The highest scoring 13 and lowest scoring 47 cells are mapped in Figure 7.6.

As with land resources and fossil fuels, non-fuel mineral reserves tend to be highly concentrated in certain cells. Figure 7.7 shows the high degree of concentration of non-fuel mineral reserves by cells, a gini value of 0.808. The 10 highest scoring cells, with about 10 percent of the world's population, have about 70 percent of all the reserves. The 50 highest scoring ones have about 98 percent.

It should be appreciated that, all other things being equal, the larger a cell in area, the larger the mineral reserves it might be expected to have. Most of the 13 cells listed in Table 7.8 as having large non-fuel mineral reserves per inhabitant also have large areas per inhabitant. There are at least two main reasons why mineral reserves, whether fossil fuel or non-fuel, are only very broadly related to total area. Firstly, some areas are much richer than others due to geological conditions and, secondly, some parts of the world have been explored much more thoroughly than other parts. In fact, fossil fuels, metallic minerals, and non-metallic minerals tend to be highly localized in occurrence in certain structural and geological conditions. It is not within the scope of this book to discuss these. Areas of probable or possible occurrence of various types of mineral are shown by Kesler (1976). A broad relationship between the distribution of minerals and features of plate tectonics is outlined by Rona (1973).

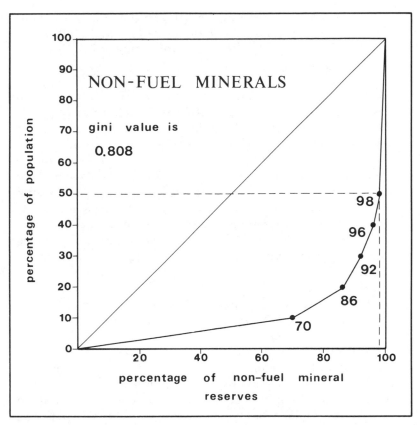

Figure 7.7 The distribution of the non-fuel mineral reserves of the world according to population

7.6 Territory

The three categories studied in Sections 7.3-7.5 cover most natural resources. It was considered that allowance should also be made for resources such as water and fishing grounds not directly included so far and also for prospective resources such as undiscovered minerals. To arrive at a satisfactory 'bonus' resource category was very difficult. A somewhat elaborate and highly subjective score was worked out for each of the 100 cells of the world for a 'resource' referred to hereafter as 'territory' (the term 'space' might also have been used).

Space in its own right is valued in a French publication. The French have long been concerned about the much lower density of population in France than in the U.K., Italy, Germany, and some other countries of Europe. If France had the same density of population as the U.K., it should have had in the mid-1970s about 125 million inhabitants, not 52 million. Brunet (Brunet *et al.*, 1974) draws attention to this fact of European demography. He notes (author's translation):

> ... the French do not lack space. Is that an advantage or a disadvantage? ... For a long time it was considered an obstacle. The possibilities for the development of certain regions seem adversely affected by a lack of people. But this is an archaic viewpoint, which considers above all the development of the countryside. In fact it is more an advantage today. The price of land is not so high. The cost of large undertakings is a little lower. The possibilities of managing space are made more easy, at least if an appropriate policy is applied. At all events, more than the other European countries, the territory of France constitutes a reserve of space, the largest reserve in Northwest Europe.

For each country the land area *in thousands of square kilometres* was taken as a base. To this were added small bonuses for length of coastline and for area of continental shelf. In addition an assessment was made of the total precipitation falling on each cell in a year and of the amount of heat or temperature accumulated during the year. From the bonuses for coast and continental shelf it was possible to take into account fishing potential and offshore minerals. A very crude assessment of water resources was included with the help of precipitation, while temperature gives credit to future uses of solar energy for generating electricity.

The lengths of generalized coastlines were worked out for each cell with a coast. These were then multiplied by 0.02 (the effect of dividing by 50). The areas of continental shelf were worked out for each cell with a coast and then multiplied by 0.2 (the effect of dividing by 5). The total land area of each cell was multiplied by a precipitation coefficient, ranging from 0 for extremely dry cells (such as Egypt) to 0.10 for cells with a very high precipitation. The effect of this calculation was to give a maximum bonus equal to one-tenth of its total area to a cell with very heavy precipitation. Finally a temperature bonus was given to each cell with a temperature coefficient ranging from 0, very cold, to 0.10 very hot. The effect of this calculation was to give a bonus equal to one-tenth of its total area to the hottest area.

Two examples will show how the calculations were made. Cell 1, England, has an area of about 130,000 km² (130 points). Its generalized coastline length is about 1000 miles; this was multiplied by

Table 7.9 Cells with the highest scores for territory resource

Rank	Cell No.	Cell name	Score
1	30	Australia, New Zealand	1520
2	29	Canada, N.W. U.S.A., Alaska	1039
3	19	U.S.S.R.: Ural, Siberias, Far East	904
4	34	Rest of Brazil, Bolivia, Paraguay	740
5	51	Northwest Africa	492
6	100	Rest of China, Mongolian P.R.	482
7	46	C. Africa	394
8	39	N. Africa	317
9	18	U.S.S.R.: Kazakhstan, C. Asia	294
10	31	Argentina, Chile, Uruguay	288
11	44	Southern Africa	281
12	43	Rest of S.W. Asia	257
13	48	Northeast Africa	238
World average			100

0.02 to give 20 points for the coast. The continental shelf area was estimated to be 250,000 km² ; this was multiplied by 0.2 to give 50 points. A rainfall conversion of 0.04 (moderate precipitation) was used to turn 130,000 km² into 130 × 0.04, or 5 points. A temperature conversion of 0.03 (not very high temperatures) was used to turn 130,000 km² into 130 × 0.03, or 4 points. The sum of points for England on this 'territory' or 'space' score was 130 + 20 + 50 + 5 + 4, or 209. Cell 30, Australia and New Zealand, scores 9431 points, nearly 50 times the points for England. The initial total land area of the two countries is 7,974,000 km², or 7974 points, to which 340 for 17,000 miles of coastline and 400 continental shelf points are added. Precipitation at 0.02 and temperature at 0.07 added 159 and 558 more points. In the final assessment, England turns out to have 14 per 10,000 (0.14 percent) of the total territory resource of the world while Australia and New Zealand have 614 per 10,000 (6.14 percent).

After the 'territory' resource of each cell had been expressed in per 10,000s, it was divided by the population of the cell, also in per 10,000s. The resulting index of 'territory' resource per inhabitant is given in column (4) of Table 7.2. Thirteen cells with twice the world average per inhabitant are listed in Table 7.9. Twenty-one have 10 percent of the world average or less. The cells that are best and least well endowed with regard to 'territorial' resource per inhabitant are mapped in Figure 7.8.

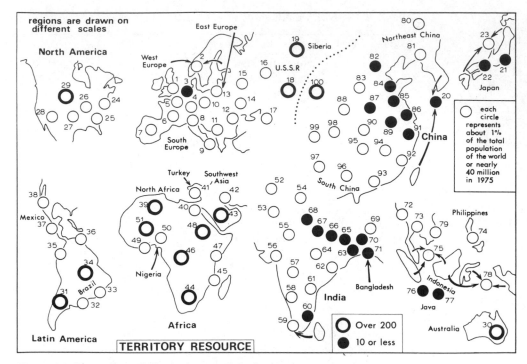

Figure 7.8 The cells with the highest and the lowest territory resource scores

The distribution of the territory resources in relation to population is shown in Figure 7.9. There is a gini coefficient of 0.694. The 10 highest scoring cells, with about 10 percent of the population of the world, have 57 percent of the territory resources.

The use of the 'territorial' resource serves as a safety net to catch extra resources not included in the three straightforward categories. It does, however, involve some double counting in the sense that the cells that are largest in area already tend to come out the best endowed in natural resources. It represents resources that are 'potential' or not discovered.

7.7 All natural resources and population

It is not claimed that all possible natural resources of the world have been covered in the last four sections. Even so it is felt that the data are good enough to give a general idea of the distribution of natural resources in the world. In order to give an overall assessment of the resources of each cell, the four sets of resources have been

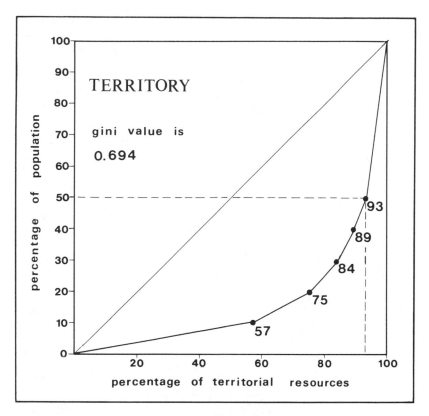

Figure 7.9 The distribution of the territory resources of the world according to population. See Tables 7.2 (column [4]) and 7.9

combined. It is regretted that some double counting occurs as a result.

The final resource/population score was calculated as follows. The proportions (in per 10,000s) of each of the resources in each cell were added. The combined total was then divided by four to give the share (in per 10,000s) each cell has of total resources. This global resource proportion was then divided by the proportion each cell has of the total population. Table 7.10 shows the best endowed cells, those with more than twice the share of world resources that they have of population, a score of 200 or more, and the most poorly endowed, those with a score of 25 or less or with only one-quarter or less resources per inhabitant than the world average.

The above cells are mapped in Figure 7.10. The 'empty' spaces of western North America, central and eastern U.S.S.R., Australia, and the interiors of South America and Africa emerge as the cells with a high ratio of resources to population. Almost all the most poorly

Table 7.10 Cells with the highest and the lowest scores for all natural resources

Rank	Cell No.	Cell name	Index
1	30	Australia, New Zealand	1355
2	19	U.S.S.R.: Ural, Siberias, Far East	1019
3	29	Canada, N.W. U.S.A., Alaska	823
4	43	Rest of S.W. Asia	443
5	18	U.S.S.R.: Kazakhstan, C. Asia	416
6	44	Southern Africa	346
7	28	U.S.A.: Texas to California	338
8	34	Rest of Brazil, Bolivia, Paraguay	317
9	27	U.S.A.: Nebraska to Florida	282
10	31	Argentina, Chile, Uruguay	271
11	51	Northwest Africa	270
12	42	Iran, Iraq	260
13	46	Central Africa	234
14	16	U.S.S.R.: Northwest, Volga-Vyatka, Volga	204
15	39	North Africa	203
71	65	India: E. Bihar	25
72	96	China: Kwangsi-Chuang, E. Kweichow	24
73	54	India: Kashmir to Delhi	24
74	84	China: N. Shantung	23
75	58	India: Karnataka	23
76	57	India: Maharashtra less N.W.	23
77	61	India: Andhra Pradesh	22
78	56	India: Gujarat and N.W. Maharashtra	22
79	53	Rest of Pakistan	22
80	8	Switzerland, Austria, N. Italy	21
81	63	India: W. Bengal less S.W.	21
82	90	China: Hupei	21
83	89	China: Anhwei	20
84	68	India: W. Uttar Pradesh	20
85	91	China: Chekiang	19
86	67	India: Mid-Uttar Pradesh	19
87	66	India: W. Bihar, E. Uttar Pradesh	18
88	59	India: Kerala and Sri Lanka	18
89	60	India: Tamil Nadu	17
90	87	China: E. Honan	15
91	85	China: S. Shantung, N. Kiangsu	15
92	82	China: N. Hopei, Peking, Tientsin	15
93	71	South Bangladesh	15
94	86	China: S. Kiangsu, Shanghai	14
95	77	East Java	12
96	76	West Java	12
97	70	North Bangladesh	11
98	20	S. Korea, Hong Kong, Taiwan	10
99	22	Japan: Osaka area	8
100	21	Japan: Tokyo area	7

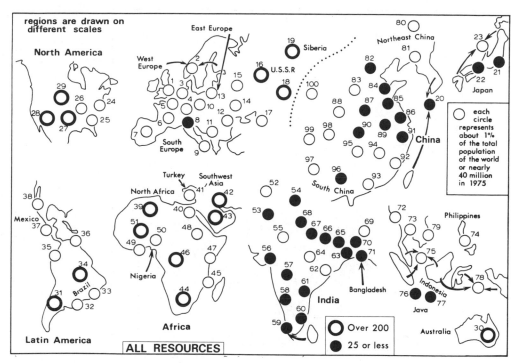

Figure 7.10 The cells with the highest and the lowest scores for all natural resources. See Table 7.10

endowed cells are in Asia. South Asia and China contain 24 out of the 30 cells scoring 25 points or less while only one is in Europe.

The gini coefficient of concentration for all four natural resources combined is 0.621. The 10 highest scoring cells (see Figure 7.11), with about 10 percent of the world's population, possess about 50 percent of all the natural resources of the world. Expressed the other way round, 90 percent of the world's population have only 50 percent of the natural resources. This fact alone is a convincing indication of the concentration of natural resources in the hands of a small part of the world's population.

The four resources were given equal weight in the above calculations. The results would have been different if some resources had been given greater weight than others. The resources could be weighted in various ways. If they were weighted according to the number of people employed in actually producing from them or to a lesser degree according to the value of production from them, land resources would have to be given much greater weight than fossil fuels or non-fuel minerals. On the other hand, if potential resources and future prospects of cells were to be taken

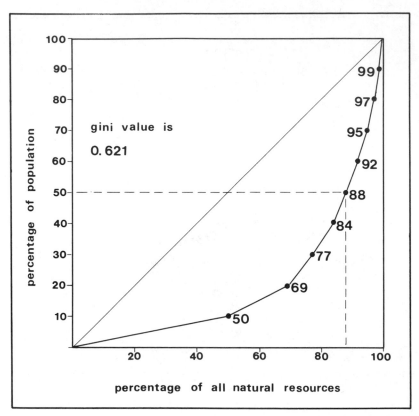

Figure 7.11 The distribution of all natural resources of the world according to population

into account then the territory resource could be given greater weight than 1/4 since cells with large land and continental shelf areas would tend to have much more in reserve than cells tightly packed with people, with intensive cultivation, and already achieving high yields in agriculture.

It was shown in Chapter 4 that the four resources, with the 'territory' resource not refined as in the previous section but simply expressed by area per population, correlated quite highly with one another in their distribution. A cell with a favourable score for one resource tends to have favourable scores on others. To some extent, then, each of the four categories has a similar distribution and some modification of weighting would not therefore make much difference.

8

The distribution of production and consumption in the 100 cells

8.1 Distributions to be described

A number of distributions are described in this chapter. To some extent their choice has been influenced by the availability of data. They all represent production or consumption rather than actual means of production. For example the production of steel is described rather than the distribution of steel-producing capacity. A proportion of productive capacity is usually idle in Western industrial countries. For example only about 70 percent of Italian steel-producing capacity was being used in the 1970s and much oil-refining and shipbuilding capacity has also been idle in various industrial countries. Even so, there is a broad enough relationship between productive capacity and production for the latter to be an adequate assessment of both. Consumption at national level, on the other hand, may differ from production on account of international trade.

In this chapter the following aspects of production and consumption are studied. It is considered that they are adequate to draw attention to major disparities in the world.

(1) The production of energy
(2) The consumption of energy
(3) The production of non-fuel minerals
(4) The production of steel
(5) The consumption of food
(6) The availability of hospital beds
(7) Gross national product

To assess the distribution of various sectors of production on the basis of the 100 cells, the procedures of calculation used in Chapter 7 have been used again in this chapter.

Table 8.1 shows the quantity of each of the above seven items related to the population of each cell. For food consumption and

247

Table 8.1 Production and consumption by 100 cells. See text for explanation

	(1) Energy production	(2) Energy consumption	(3) Mineral production	(4) Steel production	(5) Food	(6) Hospital beds	(7) GNP
1 England	145	258	9	186	3	3	254
2 North Europe	98	255	148	260	2	4	350
3 Netherlands, N. Germany	281	320	28	532	3	4	402
4 S. Germany	23	196	23	149	3	4	419
5 Belgium, N. France	40	249	29	607	3	3	391
6 Rest of France	42	172	146	103	3	4	365
7 Spain, Portugal	23	95	59	161	2	3	152
8 Switzerland, Austria, N. Italy	43	171	11	150	3	4	306
9 Rest of Italy, Greece	27	131	104	280	3	3	145
10 E. Germany, Czechoslovakia, Hungary	200	297	94	351	3	3	229
11 Yugoslavia, Bulgaria, Albania	65	131	217	100	3	3	105
12 Romania, Moldavia, S. Ukraine (U.S.S.R.)	122	190	6	183	3	3	111
13 Poland, Baltic (U.S.S.R.)	228	234	208	220	3	3	186
14 U.S.S.R.: Rest of Ukraine	330	333	241	790	3	4	168
15 U.S.S.R.: Belorussia, Centre	26	260	0	88	3	4	214
16 U.S.S.R.: Northwest, Volga-Vyatka, Volga	480	315	96	200	3	4	197
17 U.S.S.R.: Blackearth C., Caucasuses	159	233	136	144	3	3	147
18 U.S.S.R.: Kazakhstan, C. Asia	308	228	529	93	3	3	131
19 U.S.S.R.: Ural, Siberias, Far East	601	339	729	825	3	4	203
20 S. Korea, Hong Kong, Taiwan	17	49	6	23	2	1	51
21 Japan: Tokyo area	7	204	0	473	2	4	311
22 Japan: Osaka area	4	173	0	499	2	4	275
23 Rest of Japan	38	160	95	742	2	4	301
24 U.S.A.: N. Eng., N.Y., N.J.	13	581	0	161	3	3	493
25 U.S.A.: Penna. to Georgia	376	568	87	628	3	3	427
26 U.S.A.: East North Central	113	564	208	750	3	3	457
27 U.S.A.: Nebraska to Florida	826	472	355	44	3	3	422
28 U.S.A.: Texas to California	883	609	184	74	3	3	516
29 Canada, N.W. U.S.A., Alaska	449	441	1299	222	3	3	444

30	Australia, New Zealand	340	303	2408	200	3	4	376
31	Argentina, Chile, Uruguay	56	71	254	31	2	3	89
32	Brazil: Sul, São Paulo	12	48	0	45	2	2	98
33	Brazil: Rio to Pernambuco	16	32	187	74	2	2	54
34	Rest of Brazil, Bolivia, Paraguay	7	11	184	0	2	1	33
35	Colombia, Ecuador, Peru	36	31	139	9	1	2	42
36	Venezuela, Caribbean	253	87	509	22	1	2	87
37	C. America, S. Mexico	43	19	61	0	2	1	48
38	C. Mexico and N. Mexico	56	80	127	78	2	1	96
39	N. Africa	218	28	96	5	1	2	62
40	Egypt	16	20	0	5	1	2	21
41	Turkey	14	31	22	23	3	2	58
42	Iran, Iraq	624	61	17	0	1	1	95
43	Rest of S.W. Asia	1098	59	8	2	1	1	113
44	Southern Africa	89	116	891	111	2	2	71
45	Southeast Africa	1	4	8	0	1	1	15
46	Central Africa	38	5	267	0	1	2	19
47	East Africa	1	4	0	0	1	1	12
48	Northeast Africa	0	3	0	0	1	0	11
49	S. Nigeria, Benin to Ivory Coast	135	9	21	0	1	1	29
50	N. Nigeria	1	3	17	0	1	0	19
51	Northwest Africa	0	3	285	0	1	0	11
52	Afghanistan, N.W. Pakistan	7	5	0	0	1	0	8
53	Rest of Pakistan	6	10	0	0	0	0	10
54	India: Kashmir to Delhi	2	8	0	0	1	0	11
55	India: Rajasthan and N.W.M.P.	2	9	5	0	1	0	9
56	India: Gujarat and N.W. Mah.	6	8	27	0	1	0	10
57	India: Maharashtra less N.W.	5	9	4	0	1	0	11
58	India: Karnataka	2	6	16	0	1	0	9
59	India: Kerala and Sri Lanka	2	6	0	0	1	1	8
60	India: Tamil Nadu	2	7	0	0	1	0	8
61	India: Andhra Pradesh	10	10	6	0	1	0	8
62	India: Orissa and S.W. and W. Bengal	2	9	31	53	1	0	11
63	India: W. Bengal less S.W.	2	25	14	0	1	0	11

Table 8.1 (continued)

		(1) Energy production	(2) Energy consumption	(3) Mineral production	(4) Steel production	(5) Food	(6) Hospital beds	(7) GNP
64	India: Madhya Pradesh less N.W.	23	15	27	31	1	0	10
65	India: E. Bihar	52	31	14	51	1	0	10
66	India: W. Bihar, E. Uttar Pradesh	2	7	0	0	1	0	9
67	India: Mid-Uttar Pradesh	2	8	0	0	1	0	10
68	India: W. Uttar Pradesh	2	6	0	0	1	0	10
69	India: N.E., Nepal, Bhutan	13	4	0	0	1	0	9
70	North Bangladesh	0	1	0	0	0	0	7
71	South Bangladesh	1	1	0	2	0	0	9
72	Burma	1	3	0	0	2	0	9
73	Thailand	1	17	56	0	2	1	25
74	Philippines	1	16	68	0	0	1	23
75	Malaysia, Singapore, Sumatra	167	14	297	0	2	1	34
76	West Java	0	5	0	0	0	0	10
77	East Java	1	5	0	0	0	0	10
78	Rest of Indonesia, Papua-New Guinea	1	10	200	0	0	0	14
79	Indo-China	4	9	0	0	2	1	10

80	China: Heilungkiang, Kirin	109	45	11	48	1	1	26
81	Liaoning (China), N. Korea	193	106	79	141	1	1	34
82	China: N. Hopei, Peking, Tientsin	52	52	13	42	1	1	37
83	China: S. Hopei, Shansi	124	59	14	31	1	1	34
84	China: N. Shantung	17	27	13	0	1	1	23
85	China: S. Shantung, N. Kiangsu	6	26	13	0	1	1	22
86	China: S. Kiangsu, Shanghai	6	53	0	36	1	1	30
87	China: E. Honan	2	29	0	0	1	1	20
88	China: W. Honan, Shensi	23	29	8	0	1	1	29
89	China: Anhwei	23	21	0	16	1	1	20
90	China: Hupei	11	34	0	44	1	1	22
91	China: Chekiang	5	24	0	0	1	1	20
92	China: Fukien, E. Kwangtung	2	24	0	0	1	1	19
93	China: W. Kwangtung	2	33	16	18	1	1	18
94	China: Kiangsi, S.E. Hunan	8	23	30	0	1	1	20
95	China: W. Hunan	2	24	31	0	1	1	17
96	China: Kwangsi-Chuang, E. Kweichow	4	14	14	0	1	1	16
97	China: Yunnan, W. Kweichow	2	15	15	9	1	1	16
98	China: E. Szechwan	47	29	14	8	1	1	18
99	China: W. Szechwan	6	29	14	8	1	1	16
100	Rest of China, Mongolian P.R.	24	47	43	49	1	1	29

hospital beds only a very rough assessment was possible. Four levels of food consumption and five levels for availability of hospital beds are used. For hospital beds no data for China are available so a dummy low value has been given on the assumption that facilities are limited.

8.2   Energy production

It was shown in Chapter 4 that on the basis of data for the 60 largest countries of the world there is a very high correlation between estimated fossil fuel reserves per inhabitant and production of energy per inhabitant. Some degree of correlation would be expected, since countries with no fossil fuels would obviously not be able to produce any fuels from these major sources and, apart from a possible contribution from hydroelectric sources, wood, and minor sources, would not produce energy either. In fact the very high correlation indicated a close correspondence between reserves and rate of production. On the other hand, as a result of the massive world trade in fossil fuels, *consumption* of the energy per inhabitant does not correspond closely to reserves of fossil fuels or to production of energy.

In order to give a score to the production of energy on the basis of the 100 cells, the procedure used in the last chapter has been employed again. From data in the *United Nations Statistical Yearbook* on energy production in tonnes of coal equivalent the amount produced in each cell was calculated, either by joining the production of smaller countries into their respective single cells or by subdividing the larger countries into two or more cells.

Total world production of energy in 1975 was 8,560,000,000 tonnes of coal equivalent. The amount of energy produced in each cell was expressed as a share in per 10,000s of the world total. This share was divided by the share of world population in the cell, also in 10,000s. Thus for example with 173 per 10,000 (1.73 percent) of world energy production and 119 per 10,000 (1.19 percent) of total population of the world, England (cell 1) achieved an index of 145 (173 divided by 119). An index of 100 indicates that a cell has exactly the same proportion of world production of a given item as it has of population, that is a production level per inhabitant equal to the world average. The score for each of the 100 cells is shown in Table 8.1, column (1).

All cells with more than twice the average production of energy per inhabitant (score of 200 or more) are shown in Table 8.2. Sixty-six cells had scores of under 50, 43 of them with scores of under 10.

Table 8.2 Highest scoring cells according to production of energy per inhabitant

Rank	Cell No.	Cell name	Score
1	43	Rest of S.W. Asia	1098
2	28	U.S.A.: Texas to California	883
3	27	U.S.A.: Nebraska to Florida	826
4	42	Iran, Iraq	624
5	19	U.S.S.R.: Ural, Siberias, Far East	601
6	16	U.S.S.R.: Northwest, Volga-Vyatka, Volga	480
7	29	Canada, N.W. U.S.A., Alaska	449
8	25	U.S.A.: Pennsylvania to Georgia	376
9	30	Australia, New Zealand	340
10	14	U.S.S.R.: Rest of Ukraine	330
11	18	U.S.S.R.: Kazakhstan, C. Asia	308
12	3	Netherlands, N. Germany	281
13	36	Venezuela, Caribbean	253
14	13	Poland, Baltic (U.S.S.R.)	228
15	39	N. Africa	218
16	10	E. Germany, Czechoslovakia, Hungary	200
World average			100

Thus nearly two-thirds of the world's population is in cells producing less than half the world average of energy per inhabitant. The cells with the highest and the lowest scores for energy production per inhabitant are mapped in Figure 8.1. From the data for the energy production and population of each cell it was possible to calculate the Lorenz curve of distribution and the gini coefficient of concentration. Figure 8.2 shows the Lorenz curves for energy production and consumption (see next section). The 10 cells with the highest scores for energy production have about 10 percent of the population of the world but account for 60 percent of energy production. The gini coefficient for energy production is 0.768, a very high degree of concentration.

Among the cells with high production a distinction can be made between those producing predominantly oil and natural gas, in particular 36 (Venezuela), 39 (North Africa), and 42 and 43 (Middle East), and those producing mainly coal and lignite, among them 25 (Eastern U.S.A.), and 10, 13, and 14 (East Europe and the Ukraine). Cells 19 (Siberia), 29 (Canada, Alaska), and 30 (Australia) have a mixed base. The predominantly oil-based cells of the developing countries are the major source of fossil fuels in world trade.

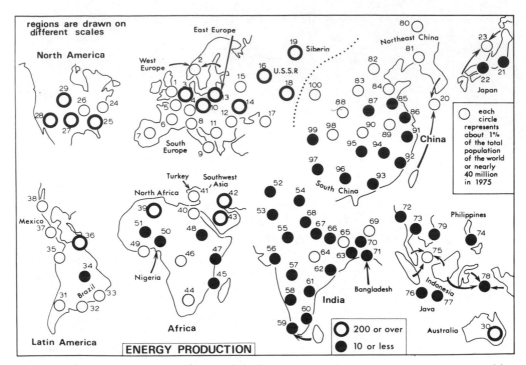

Figure 8.1 The cells with the highest and the lowest scores for energy production. See Tables 8.1 and 8.2

8.3   Energy consumption

Great variations occur in the world in the consumption of energy per inhabitant, as was shown on a country by country basis in Chapter 4 (see Table 4.1). The 100 cells are used here as a base for describing the distribution of energy consumption, data for which, in terms of coal equivalent, were obtained from the *United Nations Statistical Yearbook 1976*.

The total amount of energy consumed in the world in 1975 was estimated at 7,987,000,000 tonnes, considerably less than the amount actually produced in that year (see last section). The consumption of energy was estimated for each cell. The share of total world consumption in each was then converted to 10,000s and this figure was divided by the share of world population in the cell, also in 10,000s. Thus, for example, cell 29, Canada plus northwestern U.S.A. and Alaska, was estimated to consume 320 million tonnes of energy (in coal equivalent), or 401 per 10,000 (4.01 percent) of the total world consumption. It has 91 per 10,000 (0.91

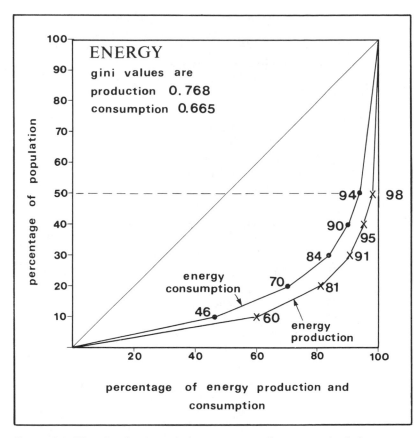

Figure 8.2 The distribution of the energy production and of the energy consumption of the world according to population

percent) of the total population of the world and therefore a score of 441. An index of 100 indicates that a cell accounts for exactly the same proportion of world energy consumption as it has of world population. The score for each of the 100 cells is shown in Table 8.1, column (2).

Table 8.3 shows the 20 cells in which the consumption of energy per inhabitant is more than twice the world average. At the other extreme, 61 cells had below half the world average, with scores of 50 or less, 29 of them scoring 10 or less. Figure 8.3 shows the distribution of cells with the highest and the lowest scores. Figure 8.2 shows the Lorenz curve for energy consumption (as well as energy production) against population. The gini coefficient is high, being 0.665, but not so high as that for production (0.768). The difference is accounted for by the dispersal

Table 8.3 Highest scoring cells according to consumption of energy

Rank	Cell No.	Cell name	Score
1	28	U.S.A.: Texas to California	609
2	24	U.S.A.: New England, N.Y., N.J.	581
3	25	U.S.A.: Pennsylvania to Georgia	568
4	26	U.S.A.: East North Central	564
5	27	U.S.A.: Nebraska to Florida	472
6	29	Canada, N.W. U.S.A., Alaska	411
7	19	U.S.S.R.: Ural, Siberias, Far East	339
8	14	U.S.S.R.: Rest of Ukraine	333
9	3	Netherlands, N. Germany	320
10	16	U.S.S.R.: Northwest, Volga-Vyatka, Volga	315
11	30	Australia, New Zealand	303
12	10	E. Germany, Czechoslovakia, Hungary	297
13	15	U.S.S.R.: Belorussia, Centre	260
14	1	England	258
15	2	North Europe	255
16	5	Belgium, N. France	249
17	13	Poland, Baltic (U.S.S.R.)	234
18	17	U.S.S.R.: Blackearth Centre, Caucasus	233
19	18	U.S.S.R.: Kazakhstan, C. Asia	228
20	21	Japan: Tokyo area	204
World average			100

of production from a few major energy-producing cells to a larger number of energy-deficient ones. In spite of the effect of trade, about 10 percent of the world's population consumes 46 percent of the world's energy and about 50 percent consumes 4 percent.

The distribution of cells with the highest and the lowest scores for consumption of energy per inhabitant in Figure 8.3 shows the familiar picture of the development gap. The heaviest consumers are North America, the U.S.S.R., and northern, rather than southern, Europe. Tropical Africa and South and Southeast Asia have the lowest levels of consumption. Latin America, North Africa, Southwest Asia, and China occupy an intermediate position, but many of the Chinese cells probably come near to the score of 10. In the allocation of consumption of energy to Chinese cells the author assumed a considerable amount of movement of coal from the main coalfields into other cells, crediting the railway system of China perhaps with a capacity it does not possess.

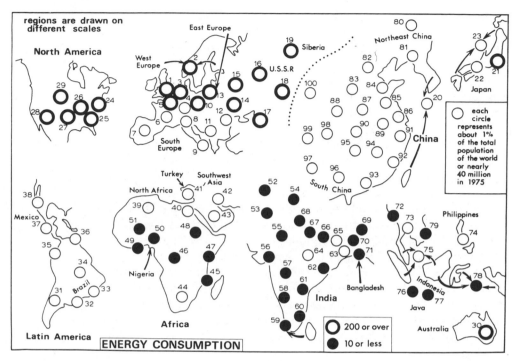

Figure 8.3 The cells with the highest and the lowest scores for energy consumption. See Tables 8.1 and 8.3

8.4   The production of non-fuel minerals

Estimates were given in the last chapter of the reserves per inhabitant of non-fuel minerals in each of the 100 cells. In this section, rough estimates are made of production. As with reserves, so with the production of non-fuel minerals, it is not realistic to assess the relative importance of each mineral according to weight. Therefore the approximate value of total world production of each mineral was used as a guide to the importance of the mineral. For the assessment of the total production of non-fuel minerals, data from the *United Nations Statistical Yearbook* for the production in 1975 of 20 minerals were used as a basis. The 20 minerals are listed below. The minerals were weighted as indicated, this being very roughly their relative value of production to one another, as described in Chapter 7, Section 5, on non-fuel mineral reserves. In the case of metals, the mineral assessed was the metal content of the ore extracted.

Copper	7	Sulphur	2	Chromium	0.5
Iron	7	Zinc	2	Antimony	0.5
Aluminium	6	Silver	1	Tungsten	0.5
Lead	2	Diamonds	1	Asbestos	0.5
Gold	2	Phosphates	1	Mercury	0.5
Tin	2	Potash	1	Molybdenum	0.5
Nickel	2	Manganese	1		

The share of world production of each of the 20 minerals was calculated on a country by country basis. The shares were then weighted according to the relative importance of each mineral and the country based information was transferred to the 100 cells. The score for mineral production for each cell was then converted to per 10,000s of the world total. This index was divided by the share each cell has of total world population, also in per 10,000s. The final assessment for each cell is shown in Table 8.1, column (3).

Table 8.4 shows each of the 16 cells that had more than twice the world average level of production of non-fuel minerals per inhabitant (a score exceeding 200). Thirty-eight cells had less than one-tenth of the world average production per inhabitant. The distribution of the highest and the lowest scoring cells is shown in

Table 8.4 Highest scoring cells according to the production of non-fuel minerals

Rank	Cell No.	Cell name	Score
1	30	Australia, New Zealand	2408
2	29	Canada, N.W. U.S.A., Alaska	1299
3	44	Southern Africa	891
4	19	U.S.S.R.: Ural, Siberias, Far East	729
5	18	U.S.S.R.: Kazakhstan, C. Asia	529
6	36	Venezuela, Caribbean	509
7	27	U.S.A.: Nebraska to Florida	355
8	75	Malaysia, Singapore, Sumatra	297
9	51	Northwest Africa	285
10	46	Central Africa	267
11	31	Argentina, Chile, Uruguay	254
12	14	U.S.S.R.: Rest of Ukraine	241
13	11	Yugoslavia, Bulgaria, Albania	217
14	13	Poland, Baltic (U.S.S.R.)	208
15	26	U.S.A.: East North Central	208
16	78	Rest of Indonesia, Papua-New Guinea	200
World average			100

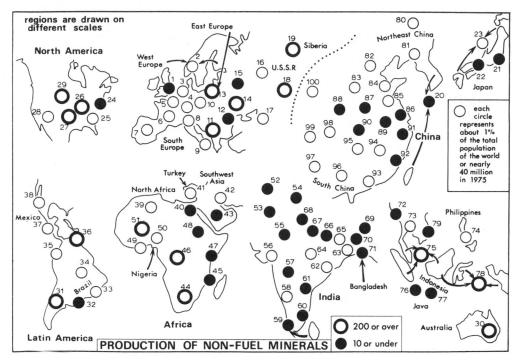

Figure 8.4 The cells with the highest and the lowest scores for the production of non-fuel minerals. See Tables 8.1 and 8.4

Figure 8.4. The Lorenz curve for non-fuel mineral production against population in Figure 8.5 shows a high degree of concentration, with a gini coefficient of 0.781. About 10 percent of the world's population produces 62 percent of the world's non-fuel minerals while 50 percent only accounts for about 2 percent.

The mix of minerals produced in each cell varies greatly. Cells 19, 29, 30, and 44 (Siberia, Canada, Australia, and South Africa particularly) produce a wide range of non-fuel minerals. In other cells with a large production per inhabitant a single mineral may account for a large proportion of total production. Bauxite is the major item in cell 36 (Caribbean) and tin in cell 75 (Malaysia and Sumatra).

On a country by country basis, Canada and the U.S.A. produce about 21 percent of the non-fuel minerals of the world, the U.S.S.R. about 17 percent, Australia and South Africa with Zimbabwe-Rhodesia nearly 9 percent each. In contrast, China only accounts for about 3 percent and India for between 1 and 2 percent of the world total.

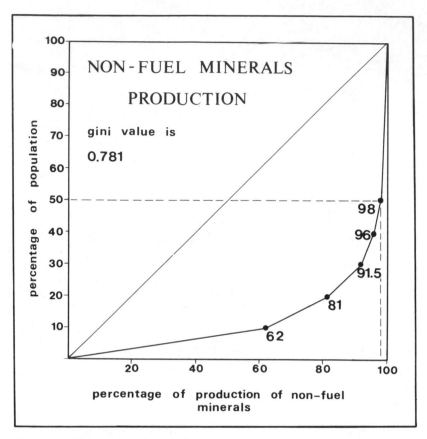

Figure 8.5 The distribution of the production of non-fuel minerals in the world according to population

8.5   Steel production

The iron and steel industry has been chosen to illustrate the development gap in heavy industry in general. Production data are easily obtainable and the product is not difficult to define. Even so, it should be noted that steel varies greatly in quality and that certain places specialize in the production of high-grade steel.

The world production of steel in 1975 was 643 million tonnes, of which the U.S.S.R. produced 141 million, the U.S.A. 106 million, and Japan 102 million. The nine countries of the European Economic Community together accounted for about 125 million.

Steel production (if any) was estimated for each of the 100 cells. The share of the world production in each cell was then expressed in

Table 8.5 Highest scoring cells according to steel production

Rank	Cell No.	Cell name	Score
1	19	U.S.S.R.: Ural, Siberias, Far East	825
2	14	U.S.S.R.: Rest of Ukraine	790
3	26	U.S.A.: East North Central	750
4	23	Rest of Japan	742
5	25	U.S.A.: Pennsylvania to Georgia	628
6	5	Belgium, N. France	607
7	3	Netherlands, N. Germany	532
8	22	Japan: Osaka area	499
9	21	Japan: Tokyo area	473
10	10	E. Germany, Czechoslovakia, Hungary	351
11	9	Rest of Italy, Greece	280
12	2	North Europe	260
13	29	Canada, N.W. U.S.A., Alaska	222
14	13	Poland, Baltic (U.S.S.R.)	220
15	16	U.S.S.R.: Northwest, Volga-Vyatka, Volga	200
16	30	Australia, New Zealand	200
World average			100

10,000s and the share of steel was divided by the share of world population in the cell, also in 10,000s. The data for the 100 cells are shown in Table 8.1, column (4). The 16 cells in which more than twice as much steel was produced per inhabitant as the world average are listed in Table 8.5. At the other extreme, 51 cells produce less than one-tenth of the world average per inhabitant, 43 of them no steel at all. The cells with highest and the lowest scores are mapped in Figure 8.6.

Steel production brings out both the development gap and the concentration of steel production in the major industrial regions. Sixteen cells each produce at least 20 times as much steel per inhabitant as each of 51 others. Figure 8.7 shows that there is a very high concentration of steel production, with a gini coefficient of concentration of 0.780 of steel to population. The 10 top scoring cells, with about 10 percent of the world's population, produce 62 percent of the world's steel, while about half produce none at all.

Much of the steel produced in some cells is actually made from iron ore and/or coking coal obtained from other cells. Virtually all steel produced in the three cells of Japan and in southern Italy (cell 9), for example, is now made from imported fuel and materials.

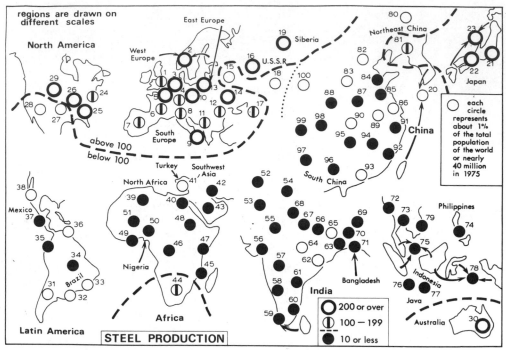

Figure 8.6 The cells with the highest and the lowest scores for the production of steel. See Tables 8.1 and 8.5

8.6   Food consumption

For obvious biological reasons the food consumption gap is much narrower than the gap in the consumption of energy, raw materials, and most manufactured goods. Even so, the dietary energy supply of the average inhabitant of the countries with the highest intake is nearly twice that of the average inhabitant in countries with the lowest intake. The estimated average kilocalorie intake for each country in the world, together with the protein supply, is given in publications of the Food and Agriculture Organisation. The food intake is then assessed in terms of actual requirements. Table 8.6 shows the 13 countries with the most marked excess and the most marked deficit in average kilocalorie dietary energy supply. The kilocalorie intake is shown, with the percentage above or below requirements, and also the protein supply.

The dietary requirement of an individual varies somewhat from country to country in view of differences in the build of the inhabitants and in climatic conditions. For example the theoretical

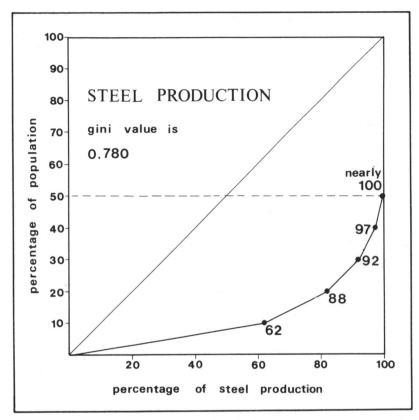

Figure 8.7 The distribution of the production of steel in the world according to population

requirement of an inhabitant of Finland is considered to be 2700 kcal per day while that of a Nigerian is 2365 kcal and of an inhabitant of Thailand 2225 kcal. The inhabitants of North America, Europe, the U.S.S.R., and Australia have high food intakes, with an excess over requirement of 20-30 percent in most countries. The countries estimated to be worst off are scattered through the tropics, a few in Latin America, and a considerable number in Africa and Asia. Indonesia and Bangladesh are two large countries in which food intake falls well below estimated requirement, while in India the deficit is 6 percent and in China 9 percent. Deficits vary from year to year, especially in poorer countries, which are unable to afford to top up when home supplies are short by importing much food.

Unfortunately there are no readily available data to allow a good estimate of food intake on the basis of the 100 cells. With the help

Table 8.6 Average daily dietary energy supply per inhabitant, 1974

		Kilocalories	% of requirement	Protein supply (g)
1	Ireland	3410	+ 36	103
2	Bulgaria	3290	+ 32	100
3	U.S.S.R.	3280	+ 31	101
4	Canada	3180	+ 29	101
5	Czechoslovakia	3180	+ 29	94
6	Greece	3190	+ 28	113
7	Belgium	3380	+ 28	95
8	France	3210	+ 27	105
9	Austria	3310	+ 26	90
10	Italy	3180	+ 26	100
11	U.K.	3190	+ 26	92
12	U.S.A.	3330	+ 26	106
13	E. Germany	3290	+ 26	87
117	Mauritania	1970	− 15	68
118	Angola	2000	− 15	42
119	Rwanda	1960	− 16	58
120	El Salvador	1930	− 16	52
121	Yemen Arab Rep.	2040	− 16	61
122	Indonesia	1790	− 17	38
123	Afghanistan	1970	− 19	58
124	Bangladesh	1840	− 20	40
125	Bolivia	1900	− 21	46
126	Somalia	1830	− 21	56
127	Haiti	1730	− 23	39
128	Algeria	1730	− 28	46
129	Upper Volta	1710	− 28	59

Source: *State of Food and Agriculture,* FAO.

of data available on a country by country basis it is, however, possible to put the cells into a number of categories. The categories are presented in Table 8.1, column (5), and are given scores of 3-0. The score of each cell is indicated in Figure 8.8.

(i) Score 3: cells in which the dietary energy supply is more than 20 percent above requirement. Twenty-five cells fall into this category, all the six in North America and all but two in Europe and the U.S.S.R., together with Turkey and Australia-New Zealand.

(ii) Score 2: cells in which the level is 0-20 percent above requirement. Seventeen cells fall into this category, six in Latin America, four in Southeast Asia, three in Japan, South Korea, and three others.

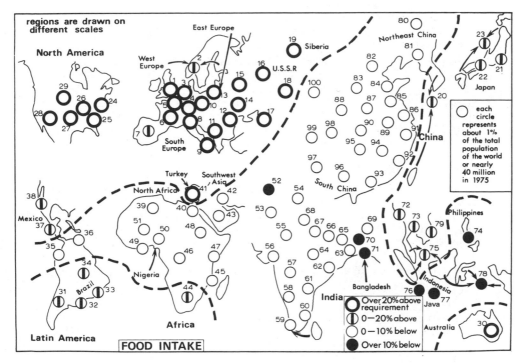

Figure 8.8 Levels of dietary energy supply in the world on the basis of the 100 cells. See Table 8.6

(iii) Score 1: about half the cells and therefore about half of the population of the world fall into the category of 0-10 percent below requirement. All of China and India fall into this category, but if data were available it is likely that they would show regional variations marked enough to drop some cells in these two large countries below the level of 10 percent below requirement.

(iv) Score 0: the 'sinks' of Bangladesh and Indonesia, together with Afghanistan, fall beyond 10 percent below requirement.

8.7 Hospital beds

Two commonly used ways of assessing the level of health services in a region are to calculate the number of inhabitants per doctor and per hospital bed. The definition of 'doctor' or 'physician' varies considerably from one country to another. Similarly, the equipment and personnel available per 'hospital bed' also vary. Hospital beds rather than doctors were chosen to represent health services in this section because the definition is more straightforward.

Table 8.7 Population per hospital bed

(a)	Selected countries with a favourable ratio			
	Sweden	66	West Germany	87
	Finland	67	France	98
	Iceland	68	Canada	106
	Norway	73	England and Wales	117
	Japan	78	U.S.A.	149
	Australia	81	Argentina	176
	U.S.S.R.	86	Spain	193

(b)	Selected countries with an intermediate ratio			
	Brazil	266	Iran	650
	Venezuela	339	Kenya	759
	Algeria	356	Mexico	785
	Ivory Coast	496	Saudi Arabia	897
	Philippines	639	Syria	1054

(c)	Selected countries with an unfavourable ratio			
	Haiti	1344	Mauritania	2727
	Nigeria	1378	Oman	2802
	Indonesia	1415	Ethiopia	3081
	South Korea	1515	Nepal	6630
	India	1517	Bangladesh	6946
	Pakistan	1871	Afghanistan	7051

Source: *United Nations Statistical Yearbook 1976,* Table 206, pp.833-7.

The availability of hospital beds in relation to population varies enormously in the world, as can be seen in Table 8.7. In Scandinavia there are only about 70 inhabitants per hospital bed while in Afghanistan there are about 7000.Even if the availability of hospital beds in Sweden exceeds basic requirements, the gap between Sweden and Afghanistan remains very large. Within Europe itself there are three times as many persons per hospital bed in Spain as in Sweden. Again, Brazil is nearly 20 times as well provided with hospital beds in relation to population as Bangladesh. Section (c) in Table 8.7 shows that apart from Haiti in Latin America the countries worst provided with beds are in Africa and in South or Southeast Asia. Comparable data are not available for China. Traditional medicine there is less based on hospital facilities than Western medicine.

The information about hospital beds has been transferred to the 100 cells in a simple way. Five categories of cell have been identified: category 4, those with under 100 inhabitants per hospital bed; category 3, those with 100-199; category 2, those with 200-499; category 1, those with 500-999; and category 0, those with 1000 or

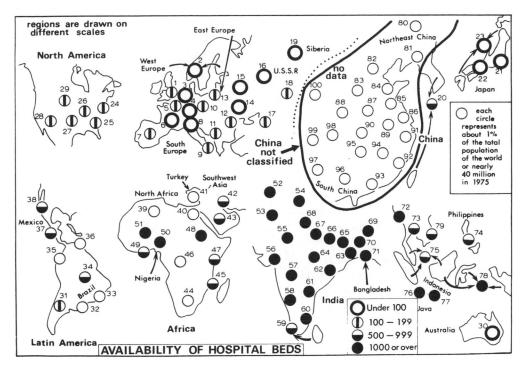

Figure 8.9 The availability of hospital beds in the world on the basis of the 100 cells

more. The category of each cell with regard to hospital beds is given in Table 8.1, column (6) and this is indicated in Figure 8.9. From the map and the supporting data in Table 8.7 it is evident that northern and central Europe, parts of the U.S.S.R., Japan, and Australia are the areas of the world with most hospital beds per population. South Asia in general and the margins of this region in particular (Afghanistan, Nepal, and Bangladesh), together with north-central Africa, are poorly provided with hospital facilities.

If less than 200 is 'adequate' and less than 100 'above requirements', then some notional form of transfer of excess hospital requirements from developed to developing countries could be envisaged, though what form it might take in reality is difficult to imagine. It would not solve the problem simply to ship off the 'excess' beds from rich to poor regions.

8.8   Gross national product

It was noted in Chapter 4 that for various reasons gross national product is not altogether a satisfactory measure of the production

Table 8.8 Highest scoring cells on gross national product

Rank	Cell No.	Cell name	Score
1	28	U.S.A.: Texas to California	516
2	24	U.S.A.: New England, N.Y., N.J.	493
3	26	U.S.A.: E.N. Central	457
4	29	Canada, N.W. U.S.A., Alaska	444
5	25	U.S.A.: Pennsylvania to Georgia	427
6	27	U.S.A.: Nebraska to Florida	422
7	4	S. Germany	419
8	3	Netherlands, N. Germany	402
9	5	Belgium, N. France	391
10	30	Australia, New Zealand	376
11	6	Rest of France	365
12	2	North Europe	350
13	21	Japan: Tokyo area	311
14	8	Switzerland, Austria, N. Italy	306
15	23	Rest of Japan	301
16	22	Japan: Osaka area	275
17	1	England	254
18	10	E. Germany, Czechoslovakia, Hungary	229
19	15	U.S.S.R.: Belorussia, Centre	214
20	19	U.S.S.R.: Ural, Siberias, Far East	203
World average			100

of goods and services. Countries with centrally planned economies assess production differently from market economy countries. Comparisons between countries are distorted by exchange rates. Gross national product misses some aspects of production. In spite of these drawbacks it was considered worth assessing the distribution of gross national product on the basis of the 100 cells. Thus the amount produced in each cell was calculated, expressed in per 10,000s of total world gross national product and divided by population, also in per 10,000s. The resulting scores for each cell are shown in Table 8.1, column (7), and are mapped in Figure 8.10. The highest scoring cells are shown in Table 8.8. There is a high degree of concentration of gross national product in the world, as shown in Figure 8.10. The gini coefficient of concentration (see Figure 8.11) of gross national product according to population is 0.642. The richest 10 percent of the world's population accounts for 43 percent of total gross national product while the poorest 50 percent has only 7 percent.

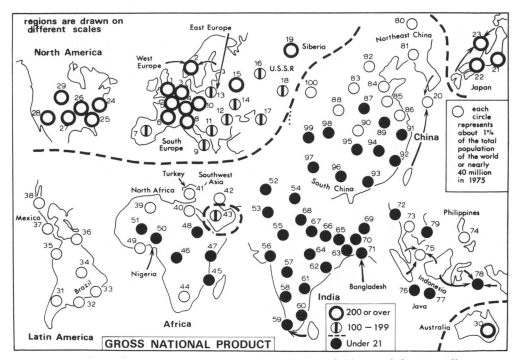

Figure 8.10 The distribution of gross national product on the basis of the 100 cells

Twenty cells have more than twice the world average gross national product per inhabitant while 42 have only a fifth of the world average or less. In other words, about 20 percent of the world's population has an average gross national product at least 10 times as high as the average of the poorest 40 percent. The poorest cells are in central and eastern Africa, in South and Southeast Asia, and in the southern less industrialized part of China.

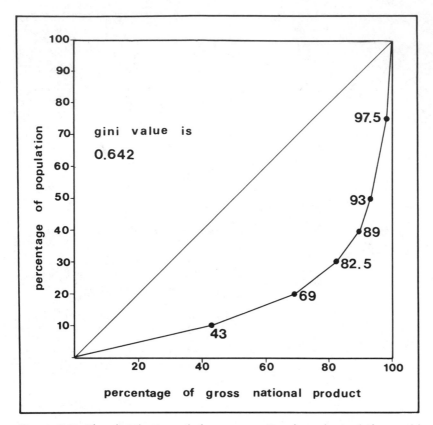

Figure 8.11 The distribution of the gross national product of the world according to population

9

The characteristics of the 100 cells

Cell profiles

Chapters 1-6 were a review of the development gap and how it came about. The spatial basis consisted of conventionally accepted areal units, the sovereign states. In Chapters 7 and 8 selected data about natural resources, production, and consumption were expressed in a new regional framework. It was felt that the presentation of data in the system of 100 regions all roughly equal in population size would bring out aspects of the development gap not normally seen. The framework gives in addition a more balanced view of the situation than that achieved through a system in which large units such as China and India are listed alongside small units like Jamaica and Gabon, which while equal in status, are several hundred times smaller in population size.

Some decades ago it was fashionable for geographers to divide the world into physical or natural regions, based partly on climatic conditions. For example since West Europe, northwest U.S.A., and south central Chile have similar climatic conditions it tended to be assumed that other features, particularly man's activities, would be similar in the regions. More recently, regional studies have tended to use sovereign states as the basis for subdivision of the world. Since sovereign states are indeed units of spatial organization there is some justification in treating each as a distinct region.

The system of equal population regions has disadvantages as well as advantages. Although drawbacks may already have occurred to the reader, some defects will be briefly noted here before the system is used in this and the next chapter to distinguish types of development region and to estimate possible transfers between cells.

It would have been possible to subdivide the world into a larger
or a smaller number of equal population cells than 100. Population
could even have been allocated differently to still arrive at a
system of 100 equal population cells. Although each cell has been
treated as an entity so far, the cells that are larger in area vary
greatly in natural conditions and availability of natural resources
from one part to another. Moreover, almost all the cells are either
composed of two or more separate smaller sovereign states or are
only part of a larger one and they are not therefore units of spatial
organization.

Each cell has been considered as a statistical entity in Chapters 7
and 8. Altogether in Tables 7.2 and 8.1 11 pieces of numerical
information are given for each of the 100 cells. Four values estimate
natural resources per inhabitant while seven give production or
consumption per inhabitant of selected goods and services. The
basis for the comparison of cells in the present chapter is the
concept that each has a 'profile' and that some pairs of cells have
fairly similar profiles. To illustrate this idea, three pairs of cells are
compared in Table 9.1. The 11 columns of data are from Tables 7.2
and 8.1. Profiles of selected cells will be represented graphically in
the next section.

Table 9.1 Profiles of selected cells

	Resource scores from Table 7.2				Production, consumption scores from Table 8.1						
	(1)	(2)	(3)	(4)	(1)	(2)	(3)	(4)	(5)	(6)	(7)
Cell 40 Egypt	39	14	0	75	16	20	0	5	1	2	21
Cell 79 Indo-China	62	0	5	51	4	9	0	0	2	1	10
Cell 31 Argentina, Chile	302	2	470	288	56	71	254	31	2	3	89
Cell 44 Southern Africa	148	57	898	281	89	116	891	111	2	2	71
Cell 19 U.S.S.R.: Siberia	385	1892	898	904	601	339	729	825	3	4	203
Cell 29 Canada, N.W.U.S.A.	648	561	1336	1039	449	441	1299	222	3	3	444

9.2   The structure of selected cells

From the 100 cells, 13 have been chosen for special consideration.
As explained in Section 9.1 and exemplified in Table 9.1, a set of 11
pieces of numerical data is recorded for each cell in Tables 7.2 and
8.1. As a row of numbers these are not easily interpreted. In this
section therefore a diagram has been drawn for each of the 13
selected cells.

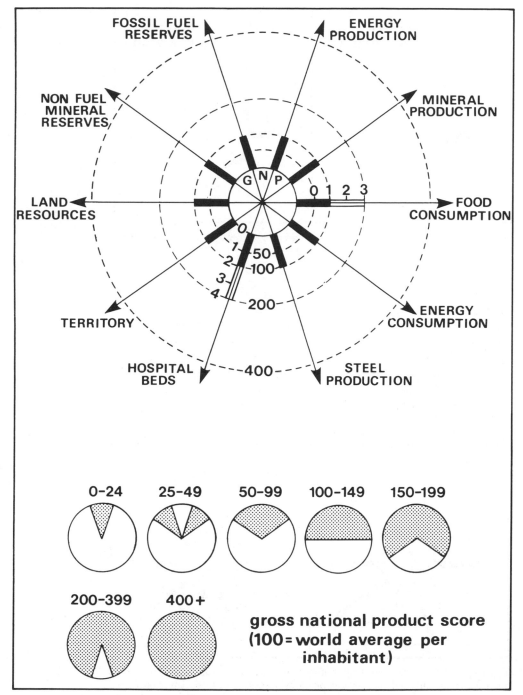

Figure 9.1 Key to the studies of individual cells in Figures 9.2-9.5

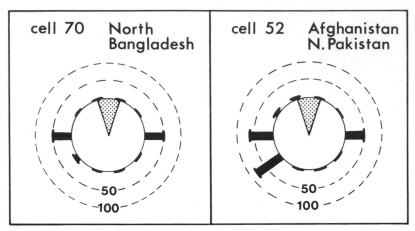

Figure 9.2 Two examples of cells that have low scores on both resources and production-consumption. See Figure 9.1 for key

The structure of the cell diagrams is explained in Figure 9.1. Four of the lines radiating from the centre of the circle, all towards the left, represent each of the four categories of natural resources per inhabitant, while the remaining six lines represent production or consumption per inhabitant. Each line is drawn out from the central part of the diagram proportional to the score that the cell has on each of the 10 measures of resources, production or consumption. A radiating line that reaches the circle marked 100 indicates that

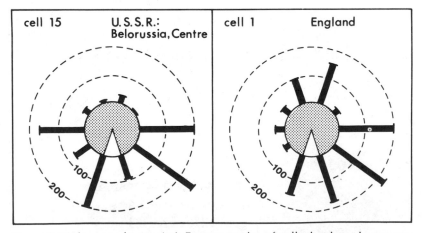

Figure 9.3 (Above and opposite) Four examples of cells that have low scores on resources but high scores on production-consumption. See Figure 9.1 for key

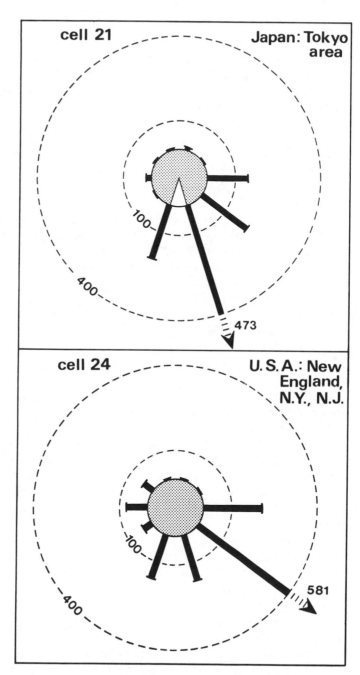

Figure 9.3 (continued)

the cell has a score of 100. This means that its share of resources, production or consumption is exactly equal to its share of world population. If it reaches to 200 then its share of the item is twice its share of world population. If it only reaches to 50 then its share of the item is half its share of world population. The lines for food (to the right) and for hospital beds (to the lower left) have been expressed differently, as the scores for each cell were whole numbers from 3 to 0 for food and from 4 to 0 for hospital beds, but their length is still related to the score. The central part of each cell is shaded according to the score for gross national product per inhabitant of the cell. It is hoped that the visual comparisons permitted by the diagrammatical representation of the cells in the form described above will make the contrasts between cells clear.

Two cells with very low scores on both resources and production are shown in Figure 9.2. Cell 70, North Bangladesh, has limited land resources and a very low level of food intake. It has and produces little of anything else. Many of the cells of India and China, as well as the two for Java in Indonesia, have profiles very similar to the profile of cell 70. Cell 52, Afghanistan and North Pakistan, also has limited land resources and a low level of food intake, but occupies a considerable territorial extent, much of which however is dry and rugged. The cell therefore scores moderately on the territorial resource line to the lower left.

Four cells with low scores on natural resources but high scores on production and consumption are shown in Figure 9.3. Cell 15, which includes the Moscow industrial region of the U.S.S.R., has a considerable amount of agricultural land, indicated by its high score on the line to the left. Cell 1, England, has considerable reserves and production of fossil fuels (coal and natural gas). The other two cells are particularly poorly endowed with natural resources. All four cells, however, have high scores on industrial production (partially represented by steel) and high levels of consumption (food, energy, hospital beds as a service). Cells 15 and 24 draw on internal sources in the U.S.S.R. and U.S.A. respectively for most of their food, fuel, and raw materials needs. Cells 1 (England) and 21 (part of Japan) trade with other parts of the world for this purpose.

The two cells shown diagrammatically in Figure 9.4 are fairly well balanced with regard to their share of natural resources and rates of production and consumption. The diagrams show both cells to have all their lines going out roughly the same distance. On average the scores of cell 16 (part of the U.S.S.R.) are twice as high as the scores of cell 38 (part of Mexico). Cell 16 has very large fossil fuel reserves

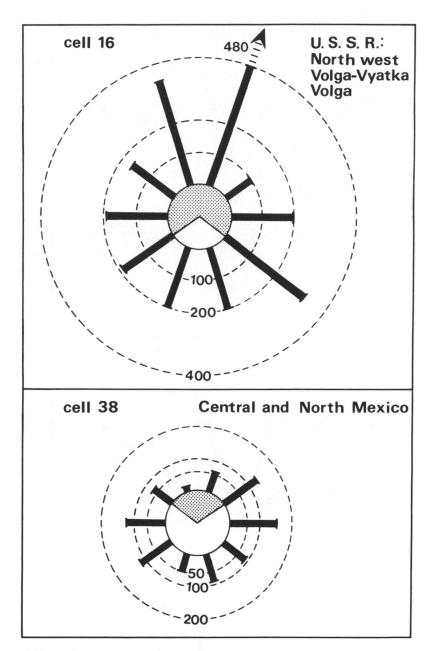

Figure 9.4 Two examples of cells in which resources and production-consumption are fairly evenly balanced

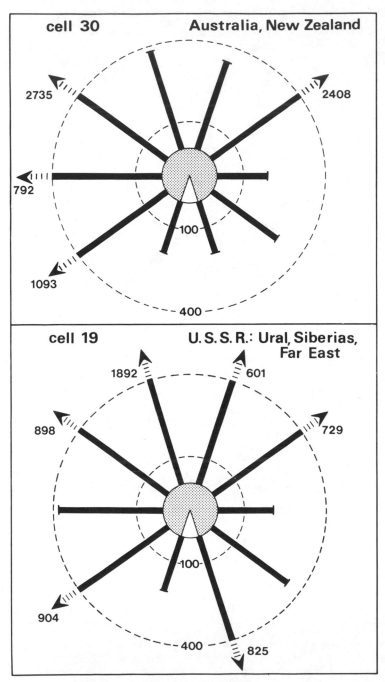

Figure 9.5 (Above, opposite and page 280) Five examples of cells that have very high scores on all or some resources and on all or some aspects of production-consumption

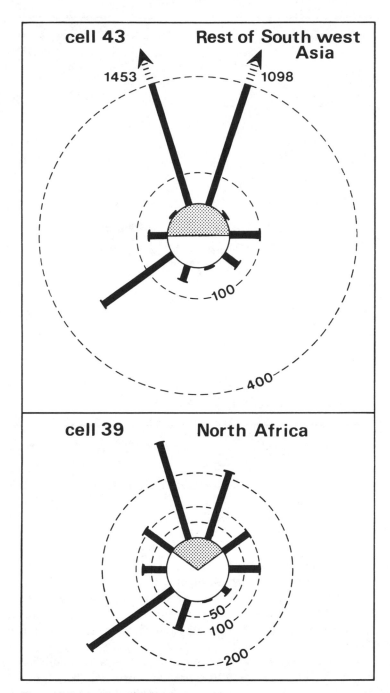

Figure 9.5 (continued)

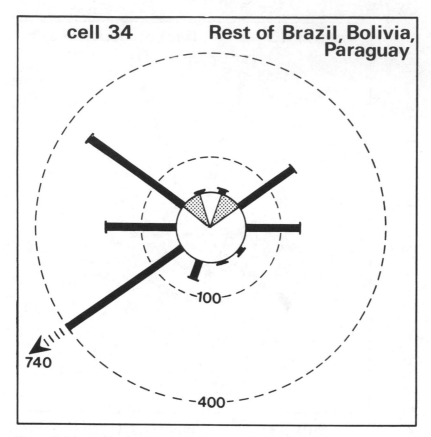

Figure 9.5 (continued)

and produces large quantities of oil and natural gas as well as coal (score here is 480).

Five cells that are well endowed with natural resources in relation to population are shown in Figure 9.5. Of these, only cell 30 (Australia, New Zealand) is also very high on gross national product per inhabitant. Cell 19 (U.S.S.R.: Ural, Siberias, Far East) does, however, also have a high level of production and its estimated gross national product does not seem to do justice to this level. Cells 30 and 19 are fairly similar in that they each score at least twice the world average on all 10 lines; some scores reach out far beyond the 400 score circle.

Cell 43 (Rest of Southwest Asia) is one of the two cells that are of particular importance with regard to world oil. Together, cells 42 and 43 have about 50 percent of all the world's oil reserves. Cell 39 (North Africa) is fairly similar in profile to cell 43 but the two top lines of cell 43 reach out far beyond the 400 score circle on account of the exceptionally large fossil fuel reserves and production of the regions, already referred to. Both cells cover large areas and therefore have a high score on the territory resource though both are largely desert or semi-desert. Cell 39 (North Africa) has a moderate score on non-fuel mineral reserves and production.

Cell 34 (Rest of Brazil, Bolivia, Paraguay) covers a very large area in the interior and northeast of South America, as its high score (740) on the territorial resources shows. It also has large mineral reserves and land resources (mainly forest) but virtually no fossil fuel reserves have yet been found. There is little industry in the region and levels of consumption are very low.

From the above brief review of the profiles of selected cells it is possible to see the great variations that exist from one part of the world to another. In the section that follows the layout of some of the cells will be examined and comparative sizes noted.

9.3 A comparison of the size and layout of selected cells

An advantage of dividing the world into regions that are roughly equal in population size is that comparability is achieved; this facilitates the study of some aspects of development. A disadvantage of using cells that are equal in population size is that their difference in territorial extent tends to be forgotten. The average area of cell is obviously 1/100 of the total land area of the world, or about 1,330,000 km² (see Table 6.16). Several of the smallest cells occupy less than 1/20 of this area while two are more than 10 times the world average. In Figure 9.6, three sizes of cell are distinguished. Those indicated with a black dot are roughly less than half the average size for the world. Those with an open circle are larger than average. The intermediate sized cells are shaded.

For comparative purposes a number of cells have been mapped in groups in which all are represented on the same scale. The correct comparative size of regions in the world is not widely appreciated. Perception of scale and area seems to diminish away from one's home region. This section consists of a brief commentary on a number of maps and some comments on differences in density of population.

(1) Figure 9.7 is a comparison of six highly industrialized cells which, however, are lacking in natural resources. The profiles of four of the cells were shown diagrammatically in Figure 9.3. Japan consists of three cells, the limits of which are shown on the map. The cell for Northeast U.S.A. (states of New England plus New York

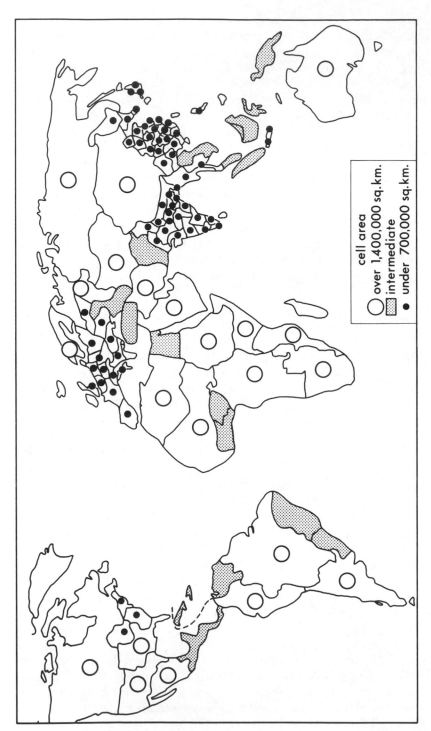

Figure 9.6 Three sizes of cell according to territorial extent

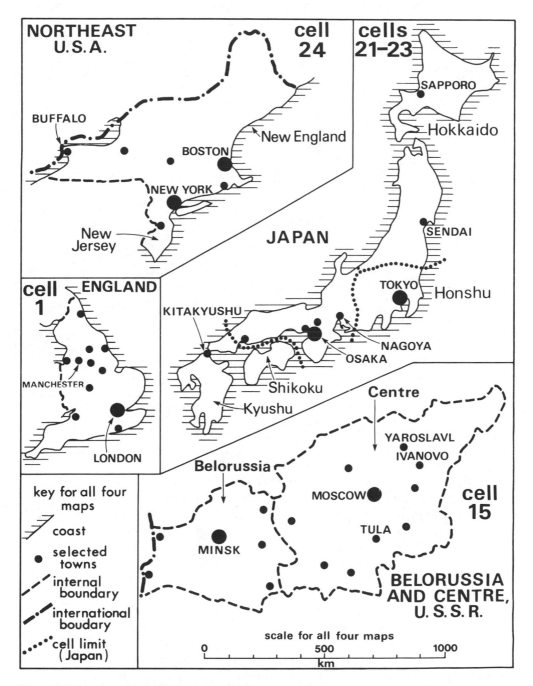

Figure 9.7 A comparison of selected cells that are small in area, comparatively poor in natural resources, but have high levels of production-consumption. All cells are drawn on the same scale

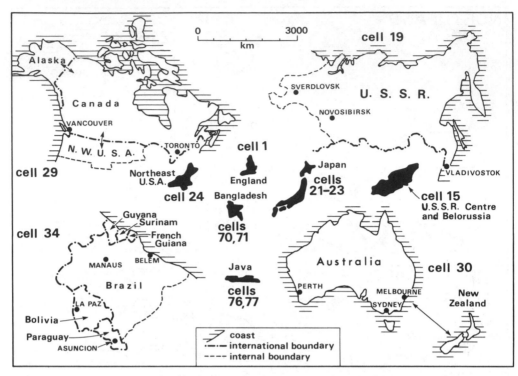

Figure 9.8 A comparison of cells that are small in area with cells that are very large in area

and New Jersey) is considerably larger in area than England, itself much larger than the Tokyo area cell. The central part of European U.S.S.R., however, is again larger even than Northeast U.S.A. All six cells in Figure 9.3 depend heavily on other cells for part of their food, energy, and/or raw materials. The cell for Northeast U.S.A. receives these mainly from other parts of the U.S.A. itself and the Centre region around Moscow likewise draws largely on other Soviet regions. Japan and England, on the other hand, depend on foreign trade for many of the materials used in their economies.

(2) Figure 9.8 compares the small, highly industrialized cells in Figure 9.7 with other small, developing areas, Bangladesh and Java, each with two cells, and with the wide open spaces of the four largest cells in the world in area. The 10 small cells, all in solid black, have about 10 percent of the total population of the world between them. The four large cells have only about 4 percent of the population of the world between them. The profiles of cells 19, 30, and 34 were shown in Figure 9.5.

(3) Figure 9.9 compares Great Britain with Southwest China. Great Britain is cell 1 (England) plus a part of cell 2 (North Europe).

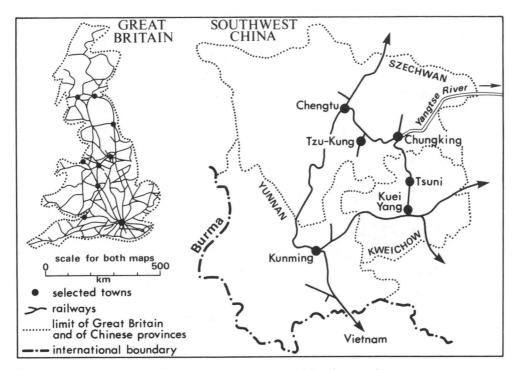

Figure 9.9 A comparison of Great Britain and part of Southwest China

Southwest China is three whole cells (97-99) and part of a fourth. The total population of Great Britain in 1975 was 55 million and that of the three provinces of China nearly 130 million. The density of population is considerably higher in Britain than in Southwest China, much of which is very rugged and virtually uninhabited. On the other hand the gross 'cell' product per inhabitant is about 15 times as high in Britain as in Southwest China.

The communication networks of the two regions are compared in Figure 9.9. What is left of the British rail network in 1978 after drastic cuts in the 1960s is shown on the map. Most lines are double track, some quadruple. The very dense road network is not shown at all. The complete rail network of Southwest China is also shown. Most lines are single track. Roads are few and of poor quality. Virtually all the railways in Southwest China have been built since the communists gained power in 1949. A little thought will show not only how weakly linked various parts of Southwest China are internally, but also how weak are its links with the outside world. One outlet is down the Yangtse River to Shanghai, another along a single track railway to Canton and Hong Kong, or to Hanoi in

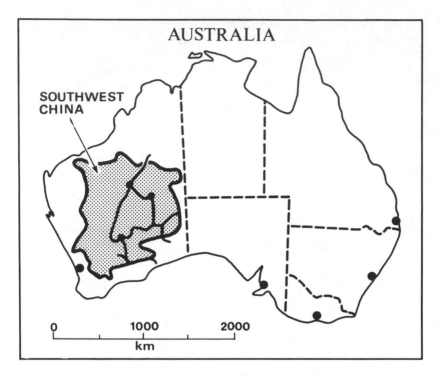

Figure 9.10 A comparison of part of Southwest China with Australia

Vietnam. It would be impossible to carry more than a very small quantity of goods between Southwest China and the rest of the world. Such inaccessibility is a feature of many cells in developing countries, and should be borne in mind by the reader when transfers are discussed in Chapter 10.

(4) Figure 9.10 compares Southwest China with Australia, Australia has about 13 million inhabitants compared with the 130 million in Southwest China. Southwest China actually fits comfortably into the state of Western Australia, which has little more than one million inhabitants. Western Australia has approximately half as much cultivated land as Southwest China, though the land is not so fertile. It has proved reserves of several non-fuel minerals that are of international significance, as well as oil. Szechwan in Southwest China has large coal reserves.

(5) Figure 9.11 compares Southwest China and Great Britain (only some railways shown) with Western Australia. With only one million inhabitants, Western Australia has a larger route mileage of railways than Southwest China with 130 million inhabitants. The iron ore extracted in the northwest part of Western Australia

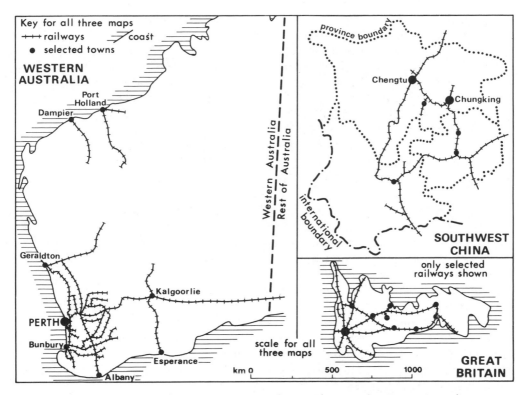

Figure 9.11 A comparison of Great Britain, Southwest China, and Western Australia

reaches the coast along specially built railways. The wheatlands of the Southwest have an ample rail system to serve them.

(6) Figure 9.12 compares parts of the developing world. Cell 34 consists of the more thinly populated parts of Brazil plus Bolivia, Paraguay, and the Guianas. Much of it is tropical rain forest. There are also extensive areas of floodplain where, if the Amazon and its tributaries could be controlled, intensive cultivation could be practised. Among economic minerals in cell 34 are oil, manganese ore, iron ore, bauxite, and tin. In a considerably smaller total area than that of cell 34 there are 20 times as many people living in South Asia, cells 52-71. It is not implied here that the density of population *should* be the same in all cells, but the natural resources available per inhabitant are far greater in cell 34, 'empty' South America, than in South Asia. Both regions in Figure 9.12 are, however, part of the developng world, in the sense that the standard of living throughout is low. Amazonia could be referred to as undeveloped because its natural resources have hardly been

used. South Asia could be referred to as overdeveloped because its natural resources are limited and are heavily used.

The great disparities in the density of population among different parts of the world, some of which have been illustrated in this section, have attracted the attention of many people. It worries politicians and the military establishment in large countries like Brazil, Australia, and the U.S.S.R. to have large 'empty' areas. The economic potential is seen to be wasted and the areas are regarded as vulnerable strategically unless seen to be adequately occupied. A low density of population over a large area may be the result of two different influences. Either there are no natural resources to be used or for some reason the natural resources of the region have not attracted settlers. Greenland may have valuable minerals beneath its icecap but it serves as an extreme example of a land mass that cannot realistically be densely populated. Most other thinly populated parts of the world probably have some natural resources.

Until the nineteenth century the western two-thirds of what is now the U.S.A. supported only a few million American Indians. Now it has over a hundred million Americans. It was 'empty' until settlement in the nineteenth century because its generous land and mineral resources were not used. In contrast, the interior and north of Australia, the north of Canada, and much of Siberia are still empty today. They do have natural resources, including minerals, and in Canada and Siberia abundant timber and water resources. The natural resources can, however, be managed and used by comparatively few people.

At least some of the disparities in the density of settlement in the world can be accounted for by the history of colonization and settlement of different continents since the rise to dominance of Europe in the sixteenth century. Some parts of the world were still inhabited by populations with a very low level of technology and with few resource requirements. The Europeans were able to move in. Rostow (1960) describes such areas thus:

> the small group of nations that were, in a sense, 'born free': the United States, Australia, New Zealand, Canada, and, perhaps, a few others. These nations were created mainly out of a Britain already far along in the transitional process. Moreover, they were founded by social groups — usually one type of non-conformist or another — who were at the margin of the dynamic transitional process slowly going forward within Britain. Finally their physical settings — of wild but abundant land and other natural resources — discouraged the

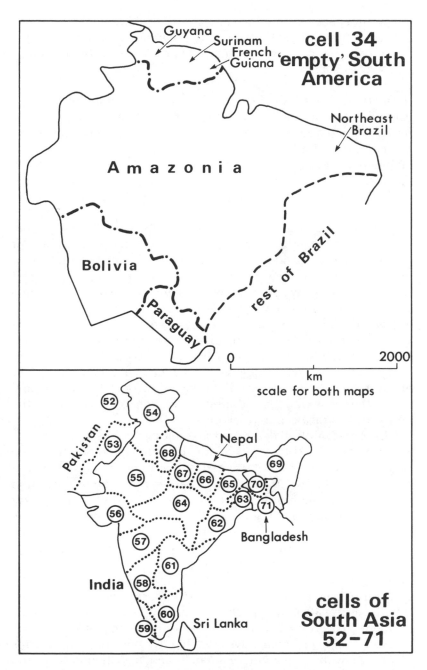

Figure 9.12 A comparison of the interior of South America with the cells of South Asia

maintenance of such elements in the traditional structure as were transplanted, and they accelerated the transitional process by offering extremely attractive incentives to get on with economic growth.

Siberia is now to some degree like the British colonies in North America were in the nineteenth century. Population growth is hoped for in the eastern part of the U.S.S.R., even though according to Khachaturov (1977) a million more people have left the Urals and Siberia than have gone there between the mid-1960s and mid-1970s. The eastern and northern half of the U.S.S.R. has vast natural resources but only a few percent of the total population of the country.

Adverse climatic conditions such as permafrost in the ground, very low temperatures, and snow make both the exploitation of resources and the conditions for living very difficult and unpleasant in Siberia. There are few communications in the region. An idea of why there are so few people in the northern and eastern parts of the U.S.S.R. may be gained from the following description of Ust-Ilimsk, a new town in East Siberia by a large hydroelectric project. The extreme continental climate has a snow cover lasting more than six months each year, temperatures that can exceed 30°C in July yet drop to -60°C in January. Fog commonly forms in summer as colder air from higher areas descends to the valley of the River Angara, where the air is warmer and moister. Winter fog occurs over the new water surface of the reservoir.

L.E. Soboleva (1974) describes the resulting depressing conditions and problems at Ust-Ilimsk. 'The city that is to be built on the shore of the tail water will be situated in the zone of maximum fog occurrence. The fog, in turn, will foster the intensive precipitation of industrial emissions. Conditions will be particularly unfavourable in heavy fog during the stable high-pressure systems that are typical of Eastern Siberia in winter. The harsh climate gives rise to a large number of negative reactions in the organism of healthy and particularly of ailing people. This is most evident among newcomers. Negative reactions are most common among those suffering from cardio-vascular disease. Their condition is usually aggravated during abrupt changes in weather elements (sudden changes in atmospheric pressure, a shift from a low-pressure to a high-pressure system, etc.), The low air temperatures combined with a great diurnal range and high humidity in the intermediate seasons tend to increase the heat loss of the organism and lead to meteo-tropic disease. Respiratory ailments occur more frequently in the intermediate seasons — spring and autumn.'

Figure 9.13 A Brazilian poster drawing attention to the empty half of Brazil. Caption: 'Now the turn of the other half has come'

Australia, Canada, and Brazil also have large areas that are virtually uninhabited. Over half of the population of Australia is concentrated in a few coastal cities. Even the proposed new city in the 'interior', Albury, turns out to be comfortably placed in the extreme southeast of the national territory, between Sydney and Melbourne, rather than at Alice Springs. There have been attempts to settle the northlands of Canada. It has been estimated by Wreford Watson (1967), however, that in the 1960s more people were moving into one suburb of Toronto, named North York, than into the whole 'empty' north.

In contrast to the U.S.S.R., Canada, and Australia, Brazil has a fast growing population. Most of the inhabitants are concentrated near the coast in the Northeast, Southeast, and South regions. The

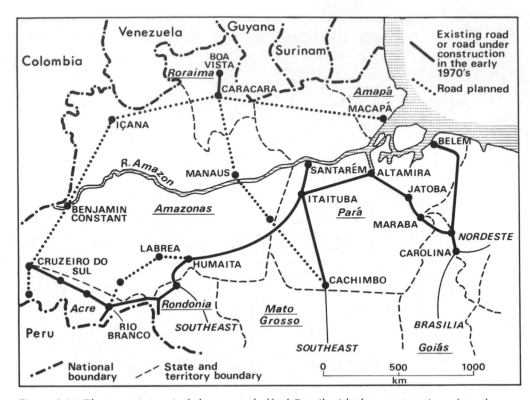

Figure 9.14 The 'opening up' of the empty half of Brazil with the construction of roads

'empty' northwestern half of Brazil seems the obvious place for settlement and development. The transfer of the national capital towards the territorial centre of Brazil in 1960 with the inauguration of Brasilia does not appear to have changed the distribution of population in the country greatly. The attempt to move people to the natural resources of Amazonia continues. Figure 9.13 shows an advertisement about the empty half of Brazil and Figure 9.14 the roads built there in the 1970s. Not long ago Amazonia was being referred to as the 'green inferno'.

The disparities in the distribution of population in relation to territory in general and to specific natural resources in particular have formed over a long period of time. Around 1500 the population of the world was distributed very much in accordance with the availability of land resources usable according to the agricultural technology of the time and the place. Thus most of the land resources in use today in Europe, India, and China were already in use then. Since then some of the land resources have been depleted in these areas (forests) while some new land has been added (reclamation, new irrigation). Yields are on the whole much higher than they were. In contrast, very large areas of potentially good agricultural land in North and South America, in Australia, and in parts of the Russian Empire were hardly cultivated at all. Examples are the prairies of North America, the pampas of Argentina, and the steppes of Kazakhstan. The indigenous population did not have the technology to use them.

Today long-settled farming areas such as the Nile Valley in Egypt, the Andes in South America, and much of Europe, South Asia, and East Asia carry a legacy of large numbers of people engaged in agriculture per unit of cultivated land. In other areas, only comparatively recently settled, including most of Canada, the U.S.A., Siberia, and Australia, the amount of farmland per farm worker is very large.

The large-scale use of inanimate sources of energy (fossil fuels such as coal and oil as well as hydroelectric power and nuclear fuels) dates only from the early nineteenth century. The same is true of mineral raw materials. Thus two centuries ago the distribution of population in the world was still largely accounted for by the distribution of land resources, with mineral resources only of local influence. Subsequent population growth has been fastest at first in the 'new' countries (the Americas, Australia, parts of Russia), between about 1840 and 1920, as a result of the boost provided by migration from Europe (which relieved pressure in Europe), and then in the developing world mainly from about 1920 to the present, with the prospect that it will continue there for some decades. Altogether, then, the population of the world is not 'well' distributed even according to the distribution of land resources and its distribution bears little relationship at all to the distribution of other natural resources.

9.4   The relationship of natural resources to production

The countries of the world can be placed on two distinct 'development' scales. They vary firstly according to the quantity of natural resources per inhabitant and secondly according to the production of goods and services per inhabitant. Similarly, the 100 cells can be scaled on these two dimensions.

For each cell an estimate of gross national product per inhabitant was given in Table 8.1, column (7), and of all natural resources per inhabitant in Table 7.2, column (5). Each of the two dimensions

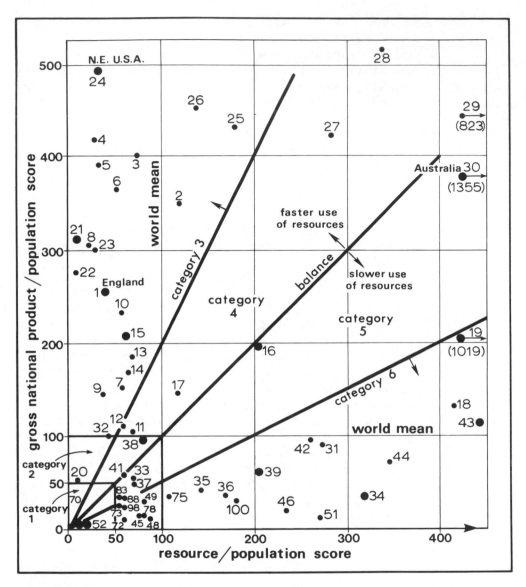

Figure 9.15 The distribution of the 100 cells according to their resource to population scores (horizontal axis) and gross national product to population scores (vertical scale). Data are from Tables 7.2 and 8.1

forms an axis in the graph in Figure 9.15. On each scale, 100 is the position at which a cell would be located if it had a share of world production (vertical axis) or resources (horizontal axis) equal to its share of world population.

Some examples will clarify what the graph is showing. Cell 16 (U.S.S.R.: Northwest, Volga-Vyatka, Volga) has twice its share of world natural resources per inhabitant *and* a gross national product per inhabitant twice the world average. Cell 16 is near the centre of the graph. In contrast, cell 19 (U.S.S.R.: Ural, Siberias, Far East) is also at 200 for gross national product per inhabitant but far to the right on natural resources, having about 10 times its 'share' of the world total according to population. At the extreme left of the graph are cells 21, 22, and 23, the three cells of Japan. These are very poorly endowed with their own natural resources but have a high level of production, about three times the world average. Although the limited natural resources of Japan are being used intensively, most of the fuel and raw materials in Japanese industry come from other cells. Thus cells 42 (Iran, Iraq) and 43 (Rest of Southwest Asia) provide most of Japan's crude oil imports. They are on the lower right of the diagram.

Gross national product per inhabitant not only measures the production of goods and services in a region. It serves as a rough measure, or meter, indicating the rate at which natural resources are being used and, in the case of non-renewable resources, used up. Three diagonal lines are shown on the graph in Figure 9.15. A cell on the central of the three lines would be using natural resources at an average rate because it has equal scores on each axis. Cell 16 (part of the U.S.S.R.) in the middle of the graph is in such a position. The closer a cell is towards the left of the graph and therefore the farther it is to the left of the central diagonal, the more heavily its economy is using up natural resources, whether its own or those from other cells. The closer a cell is to the lower part of the graph and therefore the farther it is downwards from the central diagonal, the less quickly its economy is using up natural resources. The intermediate diagonals mark the half-way distances between the middle diagonal and each of the axes.

The vertical axis arranges the cells according to how 'profligate' they are in using the natural resources of the world. The horizontal axis arranges the cells according to whether they themselves have an abundance or a lack of natural resources. The diagonals sort the cells out according to how 'profligate' they are with regard to their own natural resources or those from another cell. Six categories of cell have been identified from the graph in Figure 9.15. Examples of cells from each of these six categories have already been looked at in detail in the previous section. The 13 cells used are indicated on the graph in Figure 9.15 with extra heavy dots.

Category 1 cells have a score of less than 50 on *both* dimensions. There is not enough space to plot them all in Figure 9.15 so they

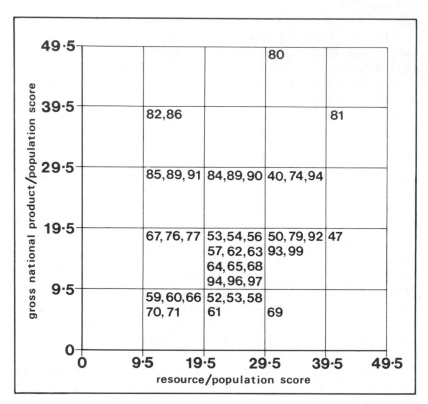

Figure 9.16 Detailed graph of the lower left-hand portion of Figure 9.15. Data are from Tables 7.2 and 8.1

have been displayed separately in Figure 9.16, which is a tabular representation of the extreme lower left portion of the large graph in Figure 9.15. These 41 cells have few natural resources per inhabitant and are little industrialized. Their main natural resource is agricultural land. All the cells of South Asia fall in category 1 together with most of the cells of China and some of those of Southeast Asia and of Africa. On the map in Figure 9.17 these cells are left as blank circles and are marked off from the rest of the cells. They are very poor, they have little part in world trade, and each is to a large degree self-sufficient.

Category 2 cells score below 100 on both axes but over 50 on one axis or on both axes. Thus although these 14 cells are below the world average with regard both to gross national product per inhabitant and to resources per inhabitant, there is greater economic activity or potential than in the 41 cells in category 1. Cells 20 (S. Korea, Hong Kong, Taiwan) and 32 (Southeast and South

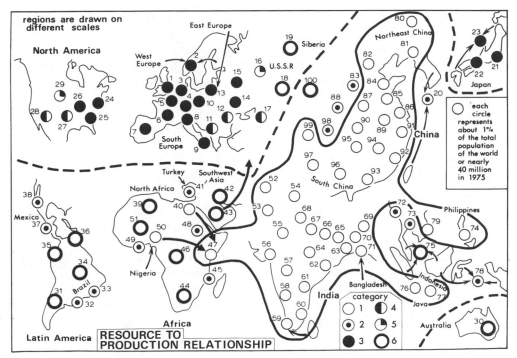

Figure 9.17 The relationship of resources per inhabitant to production per inhabitant on the basis of the 100 cells. See text for explanation

Brazil) are higher on the gross national product axis than on the resource axis. Cells 45 (Southeast Africa) and 48 (Northeast Africa) are better on the resource axis than on the gross national product axis. They are indicated in Figure 9.17 by circles with a dot inside.

The remaining 45 cells all score higher than 100 either on the gross national product axis (e.g. 21, 22, 23, Japan) or on the resource axis (e.g. 34, interior Brazil, Bolivia, Paraguay) or on both (e.g. 28, U.S.A.: Texas to California). They have been divided into four categories (3-6) according to their relationship to the three diagonal lines in Figure 9.15.

Category 3 cells are those with a high level of industrialization but limited natural resources. They are shown as black dots in Figure 9.17. There are 19 such cells. They are in Europe, eastern North America, and Japan. Their positions on the gross national product scale range from about 150 for cells 7 and 9 (southern Europe) to nearly 500 for cell 24 (Northeast U.S.A.). A large part of their gross national product is derived from industry and services.

Category 4 cells, of which there are only five, are better provided with natural resources than the cells in category 3 but cells 11, 12, and 17, which are in Eastern Europe and the U.S.S.R. (the Balkans and Caucasus), have a much lower gross national product than cells 27 and 28, southwestern U.S.A.

Category 5 contains only two cells, 16 and 29. Cell 16 has already been referred to on account of its central position in the graph and unusual position very near the middle diagonal. Cell 29 (Canada, N.W. U.S.A., Alaska) falls outside the part of the graph shown on account of its very high resource level (score 823 on the horizontal axis).

Category 6 contains 16 cells shown in Figure 9.17 with a heavily ringed circle. Two of them, 30 (Australia, New Zealand) and 19 (U.S.S.R.: Ural, Siberias, Far East), score so highly on the horizontal axis at 1355 and 1019 respectively that they fall outside the bounds of the graph. The cells in category 6, together with cell 29 in category 5, comprise the main existing or potential sources of food, energy, and raw materials for the 'profligate' but poorly endowed cells of category 3 to draw on. In short, world trade, whether international or internal, is largely a set of transactions across the graph between the cells on the upper left of the graph and those on the far right or lower right. On the world map it is between the solid black circles and the heavily ringed circles in Figure 9.17. Some flows are internal, such as those between cells in the U.S.S.R. Other flows are international, such as those between Europe and the Middle East or between Japan and Australia.

Two final observations are worth making about the graph in Figure 9.17. A cell is likely to change position on the graph through time. It would move either as a result of a change in gross national product per inhabitant or as a result of a change in natural resources per inhabitant. These changes are caused by changes in the size of means of production (turning-out GNP), of natural resources (used-up *versus* new discoveries), and of population. A second aspect of the relationships in Figure 9.17 is the remarkable way in which the cells avoid the central part of the graph. There are very few in categories 4 and 5.

10

The scale of transfers needed to reduce the development gap

10.1 Views on the development gap

From a geographical point of view the subject of inequality falls broadly into two parts, inequality within countries and inequality between countries. The difference is a political one, caused by the existence of the system of sovereign states in the world and the great influence it has on world affairs and the world economy. Many countries now have policies and institutions that are aimed at narrowing internal regional inequalities in living standards. On the other hand sovereign state boundaries act as a barrier to the flow of both trade (exchange) and aid (gifts). Such boundaries also tend to be the limits beyond which governments and most ordinary citizens cease to have a conscience about the less well-off.

There may paradoxically be some advantage in the present world system of sovereign states. Developing countries can protect themselves against forces originating in developed countries that might keep them from industrializing. It has been argued for example by people living in Northeast Brazil that their backwardness has been maintained at least until the late 1960s by the presence in the same country of the dynamic industrial state of São Paulo in the southeast. As a separate sovereign state Northeast Brazil might have started to industrialize sooner than it has.

In this section some views about the development gap are quoted and commented on. The rest of the chapter attempts to assess the net transfers that would be needed in the world to achieve something near equality in living standards.

The subject of inequality in the world as a whole and in parts of it has been discussed a great deal since the Second World War. Typically the narrowing of the development gap is seen by economists

299

as a matter of differential economic growth. If only the developing countries could achieve and sustain a very high rate of growth, then eventually results might be achieved.

One of the best known authorities on development is the Swedish economist G. Myrdal. Myrdal (1957) is very pessimistic (pp. 4-5):

> In the under-developed countries, on the other hand, where incomes are so very much lower, capital formation and invest-ment tend generally to be smaller, even relatively to their lower incomes. For equality in rate of development, they should instead be relatively bigger, since in the poorer countries the natural population increase is usually faster. The faster population increase is a result of a particular relation between fertility and mortality rates, where both are on a very high level, which, in addition, tends to make the age distri-bution of their populations relatively less advantageous. As a consequence of all this — and of the tradition of stagnation which has entrenched itself in their entire culture — their economic development usually proceeds more slowly. Many of these countries have during recent decades even moved backwards in average income.

The gap between developing and developed countries in the production and consumption per inhabitant of many goods and services has indeed become even greater in the 1970s than it was in the 1950s.

In *The Strategy of Economic Development,* A.O. Hirschman (1958) also discusses regional inequalities at both internal and international levels. He talks of 'two nations' and the 'North-South' problem. He argues that economic progress cannot appear everywhere at the same time. Once it appears it is spatially concentrated in 'poles'. Advantaged regions are therefore inevitable. Hirschman is more optimistic than Myrdal about the eventual trickling down and spread of economic progress from the original areas of growth to surrounding areas. The 'backwash' effects that he expects are, however, stronger internally than internationally. The ideas in Hirschman's Chapter 10 on Transmission in the above book seem very fresh still. Perhaps this is because little new has been said on the development gap since the 1950s.

In *The Year 2000,* H. Kahn and associates (Kahn and Wiener, 1967) recognize a 'dichotomised standard world' (p. 141). They speculate on how long it would take various countries to reach the 1965 U.S. gross national product *per capita* of $3600 (Table VIII, p. 149). While

Sweden would only need 11 years and Canada 12, it is estimated that India would need 117 years, Brazil 130, Nigeria, 339, and Indonesia 593. These time spans are interesting but, as argued throughout the present book, gross national product itself cannot be eaten and does not make machines. The time that it might take given countries to reach the 1965 or the 1980 level of gross national product *per capita* in the U.S.A. is an academic consideration. For a large part of the population of the world to reach such astronomical levels of consumption as those achieved in the 1960s by the U.S.A., vast quantities of natural resources, far in excess of those known in most developing countries, would be required.

Kahn and his associates (Kahn *et al.*, 1977) give the impression that they have put the development gap in perspective in *The Next 200 Years*. In their breathtaking view of things ahead they see a very large gap for a long time (pp. 48-9):

> Today (1975) per capita GNP ranges from about $100 to $10,000, and it would not at all surprise us if the range at the end of the 21st century were still rather large, perhaps from a basic minimum of a few thousand dollars to a maximum of 10 to 20 times greater ... But this would not be disastrous either morally or politically since there are very few peasants, workers or even businessmen in developing nations who care much about gaps (whether arithmetic or geometric), no matter how much intellectuals, academics and some businessmen may profess to do.

In Kahn's view the world will continue to be conveniently fragmented: 'The task is not to see that these societies proceed along the same path as Europe, North America and Japan, but that each should find its own way'. Later (pp. 165-6) he writes: 'Most of the current no-growth advocates argue for a redistribution of resources as opposed to continued growth as a means of improving the current quality of life ...

... our conclusion (is) that it is both safer and more rewarding to move forward with caution and prudence on the present course than to try to stop or even to slow down generally.'

The view of Forrester (1971) is also that the gap will not be closed:

> There may be no realistic hope of the present underdeveloped countries reaching the standard of living demonstrated by the present industrialized nations. The pollution and natural-resource load placed on the world environmental system by each person in an advanced country is probably twenty to fifty

times greater than the load now generated by a person in an underdeveloped country. With four times as many people in underdeveloped countries as in the present developed countries, their rising to the economic level that has been set as a standard by the industrialized nations could mean an increase of ten times in the natural-resource and pollution load on the world environment. Noting the destruction that has already occurred on land, in the air, and especially in the oceans, capability appears not to exist for handling such a rise in standard of living. In fact, the present disparity between the developed and underdeveloped nations may be equalized as much by a decline in the developed countries as by an improvement in the underdeveloped countries.

Mesarovic and Pestel (1975) also write off the prospect of closing the development gap, but with regret rather than as something desirable (p. 58): 'Not only does the economic gap between rich and poor regions not narrow, but it increases considerably in terms of ratios and appallingly in absolute terms .... If one relies on the prevailing economic patterns, trying to close the gap might as well be forgotten. The present trends and attitudes are apparently loaded heavily against narrowing. The crises in the economic gap are clearly not only persistent but even worsening.'

Eyre (1978) sees little prospect of most developing countries becoming industrialized (p. 107): 'All the evidence of the mid-1970s indicates that the imminent arrival on the world scene of new industrial nations, with few exceptions, must be regarded with scepticism'. He also draws attention to the very limited amount of aid being given by rich to poor countries: 'The point that has not been emphasized sufficiently, however, is that if the volume of this aid rises no higher than what one might call the "survival threshold", then all it can do is keep alive large numbers of people in hunger and ignorance. Far, far more is required to ensure that sufficient funds are available to reduce the number of births to a point where people do not just come into existence to suffer malnutrition or even, ultimately, to die of hunger.'

The above authors, like many others, recognize that there is a development gap, note that it is widening, and lament it. Either explicitly or implicitly, so many people assume that it is through the greed of the rich countries or for political or organizational reasons that nothing can be done about the development gap. Many talk of transferring money from rich to poor countries, but there are few references to the *real* quantities of goods or people that would have to be moved around the world to make transfers on the scale required. Keyfitz (1976), however, described the world situation in less conventional terms:

> How much economic development is possible? Surely the planet and its materials are finite and not even all its present four billion people can live like Americans, let alone the six or eight billion that on present trends will be alive when a stationary world population is established. Indeed, there is doubt whether the 250 million people expected to populate the U.S. in the year 2000 will be able to live as Americans do today. How far, then, can industrial society spread through the preindustrial world before it reaches a ceiling imposed by space, raw materials and waste disposal?

He notes the magnitude of the development gap and points out (pp. 32-3) that the inhabitant of a developed country uses five times as many resources as the inhabitant of a developing country. He assesses the implications of a strategy to share world income evenly:

> The division of a total number of dollars by a number of individuals to obtain an average per head has a long tradition; dividing one number by another is an innocent operation and without any necessary implication that everyone obtains the average, and yet it puts thoughts into people's minds. The first thought might be that things are not bad with 881 dollars per head for the entire global population — a conservative conclusion. The second thought might be that things would indeed not be bad if the total was actually divided up — a radical viewpoint that has been voiced often in recent years. Income is an aspect of a way of life, however, and only a trifling part of a way of life is directly transferable.

The above argument is reasonable in a world context, though it is reminiscent of the view of the rich that the poor would not know what to do with more wealth (or income). Given a new house with a bathroom and bath they would 'keep the coal in the bath'. Keyfitz goes on (p. 29): 'Moreover, to discuss massive transfers of capital would be futile for political reasons even if it were economically practical: the declining U.S. foreign-aid budget shows how unappealing to the major donor this path to world development is'.

In the view of the present author, the major contribution of the above paper of Keyfitz to development studies is his recognition of more than one kind of developing country. It was shown in Chapter

9 of the present book that some cells, though with low gross national product per inhabitant and a low level of technology, have large natural resources per inhabitant. Like Eyre, Keyfitz recognizes the importance of having adequate natural resources, though he does not define them at any length or distinguish between different kinds (p. 30):

> To speak of developed and less developed countries is an improvement on treating the world as being homogeneous, but it has been overtaken by the events of the past three years. Where two categories of countries once sufficed, we now find we cannot do with fewer than four.
>
> The shifts in raw-material prices have created resource-rich countries such as Abu Dhabi and Venezuela, whose wealth is comparable to that of the developed countries, which by way of contrast can be called capital-rich. Some countries that were poor have actually been developing, including Singapore, Korea, Taiwan and Hong Kong. Finally there are the many countries that are truly poor, lacking (in relation to their population) both capital and resources. We have, then, the resource-rich countries, the capital-rich countries, the developing countries and the poor countries. Specifically identifying and classifying all cases to provide numbers for population in these groups is not easy. (Indonesia has resources but not enough so that any likely rise in prices would make its 135 million people rich.) The new categories of resource-rich and developing countries might be defined in such a way that they total 200 million people each; the fact remains that most of the world's people are in countries that have no leverage through either control of capital or control of resources.

Broadly, then, the experts in developed countries accept that the development gap is here to stay for a long time. Such a view of the state of the world at the end of the 1970s is expressed in the World Bank Report, quoted by Peiris (1979) in an article with the amusing though depressing title: 'McNamara sees dark at the end of the tunnel'.

> In their view the growth figures of the economies of the developing nations for the entire decade up to 1978 do not 'provide any hope that the so-called "gap" between the developing and industrialized world might be narrowing'. More despairingly, the report predicts: 'Even if the developing countries were to manage to double their *per capita* growth

rate, while the industrialized world but maintained its, it would take almost a century to clear the absolute gap between them, so great are the differences in the capital and technological base of the two groups'.

The rest of this chapter is an attempt to show why the closing of the development gap in a few decades would be very difficult.

10.2   What transfers can be made?

Most transactions between countries and even within countries take the form of some kind of exchange. The main flows in international trade were described in Chapter 6. This chapter is about the net transfers that would have to be made between pairs of regions, the 100 cells, to achieve various goals. Such transfers take place already in the world in the form of aid or gifts, or, it could be argued, in the form of loans on favourable repayment terms. On the whole they do not involve great sacrifices on the part of the population of the donating regions. Nor do they make much impact overall. Private donations by charitable institutions from rich countries to poor ones transfer about 1/1000 as much as would be needed to change the present inequality in living standards in the world greatly. Government aid transfers amount to perhaps 1/100 of what would be needed.

In order to help to identify the transfers that are possible and meaningful a model has been constructed. There is no point in making a model unless it helps to show more clearly or in more simple terms a situation that is highly complex or a situation about which people's idea are woolly and their discussion confused. It is hoped that the model shown in Figure 10.1 covers adequately the development situation in the world and will be comprehensible to the reader. It is an elaboration of models presented in Chapter 2 in Figures 2.9-2.11.

Four kinds of ingredient are represented by four different shapes of box in Figure 10.1. The shape of each type of box has been chosen purely for convenience and has no special significance.

(1) The hexagon A represents total population.

(2) Triangular boxes B(1)-B(4) represent natural resources, subdivided as in Chapter 7 into land resources, fossil fuels (here energy), non-fuel minerals, and territory (here potential natural resources).

(3) Diamond-shaped boxes C(1)-C(5) represent means of production. The three categories C(1)-C(3) produce from natural

resources. Examples of C(1) would be tractors or fertilizers and of C(2) and C(3) mining equipment. Box C(4) represents all kinds of manufacturing establishment and C(5) all kinds of non-goods producers, such as schools and hospitals.

(4) Square boxes D(1)-D(5) represent products. One subset of products, D(1)-D(3), comes direct from natural resources. Such products usually receive some kind of processing near where they are grown or extracted (e.g. processing of sugar cane, concentrating of metal ores). Another subset of products, D(4/1)-D(4/4), comes from manufacturing. Of the four categories of product distinguished here, three categories are for producer or capital goods and one category is for consumer goods. The producer goods are used for the maintenance or expansion of productive capacity in three sectors of means of production, C(1)-C(3) to produce from raw materials, C(4) to go back into manufacturing itself, and C(5) to go to services (hospital beds, school desks). The third subset of products, D(5), consist of services, the term being used here in a very broad sense.

Various kinds of link between different boxes are indicated in Figure 10.1. The line of open circles represents discovery and incorporation of new natural resources from the potential pile, a process related to the size of the potential itself, the intensity of exploration for minerals, and the rate of 'improvement' of land for cultivation. The broken lines are the supply of labour to the five boxes representing means of production. The links indicated by the double lines and the solid black lines are the flow of goods and services. The double line symbol indicates flows within the region under consideration while the solid black one indicates flows between the region under consideration and other regions. All the internal flows are one-way, while all the external flows can be two-way.

Not all possible links are shown in Figure 10.1. For example fossil fuels from the natural resources pile for energy can be moved into the raw materials box (e.g. for plastics) and in the future, after processing, might even provide food. Means of production can be taken from one region where they have already been used (but not to the full) and transferred to another region, as for example factories from a war zone to a safe area or aircraft from the airline of a rich country to the airline of a poor one. No allowance is made in the diagram for such a transfer.

The aim of the whole system is to cater for and if possible satisfy the needs of the population of the region, represented in the hexagonal box A. Food, materials, manufactured consumer goods, and services pass into A. They end up respectively as energy to

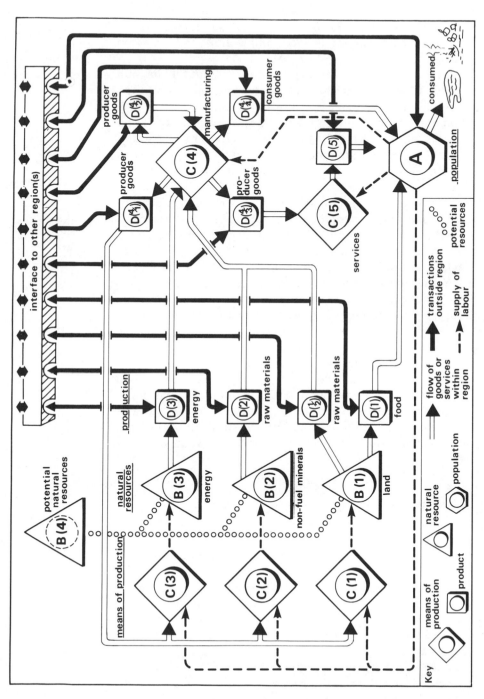

Figure 10.1 The relationship between natural resources, means of production, population, and production. See also Figures 2.9–2.11. See text for explanation

'drive' humans, as smoke from the fuel used to warm them or carry them about, on the scrap heap as worn-out appliances or as containers, or even in books on development, waiting to be read on their bookshelves.

For the purpose of this chapter, the vital point about the diagram is that it helps to show what can and what cannot be transferred between regions. Ten different possible transfers into or out of a given region are indicated in Figure 10.1. They are either goods and services produced, or people (box A). Four of the products, D(1), D(1/2), D(2), and D(3), are from natural resources and are thought of as food, raw materials (mineral or plant and animal), and fuels (or energy). Four products are from the manufacturing sector. One rather nebulous set of products comes under the heading of services. The final item is migrating population.

Trade is an exchange of products between regions. Investment is a special exchange particularly of producer goods in boxes D(4/1)-D(4/3). It could be from a developed country to be placed either in another developed country or in a developing one as a means of production. Something comes back, or is expected back, in return. In the transfer of population between two regions usually more people migrate in one direction than another, giving a bias in one direction.

It is hoped that the diagram has indicated most of the major types of possible transfer between regions. In the next section an attempt is made to assess whether it would in reality be feasible to make net transfers on a world scale large enough to eliminate or reduce the imbalances in the availability of natural resources and means of production shown in Chapters 7 and 8 to exist between the 100 cells.

10.3   World distributions of natural resources and production and possible transfers

In Chapters 7 and 8 Lorenz curve diagrams were used to show the distribution of various natural resources and production in the world and gini coefficients of concentration were given. Data are presented in a concise form in Table 10.1 to show concentration of each of 10 distributions. The theoretical transfers that would be needed to even them out in the world are estimated. Table 10.1 will now be referred to.

The column headed 'Gini' shows the gini coefficient of concentration of each distribution in the world as a whole. The columns numbered (1)-(10) each represent 10 cells and therefore 10 percent

Table 10.1 Distributions

Distribution	Gini	(1)	(2)	(3)	(4)	(5)	(6)	(7)	(8)	(9)	(10)	Transfer (%)
(i) Fossil fuel reserves	0.840	73	16	7	2	1	1	0	0	0	0	69
		+63	+6	−3	−8	−9	−9	−10	−10	−10	−10	
(ii) Non-fuel mineral resources	0.808	70	16	6	4	2	1	1	0	0	0	66
		+60	+6	−4	−6	−8	−9	−9	−10	−10	−10	
(iii) Territory	0.694	57	18	9	5	4	2	2	1	1	1	55
		+47	+8	−1	−5	−6	−8	−8	−9	−9	−9	
(iv) Land resources	0.397	34	15	10	9	7	6	6	5	5	3	33
		+24	+5	0	−1	−3	−4	−4	−5	−5	−7	
(v) All resources (i–iv)	0.621	50	19	8	7	4	4	3	2	2	1	49
		+40	+9	−2	−3	−6	−6	−7	−8	−8	−9	
(vi) Non-fuel mineral production	0.781	62	19	10	5	2	1	1	0	0	0	61
		+52	+9	0	−5	−8	−9	−9	−10	−10	−10	
(vii) Energy production	0.768	59	22	10	4	3	1	1	0	0	0	61
		+49	+12	0	−6	−7	−9	−9	−10	−10	−10	
(viii) Steel production	0.780	62	20	10	6	2	0	0	0	0	0	62
		+52	+10	0	−4	−8	−10	−10	−10	−10	−10	
(ix) Energy consumption	0.655	46	24	14	6	4	2	1	1	1	1	54
		+36	+14	+4	−4	−6	−8	−9	−9	−9	−9	
(x) Gross national product	0.642	43	26	14	7	3	2	2	1	1	1	53
		+33	+16	+4	−3	−7	−8	−8	−9	−9	−9	

of the total population of the world. A Lorenz curve is constructed on the basis of the density or concentration of a given item, in this case against population. What the table is showing can be appreciated with the help of the example of fossil fuel reserves in the first row.

The value of 73 in column (1) for fossil fuel reserves indicates that 73 percent of all world fossil fuel reserves, as estimated by the author, are concentrated in just 10 cells, with about 10 percent of the population of the world. They are the 10 cells with the highest amounts of fossil fuels per inhabitant. The next 10 cells with regard to fossil fuel reserves per inhabitant, also with about 10 percent of the world's population, have another 16 percent of the fossil fuel reserves. The most poorly provided 40 cells have virtually no fossil fuels at all, the four zeros in columns (7), (8), (9), and (10). The second row of values against each item in Table 10.1 gives the percentage of the world total that would have to be transferred from some cells (the best provided) to other cells (the less well provided) to give every cell 1 percent of the world total of a given item, or to give every 10 cells 10 percent.

The concept of redistributing a resource or a product to achieve an even distribution can be represented graphically. Ten graphs are shown in Figures 10.3-10.6. If an item were distributed evenly according to population, each column in the graph would reach the 10 percent horizontal cut-off line. In fact all the items considered are highly concentrated in a small number of cells. In each graph the diagonal shading indicates the amount that would have to be moved out of the best provided sets of cells to the cells with a deficit, which would receive the amount indicated by shading with dots.

The percentage transfer score on each diagram shows how much of the world total actually has to be transferred to achieve equality. Fossil fuel reserves in Figure 10.3 will again serve as an example. The first and second groups of 10 cells have 73 percent and 16 percent of the world's fossil fuel reserves respectively. They only 'need' 10 percent each. To achieve an even distribution of fossil fuel reserves in the world they would have to transfer their (shaded) surpluses of 63 percent and 6 percent to the other eight groups of cells. Thus 69 of the fossil fuel units would have to be transferred.

Of the 10 items in Table 10.1 the first five (item (v) is the sum of items (i)-(iv)) could not in reality normally be transferred from one region, country or cell to another, only the products from the resources. Natural resources are on or in the ground in each cell. In certain circumstances, as illustrated in Figure 10.2, a transfer of natural resources could be made. Cells x and y each have 40 million

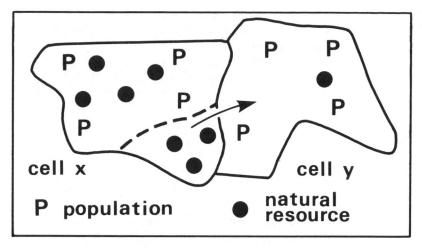

Figure 10.2 A possible way of transferring natural resources from one region to another

people but cell x has seven units of fossil fuel reserves, cell y only one. Part of the territory of cell x could be handed over to cell y. Such a philanthropic act of cession of territory with resources is almost unheard of in world history. For the purposes of this chapter it will be assumed that each cell, or in real world conditions each country, will retain all its territory and the resources therein and that a transfer of natural resources is not likely to occur.

In contrast to items (i)-(v) in Table 10.1, items (vi) to (x) can at least in theory be transferred between cells, as reference to the model in Figure 10.1 in the previous section will show. Non-fuel mineral production and energy production in that diagram are boxes D(2) and D(3) in the model. Steel production can be any of the four types of production from manufacturing. Energy consumption is energy production after a net inflow or outflow of energy from or to other regions (cells). Gross national product represents all goods and services produced, some perhaps double counted. Diagrams (6)-(10) in Figures 10.5 and 10.6 have more meaning than diagrams (1)-(5) in Figures 10.3 and 10.4 because given suitable institutions, control, and transportation facilities, the items they represent could be physically moved from cell to cell (or country to country). It is therefore interesting to note in Table 10.1 that items (vi)-(viii), non-fuel mineral production, energy production, and steel production, are all concentrated in the world to roughly the same degree, though not in exactly the same sets of cells.

The fact that energy consumption is less concentrated than energy production reflects the movement of sources of energy from energy-rich cells with high levels of production (e.g. Venezuela, Iran-Iraq) to energy-poor cells with low levels of production (e.g. France, Japan, Italy). The massive flows of fossil fuels in the world trade (international plus internal) only, however, produce roughly a limited shift in the gini coefficient. This is the difference in concentration between production and consumption in the world. This fact underlines the great increase that would have to be made in transfers of sources of energy to lower the concentration of energy consumption from its present gini coefficient of 0.655 down to zero or even to the low level of concentration of food consumption of around 0.100 (see Chapter 4). It should also be noted that the data as arranged by cells, as opposed to countries, include massive movements of energy between cells *within* the U.S.A. and the U.S.S.R., not recorded as international trade.

Gross national product, item (x) in Table 10.1, is highly concentrated, as can be seen in Figure 10.6, with a coefficient of 0.642. The degree of concentration is, however, less than when the calculation is made on the basis of countries.

10.4   The feasibility of making different kinds of transfer

It is clear that the world distributions of population, natural resources, and means of production are mismatched. In order to provide everyone with equal living standards, transfers of some kind from some parts of the world to other parts would be needed.

Four ingredients were discussed in Section 10.2 and considered to be essential in a study of development. Natural resources will not be considered as transferable in the study of transfers that follows. Products derived directly from natural resources such as coal, copper, and wheat are transferable. Similarly, means of production are regarded as fixed in location but producer goods, as means of production to be, can be moved. Thus four items will be considered as transferable between regions (countries or cells), population, producer goods, consumer goods, and services. Regions with a surplus of any of these items might theoretically make transfers to regions that are deficient in them.

Population could be moved from regions with few natural resources to regions with abundant natural resources. It could also be moved from regions with limited means of production to regions with a large productive capacity and a high level of technology. Alternatively, products could be moved to population. This movement would involve net transfers of goods, the giving away of part of the production of the rich cells to the poor ones. The transfers could take the form of the donation either of producer goods, which would enable the developing cells to build up their means of production, or of consumer goods (manufactures and food), which would raise their living standards but leave them dependent on charity.

The movement of products would be less of a problem, at least from the point of view of transportation, than the movement of population. The one-way 'trade' that would be needed to shift 'income' from rich to poor countries would involve quite different patterns and directions of flows of goods from those found in the world at present. Six general types of transfer will be discussed briefly in this section.

(1) *Population to natural resources.* Population could be moved from both developed and developing regions with poor natural resource population ratios to regions with abundant natural resources. Examples would be transfers of population from China and Japan to Siberia, from India and Indonesia to Australia, from West Europe to parts of Africa, from Northeast Brazil to the Amazon region of Brazil. Even if organizational and political obstacles could be overcome, a problem with the above kind of transfer is that some means of production would also have to be transferred with people to enable them to use the natural resources to which they were being moved. Moreover, it would hardly be humane to drop them in the middle of nowhere with no housing and amenities.

Such problems are, however, trivial compared with the task of actually moving enough people to natural resources to achieve roughly the same natural resource/population ratio everywhere in the world. Graph (5) in Figure 10.4 shows that to spread natural resources evenly according to population, about half the natural resources of the world would have to be reallocated among the 100 cells. By definition, natural resources may not be moved. The same effect could, however, be achieved by moving half of the population of the world, or some 2000 million people, from about 75 'crowded' cells to about 25 'uncrowded' ones as defined by abundance or lack of natural resources.

To put the movement of 2000 million people in perspective, flows that have actually taken place may be noted. Between the 1870s and the 1930s about 50 million people emigrated from Europe. During 1881-1930 about 8 million per decade went, 40 million altogether, mainly to the Americas and Australasia. In over three decades since the Second World War, tens of millions of temporary migrants have moved between poorer and more prosperous parts of Europe. In the U.S.S.R. a few million people have

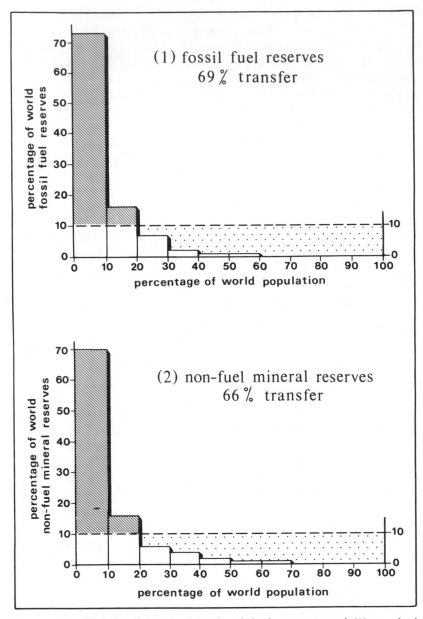

Figure 10.3 The distribution of (1) fossil fuel reserves and (2) non-fuel mineral reserves according to population, and hypothetical transfers needed to achieve equality

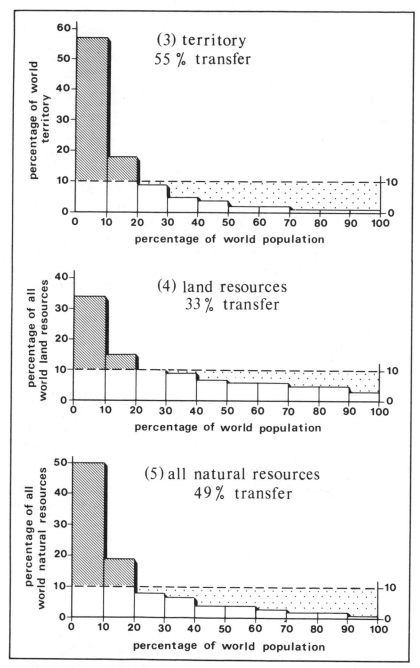

Figure 10.4 the distribution of (3) territory, (4) land resources, and (5) all natural resources according to population, and hypothetical transfers needed to achieve equality

moved from European U.S.S.R. into Asiatic U.S.S.R. in recent decades, though there has been a net migration back since the 1960s.

(2) *Population to means of production.* Population would be moved from areas with small productive capacity to areas with large productive capacity. There would be transfers of population, for example, from India to West Europe, from Latin America to the U.S.A. The possibilities of creating new jobs in a region would depend to a considerable extent in fact on the presence there of natural resources, or on products derived from natural resources in other regions.

There are at least three major reasons why it is unlikely that the movement of large numbers of people to areas with a high level of productive capacity would be acceptable. Firstly, the mechanization, and later automation, the productivity of labour has been increasing enormously in many sectors of the world economy in recent decades. A small proportion of a total population can produce enough to keep a whole population affluent. Secondly, people who migrated from a developing to a developed country would generally lack the educational levels and technical skills needed in an industrial society. Thirdly, cultural conflicts could be anticipated.

Often the 'wrong' people have been the ones to migrate internationally. An example is the large flow of doctors to the U.S.A. from developing countries described by Mick (1975). By 1973 more than a fifth of physicians practising medicine in North America had graduated from medical schools outside the region. He remarks: 'the underdeveloped nations are educating thousands of physicians who ultimately end up practising in what is perhaps the most developed nation of all'.

(3) *Producer goods to natural resources.* Such a flow of goods is a conspicuous part of world trade at present. This type of movement takes place both between developed countries (e.g. U.S. commercial airliners to West Germany and Japan) and from developed to developing countries (e.g. European mining equipment to Zambia and Bolivia). Much of the sophisticated equipment and machinery exported from developed to developing countries, especially that used in extractive industries, extracts fuel and mineral raw materials and prepares them for export back to the industrial countries. Only a limited number of the less industrialized cells are well enough endowed with natural resources to be able to make wide use of producer goods in agriculture and mining. Many of the poorer cells have few mineral reserves. Their agricultural land usually has such large numbers of

persons employed per unit of area that rapid mechanization of the agricultural sector would cause more problems than it solved. On the other hand the transfer of fertilizers, pesticides, and other such means of production from industrial countries to developing ones could produce higher yields.

(4) *Producer goods to population.* This transfer is the reverse of the transfer described in (2), the transfer of population to means of production. One is putting new jobs where people are, rather than taking people to jobs. Labour intensive activities have been located in areas with large local populations. In the nineteenth century it was not long before textile machinery made in Britain was exported to many parts of the world. Since the Second World War labour intensive jobs have been established by U.S. firms in such developing countries as Taiwan and Haiti as well as in the U.S.'s own dependency, Puerto Rico, to use the abundant cheap labour there. A somewhat bizarre example is the sending of mica to India to be split into very thin sheets by hand labour. In the U.S.S.R., many new light industrial establishments have been put in urban centres in areas with few natural resources. The application of this category of transfer would require the developed countries to be prepared to lose much of their industrial capacity to developing ones and to import far more manufactured goods from developing countries than they do at present, and presumably fewer from each other.

(5) *Consumer goods to population.* With this form of transfer the developed countries would continue to have a large share of the world's consumer goods industry but would give away part of the production. In addition to consumer manufactures, food may be regarded as a consumer item. The prospect for the next few decades seems to be that some of the developed cells will be the only ones left with a large surplus of food and they would have to transfer some of this, as the U.S.A. has done in emergencies, to many developing countries and would also have to supply food-deficient countries such as West Germany and the U.K.

(6) *Services to population.* On the whole services are provided lcoally and cannot be 'transported' far. In other words, people move to services such as hospitals and schools. Students from developing countries receiving *free* higher education in developed ones (and then returning to their countries of origin) could be transferring a service from a rich to a poor country. The transfer of a service from a developed to a developing country would involve the movement of materials (means of production) to set up and equip buildings in developing countries as well as the secondment (at the expense of the developed countries) of experts to help to

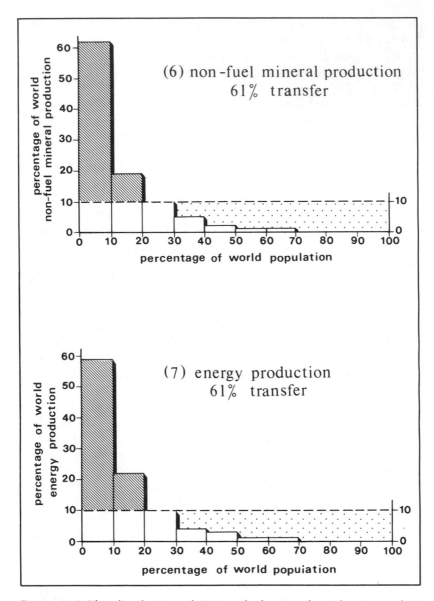

Figure 10.5 The distribution of (6) non-fuel mineral production and (7) energy production according to population, and hypothetical transfers needed to achieve equality

Figure 10.6 (Opposite) The distribution of (8) steel production, (9) energy consumption, and (10) gross national product, and hypothetical transfers needed to achieve equality

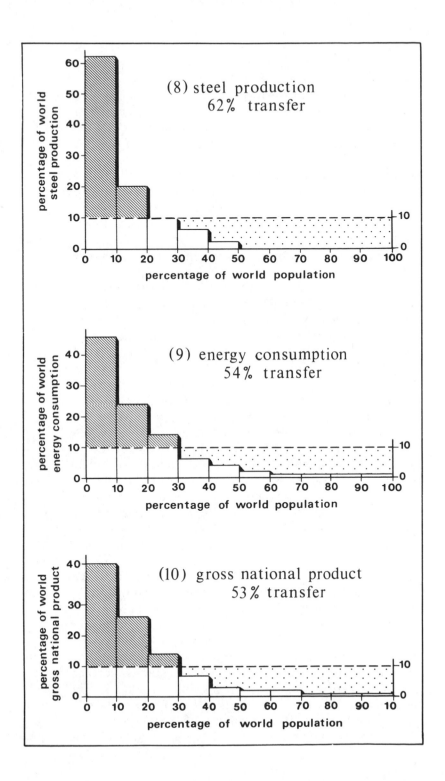

establish and initially run the service. An example is the policy of a certain publisher to sell books only in hard cover form in Britain and in (cheaper) soft cover form in developing countries.

The above account of six possible types of transfer of people or products from one region of the world to another is only a brief review of a very complex situation and problem. On the whole it is probably easier for all concerned to transfer goods rather than people and in the end more important to transfer producer goods rather than consumer goods, since producer goods help to reduce the dependence of developing countries on developed ones. The continuing transference of food and consumer manufactures from developed to developing countries would narrow the gap between the living standards in rich and poor countries but it would leave the recipients in the position of living on world aid or charity indefinitely.

The general arithmetic and logistics of what would have to be done to have an 'equal' world have now been discussed. The transfers needed, even if unanimously authorized by the representatives of the countries of the world, could not be carried out quickly. They would have to be carried out over a period of time. There follows a brief review of a hypothetical transfer of population from resource-poor to resource-rich cells, the transfer of type (1). Instead of transferring 2000 million people between cells, the number required roughly to redeploy population evenly over natural resources, a mere 400 million are transferred.

The transfer to be described is intended to reduce the pressure of people in cells poor in natural resources and to shift them to cells rich in natural resources. Although the basis is the 100 cells, there could actually be movements of people *within* cells themselves, as from eastern to northern Canada. People of all age groups and of all professions, skilled and unskilled, would have to be transferred, not just those of employable age or those with certain skills.

Ten major and 10 lesser resource-rich cells are chosen to receive population. Altogether in the mid-1970s they had some 800 million inhabitants (20 percent of the population of the world). Ten of the 20 cells would each receive about 25 million people and 10 each about 15 million. About 400 million people, or 10 percent of the total population of the world, would therefore be transferred.

The cells providing 'surplus' population are those suffering from acute pressure of population on natural resources, whether they are basically agricultural like Java and Bangladesh or highly industrialized like Japan and parts of West Europe. The eligibility of cells to lose population would be assessed on their natural resource/population ratios. About 50 cells would be eligible to send from 5 to 10 million each into the 20 receiving cells. The allocation might be as follows:

Europeans to North America

South Asians to Latin America

Chinese elsewhere within China or to Siberia

Japanese and some other East Asians to Australia

Political and cultural problems that would arise from the above mass transfers make them unrealistic in practice. The physical problems in making such shifts over three to four decades are equally formidable though less widely appreciated. To move 'enough' Russians into Siberia, several trains per day would have to leave European U.S.S.R. with migrants. To move a few million Brazilians from coastal regions into Amazonia would involve fleets of lorries and buses running over non-existent or bad roads for decades to come. How much shipping would be needed to move 10 percent of the 1975 population of the world between cells in a few decades? Ten million people *per year* is an enormous number. In peak decades of migration from Europe to the Americas and Australia in the late nineteenth and early twentieth centuries the numbers were some 10 million *per decade*.

Even the transfer of 400 million people in 30-40 years would only make a slight difference to disparities in the world. During that period there would probably be an increase through natural growth of 1200 million inhabitants in the cells losing population, in spite of the outflow described above.

10.5 Transfers of steel on a world scale

Another approach to the problem of achieving equality in the world is exemplified by a hypothetical steel-equalizing operation. It comes under the headings described in Section 10.3 of moving products, whether producer or consumer, to population. The author is neither advocating the operation nor implying that it is feasible but is using it to bring home the massive scale of transfers needed to carry it out.

A considerable amount of steel enters world trade, though usually with value added to the material itself. A tonne of steel razor blades might be several hundred times the value of a tonne of steel itself. A comparison of production and consumption of steel in developing countries shows that each year in the mid-1970s they imported, almost all from developed countries, 30-35 million tonnes of steel, much of it in the form of manufactured goods. There was also a large movement of steel, again much of it as manufactured goods, traded among developed countries themselves. The U.S.A., for example, had a net inflow of between 10 and 20 million tonnes a year in the early 1970s and Japan a net outflow of between 20 and 40 million tonnes a year in the same period, some though not all of Japan's exports going to developed countries. It will be shown that to achieve equal consumption of steel per inhabitant throughout the world about 10 times as much steel would have to be moved between different parts of the world as is moved now in trade.

The two following assumptions are made in the operation to be described: each of the 100 cells that produces a bigger share of the world output of steel than its share of world population gives away the surplus, and each of the 100 cells that produces a smaller share of world steel output than its share of world population (or produces no steel at all) receives the deficit. The calculations in this operation are only approximate. They are based on the upper diagram of Figure 10.6.

A cell can have either a 'surplus' of steel production, a 'balance' or a 'deficit'. For example cell 19, Ural-Siberia, has 1 percent of the world's population but produces 7½ percent (or 7½ units) of the world's steel. In the exercise being carried out here, 6½ units of the steel would have to be transferred from cell 19 to deficit cells. In contrast, many cells produce no steel at all and each therefore has a complete deficit, consequently requiring 1 unit. The transfers that would be needed to give an exactly even consumption of steel in the world according to population require that 62 percent of the world's steel production should be moved between cells. The situation is illustrated in Figure 10.7.

In the year under consideration, 1975, the total world production was 643 million tonnes, so each 1 percent or 1 unit is about 6½ million tonnes. Four kinds of cell are identified:

1. Those with a 'surplus'. The surplus is indicated in each cell as a percentage of total world steel production.
2. Those in which production is about 1 percent of the world's total. Such cells have a 'balance'.
3. Those which produce between about 0.25 and 0.75 of the world's steel and therefore have a partial 'deficit'.
4. Those which produce less than 0.25 percent of the world's steel and which have a near-complete 'deficit' together with those that produce no steel at all and therefore have a complete 'deficit'.

In the map in Figure 10.7 some cells have for convenience been moved from familiar positions. Cells 1-30, except for cell 20 (South

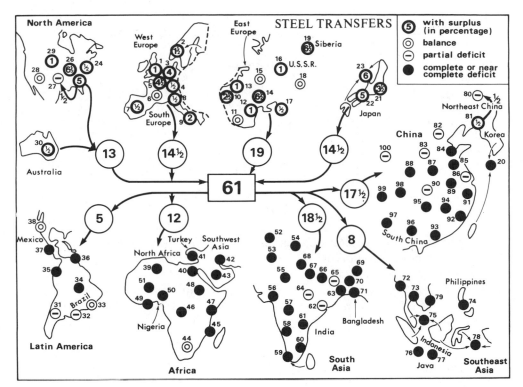

Figure 10.7 The scale of hypothetical steel transfers from 'surplus' to 'deficit' cells needed to achieve equality of steel consumption in the world

Korea, Taiwan, Hong Kong), are lined up side by side along the upper part of the map. The remaining cells are along the lower and right-hand sides of the map.

Of the 29 cells in the developed world, 23 have some 'surplus' of steel, five are roughly balanced, and one is partially deficient. Of the 71 cells in the less developed world, one in China has a small surplus, three (Mexico, part of Brazil, and South Africa) are roughly balanced, 11 have a partial deficit, and the rest, 56 in all (the black dots), have little or no production.

To even out steel consumption, two small transfers have to be made within regions, one in North America, one in China. The remaining transfers, 61 percent of all the steel produced in the world, would leave the developed cells and be transferred to cells in the developing countries. Table 10.2 shows the percentages lost and gained.

The purpose of the steel transfer operation has been to show the scale of movement of transfer that would be needed to achieve

Table 10.2 Transfers of steel

From	Percentage	To	Percentage
North America and Australia	13	Latin America	5
West Europe	14½	Africa and Southwest Asia	12
East Europe and U.S.S.R.	19	South Asia	18½
Japan	14½	Southeast Asia	8
		China	17½
	61		61

equality in steel consumption throughout the world. The exercise shows that some 400-500 million tonnes of steel would have to be moved a year. It is the feasibility of this kind of transfer that is being questioned, not the equally serious but more obvious problem of how the steel would be used in the developing regions once it arrived there.

10.6   The miniature world of the U.S.S.R.

The problems of development in the U.S.S.R. are similar in some respects to those in the world as a whole. The U.S.S.R. is the largest country in the world in area, occupying nearly a sixth of the total land area. It had 263 million inhabitants in 1979. It is very diverse culturally and very well endowed economically, with a wide variety of natural resources. The experience of the U.S.S.R. in attempting to solve its own internal development problems can serve with reservation as a guide to the prospects for a larger world community organized to tackle the development gap.

In addition to the reasons given above as to why the U.S.S.R. can serve as a useful model, some other features should be borne in mind. Within the U.S.S.R. some regions are very well endowed with natural resources while others are relatively poorly provided. Some regions are highly industrialized while others depend heavily on agriculture. Means of production are virtually all owned by the state rather than privately by individuals or companies. They can therefore be controlled by the politicians and planners of the central government. The Communist Party of the Soviet Union has not only nearly complete control over the economic life of the country but also considerable control over the lives of its citizens.

The professed aim of the Soviet Communist Party is to achieve equally high living standards throughout the country both regionally and by classes of employment. That such an aim had not been anywhere near achieved by the late 1970s, even after six decades of Soviet rule, emerges clearly from a study of postwar Soviet statistical yearbooks. The example of availability of doctors was given in Chapter 3. Regional inequalities in retail sales per inhabitant and in the availability of services such as health and higher education had been reduced by the mid-1970s to about half their level in the late 1930s. On the other hand, since virtually all the goods and services consumed in the U.S.S.R. had increased considerably during the period in question, the *absolute* gap between consumption per inhabitant in the richest regions and in the poorest regions was actually higher in the mid-1970s than in the late 1930s. If equality has not been achieved in the Soviet Union, then the prospects for the world as a whole are indeed remote. Some aspects of the Soviet system will now be examined.

One reason why Soviet planners have found great difficulty in levelling out living standards is a familiar spatial problem. In their distribution over the national area, natural resources do not match population in the U.S.S.R. Another problem, partly related to the above, is that a worker in a given sector of the economy in one region may produce two or three times as much as a worker in the same sector of the economy in another region. Natural resources are more easily used or extracted in some circumstances than in others and workers in some regions are more 'mechanized' than workers doing the same job in other regions. Thus a Kuzbass coalminer, with no extra equipment, extracts about twice as much coal per shift as a Donbass coalminer because the coal seams are easier to work. A farm worker in northern Kazakhstan produces per man-hour or per season two or three times as much grain as one in Belorussia, both because he has better equipment and because conditions are easier for the application of mechanized means of production.

Differences in productivity per worker in the same sector of the economy and between sectors are to be expected. The problem is to reconcile equal living standards for all with unequal productivity. Transfers have to be made on a large scale in the U.S.S.R. to subsidize some regions with the help of others. Until the 1960s, however, it was accepted that collective farm workers in the agricultural sector would have a low standard of living, so living standards in rural areas tended to be considerably lower than those in urban areas.

It is not within the scope of the present book to give a detailed

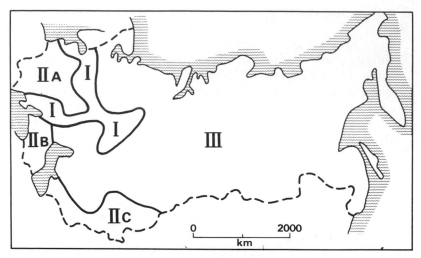

Figure 10.8 A regionalization of the U.S.S.R. See text for explanation

account of the U.S.S.R. and to bring all the evidence needed to support the points that are to be made. The subject is dealt with at some length by Cole (1981). There follows a brief account of the problem of inequality in the U.S.S.R. in which only the essential sectoral and spatial aspects are dealt with.

For the purpose of the argument that follows, three types of region may be identified in the U.S.S.R. Their location is shown in Figure 10.8. Twenty equal population cells each with about 13 million people, or 5 percent of the total Soviet population, are shown in Figure 10.9 (upper map) together with selected resources and means of production (lower map). Basic data about the three regions (I-III) are given in Table 10.3.

Region I contains most of the older industrial areas of the U.S.S.R., still highly industrialized but drawing increasingly on other parts of the country for energy, plant and mineral raw materials, and food. It is comparable on a world scale with West Europe and Japan and to some extent with Soviet Comecon partners in East Europe.

Region II is more rural and more dependent on agriculture than region I. The part of the region indicated as IIA contains a European population, consisting mainly of Ukrainians and Belorussians. Its economy was badly affected in the Second World War and it has only a slowly increasing population. Parts IIB (Transcaucasia) and IIC (Central Asia) of region II have Asian, non-Slav populations. They became colonies of the Russian Empire in the nineteenth century, are less developed than the U.S.S.R. in general, and have

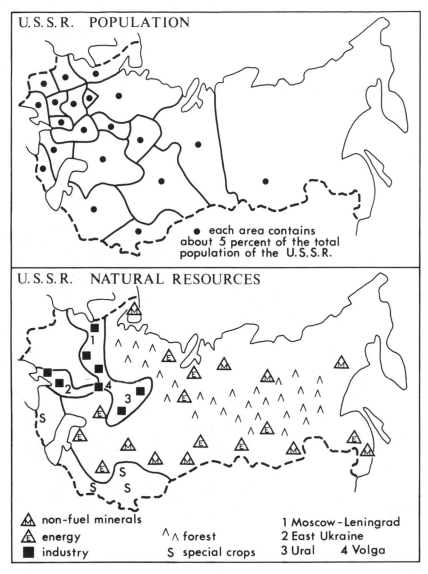

Figure 10.9 The distribution of population (upper map) and of natural resources (lower map) in the U.S.S.R.

fast growing populations. Regions IIB and IIC of the U.S.S.R. are comparable on a world scale with many developing countries.

Region III occupies about 75 percent of the total area of the U.S.S.R. but contains only about 25 percent of the total population. It has at least half of the 'land' resources of the U.S.S.R., counting

Table 10.3 Features of three Soviet regions

| | Percentage shares | | |
	Region I	Region II	Region III
Population	30	45	25
Area	10	15	75
Agricultural land	20	40	40
Forest	10	5	85
Fishing	20	30	50
Fossil fuels	15	10	75
Non-fuel minerals	5	15	80
Heavy industry	60	20	20
Light industry	60	30	10

forests and pastures as well as agricultural land, and about 75 percent of the mineral reserves of the country. It is becoming increasingly industrialized. Region III is comparable on a world scale with Australia, Canada, and part of the U.S.A.

A very generalized but basic distinction may now be made between the three regions outlined above. Region I is highly industrialized and has a fairly high level of productivity per worker but is poor in natural resources. Region II is weakly industrialized, has a low level of productivity per worker, and is poor in natural resources. Region III is moderately industrialized, has a very high level of productivity, and is very well endowed with natural resources. Under these circumstances present living standards might be expected to be high and future prospects bright for region III. In reality region I has living standards comparable with those in region III because it is subsidized by net transfers of products from region III. Region II has low living standards and is not apparently subsidized to any great extent by the other two regions.

Enormous quantities of goods are moved over great distances in the U.S.S.R. The rail system still carries about three-fifths of the tonne-kilometres but pipelines now handle most of the oil and natural gas. Since different regions specialize in different products, internal trade reflects the exchange of these, supposedly on a rational and equable basis. In the 1970s the main flows of major categories of goods in internal Soviet trade were those shown in Figure 10.10, diagrams a and b. Region III supplies region I with many kinds of primary product. Region II supplies region I with a more limited range and quantity of primary products, including subtropical items such as cotton, tea, and citrus fruits, only grown in regions IIB and IIC. In return, region I supplies regions II and III

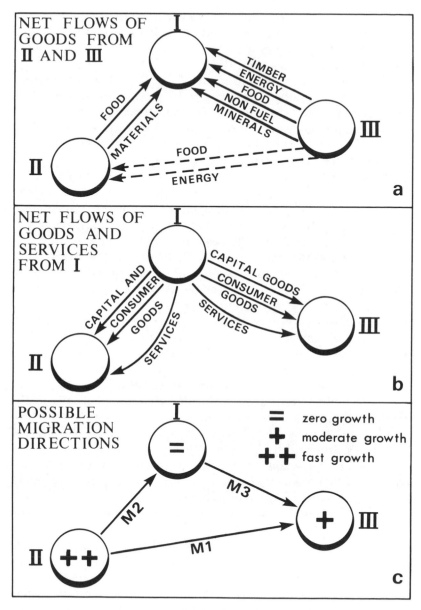

Figure 10.10 Flows of goods, services, and population between the three regions of the U.S.S.R. shown in Figure 10.8

with both producer goods and consumer manufactures as well as with services, though regions II and III do themselves also produce these items. In addition, a certain quantity of food and energy enters region IIC from region III.

When one examines the production of goods in the three regions of the U.S.S.R., it appears that region III produces about twice as much per inhabitant as region I. On the other hand, the level of consumption of goods and services per inhabitant is roughly equal in regions I and III. The level of consumption is considerably lower in region II than in the other two regions.

Although it is impossible from Soviet published data to compare precisely the value of goods sent from region I to region III and from region III to region I, there seems no doubt that the value of the latter greatly exceeds the value of the former. Region I is therefore being subsidized by region III. Put in another way, the terms of trade between regions I and III are greatly biased in favour of region I. If one looks for a comparable situation elsewhere in the world, it is as if Canada was sending its primary products to the U.S.A. and receiving manufactured goods from the U.S.A. on very unfavourable terms. Some might argue that this is what actually happens at present. It would be more 'just' for region III to subsidize region II rather than, or as well as, region I. It is perhaps no coincidence, however, that in region I most of the population is Russian while in region II most is non-Russian.

Soviet planners are faced with some difficult decisions in the next decade or two. Future investment in expanding the means of production has to be allocated both by sectors of the economy and by regions. It would help region II if much new investment were placed there, but many of the natural resources with the lowest costs to exploit are in region III. The amount of capital investment in region III is up to four times as high per inhabitant as in region II. Region I also receives more investment per inhabitant than region II.

In Section 10.4, six possible transfers between regions of the world were discussed. In the Soviet Union such transfers actually occur, though they cannot be quantified. By examining these transfers in the Soviet context, the nature of the world situation may be better appreciated. The reader should refer to Figure 10.10.

(1) *Population to natural resources.* It would be reasonable to move population from regions I and II to region III because the natural resource population ratio is far higher in region III than in the other two regions. There is little movement of population from region II to region III, though with fast population growth in regions IIB and IIC, pressure is growing on natural resources. There are both

cultural and environmental reasons against moving people from Transcaucasia and Central Asia into Siberia. On the other hand, attempts to attract large numbers of people from region I to region III have failed dismally. Living conditions on the whole are more pleasant in region I than in region III and people have drifted back to the comparatively more attractive climate and urban life of European U.S.S.R.

(2) *Population to means of production.* It might make sense to transfer population from region II to region I, from 'developing' areas with fast growing population to 'developed', industrialized areas. There seems little movement of this kind.

(3) *Producer goods to natural resources.* A great deal of investment is taking place in region III and this is a solution to the imbalance between population and natural resources. Much of the work in region III is by its nature dependent on mechanization and a comparatively small labour force is therefore required.

(4) *Producer goods to population.* This would involve putting many new industries in region II. But such a policy could be self-defeating because production costs tend to be high in region II, which would depend also on raw materials from region III for its industries. Soviet sources even refer to resistance in Asian areas to the introduction of a modern industrial way of life. A policy of modernization would benefit region II materially, but would not be advantageous to the economy of the U.S.S.R. as a whole.

(5) *Consumer goods to population.* Region II could be subsidized by consumer manufactures from region I and food from region III.

(6) *Services to population.* Region I provides services to various kinds for regions II and III.

Although the picture of the U.S.S.R. described above is very generalized and greatly simplified, the following conclusion can be drawn: region II gives little to the other two regions and gets little from them. Soviet development is a dialogue between regions I and III. This message could be of the utmost importance in a study of the world development gap. If developing countries shut themselves off from the influence of developed ones, refusing investment and turning from trade to self-sufficiency, the world trading system would be concentrated even more than now on links between resource-rich and resource-poor parts of the rich countries.

In fairness to the achievements of the Communist Party of the Soviet Union, one should point out that regions IIB and IIC, Transcaucasia and Central Asia, are probably much better off materially than they would have been if they had not been colonized and kept within the Russian-Soviet system. A comparison of the best-off with the worst-off regions of the U.S.S.R., that is

Latvia, Estonia, and Moscow with Azerbaijan and Tadjikistan, shows a disparity in living standards of at most 3 to 1. The gap between Sweden and Finland (close to Estonia) and Afghanistan (next to Tadjikistan) is anything from 20 to 1 to 50 to 1 depending on how it is assessed.

Nevertheless, if the Soviet model is anything to go by, then even in a centrally controlled world system, it could be difficult to integrate the developing countries (analogous to Soviet region II) with the developed world (analogous to Soviet regions I and III). West Europe, Japan, and Northeast U.S.A. will have prior claim to the fuels, non-fuel minerals, and food of Canada, Australia, and other 'empty' areas. The products will remain out of reach of such poor countries as India, China, Indonesia, and Bangladesh.

11

Recent trends and future prospects

11.1 Population change

The future size of the population of the world and its distribution by regions will be considered in this section. In the following sections recent trends in selected sectors of economic activity will be discussed and future prospects outlined.

In 1975 the population of the world was estimated to be about 4000 million. It was on this basis that each of the 100 cells used in this book could be given on average about 40 million inhabitants, though the estimates actually used to calculate the population of the cells were for a total world population of 3960 million.

In the late 1970s the population of the world was estimated by the Population Reference Bureau (1979) to be increasing by about 1.7 percent per year. The rate of change varies greatly from region to region in the world. As shown in Chapter 5, the fastest rates of increase are occurring in the developing countries.

There appears to be growing evidence that the rate of growth of population in some developing countries is beginning to slow down. For example during the 1960s world population was increasing by about 1.9 percent per year whereas by the late 1970s the rate had fallen to 1.7 percent per year. The absolute increase was, however, larger in 1978 than in 1970, being 73 million compared with 69 million. The increases in 1960 and 1950 were only 57 million and 43 million respectively. If a rate of increase of 1.7 percent per year were maintained for some decades the population of the world would still double in about 40 years.

Even if a downward trend in natural increase of population has started and is sustained, there is a very wide range between reasonable alternative future populations for the world. Frejka

(1973) anticipates a stationary world population of 8400 million by the year 2100 as the likely extrapolation of present world demographic trends, an estimate between two extreme projections for that year at 6000 million and at 15,000 million. Of the eventual stationary world population, less than 14 percent would live in

Table 11.1(a) Population in millions of the world 1750-2025 by regions

	1750	1925	1950	1975	2000	2025
W. Europe	105	250	290	343	388	400
E. Europe	40	90	103	130	152	160
U.S.S.R.	50	166	194	256	318	350
Japan*	40	90	114	165	212	230
N. America }	5	126	165	237	296	320
Australasia }		8	10	17	25	30
Latin America	30	100	165	324	620	770
S.W. Asia/N. Africa	50	80	121	187	364	460
Rest of Africa	60	120	155	321	660	860
S. Asia	150	360	450	819	1464	1770
S.E. Asia	70	130	173	327	599	800
China	230	380	470	840	1154	1350
World	830	1900	2410	3966	6252	7500

* Plus S. Korea, Taiwan, Hong Kong.
Source: Except 1925, 2025, Cole (1979, Table 10.1, p. 234).

Table 11.1(b) Rates of increase from data in Table 11.1(a)**

	1750-1925	1925-1950	1950-1975	1975-2000	2000-2025
W. Europe	238	116	118	113	103
E. Europe	225	114	126	117	105
U.S.S.R.	330	117	132	124	110
Japan*	285	127	145	128	108
N. America	2500	131	144	125	108
Australasia	4000	125	170	147	120
Latin America	330	165	196	191	124
S.W. Asia/N. Africa	160	151	155	195	126
Rest of Africa	200	129	207	206	130
S. Asia	240	125	182	179	121
S.E. Asia	185	133	189	185	134
China	165	124	179	137	117
World	230	127	165	158	120

* Plus S. Korea, Taiwan, Hong Kong.
** Original population = 100 each time.

Europe, the U.S.S.R., North America, and Oceania compared with about 28 percent in the early 1970s. Johnson (1979) quotes the estimate of Indian experts that India should reach zero population growth by 2071-81, by which time it would have 1600 million inhabitants. By then India alone would have more people than the whole of the developed world of the 1970s.

A regional breakdown of the population of the world is shown in Table 11.1(a) for 12 regions. The estimated or projected population is given for six different years. The data are very approximate for 1750. Those for 1925, 1950, and 1975 are based mainly on United Nations sources. The projection for 2000 is calculated from estimates of the Population Reference Bureau (*1975 World Population Data Sheet*). The population in 2025 has been estimated by the author. The percentage increase of population for each period is shown in Table 11.1(b).

Though the projected world population of about 6250 million for the year 2000 may not be reached by that year, it should be reached soon after. The figure of 6250 million has therefore been taken to be the population of the world somewhere between 2000 and 2005. The author's estimate of 7500 million for the year 2025 is based on a final stable world population of 8000 million, double the 1975 population of the world, by around the year 2050. This estimate is very 'optimistic' as it assumes a rapid change in demographic habits in developing world countries, starting in the 1970s.

It was explained in Chapter 6, Section C, how the world could be subdivided into equal population regions or 'cells'. The main features of the probable distribution of population in the world in the year 2000 can be brought out vividly with the help of a new map of cells for that year.

The population of the world in the year 2000 could be allocated to new cells in two different ways. There could either be 100 new cells, each with 1 percent of the population of the world in the year 2000, that is with an average of about 62.5 million inhabitants, or 156 cells, each with an average of about 40 million inhabitants, as in the 1975 breakdown.

It was decided to produce a new cell map for the year 2000 with 156 .cells, each with about 40 million inhabitants. The location of the new cells is shown in Table 11.2 and in Figure 11.1. To accommodate the 156 new cells, a redistricting procedure was applied to the existing system of 100 cells. Many of the 100 cells of 1975 were reduced considerably in area to make space for new ones.

Perhaps the clearest message from the above exercise is that only four new cells are needed to represent the estimated 160 million

Table 11.2

| | No. of population cells | | | |
	In year 1975	In year 2000	In year 2000 (millions)	Cells gained 1975-2000
W. Europe	9	10	390	1
E. Europe U.S.S.R. }	10	11	148 } 313 }	1
Japan plus	4	5	214	1
N. America	6	7	292	1
Australia/N.Z.	1	1	24	0
Latin America	8	15	606	7
N. Africa/S.W. Asia	5	10	382	5
Rest of Africa	8	17	662	9
S. Asia	20	35	1393	15
S.E. Asia	8	14	574	6
China plus	21	31	1241	10
World	100	156	6240	56

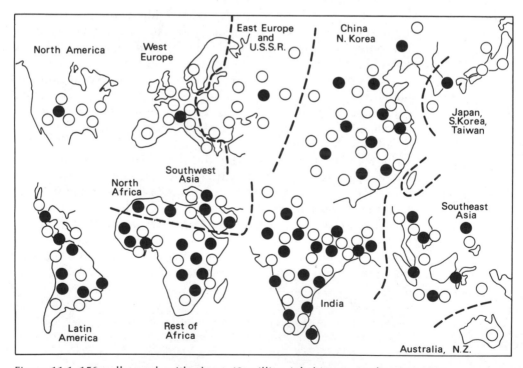

Figure 11.1 156 cells, each with about 40 million inhabitants, in the year 2000

increase in population in the 'developed' cells, numbered 1-30 in the 1975 list, while 52 new cells are needed to represent the increase in population in the 'developing' cells, numbered 31-100 in the 1975 list. The prospect of the new cells in Figure 11.1 is daunting.

Cells 1-30 in 1975 were basically developed cells, with high levels of technology and a high gross national product per inhabitant. Only about one-third of them, however, had abundant natural resources in relation to population. Most of the 70 percent of the world's population living in cells 31-100 had low levels of technology and low gross national product per inhabitant. Limited numbers of people lived in 'islands' or 'outliers' that were comparatively highly developed within some of the 70 developing cells, as in Southeast Brazil, South Africa, Singapore, and possibly parts of North China. Few of the 70 developing cells were well endowed with natural resources.

In 1975 about 1200 million people lived in the cells that were regarded as 'developed'. In the year 2000, how many of the 156 cells will qualify as developed by the standards of 1975? The question deserves some thought.

It is assumed that in the period 1975-2000 living standards in the 30 developed cells of 1975 will either rise, be maintained or fall only a little. These areas will have grown in fact to 34 cells between 1975 and 2000. One can therefore start in 2000 with 34 cells developed for sure out of 156 altogether, that is, with 22 percent of the total population in the year 2000. This is in place of 30 cells and therefore 30 percent of the world's population in 1975.

How will 70 developing cells of 1975 fare in the period 1975-2000? By the year 2000 there would be about 2100 million more people than in 1975 living in the developing countries of 1975. If things go very well for some of the developing world countries between 1975 and 2000 then they might transfer from the developing to the developed world. It is reasonable to expect some of the cells of Latin America and Southwest Asia and a few other areas to reach a level defined as 'developed' by the year 2000 with the help of oil revenues (wisely invested), an existing industrial base (Brazil, South Africa), and/or abundant natural resources. If, for example, 16 new cells 'cope' and become developed, then in the year 2000 there would be 50 developed cells altogether, with about 32 percent of the population of the world, but 106 would remain 'developing' and poor. In other words there would not only be *more poor* in the world in the year 2000 (some 4250 million) than in 1975, but more poor then than the *sum of rich and poor* in 1975.

The prospective situation in the year 2025 is more problematical. If nothing goes drastically wrong with the world by then in the form of a nuclear war, an environmental disaster, mass starvation or a drastic reduction in living standards in the developed countries, then there would be 188 cells, each with some 40 million inhabitants, and perhaps 60 percent of them still 'developing', with some 4500 million poor in them.

The above estimates of future population and levels of development have been based on the assumption that few net transfers of population have taken place between cells and that little has been deliberately or willingly done by the rich countries of the 1970s to help the poor ones in the 1980s and 1990s. Only some currently poor cells, like the big oil producers of the Middle East, by raising prices greatly, should be able to acquire capital and consumer goods on a large scale (in relation to their populations) from the industrial countries.

Increasing numbers of developing countries are feeling the need to publicize and make available various means of family planning. There are still some in which a much larger population than the existing one is regarded as desirable. On the other hand, considerable efforts have been made in both India and China, the two largest developing countries in population by far, to reduce fertility and birthrate.

It would be unfair to conclude this section on population change without putting the case for a large population for the world. Two very different authorities arrive at similar conclusions, the economist C. Clark and an 'official' Soviet view of the 1970s.

In *Population Growth and Land Use,* C. Clark (1967) puts the case for population growth as a prerequisite for economic growth in developing countries. In a review of the book, K. Davis (1968) summarizes Clark's viewpoint:

Clark's theory of population economics is eclectic. He cites Sir William Petty's idea that a dense population brings economies of scale, Everett Hagan's view that investment errors prove less costly when population is growing than they do when it is not growing, Albert O. Hirschman's thought that a growing population offers the possibility of windfall profits and expanding markets and therefore stimulates investment and Alfred Sauvy's contention that the *per capita* overhead costs of government and public services are less when population is growing than they are when it is not growing. Clark adds that a slowly growing population, with its large proportion of old people, will tend to consume capital rather than to save it, because the old save less than the young. He also suggests that the parents of large families make more effort to save, and that in such families younger sons expect less of an inheritance and therefore make great effort to accumulate for themselves.

K. Davis puts strong counterarguments, pointing out among other things that rapid population growth gives rise to a large number of young (as opposed to old) dependants.

Concern has been expressed in the U.S.S.R. about a declining fertility and natural growth since the early 1960s. The passage that follows, though it reflects the general Soviet attitude to population, refers more particularly to the Soviet situation. It should be remembered that compared with most countries the U.S.S.R. has a very favourable natural resource/population ratio and indeed has been preoccupied with moving more people into Siberia and the Far East. L. Ya. Berri (1977) writes:

> The fall in the birthrate has been significantly affected, not only by the demographic effects of the war, but also by other factors, such as urbanization, the increasing employment of women in social production, the higher cultural and educational levels, etc. A low rate of population growth has adverse socio-economic consequences. In this connection, demographic problems are becoming the object of the most careful study on the part of governmental and research bodies, and a whole series of measures are being taken with the object of maintaining and raising the birthrate in the Soviet Union.
>
> The age structure of the population also determines the size of and changes in manpower resources. From the point of view of short-term interests, it is more advantageous for society to have the very highest proportion of persons of working age. However, a low proportion of children would mean a slowing down of the rate of growth of the man-power resources in the future. In planning the size of the population of working age, account must be taken of the fact that manpower resources are affected by the birthrate that existed 16-18 years earlier. At the present time the proportion of persons in the older age-groups is increasing, while the number of young people, and especially children, is on the decrease. This phenomenon, which is characteristic of many industrialized countries, reflects the process known as the 'ageing' of the population, which is linked with an increase in the average length of life and a relative fall in fertility.

11.2 The organization of agriculture

Views on the prospects for world agriculture in the future vary greatly. The purpose of this and the following two sections is to present a framework for looking at the prospects of this vital sector of the world economy and to provide some general data on area cultivated and on yields in recent decades.

Four fictitious regions are shown in Figure 11.2. The data on which the regional differences are based are in Table 11.3. As several variables are involved it is not possible to represent the information graphically. Columns in Table 11.3 will now be referred to.

Columns (1) and (6). Only cropland is included in column (1), though in a full assessment of agriculture natural pasture would have to be taken into account as well. The proportion of cropland to total land varies greatly from one country to another, from a mere 1-2 percent in some African and Latin American countries to over 50 percent in some European countries and over much of South Asia. One might in general assume that the smaller the proportion of land under crops, the greater the potential left to develop or attempt to develop. In the view of the author, in most parts of the world the better land for crops has already been taken into use for cultivation. Regions (b) and (d) in Figure 11.2 have a large amount of cropland per total population, regions (a) and (c) not much (see column (6)).

Columns (2)-(4). Population is divided into two parts, the part in agriculture and the part not in agriculture. It would be possible to distinguish only the economically active population, but such a refinement would add an extra complication to the study here and would not add weight to the argument. Two types of region are distinguished here, regions (a) and (b) with half the population in agriculture and regions (c) and (d) with only one-tenth in agriculture. These represent developing and developed regions respectively.

Column (5). Each member of the agricultural population farms a very small area in region (a), a medium size area in regions (b) and (c), and a large area in region (d).

Column (7). In countries (a) and (b), each agricultural family supports itself and one other. In countries (c) and (d), each agricultural family supports itself and nine others. In some countries of Africa and South Asia, it takes nine agricultural families to support themselves (not very well) and only one other. In the United States in the early 1970s, each family in agriculture was supporting itself and about 50 others.

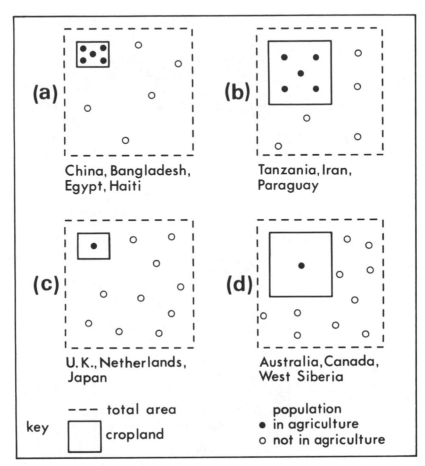

Figure 11.2 Relationships in agriculture between total land, cropland, total population, and agricultural population

Column (8). Yield represents productivity of a given piece of land. One might expect yields to be higher where cropland is limited in relation to population than where plenty of land is available. The highest yields in the world are in countries such as the U.K. and the Netherlands, with limited land *and* high levels of technology (type (c) regions).

Column (9). Production is crop area (1) multiplied by yield (8).

Column (10). When production is divided by population in agriculture, productivity (or efficiency) per worker is the result. Thanks to large area, small labour force, mechanization, and the extensive use of fertilizers, an average Australian or U.S. farmer

Table 11.3 Agricultural data in four regions

Region	Cropland area (1)	Population In agric. (2)	Not in agric. (3)	Total (4)	Cropland area Per popn. in agric. (5)	Per total popn. (6)	Support (7)	Yield (produc-tivity per area) (8)	Production Total (9)	Per popn. in agric. (produc-tivity) (10)	Per total popn. (availa-bility) (11)	Trade
(a)	20	5	5	10	4	2	2	7.5	150	30	15	Deficient
(b)	100	5	5	10	20	10	2	3	300	60	30	Adequate
(c)	20	1	9	10	20	2	10	10	200	200	20	Import
(d)	100	1	9	10	100	10	10	5	500	500	50	Export

produces up to 50 times as much as an average farmer in many developing countries. The output of a West European farmer falls short of that of a U.S. one but is still much higher than that of farmers in developing countries.

Column (11) shows how much production is available per inhabitant. If it is not adequate in region (a) then people go without an adequate diet. If it is not adequate in region (c) then food and plant raw materials are imported.

From the data in Table 11.3 it can be seen that agricultural production can be increased in two distinct ways. Firstly, more land can be brought into cultivation and, secondly, yields in existing areas of cultivation can be increased. The increase in yields may be achieved by changes in land tenure and attitude to the land combined with an increase in the application of fertilizers and other such methods. The reduction of the percentage of economically active population in agriculture releases people to other activities but does not necessarily affect production. It may *indirectly* help agriculture by allowing the production of fertilizers, tractors, and other means of production for the farming sector.

11.3 The prospects for agriculture

For convenience, the prospects for agriculture will be considered under seven headings. These are summarized in Table 11.4. Three countries, Bangladesh, the U.K., and Australia, are used for comparison with reference to each of the seven headings.

1. Economically active population in agriculture as a percentage of total economically active population

This variable has been discussed at some length in Chapter 4 and data for countries are given in Table 4.1. In Chapter 5 it was shown how in the present century the proportion of economically active population in agriculture dropped below 10 percent of the total economically active population in many of the present developed countries. In contrast, many developing countries still have more than 70 percent of their economically active population in agriculture. Even if this percentage decreases in developing countries, the absolute number of people working the land can still increase so long as population itself grows.

In the period 1937-1976 the *absolute* number of persons in the agricultural sector in three developed regions (1-3 in Table 11.5(a)) has diminished. In the U.S.A. it has fallen to a quarter of what it was,

Table 11.4 Seven aspects of agriculture

	Bangladesh	U.K.	Australia	
1 Agricultural population/ total population	High	Low	Low	Developed if low
2 Agricultural land/total land	High	High	Low	Potential if low
3 Agricultural land/total population	Low	Low	High	Export if high
4 Agricultural land/ agricultural population	Low	Medium	High	Efficient if high
5 Production/total population	Low	Low	High	As 3
6 Production/agricultural population (productivity)	Low	High	High	As 4
7 Production/agricultural land (= yield)	Low	High	Medium	Productive if high

in the U.S.S.R. to a half, and in West Europe to about 60 percent. In the five developing regions (4-8 in Table 11.5(a)) the absolute number of persons in the agricultural sector has increased during the same period, roughly doubling in Central America (including Mexico and the Caribbean) and in Africa and increasing substantially in Asia and South America.

While the area under cultivation increased considerably in North America and the U.S.S.R. during 1937-1976, the number of people working the land declined sharply. The area under cultivation in Europe changed little between 1937 and 1976 but again the number of people on the land declined greatly and yields in existing areas of cultivation increased. In Latin America and Africa the area under cultivation increased during 1937-76 but not so fast as agricultural population. In Asia, including China but excluding Asiatic U.S.S.R., the area under cultivation did not increase by much but agricultural population did. Thus owing to the difference in the rate of population growth between developed and developing countries, and in spite of a shift out of agriculture in developed and developing countries alike, the actual average number of people working a given area of land has increased in most developing countries in recent decades. In contrast it has decreased in virtually all developed countries.

Table 11.5(a) Agricultural population of the world by major regions in millions of persons

	1937	1950	1960	1970	1976
1 Europe (excl. U.S.S.R.)	133	129	109	89	79
2 U.S.S.R.	108	100	90	77	51
3 North America	32	23	14	10	7
4 Central America	24	28	38	44	45
5 South America	52	66	65	74	79
6 Africa	128	134	201	239	272
7 Asia (excl. China)	504	528	693	791	866
8 China	362	377	486	523	537
World*	1349	1412	1699	1851	1940

* Total exceeds sum of individual regions because Oceania omitted.

Table 11.5(b) Economically active population in agriculture as a percentage of total economically active population

	1937	1950	1960	1970	1976
1 Europe (excl. U.S.S.R.)	36	33	26	19	17
2 U.S.S.R.	57	50	42	32	20
3 North America	23	14	7	4	3
4 Central America	63	55	55	48	41
5 South America	62	59	45	39	35
6 Africa	76	66	74	69	68
7 Asia (excl. China)	73	64	72	64	61
8 China	76	69	75	68	63
World	62	56	57	51	47

Sources: *Food and Agriculture Organisation Production Yearbook,* Vol. 13, 1959, Table 4B; Vol. 28.1, Table 6.

In spite of the absolute increase in the number of persons in agriculture in developing regions, the proportion of employment accounted for by the agricultural sector has diminished in all regions during 1937-76. The data in Table 11.5(b) are actually for economically active population, not total population, but the percentages are very similar to those for total population.

The prospect for the world seems to be a continuing increase in the absolute agricultural population in many developing countries for some decades to come. In Asia this cannot be matched by an increase in the cultivated area. On the other hand the agricultural sector cannot shed large numbers of people without serious repercussions in other sectors of the economy because there are not the natural resources to allow a great expansion of other productive activities. In Latin America and Africa there seems to be a greater potential for increasing the area under cultivation in agriculture and there are also more natural resources for creating other productive employment.

2. Land under crops as a percentage of total land

The relationship between total land, cropland, and population in 17 selected countries is reviewed in Table 11.6 at different periods. The cropland, technically, is defined as arable land plus permanent crops. The total land area of the world is 13,075 million hectares (130,750,000 km^2). On average 1394 million hectares were used during 1961-65 for arable plus permanent crops, that is 10.7 percent of the total land area. In 1975 the area under arable plus permanent crops was 1506 million hectares and the percentage 11.5. From 1963 to 1975 the total population of the world increased from 3160 million to 3967 million. The actual area of arable land plus permanent crops per inhabitant therefore diminished.

The first seven countries in Table 11.6 are developed while the remainder are developing, though Argentina, Brazil, Mexico, and South Africa might be regarded as intermediate. Column (1) shows the total area of each country. Columns (2) -(6) show the area under arable plus permanent crops in five different years or periods. Some reservations must be made about the comparability of data in columns (2)-(6). The definition of arable varies from one country to another. The 1950 data for some countries (e.g. Thailand) seem to be estimated on different criteria from those used in later years. The actual quality of the land varies greatly from country to country, as well as within countries, and no allowance is made for this. Even so, it is felt that the data in Table 11.6 show major trends and prospects.

During a given period of time both the area under cropland and population can change. In the three European countries, 1-3 in the list in Table 11.6, the cropland area has actually diminished since the Second World War. In all the other countries it has increased. Cropland area is expressed as a percentage of total area in columns (7) and (8). Here it can be seen that the three European countries, together with India, were the ones with the largest proportion of cropland to total area in 1963.

All other things being equal, it might be expected that the countries in which only a small proportion of total area was under crops would be the ones in which there was much potential cultivable land. In many countries this does not seem to be the case

Table 11.6 Agricultural area and population in selected countries

	Total land area (m ha)	Area under crops (m ha)					Area under crops as % of total area		Population (millions)		ha/100 population	
	(1)	(2) 1950	(3) 1961-65	(4) 1966	(5) 1970	(6) 1975	(7) 1963	(8) 1975	(9) 1963	(10) 1975	(11) 1963	(12) 1975
1 France	55	21	21	20	19	19	38	34	48	53	44	36
2 Italy	30	17	15	15	15	12	50	40	50	55	30	22
3 Poland	31	17	16	16	15	16	52	48	31	34	52	44
4 Japan	37	5.1	5.9	5.8	5.7	5.6	16	15	96	111	6	5
5 U.S.A.	913	184	180	178	192	209	20	23	189	214	95	98
6 Canada	922	39	42	43	43	44	5	5	19	23	221	191
7 Australia	769	19	34	40	43	46	4	6	11	14	309	329
8 Argentina	278	30	28	30	33	35	10	13	22	25	127	140
9 Brazil	846	19	30	32	34	37	4	4	76	110	39	34
10 Mexico	202	15	25	26	27	28	12	14	38	59	66	47
11 Nigeria	92	22	22	23	24	24	24	26	56	63	39	38
12 S. Africa	122	8	13	13	14	15	11	12	17	25	76	60
13 Turkey	78	15	26	26	27	28	33	36	30	40	87	70
14 India	297	131	162	163	165	167	55	56	460	613	35	27
15 Thailand	51	5	13	13	14	17	25	33	29	42	45	40
16 Indonesia	181	11	17	17	18	19	9	10	100	136	17	14
17 China	960	91	119	122	126	129	12	13	700	823	17	16

Main sources:*Food and Agriculture Organisation Production Yearbook 1952, Table 1; 1976, Table 1.*

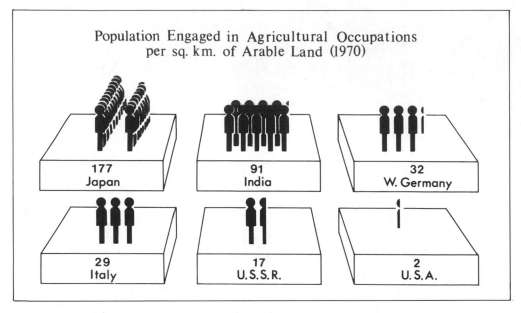

Figure 11.3 Contrasts in the number of persons engaged in agriculture per unit of arable land in 1970. Source: *Nippon* (1975)

in practice. In Japan, for example, only about 15 percent of the total area is under crops yet there is very little prospect of extending cultivation into the remaining areas, which are too rugged. On the contrary, the built-up land is eating into the limited agricultural land. A Japanese illustration comparing pressure of population on agricultural land in different countries is shown in Figure 11.3. Again, only about 11 percent of the total area of China is under cultivation. But, according to the Rand McNally *Illustrated Atlas of China* (1972):

> It appears unlikely that agricultural output can be significantly increased by bringing new lands into cultivation. Almost all cultivated land — about 11 percent of China's land area — is located in the eastern half of the country. Although some new land has been brought into cultivation during the past 20 years, it has not offset losses caused by the expansion of urban and industrial areas, the construction of reservoirs, and the salinization and erosion of productive land. The potential for opening new land in western China or the Northeast to cultivation is limited because of aridity, short growing season, and other inhibiting physical factors.

The Chinese are slowly creating additional cultivable land in various ways such as terracing hillsides and levelling the surface in areas of broken relief, see Plates 11.1 and 11.2.

The data in columns (7) and (8) show that some countries have succeeded in extending their cultivated area considerably since 1950. Thanks to a massive campaign to open up new and long fallow lands mainly in the Ural region, West Siberia, and northern Kazakhstan, cultivated area was greatly extended in the U.S.S.R. in the 1950s. The upper graph in Figure 11.4 shows the 'one-off' appearance of the addition of the new lands to total Soviet sown area in the 1950s. The lower graph shows how the sown area of the Ukraine hardly increased at all while that in Kazakhstan increased about three times.

The above Soviet example illustrates the problem of increasing the area of cropland in the world. On the whole the more easily 'improved' land is brought into use first. Additional new areas become increasingly costly to bring under cultivation. They may require the provision of roads and settlements as well as the clearance of land, drainage or irrigation. In spite of the many obstacles to the extension of the cultivated area, Revelle (1976) estimates that potentially 22 percent of the world's ice-free land surface is capable of supporting crops without irrigation. Only about 11 percent was in use in the mid-1970s. Further areas could also be irrigated, and yields widely increased. Very little of the potential, however, is in China, Japan, South Asia or Europe, the area in which some 60 percent of the world's population is concentrated at the moment.

3. Agricultural land per total population

This relationship will be dealt with very briefly by referring again to Table 11.6. Columns (9) and (10) show that in all the 17 countries included in the table, total population grew between 1963 and 1975. In contrast, columns (11) and (12) show that only in three of them, the U.S.A., Australia, and Argentina, did the number of hectares under crops per 100 inhabitants increase between 1963 and 1975. The data in Table 11.6 illustrate the creeping onset of the Malthusian nightmare. Whatever the *theoretical* limits to the cultivated area of the world, the *reality* has been a failure in the 1960s and 1970s to 'keep up' with population growth. Columns (11) and (12) in Table 11.6 also show clearly the enormous contrasts in the world from country to country in the actual amount of cropland per inhabitant. Land resources were calculated for the 100 cells in Chapter 7 and though pasture and forest were taken into account

Plate 11.2 It is common in Southeast and East Asia to find hillsides carefully terraced to provide horizontal fields that can be cultivated. The Chinese continue to build such systems of terraces. Source: *China Pictorial,* 1970, No. 9, p. 13 (Peking). (Reproduced by permission of *China Pictorial*)

Plate 11.1 (Opposite) By various processes of terracing, levelling, and the infilling of valleys and gullies the Chinese are painstakingly creating new cultivated land. The work includes the breaking up of rocks by hand (by men) and the transfer of pieces of rock from one place to another (by women). Source: *China Pictorial,* 1970, No. 9, p. 17 (Peking). (Reproduced by permission of *China Pictorial*)

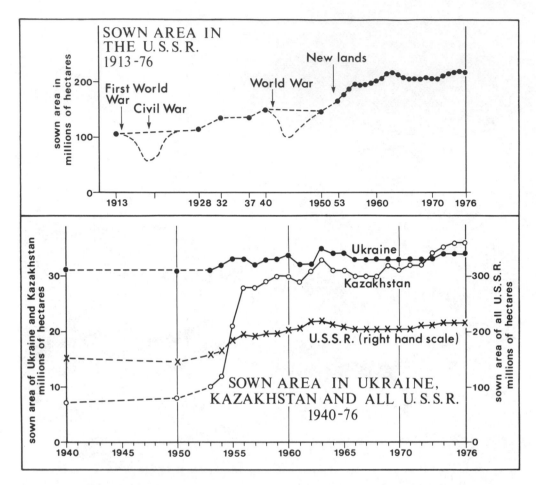

Figure 11.4 The growth of the sown area of the U.S.S.R. from 1913 to 1976 (upper diagram) and of the sown area of the Ukraine and Kazakhstan from 1940 to 1976 (lower diagram). Note the different scale on the lower diagram for the U.S.S.R. as a whole. Source: *Narodnoye khozyaystvo SSSR*, Moscow, various volumes

and cropland weighted according to quality, a similar disparity in productive land in relation to population was revealed.

4. Cropland per person economically active in agriculture

The relationship of cropland to total population was considered in the previous section. Cropland per inhabitant was seen to be limited in older industrial regions such as Europe and Japan and also in developing countries such as India, Indonesia, and China.

Cropland per inhabitant was also plentiful in some developed countries such as Canada and in some developing ones such as Argentina and Turkey. The relationship is, however, different with regard to the amount of cropland per agricultural population and more specifically per person defined as economically active in agriculture. It can be calculated that per person actually engaged in farming in Australia there is 50-100 times as much cultivated land as there is per farmer in many developing countries. Since only a small proportion of the economically active population is engaged in agriculture in Europe and in Japan there tends also to be more cropland per person working in this sector than in developing countries.

Table 11.7 The tractor gap

	Thousands of tractors in use			Persons in agriculture 1975 Thousands Per tractor	
	(1) 1961-65	(2) 1968	(3) 1975	(4)	(5)
Ethiopia	0.4	2.5	3.4	9864	2901
Tanzania	2.6	4.4	6.9	5516	799
Peru	7.7	10.0	12.5	1867	149
Venezuela	13.1	17.0	24.0	783	33
Switzerland	60.7	70.0	77.5	191	2.5
Netherlands	106.2	142.0	170.8	330	1.9
Australia	283.1	323.6	342.4	388	1.1

Sources: *United Nations Statistical Yearbook 1974,* Table 25; *1976,* Table 25.
Food and Agriculture Organisation Production Yearbook 1976, Table 3.

The disparity in productivity per worker in agriculture in different countries is illustrated in Table 11.7 by the tractor gap. The number of tractors in use is shown in thousands for three years in columns (1)-(3). Column (4) shows the economically active population in agriculture, also in thousands. When tractors are related to persons working in agriculture, a tractor gap of something like 3000 to 1 is found between Ethiopia and Australia. In 1975 there was about one tractor for every 2900 persons engaged in agriculture in Ethiopia while in Australia the ratio was roughly 1 to 1. The data show once again big differences among developing countries themselves, exemplified by the contrast between Ethiopia and Venezuela. The difference in levels of mechanization between two developed countries, Switzerland and Australia, though marked, is perhaps to

Table 11.8 Food supply in calories per inhabitant per day

	1961-65	1972-75
World	2440	2540
Africa	2170	2210
N. and C. America	3060	3230
S. America	2460	2540
Asia	2070	2200
Europe	3210	3390
Oceania	3290	3160
U.S.S.R.	3280	3470
Developed	3150	3330
Developing	2130	2170
Centrally planned Asia	2020	2280
Centrally Planned Europe plus U.S.S.R.	3250	3460
India	2050	1970
Indonesia	1930	2030
Bangladesh	1970	1950
U.S.A.	3350	3540
Brazil	2420	2540
Nigeria	2150	2070
China	2010	2070

Sources: *Food and Agriculture Organisation Production Yearbook 1976*, Vol. 30, Table 9.7

be expected given the much larger amount of land to be worked per person engaged in farming in Australia than in Switzerland.

Two further relationships, 5 and 6 in Table 11.4, will not be considered in detail here. Agricultural production per population is the question of the supply of food and raw materials. It is very difficult to compare the agricultural production of two different regions because so many 'unlikes' have to be matched. In view of the importance of food, recent trends in food supply in selected countries are given in Table 11.8. The food intake gap between major regions of the world and between selected countries, which was worked out for the 100 cells in Chapter 8, does not seem to have changed much in recent years. The contribution of animal foods to the total intake varies greatly among the regions of the world. It exceeds a third in North America and Oceania, reaches about 30 percent in Europe and nearly 20 percent in South America, but is only 10 percent in Africa and Asia.

11.4 The prospects for raising yields in agriculture

The final relationship in agriculture noted in Table 11.4 is that between agricultural land and production. At first sight there seems to be a great potential for increasing the productivity of land in agriculture. A comparison of yields in different countries shows that they are several times as high on average for the same crop in some regions as in others.

Yields can be increased in many ways, among them by using more chemical fertilizers, by the improvement of strains of plant, and by the improvement of water supply by irrigation. It is also increasingly appreciated that the raising of livestock with fodder grown on land that could otherwise be used to grow food directly for human consumption produces less food since the animals themselves use up food just to keep alive. The actual food they provide when slaughtered is according to various estimates at least several times less than the food used to raise them.

Yields of various crops have increased in a spectacular fashion in many developed countries in recent decades. It seems doubtful if yields in West Europe and Japan could be increased greatly in the future without a completely new approach to farming. On the other hand, in most developed countries (but not in Japan) there is a large livestock sector. One could hardly expect that livestock farming should be phased out altogether in developed countries, but the fact remains that the greatest potential for increasing total food production in developed countries seems eventually to be in the curtailment of livestock raising.

Latin American and African countries also have a large livestock sector in agriculture but the quality of the animals on the whole is poor. They tend to be raised on land that is not currently suitable for crop farming rather than in close association with crop production. Yields of most crops in these two continents are also low by the standards of yields in developed countries. There is therefore scope for increasing production in various ways here.

In South and Southeast Asia and in China the raising of livestock tends either to have a restricted purpose, as in India, where a main function is to provide draught animals, or to be very limited, as in China. The best prospect for most of the developing countries of Asia is to increase yields in crop farming. Much capital is needed as well as willingness and knowhow among farmers to allow them to change their methods. Some improvements in yield have been achieved in various parts of South and East Asia with the spread of high-yielding varieties of cultivated plant, but much assistance from developed countries seems to be necessary.

It is tempting to estimate how much the output from the agricultural sector could be increased if every country produced the same
yields for every crop as the country in the world currently achieving
the highest yields. This admirable but dubious idea is applied here
to wheat yields, for which data are given for selected countries
during the postwar period in Table 11.9. The graph in Figure 11.5
shows that yields in the U.K. and France (and also Switzerland)
have roughly doubled between the late 1940s and the mid-1970s.
When the year-to-year fluctuations in yield in the U.K. and France
are smoothed out it is evident that a limit was reached in the U.K.
by the early 1960s and in France by the early 1970s. It is common
sense and common knowledge that diminishing returns apply in the
use of fertilizer. Australia continues to achieve wheat yields only a
third as high as those in the U.K. and France because the physical
conditions in the wheat belt are less favourable than in Europe and
also because less effort is made to raise yields with fertilizers.

Table 11.9 Wheat yields in selected countries 1934-38 and 1948-77 in
kilogrammes per hectare. Yearly averages for five-year periods

	U.K.	Switzerland	France	Australia	Mexico	India
1934-38	2310	2310	1560	800	760	650
1948-52	2730	2670	1820	1120	880	650
1953-57	3110	2890	2190	1100	1200	730
1958-62	3630	3280	2530	1250	1590	790
1963-67	4050	3440	3110	1210	2420	990
1968-72	4070	3880	3830	1140	2780	1280
1973-77	4480	4100	4190	1280	3650	1320

Source: *Food and Agriculture Organisation Production Yearbook,* various years.

The contrast in performance between Mexico and India is of
interest. Wheat is grown mainly in the north of Mexico, the most
'developed' part, and much of it on good quality irrigated land.
Even so, improvements in wheat strains and the use of chemical
fertilizers have raised wheat yields four times in three decades.
How widely can this kind of transformation be made in developing
countries? Certainly in India nothing comparable has been widely
achieved. Maize yields in Mexico have not changed much in the
same period either, yet maize is far more widely grown in Mexico
than wheat. It is still too early to say precisely to what extent the
developing countries could raise their yields towards the highest
found currently in developed countries.

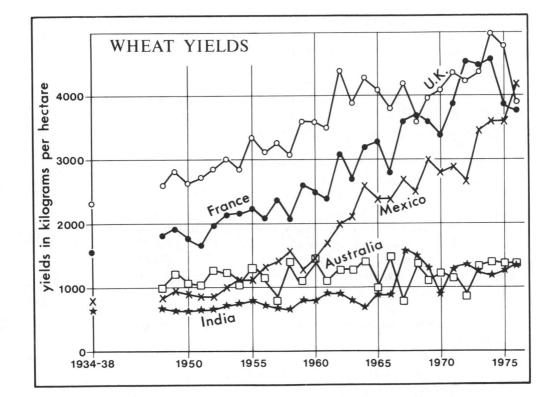

Figure 11.5 Wheat yields in selected countries from 1934-38 to 1976. See Table 11.9 for period averages. Source: *Food and Agriculture Organisation Production Yearbook,* various numbers

11.5   The loss of agricultural land

In a short but wide-ranging review of world agriculture in the second half of the twentieth century, L.R. Brown (1978) draws on many sources of evidence to argue that the prospects for the last quarter of the century are not so good as the situation during 1950-75 (p. 10).

> During the third quarter of this century, world population increased by 1.5 billion, or 59 percent, while the area in grain expanded from 602 to 731 million hectares, a gain of 21 percent. This was almost certainly the first generation during which the growth in human numbers so greatly exceeded the growth in cropland. It led to a precipitous drop in area per person from 0.24 hectares to 0.18 hectares. Such a drop did not

pose any problems because the yield per hectare was rising
rapidly throughout most of this period. Once that began to
slow, however, as it did in 1972, a global food shortage
developed.

There are at least three major reasons why the situation has
changed in the 1970s. Population is expected to continue to grow
by a greater absolute amount during 1975-2000 than it did between
1950 and 1975. The loss of cropland is becoming a serious problem.
Yields have reached towards an economic ceiling in many
developed countries.

Agricultural land is being lost for two main reasons:
encroachment by other users and reduction of fertility or
abandonment. Encroachment is resulting from the continuing
expansion of both urban and rural settlements on cultivated land,
the construction of reservoirs and strip mining, and the building of
transportation links. On the abandonment of land, L.R. Brown
(1978, p. 16) notes:

> the amount of cropland abandoned may also be at a record
> level. The reasons for cropland abandonment, usually the
> product of economic pressures interacting with ecological
> prices, include desertification, severe erosion, waterlogging
> and salinization of irrigated land, and the diversion of irrigation
> water to nonfarm uses.

Desertification is especially prevalent on the fringes of the Sahara
Desert of Africa. Overgrazing, deforestation, and overploughing are
widespread in the world and may lead to the development of
processes that cause loss of land. Stream erosion, for example, is a
problem in such widely differing areas as the Andes, East Africa,
and the Ukraine. Wind erosion has been especially noticeable in the
central agricultural belt of the U.S.S.R. Topsoil is being washed
away in large quantities in Iowa and in Ethiopia for example.
Problems of waterlogging and salinity occur in Pakistan, Iraq, and
Southwest U.S.A.

Brown (1978) estimates that in addition to the actual loss of
cropland in the ways outlined above, about one-fifth of the world's
cropland is losing its natural soil fertility. He reminds us that soil is
a mere foot thick in many areas of cultivation and is very fragile. An
inch may be lost easily and quickly. It takes a century, even with a
conscious effort, to create an inch of good topsoil.

Many 'bad' practices in agriculture in the 1970s could be
attributed to the sheer need for growing populations in developing

countries to cultivate more intensively the existing cropland or to move into areas increasingly vulnerable to degradation under cultivation. Farmers in developed countries could also be blamed for overcultivation. It was particularly tempting in the U.S.A. to respond to rising cereal prices by taking risks, though short-sighted when the needs of future generations are taken into account.

Brown summarizes the prospects as follows: 'During the final quarter of this century, population is projected to increase by 58 percent; although slightly smaller in percentage terms, the expected addition of 2.3 billion people would be half again as large as the 1.5 billion added during the third quarter. As the final quarter of this century began, cropland was being lost to nonfarm purposes at a record rate. The abandonment of agricultural land because of severe soil erosion, degradation and desertification was at an all-time high. The potential for substantial net additions to the world's cropland base was not so good.'

11.6 Trends in mineral production

The purpose of this section is to examine recent trends in the production of selected fossil fuels and non-fuel minerals and to speculate about future prospects. The general picture has been one of growth in production. A more detailed examination of data shows that the situation is very complicated and that for some regions a decline in production has set in.

Table 11.10 Coal production in seven industrial countries in millions of tonnes

	W.Germany*	France	Belgium	U.K.	Japan	U.S.A.	U.S.S.R.
1938	186	46	30	231	49	355	133
1948-52	124	51	28	222	39	501	178
1953-57	148	55	30	227	46	441	276
1958-62	144	55	23	204	51	389	371
1963-67	132	50	19	188	50	472	417
1968-72	113	37	12	148	39	521	433
1973-76	99	24	8	124	20	556	478

* Saar included in West Germany after 1951.

11.6.1 Coal production in industrial countries

Table 11.10 gives coal production for seven highly industrialized countries in 1938 and from 1948 to 1976. The data are shown

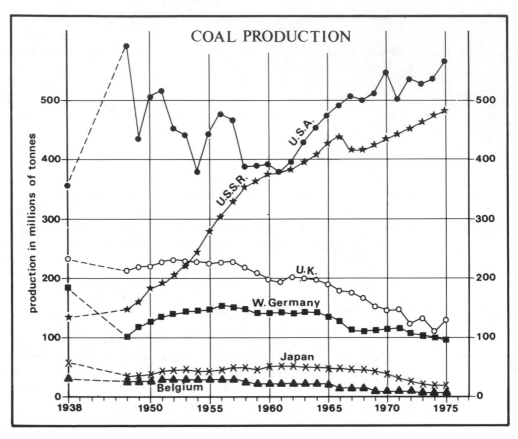

Figure 11.6 Coal production in selected countries 1938-1975. See Table 11.10 for period averages. Source: *United Nations Statistical Yearbook,* various numbers

graphically for six of the seven countries in Figure 11.6 (France follows Japan remarkably closely). In all seven countries the contribution of coal to total energy consumption (in coal equivalent) has diminished during all or most of the period surveyed, largely in favour of oil and natural gas. In the West European countries and in Japan total coal production has declined while total population has grown, though comparatively slowly. Coal production in the U.S.A. began to fall soon after the Second World War but picked up again in the early 1960s. In the U.S.S.R. there has been a fairly steady increase in coal production (lignite is not included here) but the rate of growth has been slower in the 1960s and 1970s than it was up to the late 1950s, when a fundamental change in energy policy brought the 1956-60 Five-Year Plan to a premature end.

At first sight there appear to be two main reasons for the changes in coal production in the seven countries studied, but it will then be seen that the two reasons are of the same origin. Firstly, coal production has been run down in many coalfields in the world either because commercial reserves have run out or because the more accessible and cheaply extracted seams have been used up. That is what has happened in many coalfields in Europe (e.g. South Wales, North France, the Donbass in the U.S.S.R.) and in Japan. France, Belgium, and Japan only have limited reserves left, so it is impossible for production there to be boosted greatly in the future. Secondly, coal production in the other four countries has dropped, or failed to rise as fast as at one time envisaged, not because reserves are lacking but because oil and/or natural gas could be extracted at home more cheaply than coal or could be imported more cheaply.

Home production of oil and natural gas could not continue to rise indefinitely in the U.S.A. at the high rate of the 1960s and home-produced coal became attractive again. It is expected that coal production in the U.K. will be increased again, as extensive coal reserves are known (as at Selby in Yorkshire and the Vale of Belvoir

Table 11.11 Oil and natural gas production. Oil in millions of tonnes, natural gas in cubic metres $\times 10^9$

Year	U.S.A. Oil	U.S.A. Natural gas	Venezuela Oil	Year	U.S.A. Oil	U.S.A. Natural gas	Venezuela Oil
1938	171	67	28	1962	362	391	167
1948	273	146	70	1963	372	415	170
1949	249	153	71	1964	377	438	178
1950	267	178	80	1965	385	454	182
1951	304	211	91	1966	409	487	176
1952	309	227	97	1967	435	515	185
1953	319	238	92	1968	450	547	189
1954	313	248	99	1969	456	586	188
1955	336	266	113	1970	475	595	194
1956	354	285	129	1971	467	612	185
1957	354	302	146	1972	467	612	168
1958	331	311	136	1973	454	615	176
1959	348	339	145	1974	433	587	156
1960	348	360	149	1975	413	551	122
1961	354	373	153	1976	401	550	120

Sources: *United Nations Statistical Yearbook 1954,* Tables 40, 41; *1963,* Tables 47, 48; *1967,* Tables 72, 73; *1971,* Tables 69, 70; *1975,* Tables 53, 54.

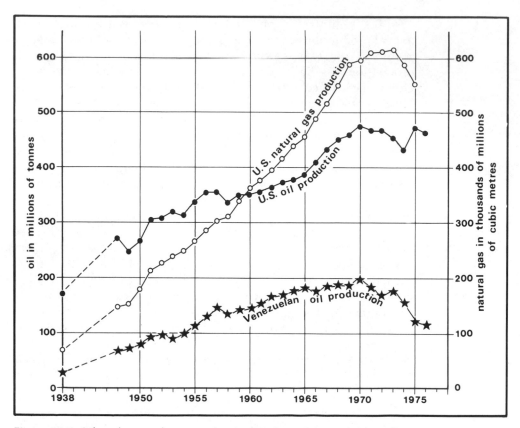

Figure 11.7 Oil and natural gas production in the U.S.A. and oil production in Venezuela, 1938-1975. See Table 11.11. Source: *United Nations Statistical Yearbook,* various numbers

in Leicestershire). Coal production is likely to start to rise again in West Germany and the U.K. and to continue to rise in the U.S.S.R. and U.S.A. Reserves in the two West European countries could last at least for many decades and reserves in the U.S.A. and U.S.S.R. at least for centuries. Thus major adjustments in coal production have been taking place in the world since the Second World War particularly in response to known reserves and to production levels of oil and natural gas. These two fossil fuels will be considered next.

11.6.2 Oil production in the U.S.A. and Venezuela and natural gas in the U.S.A.

Three examples have been chosen of fossil fuel reserves that have been used in very large quantities for some time and which have only short lives left. Production data are given in Table 11.11 and are shown graphically in Figure 11.7. U.S. oil reserves in 1975 were estimated to be 4417 million tonnes (*United Nations Statistical Yearbook 1976,* Table 52) and would only last 10 years at the rate of production of the early 1970s. A 1979 estimate indicated that if the U.S.A. did not import any oil but its consumption level stayed the same then it would have enough home oil for five years. Venezuelan oil reserves were 2643 million tonnes in 1975 and would last barely a decade at the peak 1970 rate of production, but nearly two decades at the 1976 rate. The 1974 estimate of U.S. natural gas reserves was 6715 thousand million cubic metres, which would last about 11 years at production rates of the early 1970s.

The reaction to the short life of U.S. and Venezuelan hydrocarbons can be seen in Figure 11.7. U.S. oil production levelled out in the 1970s while oil imports have increased greatly. Venezuela, however, has not obligingly responded to the U.S. need for more oil. Since the rise in oil prices in 1973, Venezuela has been able to cut production greatly while still being paid much more. Saudi Arabia, Iran, and various other Middle East and African countries continued to increase production into the early 1970s but production in Kuwait dropped after 1972. The cut in production in Venezuela gives that country a breathing space to search for more oil and to develop the tar sands it has in the Orinoco region.

Natural gas production has faltered and then diminished in the U.S.A. but it is doubtful if liquefied natural gas from such possible suppliers as Algeria or the U.S.S.R. could make much contribution to natural gas supplies in the U.S.A. for some years. As the U.S.A. approaches the end of its oil reserves there is a tendency to assume that it can obtain oil from somewhere else. Many industrial countries already depend heavily on imported oil. By the 1990s others will be in the same position as the U.S.A., including perhaps the 'somewhere else'. The extensive research and massive construction work on processing plant needed to produce oil in large quantities from the oil shales and tar sands known to exist in the U.S.A., U.S.S.R., Canada, and Venezuela precludes their widespread use for perhaps two to three decades. Theoretically they contain large oil reserves but in reality little is being done to develop them.

11.6.3 Nuclear energy

As oil and natural gas are likely to be used up in a few decades and coal, though abundant, is 'difficult' to extract on account of

Table 11.12 Electricity generated in nuclear power stations in thousands of millions of kWh

	1966	'67	'68	'69	1970	'71	'72	'73	'74	'75	'76	All electricity 1966	1975	% from nuclear 1975
1 U.S.A.	6	8	13	14	22	38	54	83	113	171	191	1249	2001	9
2 U.K.	22	25	28	29	26	28	29	28	34	30	36	203	272	11
3 Japan	1	1	1	1	5	8	9	10	20	25	34	215	476	5
4 W. Germany	—	1	2	5	6	6	9	12	12	21	24	178	302	7
5 France	1	3	3	4	5	9	14	14	14	17	15	106	179	9
6 Sweden	—	—	—	—	—	—	1	2	2	12	16	51	81	15
7 Canada	—	—	1	—	1	4	7	14	14	12	16	158	273	4
8 U.S.S.R.	2	2	3	3	4	4	5	8	9	11	14	545	1039	1
9 Switzerland	0	0	0	—	2	3	4	6	7	7	8	28	42	17
10 Belgium	—	—	—	—	—	—	—	—	—	7	10	23	42	17

Sources: *United Nations Statistical Yearbook 1976*, Table 144; 1977.

unattractive work conditions and inaccessible locations, as in Siberia, other sources of energy must be developed. The 10 leading producers of electricity from nuclear power stations in 1975 are shown in Table 11.12, with production data for 1966-1976. In the mid-1960s the U.K. was producing about half of the world's electricity generated in nuclear power stations. In 1975 the U.S.A. was in that position and obtained 9 percent of all its electricity from nuclear sources, more than half as much as from hydroelectric sources.

The Western industrial countries, whether those with very few fossil fuel reserves such as Japan, France, Sweden, and Switzerland or those with large reserves like the U.S.A. and U.K., were developing nuclear power until the mid-1970s. According to Pryde (1978), even the U.S.S.R. has at last embarked on a massive programme for building nuclear power stations, in spite of its large fossil fuel reserves. As usual, the developed countries can find means of coping with crises in the supply of fuel and raw materials. Most developing countries remain with very low levels of consumption, unable to import much oil and unable for technological and financial reasons to develop more than token nuclear power programmes. Brazil's first nuclear power station near Rio de Janeiro has been criticized for lack of adequate safety precautions.

11.6.4 The mining of metallic ores

The industrial countries of the world have come to depend increasingly on non-fuel minerals either from developing countries, such as Chile, Zambia, and Malaysia, or from large developed countries with small populations, especially Canada and Australia. Nevertheless there is always some satisfaction in using one's own raw materials, a necessity indeed for a time in the Second World War for Germany, Italy, and Japan in particular. Many of the reserves of non-fuel minerals in Europe have been worked for a long time. Table 11.13 (three left-hand columns) shows data for two minerals in three selected countries. Production is barely being maintained or is actually declining. The data are shown graphically in Figure 11.8.

Japan has pushed up home production of zinc ore to satisfy national needs as far as possible but in 1971 its production started to fall. Italian production of zinc ore has been faltering then declining. In the production of lead ore, Bulgaria just manages to

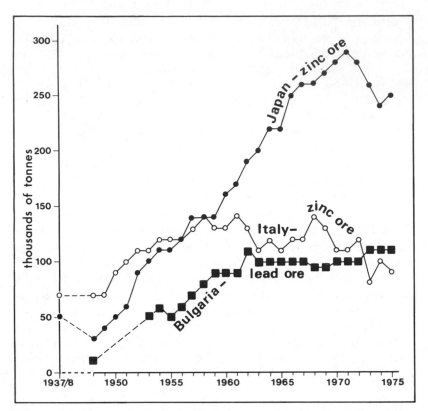

Figure 11.8 The production of non-ferrous metals in selected countries during 1937/8-1975. See Table 11.13 for period averages. Source: *United Nations Statistical Yearbook,* various numbers

Table 11.13 Production of selected primary products, yearly average for periods indicated

	Zinc ore		Lead ore	Guano	Fish
	Japan	Italy	Bulgaria	Peru	Peru
	(thous. of tonnes)				(millions of tonnes)
1937	50	70	n.a.	170	neg.
1948-52	50	90	n.a.	210	0.1
1953-57	120	120	60	300	0.3
1958-62	160	130	90	170	3.7
1963-67	230	120	100	140	8.6
1968-72	280	120	100	30	9.5
1973-76	250	90	110	neg.	3.8

neg. no production recorded.
n.a. not available.
Sources: *United Nations Statistical Yearbook 1956,* various tables; *1963,* Tables 52, 53; *1967,* Table 71; *1972,* Tables 63, 73; *1976,* Table 72.
Peru data from Cole and Mather (1978).

keep output level. Europe and Japan are reaching the limits of production of many of their known reserves of non-fuel minerals.

11.6.5 The production of guano and the fish catch of Peru

This provides an interesting study of the interaction of ecology and economics. Table 11.13 (two right-hand columns) shows production of the two items and the data are presented graphically in Figure 11.9. In the Pacific off the coast of Peru there is a very large fish population. Most of the fish are a small species, the anchovy, which for technical reasons is difficult to prepare for human consumption. The anchovy can, however, be processed into fishmeal for fertilizer. Sea birds feed on the fish. Since the middle of the nineteenth century the droppings of the sea birds, *guano* in Spanish, have been collected and used as a fertilizer in the cultivated coastal oases of Peru, or have been exported.

Guano was still being extracted after the Second World War and the amount collected actually rose until 1956. At that time the Peruvian fishing industry began to expand greatly, as shown in Figure 11.9. From the later 1950s to 1970 the fish catch rose dramatically and in the 1960s Peru became the leading fishing country in the world, though nearly all the catch consisted of anchovies which are almost all made into fishmeal.

As the fishing industry took more and more fish the sea birds were increasingly deprived of their food supply and their numbers diminished. The extraction of guano had almost ceased by the early 1970s. By the late 1960s it seems that an excessive quantity of anchovies were being caught. At the same time a periodic, temporary change in the current from cold to warm off the coast of Peru affected the food supply of the anchovies and cut their numbers. Since 1971 the annual Peruvian fish catch has only been about a third its peak size of over 12 million tonnes in 1970, when it was almost 20 percent of the total world fish catch. Severe restrictions were put on the size of catch, particularly by restricting fishing to a few weeks at a time. The fishing industry, fishmeal processing, and the export of fishmeal were cut drastically..The fish catch for 1976 was 4.4 million tonnes and for 1977 4.8 million tonnes.

The above example of the danger of overusing a 'renewable' (as opposed to a 'non-renewable') natural resource is not the first such event in history. Its recent occurrence and scale make it one worth considering in the context of this chapter. There is a 'natural' limit to the population size of the fish off the coast of Peru (or anywhere else) and various problems arise if this is abused. The ultimate result would be the disappearance of a particular species.

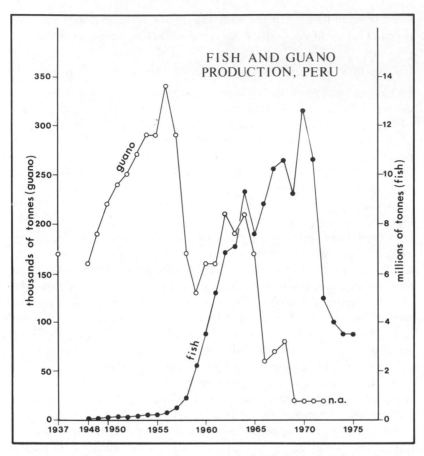

Figure 11.9 The production of guano and of fish in Peru, 1948-1975. Note the separate scales for guano (left) and fish (right). For main source refer to Table 11.13

11.7   Closing the energy gap

In the last section the production of energy was seen to be faltering in major industrial countries either because reserves were small or inaccessible or because new sources of energy had not been developed fast enough to replace traditional ones. Most of the 100 cells in the world have very few fossil fuel reserves and a low consumption of energy per inhabitant. The energy gap was used in Chapter 1 to answer the question: 'Is the gap between rich and poor countries widening?' In Chapter 10, the arithmetic of closing the steel gap by distributing production according to population was seen to involve enormous transfers of steel. In this section, the closing of the energy gap in the future to give every country the same consumption of energy per inhabitant is investigated.

It is only of theoretical interest to consider what the world would be like now if everyone had exactly the same standard of living and to imagine what would have to be done for everyone to have the same standard of living as the average North American. When, however, one is looking at the next few decades it becomes of practical importance to calculate the changes needed to make living standards more equal in the world. In this section energy consumption is used to represent level of development and living standards because a tonne of energy in coal equivalent is a more constant unit through time than a dollar or some other currency measure.

The amount of energy that would have to be transferred between the 100 cells to give every part of the world the same consumption of energy per inhabitant is shown in Figure 11.10(a). The shaded parts of the first three columns would have to be moved into the dotted part above the seven remaining columns. Fifty-four percent of the world's energy would have to be transferred. Figure 11.10(b) shows what would happen if no part of the world was permitted to consume more than twice the world average consumption of energy per inhabitant. The shaded portions of the two left-hand columns could be moved into the dotted area above the six right-hand columns. Thirty percent of the world's energy would then have to be transferred and the parts of the world below the average originally would all consume rather more than 70 percent of the world average.

Figure 11.10(c) shows the topping up that would be needed to give everywhere in the world the same level of energy consumption per inhabitant as that 'enjoyed' by the top 10 percent of the world's population. This group comprises the six North American cells plus four others, three in the U.S.S.R. and one for the Netherlands and North Germany. Since the top 10 percent of the world's population has a consumption 4.6 times the world average, the blank area with arrows pointing to the level of the top 10 percent is 4.6 times as large as the shaded area of the columns. The total height of the columns is equal to 100 units. In 1975 world energy consumption was calculated to be almost exactly 8000 million tonnes of coal equivalent. From the above information it can be calculated that for every part of the world to have the same level of energy consumption as the 10 percent with the highest level, in 1975 the world would have had to consume 4.6 × 8000 million tonnes, or nearly 37,000 million tonnes of coal equivalent.

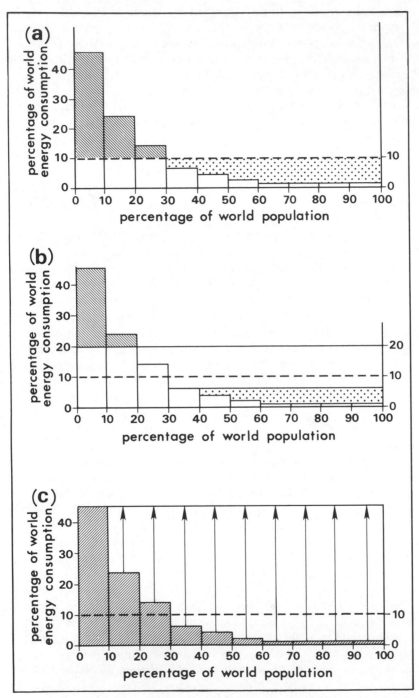

Figure 11.10 Aspects of world energy consumption. See text for explanation

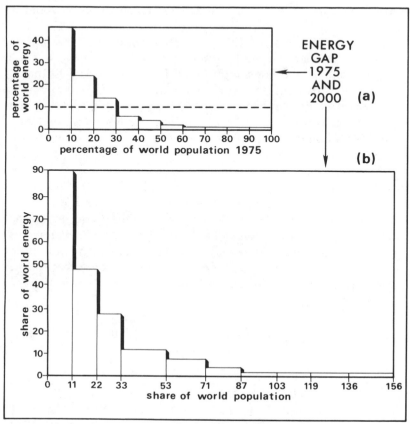

Figure 11.11 The energy gap in 1975 and in 2000

What are the prospects for the future? Figure 11.11 presents one possible future. It was shown in Section 11.1 that a reasonable estimate of the population of the world for the year 2000 would put the total at 56 percent more than that for 1975. Fifty-six new cells, each with 40 million inhabitants, have been introduced into appropriate regions of the world of the 100 cells of 1975. In Figure 11.11 the upper diagram is the same as that in Figure 11.10(c). The lower diagram (b) is a 'replica' of (a) but for the year 2000. The population scale has been extended horizontally. By the year 2000 the number of cells has increased in some of the columns (each with 10 percent of the world's population in 1975) by more than in others. In the diagram the assumption is also made that everywhere the consumption of energy per inhabitant has doubled, a very dubious one in the view of the author but not incompatible with some projections, hopes or aspirations expressed since the Second

World War. To cater for the increase envisaged above it would be necessary to consume (and therefore produce) 2 × 1.56 × 8000 million tonnes (a year) in the year 2000, or some 25,000 million tonnes. To provide the whole expected population of the world in the year 2000 with a consumption per inhabitant equal to that of the highest 10 percent, the empty part above the columns in diagram (b) would also have to be filled. The arithmetic is such that about 115,000 million tonnes would have to be consumed *each year*. This amount is larger than the *total* estimated oil reserves of the world in the mid-1970s.

The above energy gap can be viewed differently through the eyes of individual countries. Peru has been taken as an example. As already noted in this book it is one of the more developed developing countries. Its 1975 energy consumption per inhabitant was more than 20 times as high as that for Ethiopia (680kg against 30kg) but only one-third the world average of 2030kg and far below the U.S. value of 11,000kg per inhabitant. In the study that follows various possible goals for energy consumption in Peru in the year 2000 are considered.

Table 11.14 Energy consumption (millions of tonnes of coal equivalent)

	Total				kg per inhabitant			
	1950	1960	1970	1975	1950	1960	1970	1975
Peru	1.6	3.8	8.6	10.7	190	380	609	682
Mexico	15.4	31.9	60.7	73.4	600	914	1205	1221
Venezuela	3.9	19.3	25.6	31.7	770	2644	2500	2640
Ethiopia	0.1	0.2	0.8	0.8	5	10	32	30
Tanzania	0.2	0.4	0.8	1.0	30	44	62	70
Australia	26	40	67	88	3120	3810	5425	6490
Switzerland	10	10	22	23	2130	1850	3350	3640
U.K.	223	258	300	295	4420	4930	5360	5270

Table 11.15 Energy data for projections

Projection	General aim for the year 2000	Situation for year 2000		Accum. consumption 1970-2000
		kg per inhabitant	millions of tonnes	
1	Total as 1970	310	9	270
2	Per inhabitant as 1970	630	18	400
3	Mexico 1970 per inhabitant	1220	34	580
4	Venezuela 1970 per inhabitant	2500	70	890
5	Australia 1970 per inhabitant	5425	152	1650

Table 11.16 Total production in millions of tonnes achieved or needed by Peru per 5-year period to achieve goals shown in Table 11.15

	1951-55	56-60	61-65	66-70	71-75	76-80	81-85	86-90	91-95	96-2000
1	17	20	29	40	45	45	45	45	45	45
2	Peru 70				48	56	63	70	77	85
3	Mexico				50	63	80	100	125	160
4	Venezuela				52	75	110	150	205	300
5	Australia				56	90	160	275	400	670

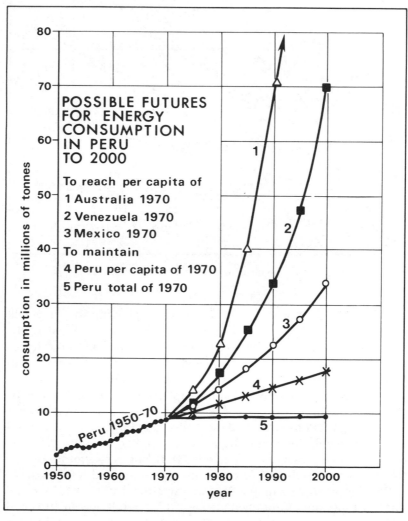

Figure 11.12 Possible futures of energy consumption in Peru to the year 2000

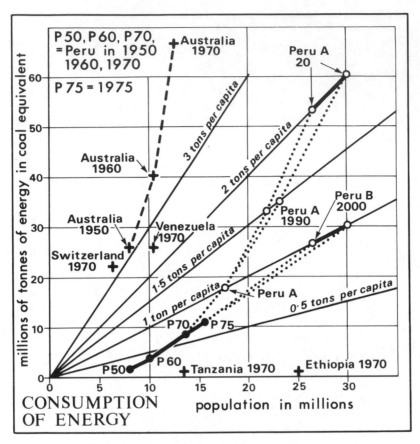

Figure 11.13 Goals for levels of energy consumption in Peru

Table 11.14 shows levels of energy consumption in eight countries. What level of consumption might Peru hope for in the year 2000? Recent trends in Peru show that oil production faltered in the early 1970s, and that this main domestic source of energy was being supplemented by increased imports. Hydroelectric projects were under construction and consideration but progressing slowly. Coal production was small and declining. Unless Peru could exploit oil and/or gas deposits beyond the Andes, any large increase in total energy consumption would have to be supplied by imports. Large amounts of capital have been needed to finance the exploitation of the interior oilfields and to construct a pipeline and refineries.

Possible energy goals for Peru are given in Table 11.15 and the implied *total* amount of energy to be consumed between 1970 and 2000 is taken into account in Table 11.16. Five projections are shown graphically in Figure 11.12. The area under each curve measures roughly the *total* to be consumed during 1970-2000.

Figure 11.13 shows graphically some of the information in Tables 11.14-11.16. Each country occupies a unique position on the graph in a given year. The position is determined by the total population of the country on the horizontal axis and its total energy consumption on the vertical axis. Thus in 1960 Peru had a population of about 10 million and a consumption of energy of just under 4 million tonnes, while in 1975 its population was nearly 16 million and its consumption of energy nearly 11 million tonnes. The dotted lines continue the energy future of Peru along two alternative courses, Peru B to reach a consumption per inhabitant of 1000kg in the year 2000 and Peru A to reach 2000kg per inhabitant that year. Each projection has a range for the year 2000 to allow for the energy required to be read off a particular population range expected and eventually reached. Even from the limited evidence given it seems that the chances that Peru could approach the Australian or Swiss levels are very slight. Equally, Tanzania and Ethiopia might well look in despair at the unattainable Peruvian level.

11.8 Steel as an indicator of the development gap

The growth of steel consumption and production in developing countries is reviewed in this section. From recent trends some idea may be obtained of what can be expected in the future. Steel consumption is an indicator of level of economic development. It may be taken to represent both producer and consumer goods.

Table 11.17 Steel consumption in oil-producing countries. Average consumption in kilogrammes per inhabitant per year during periods indicated

	Saudi Arabia	Iran	Venezuela	Nigeria*	Iraq
1936-38	n.a.	8	37	2	n.a.
1949-53	16	6	82	4	n.a.
1954-58	12	14	145	5	28
1959-63	16	20	83	5	34
1964-68	34	40	131	6	36
1969-73	56	60	168	10	46
1974-76	164	134	219	19	149

* Figures for Nigeria to 1958 are for British West Africa.
n.a. not available.
Source: *United Nations Statistical Yearbook 1953,* Table 171; *1956,* Table 131; *1958,* Table 130; *1961,* Table 130; *1966,* Table 169; *1971,* Table 167; *1976,* Table 171; *1977,* Table 175.

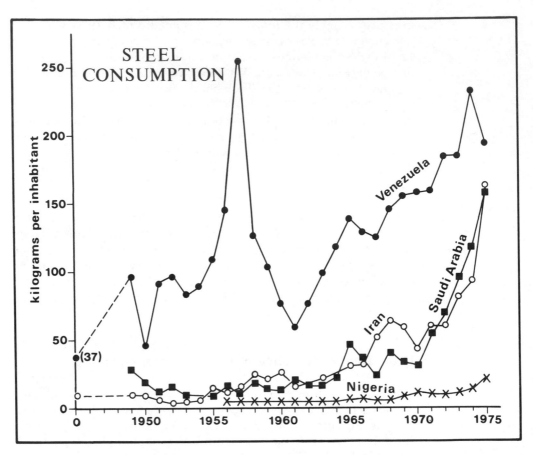

Figure 11.14 The consumption of steel in oil-producing developing countries 1949-1975. See Table 11.17 for period averages. Main source: *United Nations Statistical Yearbook,* various numbers

Steel consumption per inhabitant is shown in Table 11.17 for five major oil-exporting countries of the 1970s. Given that the price of oil rose several times in 1973 and the end of the 1970s it might be expected that the importation of steel and steel goods (or goods with steel in them) would increase greatly thereafter in those countries. Of the five countries only Venezuela is a producer of steel, though it is still a net importer.

The great increase in steel consumption per inhabitant in Saudi Arabia and Iran in the mid-1970s is shown in Figure 11.14. Venezuela has been a large consumer of steel for much longer, having exported large quantities of oil for a longer period than the Middle East countries. In Nigeria the total population is so great that the impact of oil exports on steel imports in per inhabitant terms does not look impressive.

Table 11.18 Steel production in selected developing countries. Total production of steel in thousands of tonnes, yearly average during periods indicated

	India	Brazil	Mexico	Colombia	Venezuela
1938	980	90	140	—	—
1948-52	1450	730	410	—	—
1953-57	1700	1200	540	90*	—
1958-62	3370	1840	1460	150	100**
1963-67	6280	3220	2500	200	530
1968-72	6430	5460	3750	240	940
1973-76	7690	8010	5040	260	990

* 1955-57
** 1959-62
Sources: *United Nations Statistical Yearbook 1954*, Table 109; *1963*, Table 115; *1967*, Table 127; *1976*, Table 126.

Only a few percent of the total population of the developing countries live in the major oil-producing regions. Steel consumption has actually declined in some developing countries in the 1970s. The great rises in oil prices seem only likely to affect directly the material standards of something like 100 million people. They have had a detrimental effect on much of the rest of the developing world where even at the best of times many countries were only able to import minimal quantities of oil. It has been widely assumed or at least hoped that the developing countries would be able to 'take off' by industrializing. Even if they could not expect to catch up with the most highly industrialized countries, at least they should have a respectable industrial base. It was shown in Chapter 8, Section 8.5 and Figure 8.6, that on the basis of the 100 cells in 1975, the 30 developed cells all produce some steel while out of 70 developing ones 50 produce virtually no steel at all. Most of the steel produced in developing countries comes from a few Latin American countries, from part of India, and from several provinces of China.

The data in Table 11.18 and the graph in Figure 11.15 show that three of the five developing countries chosen for consideration as steel producers have achieved some success in developing an iron and steel industry while two have made doubtful progress. It must be appreciated that the five countries differ enormously in total population size (1975 population in millions: India 598, Brazil 107, Mexico 60, Colombia 24, Venezuela 12). The amount of steel produced should therefore be considered in relation to the very large population size of India and the small size of Colombia and Venezuela.

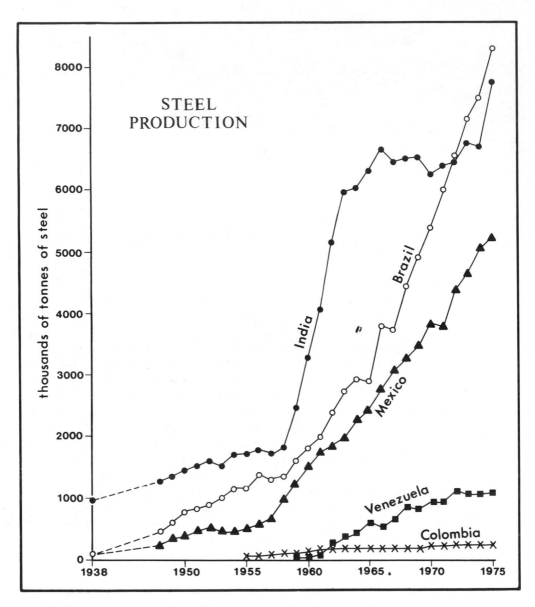

Figure 11.15 The production of steel in selected developing countries 1938-75. See Table 11.18 for period averages and sources of data

In spite of the growth of the iron and steel industry of India between the early 1950s and early 1960s, the amount produced per inhabitant is now only about 1/60 as much as the amount produced per inhabitant in Japan. While the needs of the two countries differ greatly, the gap is nevertheless very marked. To be producing as much steel per inhabitant as Japan does, India would itself have to produce nearly as much steel as the whole world produces.

By the mid-1970s, Brazil and Mexico were producing roughly one-tenth as much steel per inhabitant as Japan, still a very large gap. Colombia and Venezuela are included to provide a contrast between two countries which have broadly similar histories and physical environments. Venezuela has coped much better than Colombia with the development of iron and steel production. It has capital to invest from its oil revenues and large deposits of high-grade iron ore. In Colombia the ingredients for iron and steel production are limited and the location of the works near Bogota, the capital, is a difficult one.

11.9   Has the gap between rich and poor countries been widening?

From the examples given in this chapter it can be seen that many different trends have occurred in the period since the Second World War and that there has not been a straightforward expansion of production in all sectors and all countries. West European countries and Japan are using up limited natural resources while even the comparatively well-endowed U.S.A. is increasingly importing both fuels and non-fuel minerals, paying not only with manufactures but also with agricultural products. Only a few of the developing countries are industrializing at a rate that could bring them quickly towards present levels of industrialization in currently developed countries. The developing countries used as examples in this section have on the whole been the more successful ones.

It is important, therefore, to consider again whether the development gap is showing signs of narrowing. In anticipation, it will be shown that in a relative sense it has changed little, while in an absolute sense it has grown. If that has been the trend in the last few decades, why and how might it suddenly change fundamentally?

It was shown in Chapter 1 and again in Chapter 5 that differentiation between developed (of the time) and developing (really colonial) countries was already considerable towards the end of the

Table 11.19 Absolute data for population and energy consumption

| | Population (millions) | | | | Energy consumption (millions of tonnes of coal equivalent) | | | |
	1937	1950	1962	1974	1937	1950	1962	1974
India*	304	362	449	586	27	36	73	118
U.S.A.	129	152	187	212	759	1140	1542	2433
Indonesia	73	69	98	128	4	4	11	20
Japan	70	82	95	110	66	64	132	421
Brazil	39	52	75	104	5	12	28	67
Nigeria**	20	28	36	61	0	1	2	6
Mexico	19	26	37	58	8	15	34	74
Germany***	68	50	55	62	205	127	221	353
Italy	42	47	50	55	28	30	71	179
U.K.	47	51	53	56	202	224	265	307
France	42	42	47	53	88	85	122	228
Thailand	14	20	28	41	0	0	2	12
Philippines	15	20	29	41	1	2	5	13
Turkey	17	21	29	38	2	5	8	24
Egypt	16	20	27	36	2	4	8	12
Spain	25	28	31	35	10	16	31	73
Poland	34	21	30	34	26	52	99	158
Burma	17	18	23	30	1	0	1	2
Ethiopia	12	16	21	27	0	0	0	1
Argentina	14	17	21	25	9	13	26	47
South Africa	10	12	17	25	15	26	45	77
Zaire	10	11	15	24	0	1	1	2
Colombia	9	11	15	24	1	3	9	15
Canada	11	13	19	22	54	90	112	221

* Prewar India includes Bangladesh and Pakistan.
** Nigeria includes part of Cameroon.
***All Germany before war, West Germany only after war.
Sources: *United Nations Statistical Yearbook 1952; 1963; 1975.*

eighteenth century. By the end of the nineteenth century the gap was already very marked. On account of the lack of adequate data it is difficult to measure the extent of inequality in the world with regard to production and consumption until the interwar period. In this section the Lorenz curve technique, already used in Chapter 4 and illustrated in Appendix 1, is employed to show how inequality has changed between the 1930s and the 1970s.

The world distribution of each of four items has been compared in four different years, 1937, 1950, 1962, and 1974. The consumption of energy and steel and the production of cement and passenger

Table 11.20 Gini coefficients for world distributions in selected years

Reference	Situation		No. of countries	Gini coefficient
EN 1	Energy consumption:	1937	24	0.684
EN 2		1950	Same	0.710
EN 3		1962	Same	0.680
EN 4A		1974	Same	0.678
EN 4B		1974	50	0.665
ST 1	Steel production:	1937	19	0.644
ST 2		1950	19	0.715
ST 3		1962	22	0.617
ST 4		1974	24	0.625
CM 1	Cement production:	1937	24	0.591
CM 2		1950	24	0.605
CM 3		1962	24	0.553
CM 4		1974	24	0.577
PC 1	Passenger cars:	1937	23	0.804
PC 2		1950	23	0.818
PC 3		1962	23	0.758
PC 4		1974	23	0.716
FD 4	Food consumption:	1974	50	0.104

cars in use have been measured against population on the basis of the 24 countries of the world with the largest populations in 1974, excluding China and the U.S.S.R. for which data were not readily available. The data used for the energy calculations are shown in Table 11.19. The consumption of energy for each country in each of the four years is measured against the population of the country in the same year. The resulting gini coefficients are shown in Table 11.20 together with those calculated from similar data for steel production, cement production, and passenger car production. The data for these other three variables are given in Table 11.21. In some of the calculations, certain countries were dropped. The number of countries included is given in Table 11.20.

The gini coefficients for energy consumption show clearly that the world distribution has hardly changed at all over the last four decades. The gini coefficient measures the relative, not the absolute gap. The data in Table 11.19 show that in fact the amount of energy consumed in almost all the countries listed has grown faster than population. The gap between the absolute amount consumed per inhabitant in the developed countries and in the developing countries is much wider now than it was in the 1930s.

Table 11.21 Steel consumption, cement production, and passenger cars in use

	Steel consumption (millions of tonnes)				Cement production (millions of tonnes)				Passenger cars in use (millions)			
	1937	1950	1962	1974	1937	1950	1962	1974	1937	1950	1962	1974
India	1	2	6	8	1	3	9	14	–	–	–	1
U.S.A.	41	86	91	144	20	39	59	73	25	40	66	104
Indonesia	–	–	–	1	–	–	1	1	–	–	–	–
Japan	6	4	23	76	6	4	29	73	–	–	2	16
Brazil	–	1	3	13	1	1	5	15	–	–	1	4
Nigeria	–	–	–	1	0	0	–	1	–	–	–	–
Mexico	–	1	2	6	–	2	3	11	1	1	1	2
Germany	18	10	28	42	13	11	29	36	1	1	6	17
Italy	2	3	12	24	4	5	20	36	2	2	3	14
U.K.	11	14	18	23	7	10	14	18	2	2	7	14
France	5	7	15	24	4	7	17	32	2	2	7	15
Thailand	n.a.	n.a.	–	1	–	–	1	4	–	–	–	–
Philippines	–	–	–	1	–	–	1	3	–	–	–	–
Turkey	–	–	1	2	–	1	2	10	–	–	–	–
Egypt	–	–	–	1	–	1	2	3	–	–	–	–
Spain	n.a.	n.a.	3	12	1	2	7	24	–	–	–	4
Poland	n.a.	n.a.	7	17	1	3	8	17	–	–	–	–
Burma	n.a.	n.a.	n.a.	–	0	0	–	–	n.a.	n.a.	n.a.	n.a.
Ethiopia	n.a.	n.a.	n.a.	–	0	0	–	1	–	–	–	–
Zaire	n.a.	–	–	–	–	–	–	1	–	–	–	–
Argentina	1	1	2	4	1	2	3	5	–	–	1	2
South Africa	1	1	2	6	1	2	3	7	–	–	1	2
Colombia	–	–	–	1	–	1	2	3	–	–	–	–
Canada	2	4	6	16	1	3	6	11	1	2	5	8

n.a. not available.
— less than 500,000.
0 no production.

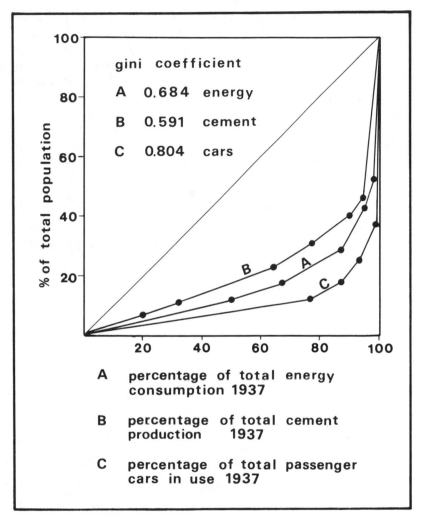

Figure 11.16 The distribution of energy consumption, cement production, and passenger cars in use in 1937 according to population. See Table 11.19 and 11.21 for data and sources

When energy data for 1974 were taken for 50 instead of 24 countries a slightly lower gini coefficient was obtained (reference EN 4B in Table 11.20).

The gini coefficients for steel consumption and for cement production, like those for energy consumption, show little change during the last 40 years. The production of passenger cars, on the other hand, was somewhat less concentrated in 1974 than in 1962 or 1950 but the deconcentration here is the result of the rapid growth of car manufacturing and ownership in West Europe and Japan since the 1950s to bring them closer to the U.S. level than they were in 1937 or 1950. It does not reflect much change in the relationship of developed to developing countries. The data used to calculate the coefficients of concentration are given in Table 11.21 but the population data, already given in Table 11.19, are not repeated. The gini coefficient for food consumption in 50 countries in 1974 is shown in Table 11.20 (reference FD 4). The figure is included for comparative purposes. Three Lorenz curves for 1937 are shown in Figure 11.16. All the curves are so similar that it is superfluous to represent the others graphically.

In the view of the author, even the limited evidence of Table 11.20 is adequate to show clearly that there is a very stable situation in the world, or at least the world excluding the two major socialist countries, the U.S.S.R. and China. A very great change would have to come about in the future for the coefficients to begin to drop far enough below their present levels for some significant change in the present development gap to be brought about.

12

The development gap in perspective

12.1 Early views on natural resources and population

It was suggested near the beginning of the book that much of what has been said and written about development since the Second World War is related to three main themes, themselves interconnected. These are the relationship of population to natural resources, the gap between rich and poor countries, and the concept of stages of growth. All three themes have been discussed at various points in the book. The theme of population and natural resources will now be taken up again.

It is widely accepted that some natural resources are likely to run out in the not too distant future while others could last hundreds and even thousands of years. What does not seem to be widely appreciated and is certainly not often referred to explicitly is the wide disparity in the availability of natural resources to population in different regions of the world. Estimates of the extent and nature of the natural resource gap in the world have been made in the present book.

The theme of the eventual occurrence of overpopulation in the world through the differential rates of growth of population and of land for agriculture is popularly attributed to Thomas Malthus (1776-1834). Adam Smith (1723-90) is associated with the theme of productivity of labour. Some quotations from the two authors will show that Smith actually referred to the pressure of population on natural resources before Malthus did. The following passage by Adam Smith (1776) is quoted because these words and the text that immediately follows appear to be widely interpreted as meaning that he implies that the productivity of labour is what brings prosperity and that natural resources need not be taken into account.

The annual labour of every nation is the fund which originally supplies it with all the necessaries and conveniences of life which it annually consumes, and which consists always either in the immediate produce of that labour, or in what is purchased with that produce from other nations.

According therefore as this produce, or what is purchased with it, bears a greater or smaller proportion to the number of those who are to consume it, the nation will be better or worse supplied with all the necessaries and conveniences for which it has occasion.

But this proportion must in every nation be regulated by two different circumstances; first, by the skill, dexterity and judgment with which its labour is generally applied; and, secondly, by the proportion between the number of those who are employed in useful labour, and that of those who are not so employed. Whatever be the soil, climate, or extent of territory of any particular nation, the abundance or scantiness of its annual supply must, in that particular situation, depend upon those two circumstances.

Adam Smith (1776, p. 182) seems to imply that it is because people are uneducated that they are poor, not because there is not enough land to go round to feed everyone. He refers to the very high mortality rate in the Highlands of Scotland: 'It is not uncommon, I have been frequently told, in the Highlands of Scotland, for a mother who has borne twenty children, not to have two alive'. Further on he concludes: 'Every species of animals naturally multiplies in proportion to the means of their subsistence, and no species can ever multiply beyond it. But in civilised society it is only among the inferior ranks of people that the scantiness of subsistence can set limits to the further multiplication of the human species; and it can do so in no other way than by destroying a great part of the children which their fruitful marriage produces.'

At many points later in *The Wealth of Nations* Adam Smith does, however, implicitly take into account the ratio of natural resources to population and the accessibility or ease of extraction of particular materials. Thus two contradictory themes may be detected. They are briefly exemplified with quotations. Smith (1776, p. 173) apparently associated a growth in prosperity with a growth in population, though in the following passage, which causes which is not clear. The relationship seems circular. The situation of North America 200 years ago was special, however, because land resources, greatly underused by the indigenous American Indian population, were being taken up by the European settlers, who were much more advanced technologically.

> But though North America is not yet so rich as England, it is much more thriving, and advancing with much greater rapidity to the further acquisition of riches. The most decisive mark of the prosperity of any country is the increase of the number of its inhabitants. In Great Britain, and most other European countries, they are not supposed to double in less than five hundred years. In the British colonies in North America, it has been found that they double in twenty or five-and-twenty years. Nor in the present times is this increase principally owing to the continual importation of new inhabitants, but to the great multiplication of the species.

Adam Smith may not have been advocating population growth as an incentive to economic development, but certainly population was needed to settle and run the empty parts of the world occupied by Europeans from the sixteenth to the eighteenth century. However, Smith (1776, p. 174) described China as stagnating, having apparently changed little over several centuries since Marco Polo first described it to Europeans. In Smith's words:

> It (China) had perhaps, even long before his (Marco Polo's) time, acquired that full complement of riches which the nature of its laws and institutions permits it to acquire. The accounts of all travellers, inconsistent in many other respects, agree in the low wages of labour, and in the difficulty which a labourer finds in bringing up a family in China. If by digging the ground a whole day he can get what will purchase a small quantity of rice in the evening, he is contented.

Here it is implied that, with the technology of the time, the limits to cultivation and food production, had been reached. A little further on, Smith (1776, p. 175) continues:

> China, however, though it may perhaps stand still, does not seem to go backwards. Its towns are nowhere deserted by their inhabitants. The lands which had once been cultivated are nowhere neglected. The same or very nearly the same annual labour must therefore continue to be performed, and the funds destined for maintaining it must not, consequently, be sensibly diminished. The lowest class of labourers, therefore, notwith-

standing their scanty subsistence, must some way or another make shift to continue their race so far as to keep up their usual numbers.

Since wealth was largely derived from the land (or was the land) then there was no great concern about the using up of non-renewable resources. Elsewhere Smith (1776, pp. 175-6) did, however, note that in Bengal population was growing but agricultural production and presumably cultivation land were not.

Thomas Malthus was more explicit and emphatic than Adam Smith about the pressure of population on land resources. The quotations that follow are from a work published in 1830 (pp. 13-15).

> In taking a view of animated nature, we cannot fail to be struck with a prodigious power of increase in plants and animals ... whether they increase slowly or rapidly, if they increase by seed or generation, their natural tendency must be to increase in a geometrical ratio, that is, by multiplication.

Malthus then makes an analogy between humans and sheep which, according to his estimate, could produce a situation where 'the whole earthy part of the globe might be completely covered with sheep in less than seventy-six years'. Mankind could grow in a similar fashion 'and the rate of increase would still be enormous, till it was checked either by the natural want of will on the part of mankind to make efforts for the increase of food beyond what they could possibly consume, or, after a certain period, by their absolute want of power to prepare land of the same quality so as to allow for the same rate of progress'.

To Malthus, the limits to the human population of the world were set by the amount of food that could be produced. This is of course true today as well, but far more food is being produced altogether in the world now than early in the nineteenth century, firstly because new areas have been brought into cultivation and secondly because chemical fertilizers have become widely available in developed countries and yields have risen (see Chapter 11). The increase in the use of chemical fertilizers has been possible thanks to the use of non-renewable natural resources.

Further on in this essay, Malthus (1830, pp. 58-9) writes: 'It has been thought that a tendency in mankind to increase beyond the greatest possible increase of food which could be produced in a limited space impeaches the Goodness of the Deity, and is inconsistent with the letter and spirit of the Scriptures'. Almost his final pronouncement is one that would hardly go down well in the permissive society of today: 'First, it appears that the evils arising from the principle of population are exactly of the same kind as the evils arising from the excessive or irregular gratification of the human passions in general, and may equally be avoided by moral restraint'. It is widely agreed and accepted that the 'geometrical' growth of world population cannot continue indefinitely.

12.2 Recent views on natural resources and population

Even from the few passages quoted from Adam Smith and Thomas Malthus it is evident that 150-200 years ago there was an awareness of differences in the availability of natural resources in relation to population. Some of the consequences were appreciated. Between the period when Smith and Malthus both drew attention to the possible eventual limits to land that could be economically cultivated and the early 1970s, there have been sporadic references to the limits of land resources and the running out of non-renewable resources such as oil and metallic ores.

The whole of the *National Geographic* of January 1916 was devoted to the question of food. It was remarked:. 'many men are inclined ... to predict that the day has at last come when the human race must cease to expand its numbers or face inevitable hunger'. It is fair to say that the article also contained examples of the hopeful technological developments of the day and indicated areas of the world where production could be increased. A great potential was seen, in particular, in Russia:

> When the day comes, as come it certainly will, that Russia produces as much per acre as Germany and England, and when the untold millions of acres of undeveloped land are opened up and settled, as they are destined to be, alone she can supply the world's present needs in cereals except rice and corn ...
>
> But as full of possibilities as the wheat growing industry of the United States may be, they are few in comparison with those of Russia. That wonderful country, possessing more latent agricultural resources, perhaps, than any like area in the world, has 288 million acres of excellent wheat land .... Russia alone could produce more wheat than is raised in the entire globe today .

Ironically, in the 1970s the U.S.S.R. was importing large quantities of grain from the U.S.A. Such are the fortunes of forecasting. M.K.

Hubbert has frequently been quoted in the 1970s for his foresight in pointing out the limits to world oil reserves two decades previously. The present author recalls vividly having a discussion in 1950 with colleagues about the prospect that the world's sources of petroleum suitable for making lubricating oil would soon run out.

In the 1970s the debate on natural resources and population growth flourished. Views ranged between highly optimistic and highly pessimistic. Often the basic problem is seen to be the global relationship of natural resources to population, not their uneven regional distribution. Some optimistic views will first be quoted briefly; these will be followed by pessimistic ones.

In *The Next 200 Years,* H. Kahn and his associates (Kahn *et al.,* 1976, p. 181) put very strongly the view that there has been undue concern in the early 1970s about the limits of economic growth. Near the end of the book they write: 'At this point, hopefully, the reader is at least aware of our various arguments that any limits to growth are more likely to arise from psychological, cultural or social limits to demand, or from incompetency, bad luck and/or monopolistic practices interfering with supply, rather than from fundamental physical limits on available resources'. They consider that there is room for guarded optimism with regard to the world resource/population ratio, not the abject pessimism of some widely publicized views of the early 1970s.

Some of the arguments of Kahn and associates seem naive, as (p. 32): 'It should be noted that there is plenty of room in almost all countries for everybody to have a suburban style of life'. On the other hand, depending on what 'requirements' means in the quotation (presumably the current uneven distribution of energy consumption in the world), the following estimate seems reasonable (p. 34): 'Allowing for the growth of energy demand estimated earlier, we conclude that the *proven reserves* of these five major fossil fuels (oil, natural gas, coal, shale oil and tar sands) alone could provide the world's total energy requirements for about 100 years, and only one-fifth of the *estimated potential* resources could provide for more than 200 years of the projected energy needs!' Kahn and his associates also argue (pp. 97-8) that non-fuel minerals are adequate for a long time to come. Their complacency about non-renewable natural resources is based on another assumption about the future: that the development gap will remain for many decades to come. There is no expectation that every country would be consuming materials at the level of the developed countries of today.

Kahn and associates (1976, p. 126) are also of the view that world food production could be increased between 20 and 110 times by increasing the area cultivated, multicropping, and improved uses of fertilizer, irrigation, and high-yielding varieties of plants. No wonder a world population of somewhere between 7500 and 30,000 million could be supported without difficulty. They stretch the limits of common sense if not resources by stating, however, that the rich countries will be so rich in the future that they will be able to 'afford' all the food they need!

On the side of the optimists with regard to population and natural resources, though more cautious in their statements and perhaps more painstaking in presenting their arguments than Kahn and associates, are the Social Science Policy Research Unit of Sussex University in their book *Thinking About the Future,* edited by H.S.D. Cole (Cole *et al.,* 1973). The book is sandwiched chronologically between two pessimistic publications sponsored by the Club of Rome. Of the many important points made by Cole and associates, several are particularly worth noting. They consider that there need be no food problem for the next 100 years, admitting (p. 57), however, that 'There are diminishing returns to investment in both agricultural inputs and the development of new land' in the long run. The technical progress needed to discover, invent or release new natural resources is limited (pp. 10-11) because half is spent on largely unproductive military research and only 2 percent on agriculture in less developed countries. They believe that (p. 156): '... today's Malthusianism can be viewed as in the interests of the materially well-off in the rich countries. It may also have the effect of giving the rich countries a clear conscience about their selfish behaviour towards the poor.' The general impression given by *Thinking about the Future* is that its authors consider there to be no great problem with regard to the exhaustion of natural resources. For political and organizational reasons, however, it may be difficult to realize the potential of natural resources available and for the same reasons impossible to do much to reduce the gap between rich and poor regions.

The strongest set of pessimistic views on population and natural resources in the early to mid-1970s came from teams of researchers sponsored by the Club of Rome. To them the overriding problem was the prospect of a breakdown of the world system from one or a combination of several causes. The problem of how to narrow the development gap by bringing up the poorer countries towards the level of the richer ones was an academic one.

D.H. Meadows and associates (Meadows *et al.,* 1972) argued in *The Limits to Growth* that (p. 188) 'it is through knowledge of wholes that we gain understanding of components and not *vice versa'*. Their book is an attempt to simplify and popularize the work of

Forrester (1971). From a large number of variables identified, quantified, and changed through time with the help of a system model, five main themes or processes serve to illustrate what they see to be the prospect for mankind: industrialization, population growth, food and malnutrition, the use of non-renewable natural resources, and a deteriorating natural environment. An increase in population requires an increase in industrialization and in food production. Increased industrialization uses up non-renewable natural resources more quickly and pollutes the environment.

Only a stable world population, using renewable natural resources and not doing anything detrimental to the natural environment, could last for very long. Otherwise, whatever assumptions are made about rate of growth (or change) in the future, the world system breaks down. Meadows and associates put the view that part of the problem is organizational: 'While technology can change rapidly, political and social institutions generally change very slowly. Furthermore, they almost never change in *anticipation* of a social need, but only in response to one'.

In *Thinking about the Future,* H.S.D. Cole and others (1973) picked out flaws in the Forrester-Meadows model and assumptions. They implied that assumptions were (consciously or not) chosen to support the results desired (p. 133): 'The mental model one chooses to describe the real world (especially the human world) is an inextricable part of one's values, interests, hopes and fears'.

The Club of Rome sponsored another project, outlined in *Mankind at the Turning Point* by M. Mesarovic (Mesarovic and Pestel, 1975). The hopeless future worked out in *The Limits to Growth* was watered down somewhat with the offer of hope of a kind if something was done at once, that is, from 1975 on. One defect of *The Limits to Growth* was that it treated the world as a single entity, undifferentiated regionally. In *Mankind at the Turning Point,* regional contrasts and regional problems were identified. The world was subdivided into 10 regions, similar to ones that the present author himself has used in *Geography of World Affairs* (various editions). Though the regions are not used much, the idea is there. Rich and poor ('North' and 'South') are recognized and the point is made that some regions could 'go under' before others.

Mankind at the Turning Point also stresses more explicitly than *The Limits to Growth* the view that the gap between man and nature is as much a problem as the gap between rich and poor. The authors argue the need for harmonious growth (pp. vii–viii). 'It is most urgent that we do not avert our eyes from the dangers ahead, but face the challenge squarely and assess alternative paths of development in a positive and hopeful spirit. Starting early enough on a new path of development can save mankind from traumatic experiences if not from catastrophe ... were mankind to embark on a path of organic growth, the world would emerge as a system of independent and harmonious parts, each making its own unique contribution, be it in economics, resources or culture'. There are few specific recommendations as to how to cope with the natural resources/population question.

The Club of Rome held its tenth Anniversary Meeting in July 1978. The President, Signor Aurelio Peccei, is quoted (*The Times,* 14 July 1978) as saying that: 'the greatest single problem was global over-population due to modern man's incapacity or unwillingness to control his own runaway numbers. Demographic pressure was subjecting the human system to new, unbearable burdens when its condition was already critical. More than one third of the population lived below the poverty line. There were no long-term plans to settle the new waves of population decently.' One side, at least, of the natural resources/population relationship is mentioned explicitly. We have or shall have a lot of people, too many if we do not try to cope quickly.

A.R. Flower (1978) carried out a study of one natural resource, oil. The conclusion he reached about the world's oil reserves and their limits was very similar, in miniature, to the conclusion of *The Limits to Growth*: whatever assumptions you make about a non-renewable natural resource, it will be used up at some stage; it is just a matter of time. Taking into account various assumptions about new discoveries of oil, about recovery rates and about production rate, he anticipated a difference of only a few years in the exhaustion of reserves between 'favourable' or 'unfavourable' conditions. Although production could fail to meet demand somewhere between 1990 and 2004.

S.E. Kesler (1976) makes a thoughtful and thought-provoking study of both fuel and non-fuel mineral reserves in *Our Finite Mineral Resources*. From his study of various minerals it becomes clear that some are much more abundant, in the sense that at current or any reasonably foreseeable production rates, some would last much longer than others. Concern should therefore be felt about some minerals rather than others. The argument in *Mankind at the Turning Point* that all the various, diverse parts of the world should not be lumped into one world system but that each should be examined in its own right is similar to the argument of Kesler and others that sectors and commodities must also be considered separately. Among key world minerals, the 'lives' of oil, industrial diamonds, gold, mercury, and sulphur seem to be short. There is no reason to be complacent about copper ore or lead ore. On the other hand there is plenty of coal, iron ore, bauxite, phosphate rock, nickel ore, chrome ore, and molybdenum, while salt (sodium chloride) and potash are 'unlimited', as is water. As shown in Chapter 7 of the present book, however, both fuel and non-fuel mineral reserves are highly concentrated in certain regions, countries or cells.

Still specifically on the availability and life of non-renewable natural resources, G. Alexandersson (Alexandersson and Klevebring, 1978) estimates (p. 15) that fossil fuels could supply the world's energy needs at least for 200 years, fissionable ones only four years unless breeder reactors are used, in which case they would last 600 years. However, if fusion energy could be produced commercially there would be enough deuterium in the sea to serve for a million years. Everyone has lapses, especially when speculating about the future, and Alexandersson (pp. 9-10) reveals exceptional powers of prediction when he says: 'In the LDCs ('less developed countries') most mineral deposits have not yet been discovered. Systematic prospecting has never occurred.'

The theme that man is using up natural resources at too fast a rate and in so doing comes into conflict with nature in a number of ways has led to some very bitter expressions of concern for mankind and disdain for those not concerned with the inevitable downfall of modern industrial society. In *Small is Beautiful*, E.F. Schumacher (1974) takes an unusual view of natural resources (pp. 10-13). He points out that the problem of production has not been solved. The reason is that development is in fact a race to use up natural 'capital' as income. In so doing, 'modern man does not experience himself as part of nature but as an outside force destined to dominate and conquer it'. Development is aimed at maximizing, not minimizing the use of raw materials, or irreplaceable capital. The rich are making the big dent in non-renewable resources. To Schumacher (p. 36) it is 'inherent in the methodology of economics to *ignore man's dependence on the natural world'*. One is inclined to ask whether using up natural resources slowly rather than fast is an answer to the resource population problem. It seems self-defeating to leave them in the ground for ever.

In *Ecology and the Politics of Scarcity*, W. Ophuls (1977) starts with the statement (p. 1): 'We begin to understand in our bones that, whatever the causes of this particular crisis, there might not always be enough material and energy to support even current levels of consumption, much less the higher levels many aspire to'. Ophuls puts the world's nutritional limits (p. 55) at 8000 million inhabitants. He criticizes the way man has set about modifying the natural environment or world ecosystem, describing him (pp. 36-7) as: 'a breaker of climaxes, which contain the stored wealth of the ages in their plants, animals, and soil and which in their natural state do not yield rapidly enough for his civilised wants. In other words, instead of living on the income of the biological capital inherited by the species, man invaded the capital itself.' Cultivation and grazing may 'simplify' the ecosystem thereby 'improving' land for agriculture and making production of plants more efficient, but at great risk to the natural environment in the long run.

So between them, Schumacher and Ophuls see man using up all natural resources in an unsatisfactory way. Such also is the theme of S.R. Eyre's (1978) *The Real Wealth of Nations.* Eyre's book differs from most others on the subject of the world prospects for resources and population in its concern with breaking down the world into regions, in his case the sovereign states, and taking a look at things on the ground. The approach of the geographer with ecological rather than economic leanings is down to earth in that the reader is made to realize that conditions differ greatly between different parts of the world. His theme is that too much attention has been paid since the time of Adam Smith to the production of labour and too little to natural resources.

Eyre's broad conclusion from his assessment of the resources of the land is (see Section 7.2) that: 'It seems inescapable that by the year 2000 A.D., given a continuance of present trends, more than half the population of the earth will be living in political units which are incapable, no matter how they might try, of being self-sufficient in the amount of organic materials which they would require to maintain a standard of living equal to the one they enjoy at the present time'.

Eyre also looks at national mineral wealth. He does not distinguish between fossil fuel and non-fuel mineral groups and his conclusions about future prospects for non-renewable resources are based on rates of production rather than on reserves. In this respect his assessment of the prospects of different countries, while useful, does not bring out the degree of concentration of reserves shown by the present author on a country by country basis in Chapter 4 or by the 100 cells in Chapter 7. Eyre does, however, emphasize the fact that the number of really large mineral deposits found in recent decades has not been great, a point also expressed by G. Manners (1978), who argues that Western industrial countries should be more concerned in the immediate future about the lack of effort on the part of Western mining companies to look for new mineral reserves, especially in insecure parts of the world like Africa, than in the long-term exhaustion of some minerals with comparatively short lives.

Section 12.1 started with the views of Adam Smith on natural resources *versus* population. It seems appropriate now to quote Eyre (p. 8) *on* Adam Smith:

> At the present time it seems as though large numbers of people have reached that unrealistic state of mind where they wish to have the best of both worlds: they would like to retain Adam Smith's *laissez-faire* with regard to both resource exploitation and having children, and at the same time to build up an infallible system of social welfare to ensure that no one goes hungry or suffers an untimely end because of neglect or disease. In the final assessment, since the earth is of finite size, it is axiomatic that the two are incompatible.

12.3   Great expectations

The gap in material living standards between rich and poor countries was wider than ever in the 1970s. Both natural resources and productive capacity are very unevenly distributed according to population among different parts of the world. Some mineral natural resources are being used up fast while agricultural land is threatened in various ways. The concept of take-off and stage of growth seems to have been applicable only to a limited set of countries, the developed ones. In view of the above features and restraints it is perhaps surprising to find the assumption still widely held in the 1970s that poor countries expect to catch up rich ones.

At the time of writing, late in 1979, there seemed to be a conspiracy among national governments and international bodies like the United Nations to maintain the illusion that something would eventually happen to change conditions in developing countries. In developed countries, governments have to promise further growth in their own economies but they are happy also to express the hope that economic growth will continue in developing countries. For governments of developing countries it is desirable to promise future economic growth. Growth is the 'right' of every country. Unfortunately the concept of stages of growth may be self-defeating because some regions, by developing rapidly in the last one or two centuries, have perhaps stunted the growth of other regions. While the technology of the now developed regions has spread to the developing regions, much of it has been employed to extract raw materials, fuels, and food from them.

Four examples of the view that positive changes are expected in developing countries may be quoted to illustrate the above points.

In a geography of Ethiopia published in 1970 an Ethiopian geographer, Wolde-Meriam (1972), uses the words 'when industrialization comes' with reference to his country. The British Cabinet Office (1976) produced a paper on *Future World Trends*. It includes the following statement: 'However, the developing countries may find it difficult, as they go through the early stages of industrialisation, to meet the pollution standards adopted by developed countries'.

In 1968 the armed forces took over the government of Peru, not for the first time. The aim was to change the country socially and to give the Andean Indians a fairer share of production. In 1976 President Bermúdez (*Comercio,* 15 July 1976) stated that Peru was 'determined to put an end to the evils of underdevelopment'. The prospects for development of Peru have been used as an example in Chapter 11. In the mid-1970s the country was experiencing a serious economic crisis. The estimates of the electoral population in 1978 showed that of the population of Greater Lima in that year little over a quarter belonged to socio-economic levels defined as high or medium. The proportion must be much lower in the rest of the country. In absolute numbers there were more people of low or very low socio-economic levels in Peru in the late 1970s than a decade or two earlier. What is there to make the trend change suddenly in the 1980s or 1990s? The Peruvian situation is typical of that in many developing countries.

The fourth example of the presumption that developing countries will improve will be discussed at some length. It illustrates the contradictory thinking that seems widely found. Johnson (1979) has produced an informative and readable regional geography of India. He states (p. 30):

> At the outset Indian planners had at their disposal vast resources of land, materials and manpower, but a dearth of capital, experience, enterprise and technological know-how.

He does not assess the vast natural resources in terms of the total population. That is enough, however, for the following assumption (p. 25):

> As Indian diets improve succeeding generations will be bigger boned and heavier, and their food needs will therefore increase.

It is not clear which is to come first, more food or bigger Indians. So far so good, but elsewhere in his book (p. 24) Johnson quotes

Indian demographers who expect an increase of two and a half times in total population, to reach 1600 million by 2071-81. According to Johnson (p. 48) agriculture is the mainstay of the Indian economy and is likely to remain so in the forseeable future. Yet he says (p. 88):

> The land-holding system has been the subject of much legislation. There is not enough land for those who are or who would be farmers, and the country suffers from intense rural over-population.

Land is not the only natural resource that is lacking. Johnson notes (p. 61):

> Water is a limited resource the efficient use of which is of increasing importance as the demand expands from agriculture, industry and a water- and power-using population with rising living standards. India cannot afford to allow water to run to waste and must strive to bring under control as much of its water resources as possible.

Compared with other parts of the world, and given its large population size, India is also very poorly provided with reserves of minerals.

For India to develop along the lines of West Europe or North America, and to have comparable levels of consumption, it would need to reduce greatly the size of its labour force in agriculture, and to expand greatly large-scale industry, possibly at the expense of small-scale industry and domestic crafts. It would have to consume far greater quantities of fuel and raw materials than it does now and to produce several times as much food. Otherwise, to return to the beginning, it will not have its bigger boned and heavier population.

12.4   Population, natural resources, and production

It is intended in the last sections of this chapter to summarize the main points made in the book and to draw some tentative conclusions. Before doing so it is useful to recapitulate briefly. The relationship to one another of population, natural resources, and production was discussed in Chapter 9. Cells were plotted graphically in Figures 9.15 and 9.16 according to natural resources per inhabitant and production per inhabitant. Some cells were

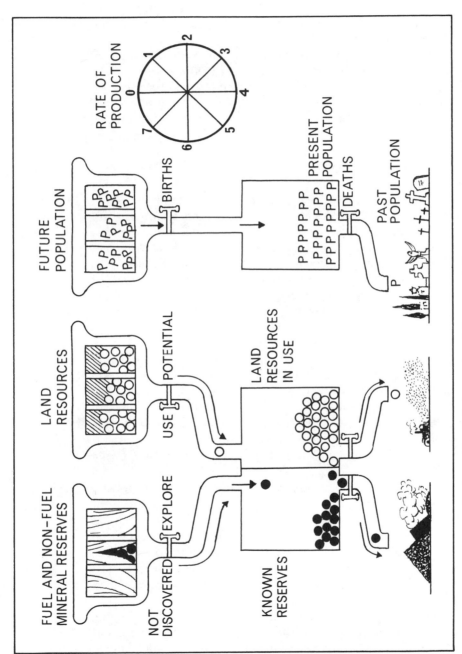

Figure 12.1 Resources, production and population, a pictorial representation

shown to be much better off than others with regard to their resource/population ratios and some were producing much more per inhabitant than others. The ideas in the graph will be further developed in this section.

The population of the world at any moment in time can be divided into three classes, those alive (nearly 4000 million in 1975), those who died before 1975, and those not yet born by 1975. People are represented in Figure 12.1 by the symbol P. The two taps in the model are fertility and mortality rates. An unchanging total world population would have both taps allowing the same number of people through in a given period. At present the fertility tap is allowing a faster flow than the mortality tap on account of high fertility in developing countries.

Natural resources have been divided into two types in Figure 12.1, mineral reserves and land resources. The minerals are thought of as non-renewable, the land resources as renewable (or not exhaustible). It was pointed out in Chapter 11, however, that agricultural land can be lost and its fertility reduced unless it is restored through proper management. Moreover, the level of production from the land is related to a considerable degree to the addition of non-renewable resource inputs (fertilizers, fuel to drive machines).

In Figure 12.1 the two left-hand boxes represent the known (proven, commercial) reserves of useful minerals (left) and the land actually in use (right). Above the known reserves of minerals is a container with an unknown but finite quantity of as yet undiscovered minerals of current or future use to man. They are hidden behind curtains. As they are discovered (by opening the tap) they join those in the box below, containing the known reserves. As they are used up they pass out of the box into the waste pile below.

In contrast to the mineral resources, land resources are mostly known now and can therefore be assessed. It is roughly known, for example, how much new land could theoretically be irrigated and how much pasture and other currently uncultivated land might be brought into cultivation. Thus land can be brought, through the process of 'improvement', from the container above into the box. By misuse or overuse, land resources can be lost. They then drop out of the bottom of the box.

The meter on the right in Figure 12.1 measures the rate at which production is taking place or the rate at which reserves and resources are passing through the taps into the waste piles below. Gross national product is roughly what the meter is measuring. Man's capacity to produce goods and services has grown greatly in

Table 12.1 Development in four regions

	Resource units	Population	Rate of use per inhabitant	Units used
Region (a)				
1975	1000	1	4	4
1976	996	1	4	4
1977	992	1	4	4
1978	988	1	4	4
1979	984	1	4	4
1980	980			
Region (b)				
1975	1000	1	4	4
1976	996	1	5	5
1977	991	1	6	6
1978	985	1	7	7
1979	978	1	8	8
1980	970			
Region (c)				
1975	1000	1	4	4
1976	996	1.1	4	4.4
1977	991.6	1.2	4	4.8
1978	986.8	1.3	4	5.2
1979	981.6	1.4	4	5.6
1980	976.0			
Region (d)				
1975	1000	1	4	4
1976	996	1.1	5	5.5
1977	990.5	1.2	6	7.2
1978	983.3	1.3	7	9.1
1979	974.2	1.4	8	11.2
1980	963.0			

the last two centuries and especially since the Second World War. The application of technology capable of boosting or replacing human muscles is now being supplemented by devices to boost or replace human brains. As production in the world continues to grow and technology becomes increasingly sophisticated, natural resources become the potential limit to economic growth. The above model can perhaps help the reader to see the 'inevitability' of certain things happening in the world. In the end, by definition, so long as they are being used at all, non-renewable natural resources will run out. This will happen whether the population of the world continues to grow, becomes stable or even diminishes.

Four fictitious situations are shown in Table 12.1. The position of a country or a region is seen in relation to three variables: total resource units, total population, and rate of use of resource units. The four regions (a), (b), (c), and (d) all start with the same initial total of resource units, inhabitants, and rate of use of resources. In all four regions, no new natural resources are discovered though allowance could be made for new resources. The units used up and deducted each year are the result of multiplying population by rate of use (or production).

In region (a), population and rate of use of natural resources remain unchanged. Each year the store of known reserves of natural resources drops by four units.

In region (b), the rate of use of resources increases and the store is used up faster.

In region (c), population increases and the effect is the same as in region (b).

In region (d), the reserves are being used up fastest because both population and rate of use per inhabitant are increasing.

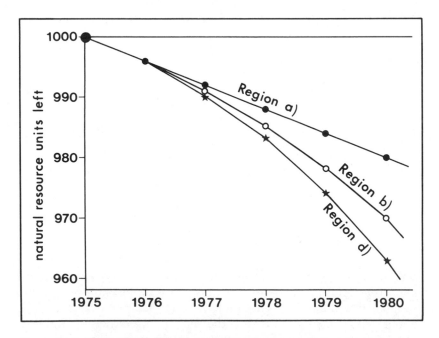

Figure 12.2 The rate of utilization of natural resources according to various assumptions. See Table 12.1 for data and text for explanation

What is happening in regions (b)-(d) has been referred to, perhaps rather unfortunately, as exponential growth. The important point is that in *all four* situations, so long as there are some people and they are producing something from non-renewable natural resources, the ultimate store of non-renewable resources will continue to be reduced. Thus in region (a) in the above example, even when population and production levels do not change, non-renewable natural resources are being used up, an important point stressed by Beckerman (1979) in his criticism of the *limits of growth* model. The process can be seen in Figure 12.2, in which three of the four regions in Table 12.1 are following a path from their initial 1000 resource units towards zero. Even if additional non-renewable natural resources are discovered and added to the store, this is simply taking something from the ultimate finite number of resource units in the curtained container at the upper left of Figure 12.1. The model can easily be modified to represent specific situations in various regions and countries of the world.

What is the answer? There is no point in just sitting back and leaving the oil and the copper in the ground because they are non-renewable. Nevertheless, it is desirable in the not too distant future to reach a state in which most of production is from renewable or non-exhaustible natural resources.

12.5 The new significance of natural resources

In Chapters 7-9 the resource and production make-up of the 100 cells was described and illustrated diagrammatically. In Figure 9.15 each cell was placed on a graph according to its share of world gross national product and its share of world natural resources. Many cells scored low on both criteria, as for example most of those in India and China. Some cells scored high on GNP per inhabitant but low on resources, as for example most of Western Europe. A number had low GNP but large resources, including the Middle East. A few 'privileged' cells had high GNP *and* high resources. Canada, part of the U.S.A., Australia, and Siberia plus the Soviet Far East stood out as exceptionally well-endowed regions.

The present great disparities in GNP and in resources in the world could broadly be explained by the history of settlement and population growth in the last few centuries. Of those parts of the world in which large numbers of people were concentrated in heavily used agricultural resources, Europe escaped from the poverty trap by developing technology to increase production per worker and acquired control over natural resources in other parts of the world. Underused regions of the Americas, Australia, and Siberia were settled by Europeans, but in comparatively small numbers. In contrast, large numbers of people live in the old agricultural societies of the world, without adequate natural resources of their own to expand production greatly and, apart from Japan, without the chance to draw on fuels, raw materials, and food from other regions.

What are the prospects for the cells in the future? A selection of cells from Figure 9.15 has been placed on the graph in Figure 12.3. Two pieces of information are used to fix the position of each cell on the graph: its GNP divided by population and its natural resources divided by population. As time passes, three elements can change, population size, production size, and natural resources size. It is proposed now to examine and speculate about changes in the three elements.

For simplicity three possible prospects are allowed for each element. It is possible either to increase, to stay the same or to decrease. One might assume, for example, that the population of England will stay roughly the same size in the next two to three

Table 12.2 Possible future positions of countries in Figure 12.3

	Population	Resources	Production		Population	Resources	Production
1	−1 NE	−1 W	−1 S	15	0 0	0 0	−1 N
2	−1 NE	−1 W	0 0	16	0 0	+1 E	−1 S
3	−1 NE	−1 W	+1 N	17	0 0	+1 E	0 0
4	−1 NE	0 0	−1 S	18	0 0	+1 E	+1 N
5	−1 NE	0 0	0 0	19	+1 SW	−1 W	−1 S
6	−1 NE	0 0	+1 N	20	+1 SW	−1 W	0 0
7	−1 NE	+1 E	−1 S	21	+1 SW	−1 W	+1 N
8	−1 NE	+1 E	0 0	22	+1 SW	0 0	−1 S
9	−1 NE	+1 E	+1 N	23	+1 SW	0 0	0 0
10	0 0	−1 W	−1 S	24	+1 SW	0 0	+1 N
11	0 0	−1 W	0 0	25	+1 SW	+1 E	−1 S
12	0 0	−1 W	+1 N	26	+1 SW	+1 E	0 0
13	0 0	0 0	−1 S	27	+1 SW	+1 E	+1 N
14	0 0	0 0	0 0				

			Change expected			Change in graph		
(a)	11	England	0	−1	0	0	W	0
(b)	12	Japan	0	−1	+1	0	W	N
(c)	27	Australia	+1	+1	+1	SW	E	N
(d)	20	Saudi Arabia	+1	−1	+1	SW	W	N
(e)	21	Bangladesh	+1	0	0	SW	W	0

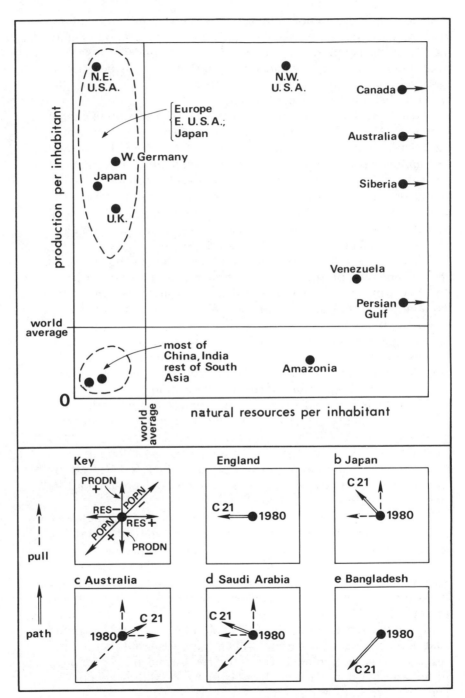

Figure 12.3 The changing position of cells in relation to population, production, and natural resources

decades, that production will stay the same, and that natural resources will decrease. England's position on the graph in Figure 12.3 would therefore change in the future under the above assumptions because it would shift to the left. This is because as resources are used up (and presumably others not found) the quantity per inhabitant would diminish.

Since there are three kinds of prospect for each of the three elements, 27 possible combinations exist. These are given in Table 12.2. The symbol −1 indicates a decrease, 0 (zero) no change, and +1 an increase. The change can be translated into a movement of the cell on the graph. If population decreases, the cell moves to the upper right (or NE). If population increases, the cell moves to the lower left (or SW). A change in resources results in a shift of the cell to the left (W) or the right (E). A change in production results in a shift of the cell upwards (N) or downwards (S).

The fortunes of five cells or groups of cells will now be described in terms of their prospects. Their assumed prospects are shown in the lower part of Table 12.2 and their changing positions on the graph in Figure 12.3 are indicated in individual diagrams below the main graph.

(a) England is the simplest cell under the assumptions made. It moves to the left because resources are being used up but population and production are assumed to remain unchanged and they therefore do not cause a change of position on the graph.

(b) Japan is assumed to have little change in population size (actually its population is likely to grow). Its natural resources will continue to be used up in the future (use of minerals, loss of land to urban development). Its productive capacity will continue to grow. Under these assumptions Japan will be pulled to the left by diminishing resources and upwards by increased production. Its path will therefore be to the upper left (NW).

(c) Australia is assumed to experience growth in population, production, and natural resources for some time to come. The growth in natural resources results from an excess of new discoveries over natural resources used up. Graph (c) in Figure 12.3 shows three forces working on Australia, population growth pulling it SW, production increase N, and extra resources E. The combined effect is to pull it some way E and a little way N.

(d) Saudi Arabia is part of oil-rich cell number 43. It is assumed that population and production will both increase, but that natural resources will be depleted. The three forces and their combined effect are shown in diagram (d) of Figure 12.3. Saudi Arabia moves some way W and a little N.

(e) Bangladesh is expected to experience further population growth, no change in the size of natural resources, and no change in production. Because population grows, production per inhabitant *and* natural resources per inhabitant diminish. Bangladesh moves SW.

What is happening in the world according to the situation illustrated above by the changes in the positions of selected cells? Once it is accepted that natural resources are not unlimited (or so big that their limits need not be considered) it becomes vital to view the total natural resource inventory of the world when discussing development. Most of the population of the world is living in cells in which the natural resource to population balance is deteriorating. Any cell that is moving to the left, whether SW, W or NW on the graph, is experiencing a reduction in its natural resource/population ratio.

The cells in the upper left half of the graph have high levels of production per inhabitant but relatively few natural resources. They use their own resources to some degree but also depend heavily on primary products from cells on the right-hand side of the graph. The cells in the lower left-hand part of the graph are in countries like India, China, and Bangladesh, which hope for some industrialization and higher production and standards of living. If they 'developed' greatly they also would have to depend on cells on the right-hand side of the graph.

In the view of the author there are not enough cells on the right-hand side of the graph even to keep the cells of Europe and Japan at their present high levels of consumption, let alone to enable the many of the lower left to develop. The cells on the upper right are few in number. In a conference held in Australia in 1973 on the use of the country's natural resources, concern was expressed that these should not be used up too quickly. If Australians are right to be concerned about the limits to their natural resources, nearly everywhere else ought to be desperately worried. The countries on the lower right of the main graph would themselves prefer to use fuel, materials, and food produced from their own natural resources rather than to export these to pay for manufactured goods. Since the natural resources of the world are limited, industrialization in cells in the lower right-hand side of the graph resulting in their climbing upwards could have the effect of pulling production down in the cells at the upper left of the graph.

The cells at the upper left are the most vulnerable of all in the world. Until recently their position was seen to be both desirable (high living standards) and strong because they provided the manufactured goods and technology for countries that they ran either as recognized colonies or in effect as economic colonies. Such colonies have been referred to as the dependent countries and the industrial countries as dominant. It could now be argued that the countries of the upper left of the graph are the ones that are 'dependent'.

The present precarious position of Europe and Japan depends on two assumptions: first that the countries at the lower right and upper right of the graph will continue to be willing to export surpluses of fuel, raw materials, and food, and second that the countries at the lower left will not industrialize, thereby diverting much of the fuel and many of the raw materials produced in the resource-rich cells from flowing to the currently industrialized cells. World trade can be seen in a new light if Europe (including European U.S.S.R.), Japan, and increasingly the U.S.A. are now seen as 'dependent' countries. It will now be examined in the light of this idea.

Fuel, raw materials, and food are derived directly from natural resources. Secondary and tertiary products, manufactures and services, are widely exchanged for primary products in world trade. There are also intermediate products, semi-manufactures, which may be primary products processed for export. Definitions of these basic classes of product are not entirely clearcut. From United Nations data it is, however, possible to calculate roughly for each

Table 12.3 The composition of the imports of selected countries (percentages)

	Imports	RM	MF		Imports	RM	MF
1	Japan	89	11	12	Indonesia	56	44
2	Bangladesh	82	18	13	Afghanistan	55	45
3	India	79	21	14	Switzerland	55	45
4	Brazil	71	29	15	Ivory Coast	52	48
5	Hong Kong	67	33	16	Mexico	45	55
6	France	67	33	17	Australia	44	56
7	U.K.	66	34	18	Venezuela	43	57
8	West Germany	64	36	19	Saudi Arabia	40	60
9	U.S.A.	62	38	20	Canada	38	62
10	Tanzania	62	38	21	Mozambique	33	67
11	Ethiopia	57	43				

RM, Food, industrial supplies, fuel as % of total imports.
MF, Manufactures as % of total imports.
Source: *Yearbook of International Trade Statistics 1977*, Vol.1 Trade by Country, U.N., New York, 1978, various tables.

Table 12.4 The composition of the exports of selected countries

	(1) Agri.	(2) Food	(3) Mining	(4) Metals	(5) Textiles	(6) Wood, paper	(7) Chems.	(8) Non-metal	(9) Metal manuf.	(10) Other manuf.	(A) Primary	(B) Secondary
Saudi Arabia	0	0	951	0	0	0	47	0	2	0	95	5
Ethiopia	794	150	5	0	10	2	32	2	3	2	95	5
Peru	103	270	184	366	17	3	46	1	9	2	92	8
Chile	26	25	123	743	0	50	27	0	7	0	92	8
Tanzania	800	65	45	1	29	3	55	0	2	0	91	9
Thailand	301	425	33	55	84	28	11	10	31	24	81	19
Australia	225	210	262	90	22	12	93	2	61	22	79	21
Argentina	417	309	2	24	75	8	43	3	117	1	75	25
Brazil	342	284	96	24	69	20	26	4	125	10	75	25
Venezuela	7	3	710	1	0	1	275	0	2	0	72	28
Bangladesh	376	5	1	0	593	7	9	0	3	7	38	62
U.S.A.	157	62	40	24	26	36	121	8	501	24	28	72
U.K.	20	57	97	57	66	23	175	16	448	41	23	77
Czechoslovakia	18	27	41	100	66	25	75	30	561	22	19	81
Japan	4	9	1	142	56	10	80	14	657	27	17	83
West Germany	12	44	19	78	97	25	157	18	559	32	15	85
Switzerland	7	40	46	41	75	25	219	7	493	47	13	87
Hong Kong	12	10	4	3	491	14	37	3	283	143	3	97

Source: *Yearbook of International Trade Statistics 1977*, Vol. 1 Trade by Country, U.N., New York, 1978, various tables.
Notes: 1. Data are for 1977 for most developed countries, 1974-76 for most developing ones.
    2. Values in columns (1)-(10) are in per thousands of total exports accounted for by each category.
        Values in (A) and (B) are totals of (1)-(4) and (5)-(10) respectively and are percentages.
    3. Categories (1)-(4) are *mainly primary products*, categories (5)-(10) *mainly secondary products*.

country of the world the percentage of the value of its imports and of its exports accounted for by primary products.

The proportions of primary and secondary products in the imports of selected countries are shown in Table 12.3. The column RM .in the table includes food, fuel, and industrial supplies. Even the limited information given about countries reflects clearly the distribution of countries in the graph in Figure 12.3. Countries that depend heavily on the importation of primary products include both developed resource-poor countries like Japan and the U.K. and developing resource-poor countries like Bangladesh and India, the upper left and lower left areas of the graph in Figure 12.3. Similarly, countries that import comparatively few primary products include developed resource-rich countries like Australia and Canada as well as developing resource-rich countries like Venezuela and Saudi Arabia.

The composition of the exports of selected countries is shown in Table 12.4. The classification of commodities is unfortunately different from that used above for imports. The division into primary and secondary products is not precise. Even so, it is clear by the break between Venezuela and Bangladesh in columns (A) and (B) which countries are basically suppliers of primary products. Europe, Japan, and the U.S.A. depend heavily on the export of manufactured goods. They export these *because* they need to import primary products.

In conclusion, the 'dependence' of the developed but resource-poor countries may once again be underlined. The developing, resource-rich, countries like Venezuela, Saudi Arabia, and Zaire could continue to exist even if they cut down their exports of fuel and raw materials. In contrast, living standards as we know them in the developed but resource-poor countries would fall very quickly without the supplies from the resource-rich regions of the world. If this situation were better appreciated and publicized in the developed countries, then they might take even more seriously the need to look for alternative resources and different ways of life. They would also perhaps be even less generous than they actually are in aiding the poor countries.

12.6   The decade of uncertainty

Until the 1970s the prospects for arriving eventually at a world with an adequate standard of living for all its citizens seemed reasonable to many people. Suddenly, in a few years, views changed completely. The same situation was perceived differently.

In this section it is proposed to examine briefly some of the aspects of the world economy that have been a cause of concern and speculation in the 1970s. For convenience subheadings have been used.

1. *Where will new natural resources be found?*

The plant and animal resources of the oceans are limited biologically because of the restricted scope for plant growth in water. Only the surface of the ocean floors can be 'scratched' and only certain commercial minerals (e.g. manganese ore) seem to be there in abundance. The possibility of obtaining any materials on a commercial basis either from the moon or the planets seems utterly remote. New natural resources will mostly have to be found and used within the land areas of this planet and in shallow offshore seas. Information from satellites is a useful addition to the means used to locate prospective mineral-rich areas.

All other things being equal, most new reserves of minerals should be found either in the large territories of such developed countries as Canada, the U.S.S.R., and Australia, or in developing countries, where exploration has so far been limited. They are least likely to be found in large quantities *per inhabitant* either in Japan, Europe or Northeastern U.S.A., or in South and East Asia.

2. *The hermit syndrome*

Whether the present developing countries attempt to industrialize or choose to remain as they are, they may find it necessary to withdraw from the world trading system in order to conserve their own natural resources. If they decide in the future to industrialize they will then still have resources on which to base industrialization.

On the whole the developed countries are the ones that have promoted the growth of international trade. Highly industrialized countries with limited natural resources have been compelled to seek raw materials, energy, and food elsewhere. Until the 1960s much of the developing world had colonial status. The colonial powers could organize trade with their colonies. A number of developing countries have, however, already shown signs of opting out of the world trading system. Burma is an example of what might be termed a hermit country. The value of its exports dropped from $270 million in 1963 to $108 million in 1970. Its trade was increasing in the mid-1970s but in real terms had not returned to the level of the early 1960s. Kampuchea (formerly Cambodia) never traded

much but it also seems to have been shutting itself off from the rest
of the world. On a much larger scale it can be estimated that
something like half of the population of the developing world lives
in whole countries, or in regions in large countries such as India and
China, that are hardly involved at all in the world trading system.

3. *The replacement option*

As various raw materials have for one reason or another become
scarce in the world economy attempts have been made to find
substitutes or replacements, or to do without them. There is often,
however, an element of circular thinking in the process of
replacement, as will be shown in some responses to the world oil
shortage.

Everyone (nearly) agrees that oil (petroleum) is non-renewable
and likely to run out sooner or later. Motor vehicles mostly run on
petroleum products. Fuel oil is widely used to fire electric power
stations. The response of Brazil to its own weak energy position,
depending heavily on imported oil, has been to launch a
programme to grow more sugar cane in order to extract from it
alcohol, suitable for internal combustion engines. In so doing Brazil
is taking land from other crops. Yet the country itself has problems
some years in satisfying its own food needs. Ironically experiments
are being carried out elsewhere in the world to produce human
food from hydrocarbons, including oil itself.

Like Brazil, Sweden depends heavily on imported oil. Its
proposed response to a world oil shortage is to grow wood for fuel.
The world in general is, however, likely to become short of
softwood timber. Moreover Sweden is putting the clock back. One
of the early 'advances' in the Industrial Revolution was to replace
wood as the major fuel by coal. However widely and efficiently the
cultivation of trees and of such field crops as sugar to produce fuel
is developed, plants could never supply more than a small fraction
of the quantity of energy now derived in the world from fossil fuels.

At the rate the United States is consuming oil it would use its own
reserves up very soon. It has at least four options: to cut energy
consumption drastically (unlikely), to import more oil than it
actually does (difficult politically and economically), to search for
more home oil (costly) or to replace oil by other fuels. It is
technically possible to produce petroleum product substitute from
the vast reserves of coal and from the oil shales available in the
U.S.A. itself. The following findings show how in this case a country
has not prepared itself to go over quickly to a substitute.

In 1979 President Carter announced a massive programme of synthetic fuel development. It was found that coal, oil shales, and tar sands are all difficult to develop. Jackson (1979) puts coal in perspective thus:

> The main natural resource available to America is its coal. One ton can produce 2.5 barrels of oil by a variety of processes. In South Africa, which has had a plant in operation for some 25 years the cost is an official secret but is thought to be about 25 dollars a barrel. American estimates run at near 35 dollars a barrel. The South African operation turns out 20,000 barrels a day: American consumption is nearer 20 million a day.
>
> The current guess is that an industrial plant designed to produce 100,000 barrels a day would cost 3,000 million dollars and that Mr. Carter's target of 2.5 million barrels would need 15 coal conversion units — an investment of 45,000 million dollars to produce oil costing 40 percent more than the current (mid-1979) OPEC price. But there would also need to be an increase in coal production of around 218 million tons a year, 35 percent above today's figures.
>
> One expert in the industry has calculated that this would require 115 new mines, 23,300 new railway hopper wagons, 5,330 conventional freight wagons, 85 large river barges, and 1,500 large lorries — all at a further cost of 20,000 million dollars. Many of the new mines would be strip operations, causing further environmental problems.

At least it is known that large reserves of energy are available in coal, oil shales, and tar sands. The question of research and production of renewable sources such as wind, wave and solar power is much more problematical and one suspects that the quantity of energy that can realistically be expected from these sources is quite limited.

Yet another response to the oil shortage is the attitude that when a country has used up its own reserves it will be able to start or restart importing oil from elsewhere. What if 'elsewhere' has been running out too? This rather short-sighted view seems to be reflected in thinking in the U.K., which actually became self-sufficient in oil in 1979-80. Its self-sufficiency is not expected to last long, so it will have to start importing again. One reason given by the Chancellor of the Exchequer for removing exchange controls (October 1979) was that it might encourage individuals to invest abroad in anticipation of the running out of British North Sea oil reserves. He may not have been thinking specifically of investment in oil itself but at least he assumed that there would be some developments elsewhere in which the 'resource-poor' U.K. investor could put his money.

In the early 1970s the official world reserves of oil were estimated to be 80-90,000 million tonnes. Had world production continued to rise at 7-8 percent a year, as it was doing before 1973, those reserves would have lasted 15-20 years. In fact, production levelled off in the later 1970s.

It was estimated by the CIA (*El Pais,* 15 Dec. 1979, Madrid, p.48) that counting existing proved reserves of oil, the contribution from more complete recovery methods, and the addition of reserves not yet discovered, possible total world oil reserves stood at about 300,000 million tonnes in the late 1970s. Production was about 7000 million tonnes a year, a rate that could theoretically be sustained for about four decades. Given the great dependence of all the developed countries on oil and the close relationship between economic growth and energy consumption, little further economic growth could be expected without the development of other sources of energy. To achieve even a modest increase of energy consumption in Africa, South and Southeast Asia, a substantial proportion of the world's oil production would have to be diverted to these areas, with their very low energy consumption levels, and containing about a third of the world's population.

4. *De-development*

Alternative and radical technology are terms that imply a rediscovering backwards. G. Boyle (Boyle and Harper, 1976) prefaces his book *Radical Technology* with the words: 'This is a book about technologies that could help create a less oppressive and more fulfilling society. It argues for the growth of small-scale techniques suitable for use by individuals and communities, in a wider social context of humanised production under workers' and consumers' control.' Alternative technology is a similar concept, advocating for example the use of renewable energy resources and the conservation of energy (trains as opposed to the private car, heavily insulated buildings).

In the view of the author, development is indivisible. In the same way, 'de-development' is indivisible. It is not possible suddenly to scrap the less desirable, more wasteful, material features of the affluent society and to keep the more desirable ones. Many people might be glad to see the end of certain luxuries, but few would want to lose electricity. It is not possible to put the clock back to the Middle Ages. It is however certainly worth preparing for more austere conditions in the developed countries.

The economy of the Western developed countries is geared to increasing the consumption of goods and services. The U.S.S.R. aims to achieve even higher living standards than the Western countries, though up to now the Soviet system has not been too generous to the consumer. There are, however, no doubt many older people in the Western industrial countries who can remember poorer times and the austere conditions in the Second World War. They may feel that the prosperity of the 1970s cannot last. There has been a weak counter-movement in Western industrial countries towards more austere standards. In the Puritan-minded sections of the Western industrial countries austerity even has a strong appeal. Many people might readily accept some tightening of the belt so long as they knew that everyone was getting equal reductions, but no political party could fight an election on greater austerity.

5. *Protection of the environment*

In the 1960s and 1970s awareness has grown of the way the exploitation of natural resources threatens the environment. New regulations tend to curb the use of natural resources and to raise the cost of production of energy and the processing of materials. In the U.S.A., alternative energy supplies to oil have development problems. The large-scale extraction of coal in the Western states meets local resistance. The refining of oil shales creates environmental damage. Nuclear power stations are suspect.

Even in the U.S.S.R., where state plans can theoretically override local resistance, geographical publications of the 1970s include numerous examples of pollution and new concern over adverse effects of development on the environment. Large-scale water transfer schemes have been delayed or shelved and there are reservations about the development of areas with permafrost. The creation of large reservoirs can adversely affect other resources and also climatic conditions. Pollution and lack of care of the environment is also noted, for example, in the contamination of the waters of Lake Baykal by pulp mills and of roadside vegetation by lead from petrol fumes. Picnickers cut wood for camp fires from protected woodland.

In the U.K., where the resource/population balance is very modest indeed, virtually any move to develop a new natural resource meets opposition. Plate 12.4 shows a protest sign against the sinking of three coalmines in the Vale of Belvoir, Leicestershire, to work what is described as one of the best coal deposits in Western Europe.

Plate 12.1 Increasing concern over the prospect that world oil and natural gas reserves could run out in several decades has led to experiments in the development of 'renewable' sources of energy. Solar panels and wind energy facilities are exhibited in the Centre for Alternative Technology, Machynlleth, Wales

Plate 12.3 (Opposite bottom) The conservation house in Plate 12.2 is sheer fantasy; it is enough trouble to rehouse the population of the U.K. in ordinary houses. One way of solving a housing shortage is to give a facelift to old property. This row of coalminers' houses in Eastwood, Nottinghamshire, dates from the nineteenth century. It was found more satisfactory to restore houses designed ironically to be heated by coal fires from abundant coal than to demolish them and rebuild. On a much vaster scale, modification of existing means of production, dwellings, and transportation links is more realistic than their complete replacement by new structures and equipment

Plate 12.2 (Above) A house by Wates Built Homes Ltd designed to conserve energy has extra thick walls, quadruple glazing, and a large space inside with batteries to store electricity from a wind-powered generator. The cost in energy of baking the extra bricks to make the walls thick should not be forgotten. Even so, only one-fifth of the energy in a similar sized conventional house would be needed. The penalty: a large metal windmill in your back garden to provide the energy. Location: as in Plate 12.1

Plate 12.4 The U.K. faces the prospect of rapidly diminishing reserves of natural gas and oil. It has abundant coal reserves. To bring coal reserves in the Vale of Belvoir, Leicestershire, into use would require the sinking of three pits. Such a development would upset the social life of several thousand local inhabitants and spoil an area of scenic beauty. The economic benefit to several tens of millions of people would be considerable. Not surprisingly, however, the people of the Vale of Belvoir object

6. *The arms race*

It was felt necessary to refer here to the enormous amount of production that is wasted through the development of armaments. Given the experience of the U.S.S.R. and U.S.A. at the hands of Germany and Japan respectively in the Second World War, it is hardly likely that either superpower will now contemplate any reduction in arms that would weaken its position. What is unfortunate is that most countries of the world now commit natural resources, products, and research facilities to developing their own armed forces.

7. *The multinational companies*

It is very difficult to gain an impartial view of the extent to which the Western-based multinational companies affect the development gap. There is no doubting their ability to produce large quantities of goods, whether from the agricultural, mining or manufacturing sectors of the economy. As they are essentially based in and financed by developed countries it could be that they help to perpetuate the development gap. They are not necessarily controlled by the governments of the countries in which they function. They are therefore an obstacle to the formation of a world body to coordinate measures to reduce the development gap, adding to the already formidable obstacle of the individual sovereign states themselves.

8. *The developing countries themselves*

So far in this section the world has largely been seen from the viewpoint of the developed countries. In this final subsection the acute problem of creating jobs in developing countries is discussed. As exporters of primary products, such countries are often losing materials to which they themselves might add value. Most of the population of the developing world was seen to be living in regions with very meagre natural resources per inhabitant (see Chapter 7). Yet in some instances, a large amount of investment is placed in certain localities and sectors in developing countries only to create comparatively few jobs.

The export of high technology to developing countries creates high-cost jobs. In the late 1960s it was found that each new job created in a new industrial estate in Salvador, Northeast Brazil, with the help of investment from the Brazilian government and from industrialists in Southeast Brazil, was costing $16,000. Large-scale

mining projects in developing countries use imported equipment
and create few jobs. One estimate for mining developments in
Central Peru required an investment of U.S. $1300 million, which
would greatly increase mineral sales but would only need 4000 new
jobs, at a cost therefore of some $300,000 each. In the late 1970s it
was estimated in Venezuela that there is a net increase in the labour
force of males of 120-150,000 a year, yet half of the capital
investment is used up to create employment for only a tenth of this
number.

In *Mankind at the Turning Point* (Mesarovic and Pestel, 1975), the
authors state: 'What is actually needed is what is called an
"intermediate technology", which requires capital per job approximately equal to the annual income per employee; furthermore,
such a technology should not be conditioned by the availability of
high quality materials nor should it demand high accuracy, large
organizations or long elaborate training for potential employees'.
One could say that there is no 'room' for high technology in many
developing countries. There are too many people already, using too
little land and having locally too few sources of energy and non-
fuel minerals. Yet it is hardly realistic to expect to mine copper or
oil in the way the Brazilian *faiscadores* are searching for gold in
Plate 12.5.

Perhaps different parts of the world should 'develop' on different
lines. The consciences of the rich could become clearer as they
heave a sigh of relief and accept that it is better and kinder to allow
each country to determine its own future. Why upset them, destroy
their culture and way of life? You have to build on what is there, an
idea growing perhaps in Africa at the moment and certainly one
taken up by President Nyerere of Tanzania in the 1970s.

9. *Future generations*

Since the Second World War the citizens of the developed
countries have become aware of the plight of the poor in the
developing countries. They have done very little directly or
consciously to help them. Only in the 1970s has concern been
expressed about another equally large set of people, future

Plate 12.5 (Opposite) Brazilians search river beds for gold dust and
precious stones in Northeast Brazil. Large numbers of people congregate
temporarily where useful minerals have been found. Even such mineral-
extracting activities could to some degree be mechanized. Note the bullock
cart and its solid wheels. Source: Lau (1969). Reproduced by permission of
Instituto Brasileiro de Geografia e Estatistica

Plate 12.6 Cultivation on the fertile volcanic soils of Mount Kilimanjaro, Tanzania, takes place in small fields. Several levels of plant are grown on the same patch of land: beans, maize, coffee bushes, banana plants, and taller trees for shelter. To transform such an agricultural landscape to make it amenable to mechanized methods of cultivation is quite unrealistic

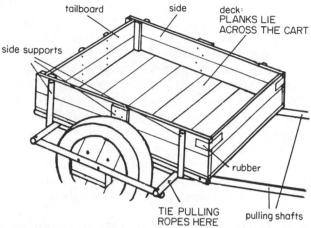

Plate 12.7 How to make a donkey cart in Tanzania. One finds it hard to appreciate why techniques used in Europe centuries ago are being diffused and taught in Africa now. Note the inefficient solid (rather than spoked) wheels. Source: Macpherson (1975, p. 105). Reproduced by permission of Tanzania Publishing House

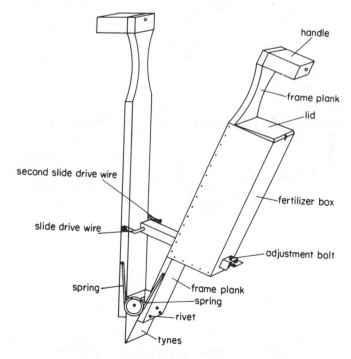

Plate 12.8 A modest piece of technology designed to ensure the efficient spreading of fertilizer, also for use in Tanzania. Source: Macpherson (1975, p. 161). Reproduced by permission of Tanzania Publishing House

generations in the developed countries themselves. W. Beckerman (1979) observes:

> The philosophical problem of how far people regard themselves to being responsible for future generations, even of their own descendants, or how far societies and individuals can regard themselves as having a continuous identity, so that their welfare could be conceived of, as it were, as being accessible by some 'outside body' which attached no importance to the particular points in time at which benefits and costs are incurred, is obviously a difficult one, but is one which seems inescapable if one is to handle social choice problems such as those arising from the problem of nuclear waste.

The rise in the price of oil since 1973 is an example of the dominance of politics over economics. The price at which Middle East oil was selling in 1979 in no way reflects either an immediate scarcity or the cost of producing it. Oil and natural gas can generally be extracted very cheaply relative to other fuels. The artificially high price, economically speaking, reflects the future scarcity of oil and the prospect for future generations of people in the oil-producing countries when the oil runs out. It protects future generations. Similarly, it is essential that cultivated land is not overused and degraded or destroyed as a result of wrong use now.

12.7   How can the rich regions help the poor ones?

It is accepted as a fact that material standards differ greatly from one part of the world to another whether at national, regional or local level. What is more, the development gap has existed for a long time. Since the Second World War, many people, though not all, have felt that something ought to be done to narrow the gap. Views vary greatly, however, with regard to the prospects of actually changing the situation.

During more than four centuries of growing European influence in the world since Columbus discovered America in 1492, European colonial powers regarded their colonies as places to use for their own benefit either to develop with their own settlers or from which to obtain raw materials and food. The influence of Christian thinking on the attitude and conduct of European administrators and settlers towards the indigenous population of their colonies has tended to be concerned with the spiritual rather than the material well-being of the natives.

The Roman Catholic men of religion who accompanied the Spanish Conquistadores as they took much of the Americas for Spain have subsequently been criticized for their failure to help the American Indians materially. It has been said, perhaps unkindly, that in Africa during the main period of colonization a century ago the Europeans gave the Africans the Bible and took away their land.

Thus even the sectors of the colonizing population that might have shown concern about the original non-European population in European colonies did not make much impact on the development gap. Charities run by the various Christian churches to improve material conditions in developing countries are mostly comparatively new. These, together with non-religious institutions, make appeals to the inhabitants of rich countries for help for the poor countries on moral, social and philanthropic grounds. Gifts from private individuals to charities such as Oxfam in Britain have been small. Public support for foreign aid has also been sought by politicians on the grounds that it is in the interest of the developed countries to help the poor ones.

It has been argued that if the economies of developing countries expanded greatly the developed countries would also benefit, through greater trade. Another line is that it is necessary to help poorer countries in order to dissuade them from taking military action to overcome the rich countries. A straight world conflict between poor and rich countries seems a dubious prospect on both military and geographical grounds. Even if the developing countries could come together and organize themselves into one cohesive body their military resources are very unsophisticated. W. Warantz (1975) clearly sees the prospect differently. After describing various deficiencies in the poor countries he concludes:

> Two-thirds of the world's preschool children suffer from malnutrition that is physically disabling. It affects them permanently, both physically and mentally. A very long list of similarly depressing deficits could be compiled. Explanations for this state of affairs usually relate levels of technology and resource availability to number of people, so that overpopulation, underpopulation and optimum population are discussed in these terms.
>
> The gaps listed above can be closed. The technology exists, but the determination to do so may not exist. The affluent will not close the gaps unless they are pressured to do so. But the aspirations of certain deprived groups are being increased by their own perceptions of the gaps. Once these gaps are perceived then a new source of power comes into existence; the gaps will be closed.

In spite of the general feeling that something ought to be done to help the poor countries, at least three serious kinds of reason have been put forward to justify not trying to interfere with the present development gap. One set of arguments is based on the view that the rich countries deserve to be rich because it is through their own inventiveness, effort and efficiency of their citizens that they have reached high levels of productivity. The rich countries are under no obligation to help the poor, especially when much aid is apparently misplaced, misused, wasted or just lost. Anyway, it is bad to help beggars. Another set of arguments is based on the idea that Europe has manipulated the rest of the world to its own ends for long enough and modified the economies and societies of other parts of the world for its own purposes. Let other parts of the world now develop in their own ways. Yet another argument is that there are not enough natural resources to go round in the world and the more the developing countries expand their economies, the less there will be for the developed countries to have.

It seems likely that many people in poor countries are increasingly becoming aware of what they are missing. They cannot help gaining an insight into the ways of the affluent society if they move to towns in their own countries and especially if they take up domestic service in the homes of the rich. Increasing mobility and the widespread diffusion of broadcasts through transistor radios have made the rural poor even in remote areas of the developing countries appreciate the standards of people in rich families in their own countries. It is perhaps more difficult for them to appreciate that the majority of people in the industrial countries receive many of the material advantages available only to a minority of well-off people in their own countries.

At the same time, again through broadcasting, especially television pictures, and through the press, it is increasingly difficult for people in rich countries to avoid seeing or reading from time to time about poor conditions in developing countries. Glimpses of starving people in rags and with flies crawling over them have come from parts of Africa in the 1970s. Programmes on shanty towns and slums in fast-growing urban centres of the developing world are also commonly broadcast.

What, then, can the rich do? Rarely in history have the wealthy given up their wealth unless compelled to do so. Rarely does a person with a large income voluntarily give away more than a tiny proportion of it to charity. Distributing wealth is difficult also because even if you wanted to you could not pack up the leavings from your meal and send them to starving people in Chad or Bangladesh. It would be meaningless for the affluent American to

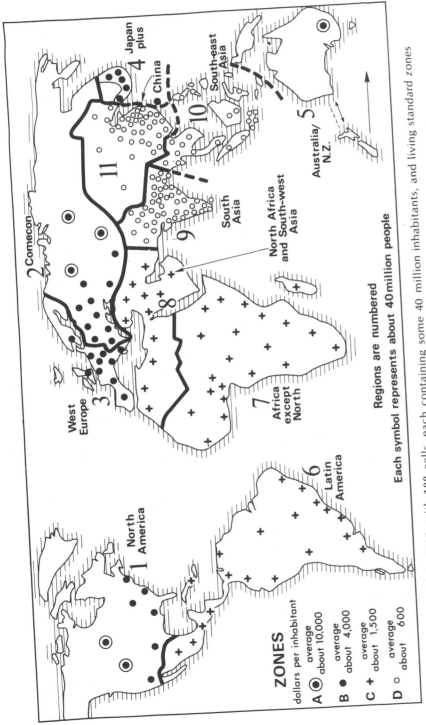

Figure 12.4 The world in 2025, with 188 cells, each containing some 40 million inhabitants, and living standard zones

Regions are numbered

Each symbol represents about 40 million people

ZONES

dollars per inhabitant

A ⦿ average about 10,000

B ● average about 4,000

C + average about 1,500

D ○ average about 600

Japan plus 4

China

South-east Asia

South Asia 10

North Africa and South-west Asia 9

Australia/ N.Z. 5

Comecon 2

West Europe 3

8

Africa except North 7

Latin America 6

North America 1

11

donate one of his two automobiles to a poor Brazilian or Indonesian farmer.

Whatever kind of redistribution of wealth or income is hoped for in the world the problem remains of actually how to move things about. If everyone lived in one place, the problem of redistribution would largely be one of persuading people to give away or receive something. In spite of the continuing improvement of the world transportation system, there is a great deal of friction in distance between places. People, natural resources, and means of production are very unevenly scattered over the earth's surface. Wealth and poverty are a spatial problem as well as a social one.

The main purpose of the present book has been to describe the uneven distribution of the ingredients of development and to show how difficult it would be to make substantial transfers between different parts of the world even if the rich suddenly accepted that they should give away much of their present wealth or forgo future increases in it. In spite of the virtual impossibility of making a substantial change in the development gap in a short time it is the view of the present author that it is better to try to do something than to do nothing at all. It is important to try to increase the transfer of aid from rich to poor countries and also to improve the terms of trade in favour of the exporters of primary products. Such measures, if adequately applied, might at least provide the very poor regions of the world with a minimum standard of living.

In the 1970s there has indeed been a more pragmatic approach to the development problem than previously. For example, the policy to channel much foreign aid to the poorest developing countries seems sensible, given the limited amount of aid expected to be available. The plan to double rice production in Asia in 15 years (*The Times,* 23 August 1978) recognizes that food is more urgently needed than steel in the poorest parts of the world.

While it is difficult to imagine large transfers of products from developed to developing countries it should be possible to organize limited transfers. Given willingness on the part of the developed countries and an adequate organization it might be possible to cut 'excessive' consumption in the more affluent developed countries without changing living standards greatly and to divert this to developing countries. For example in many parts of Africa and in regions of Asia and Latin America, trees are being cut and land being exposed to erosion to provide nothing other than fuel for cooking. Many people in developed countries, on the other hand, go around in far larger cars than are actually needed to convey them, the present author included. An energy saving of 10-20 percent in developed countries could, if successfully transferred to developing countries, help in a great variety of ways. Similarly, it is estimated that the average food intake per inhabitant in developed countries is 10-20 percent higher than it need be (see Chapter 8). Food is short and diet inadequate in many developing countries.

The above kinds of limited transfer would not be difficult in terms of transportation needs. On the other hand they implicitly preserve the development gap largely intact. What is more, they consist unfortunately of consumer goods sent as gifts, thereby reflecting the perpetuation of the development gap. The world in 2025 to be described in the next section, is the only proper scenario presented in this book. It is the author's best estimate of a world in which the limited transfer strategy has been put into practice. The very poor cells are subsidized while only a few cells are very rich.

12.8   A limited transfer scenario

In this section I will put a few of my own views on the prospects for the world in the next 50 years. I hope that my two sons will be alive to look at these words in the year 2025. For their sakes I have to look at prospects with guarded optimism.

In the 1970s, some regions of the world were clearly better off than others. It was suggested early in this book that there were various reasons why this is so.

(1) Some regions have a superior natural resource/population ratio to others.

(2) Some regions are better located than others in the world as a whole or in their own national frameworks.

(3) Some regions use more advanced technology than others and achieve higher productivity per worker.

(4) Some regions are organized more efficiently than others.

It seems reasonable to assume that in the 2020s the above reasons will still be valid and operative and that great regional differences will still be observed in the world. In the view of the author there will be four broad types of region in the 2020s, related firstly to the availability of natural resources in relation to population and secondly to the sophistication of technology. Many of the sovereign states of the early 1980s will have come together to form larger supranational groupings.

Between 1975 and 2025 the population of the present developing countries will probably roughly double while the population of the present developed countries will not grow much. International migration within the next 50 years will be on a very limited scale (see Chapter 10). Inevitably, therefore, the natural resources of the

developing regions will be supporting a much larger popula than now, yet will have been considerably depleted by 2025. natural resources of the developed regions are tending to be u up more quickly than those of most developing regions so t resource/population ratio will also be worse in these. By 202 present developing regions with large natural resources, such as th Middle East and parts of Africa and Latin America, will b conserving them and reluctant to part with them to resource-poo developed regions such as Europe and Japan. The present devel oped, industrialized countries will have tried out and applied all kinds of technology to enable them to switch to 'renewable' resources, to make fuller use of raw materials, and to save agricultural land from deteriorating.

The development gap will still be very marked, but some kind of agreement will have been worked out, a compromise to prevent any region from being very affluent and wasteful with materials and to keep every region from being very poor.

In 2025 world population will be much larger than now but many of the towns, factories, and railways of today will still be there. The replacement rate of such hardware is fairly slow. What is more, probably half of the people alive in 1975 will still be alive in 2025. There will be many more 40 million population cells crowding on the earth's surface.

The scenario to be described is a coping scenario. There has not been a drastic natural catastrophe between 1975 and 2025, nor a Third World War. Famines have occurred in places. The population of the world has increased from 4000 million in 1975 to 7500 million in 2025. There are 188 cells in 2025, each with about 40 million people (see Table 12.5 and Figure 12.4), compared with the 100 in 1975 (see Figure 9.6) and the 156 in 2000 (see Figure 11.1).

In Chapter 9 some of the 100 cells were represented diagrammatically (see Figures 9.2-9.5). They looked like insects with 10 legs, or 'decapods'. Figure 12.5 shows some of the decapods of the year 2025, distributed on the earth's land surface. Many still have short legs in all directions, some have long legs on the production side but not on the resource side, while some still have long legs in all directions. How does the world of 188 decapods cope in 2025?

Food production in 2025 should be roughly two and a half times as large as it was in 1975. Total production of goods and services should also be about two and a half times what it was then.

The idea of achieving equal living standards all over the world was abandoned in the 1980s. Instead a maximum and a minimum regional product was established for the world. In U.S. dollars equivalent to 1975 values, total world GNP around 2025 is about

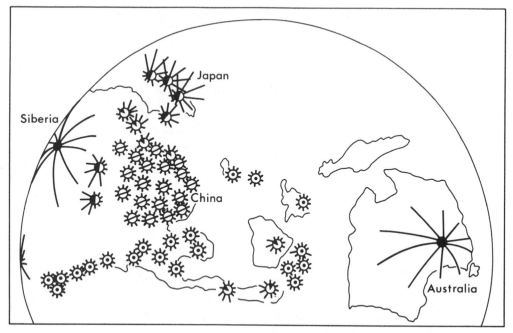

Figure 12.5 The decapods of 2025 in part of the world. Refer back to Figures 9.1-9.5

$15 × 10^{12}$ a year. This gives a world average of a little over $2000 per inhabitant. The minimum gross regional product per inhabitant permitted in 2025 is $600 and the maximum $10,000. This contrasts with extremes in 1975 of $100 and $10,000.

The following zones are recognized:

A, areas with large natural resources per inhabitant in richer regions

B, areas with limited natural resources per inhabitant in richer regions

C, self-contained areas

D, supported areas.

The world is organized in 11 regions. Table 12.6 gives population and income data for the 11 regions and Figure 12.4 shows the distribution of the 188 cells of 40 million inhabitants each.

Throughout the book, four types of region have been recognized in the world:

(i) developed, rich in natural resources (e.g. Australia, Canada, Siberia)

(ii) developed, poor in natural resources (e.g. U.K., Japan, Northeast U.S.A.)

(iii) developing, rich in natural resources (e.g. Venezuela, Zaire)

Table 12.5 The regional distribution of population in the world in 1975 and 2025. Population is in cells each with about 40 million people

'Developed'	1975	2025	'Developing'	1975	2025
West Europe	9	10	Latin America	8	19
East Europe U.S.S.R.	10	4 / 9	Southwest Asia, N. Africa	5	12
Japan plus*	4	6	Rest of Africa	8	21
North America	6	8	South Asia	20	44
Australia, N.Z.	1	1	Southeast Asia	8	20
			China	21	34

(iv) developing, poor in natural resources (e.g. India, most of China). These correspond to zones A, B, C, and D in 2025. Regions 1 and 2 are subdivided into A and B zones. The world is organized by regions roughly as follows:

Region 1. The resource-rich zone A of North America has very high living standards. Zone B of North America has prior claim to the food, energy, and non-fuel mineral surplus of zone A. Region 3, West Europe, is allowed some of the surplus from North America's A zone.

Region 2. The resource-rich zone of Comecon has very high living standards. Zone B of Comecon has prior claim to the food, energy, and non-fuel mineral surplus of zone A. Regions 3 and 4, West Europe and Japan, are allowed a small part of the surplus from Comecon's A zone.

Region 3. West Europe has limited natural resources, very little world influence, and living standards lower in 2025 than in 1975, with austerity compelled by its reduced means. England was declared a world industrial museum in 2017. West Europe provides means of production and knowhow to keep regions 9, 10, and 11 above the $600 per inhabitant 'rice-line'.

Region 4. Japan plus South Korean and Taiwan has very limited natural resources. It has become difficult to get primary products from elsewhere. Conditions in the region are similar to those in West Europe.

Region 5. Australia and New Zealand, all zone A, provide some surplus of primary products to West Europe and Japan.

Regions 6, 7, and 8. Latin America, Africa, and Southwest Asia have each become largely self-contained, neither exporting much in the way of primary products to regions 1-4 as they used to in the twentieth century nor importing many manufactured goods as they used to.

Table 12.6 Population and gross national product by 11 regions in 2025

	2025 population (millions)	Population by zones (millions) A	B	C	D	Gross regional product Per ($) inhabitant	×10⁹
1 North America	320	80	240			A 10,000	800
						B 8000	1920
2 Comecon	510	120	390			A 8000	960
						B 6000	2340
3 West Europe	400		400			4000	1600
4 Japan plus*	230		230			3000	690
5 Australia, N.Z.	30	30				10,000	300
6 Latin America	770			770		2500	1925
7 Rest of Africa	860			860		1000	860
8 N.Africa, South-west Asia	460			460		2000	920
9 South Asia	1770				1770	600	1060
10 Southeast Asia	800				800	800	640
11 China	1350				1350	700	945
World	7500						14,960

* Includes South Korea, Taiwan.

Regions 9, 10, and 11, containing over half of the population of the world in 2025, or 98 cells, with nearly 4000 million people, are still very poor but are kept above a minimum level by their own efforts plus assistance as needed, in the form of food and manufactured goods. It is sobering to find that these last three regions have roughly as many inhabitants in 2025 as the whole world had in 1975.

The above scenario has been worked out to provoke thought rather than to be a carefully reasoned estimate of the human geography of the world in 2025. Constant 1975 dollars have been used to measure the level of development and the development gap in 2025 because they are simple to calculate. It would be interesting to develop the scenario to work out what kinds of product will be turned out in each region, which natural resources of 1975 have already run out, and what kinds of flow of goods and services take place between different cells.

12.9 A bleak outlook

Until the 1970s much of the literature on development was produced by economists. The discipline of economics provides a suitable vocabulary for talking about the subject. It does not give economists a monopoly of the field. In spite of flaws in its concepts and findings, quickly noted by economists, the systems model of Forrester (1971) has shaken people's complacency about the world situation in a way that economists could not do.

One defect of many economists is that they give little attention to ecological and spatial problems. With his background as a bio-geographer, S.R. Eyre has attempted to assess the relationship between development and the natural environment. In the present book an attempt has been made to stress the spatial problems of development.

Some decades ago, geographers made comparisons between different natural regions of the world. In the present book the emphasis has been on the comparison of regions, in the form both of sovereign states and of artificial equal population cells, according to their population, natural resources, and productive capacity.

By carefully comparing different parts of the world it becomes clear that disparities in natural resources and in production as measured against population are very great. For example on average an Australian farmer works an area of agricultural land 100-200 times as large as a farmer in Haiti, Bangladesh or Japan. Australia and New Zealand have about 0.4 percent of the total population of the world but about 4 percent of all the natural resources of the world. If the world as a whole had the natural resources/population ratio that Australia had, then it would have (mid-1970s) 400 million inhabitants, not 4000 million. Such comparisons are only of theoretical interest since it is neither possible nor desirable to talk of eliminating nine-tenths of the population of the world. It is hoped that they are also thought-provoking.

The gap in production and in consumption between developed and developing countries is also notable. For a more developed developing country like Peru to reach the current level of production and consumption in Western Europe in the future, production would have to be increased about 10 times. For the whole world to have a gross national product per inhabitant in 2010 equal in real terms to that in the U.S.A. in the 1970s, the total production of goods and services would have to be about 10 times as large as it is now. Even if such an astronomical increase could be achieved, it has been pointed out in the present book that to redistribute people and/or products to give equality of living standards everywhere would be physically or geographically impossible.

If the U.K. and the U.S.A. could somehow give away to poorer countries all their consumption of goods and services above the

Plate 12.9 A rural scene on the central plateau of Ethiopia. Dung is collected and made into 'cakes' for burning. It should be returned to the ground. The pasture is greatly overgrazed. In the background, eucalyptus trees of Australian origin are gradually replacing the natural woodland of Ethiopia. If such an area were in Australia, farming practices would be utterly different. Fields would be very large, pastures fenced off, and machinery used for cultivation and harvesting. To transform Ethiopian agriculture to the Australian pattern, at least 90 percent of the labour force in agriculture could be dispensed with. A more realistic approach is to modify the existing structure of Ethiopian farming

Plate 12.10 The site of the Roman amphitheatre in Lucca, Italy, symbolizes the endurance and resilience of old patterns anywhere in the world. Even though the structure of the amphitheatre itself has largely been replaced by houses, the form is still to be seen on the ground

Plate 12.11 M.C. Escher's 'Waterfall' makes sense if you look at each part separately. The whole situation is physically impossible. Reproduced in *The Graphic Work of M.C. Escher* (fifth printing 1974), Pan/Ballantine, London, Plate 7B. (Reproduced here by permission Collection Haags Gemeentemuseum — The Hague. S.P.A.D.E.M., Paris, 1980)

world average level of consumption, the former would have to forgo about two-thirds and the latter about four-fifths. The citizens of the rich countries do not only have to take into account the poor countries, on which they depend to varying degrees for primary materials but from which they stand so far apart in living standards. They must also think of their own descendants, the future generation of citizens in their own countries.

Altogether, room for manoeuvre seems limited in the world. Both market economy and centrally planned developed countries are facing a slowing down of economic growth, the former from the earlier 1970s, the U.S.S.R. in the late 1970s. Even if growth ceases and they only maintain their present levels of productive capacity, it seems unlikely that the development gap will narrow greatly in the next few decades. The transformation needed within developing countries to make them resemble developed ones is so great that the means to achieve it are not available (see Plate 12.9). A slow transformation of parts of the developing world may be expected. Many of the basic features will remain beneath the new structure. By analogy, a town may change its buildings gradually but the underlying street plan may stay the same. Plate 12.10 shows the Roman amphitheatre in Lucca, Italy, as it has been fossilized. Its structure has been replaced by dwelling houses but its oval layout has been preserved.

A group of Brazilian economists estimated that if *all* international aid and investment from developed countries were channelled exclusively into Brazil, then it could be transformed into a developed country. But the developing world is equivalent in population to about twenty-five Brazils.

Perhaps the world development situation can be compared with the drawing of the Dutch artist M.C. Escher in Plate 12.11. Looking at any particular part of the developing world you can argue that it could become developed. When you look at the whole then you see the impossibility of the task. In Escher's picture each part makes sense but the whole is impossible.

Appendix 1
The construction of the Lorenz curve

The construction of the Lorenz curve and calculation of the gini coefficient is illustrated with two examples. Throughout the book the Lorenz curve has been constructed with the proportion of population on the vertical axis and of resources, production or consumption on the horizontal axis. It is customary to have the horizontal axis for population.

For the two examples in this appendix, six countries have been used. The first example shows the relationship of area to population, the second that of steel production to population. Columns (1)-(3) in Tables A1 and A2 show the initial data sets. From the different indices in column (3) of each table it can be seen that neither area nor steel production is shared out evenly according to population.

In columns (4)-(10) the six countries are reranked in descending order of area (Table A1) and steel production (Table A2) per population. Column (4) shows the amount per inhabitant in column (3) reordered. Column (5) shows the total population in each table and column (6) the total area (Table A1) and steel production (Table A2). In columns (7) and (8) the absolute values of population, area, and steel production are reexpressed as percentages of the total for the six countries.

In columns (9) and (10) the percentages are accumulated. The values in column (9) are the coordinate positions of each country on the vertical, population axis of a square graph. The values in column (10) are the corresponding area and steel production coordinates on the horizontal axis. The two Lorenz curves are drawn in Figure A1.

The curves may be interpreted as follows. If each country had exactly the same percentage of area or of steel production as it has

Table A1 Population and area of six countries

		(1) Population (millions)	(2) Area (thous. km²)	(3) Area (km²/1000 people)
1	Indonesia	128	1490	12
2	West Germany	62	250	4
3	Ethiopia	27	1180	44
4	Romania	21	240	11
5	Peru	15	1290	86
6	Australia	13	7700	592
		266	12,150	

		(4) Area (km²/ 1000 people)	(5) Popn. (millions)	(6) Area (thous. km²)	(7) % popn.	(8) % area	(9) Cumulative % popn.	(10) Cumulative % area
6	Australia	592	13	7700	5	63	5	63
5	Peru	86	15	1290	6	11	11	74
3	Ethiopia	44	27	1180	10	10	21	84
1	Indonesia	12	128	1490	48	12	69	96
4	Romania	11	21	240	8	2	77	98
2	West Germany	4	62	250	23	2	100	100
			266	12,150	100	100		

of population, each would fall exactly on the diagonal across the graph running from the lower left to the upper right. The further away the countries are from the diagonal towards the lower right-hand corner of the graph (the more the curve sags), the greater the concentration of a given item with a small proportion of the population.

The gini coefficient is calculated by expressing the area between the diagonal and the curve as a proportion of all the area on the graph to the lower right of the diagonal, exactly half the area of the total square. The gini coefficient lies between 0.0 (perfectly even distribution) and 1.0, complete concentration. It has been calculated in all the examples in the present book by measuring geometrically the polygon between the diagonal and the curve (a triangle and a set of trapezia). All the calculations have been made with the help of an appropriate computer program.

In Figure A1 it can be seen that both area and steel production are highly concentrated. There is a great concentration of area (per inhabitant) in Australia and of steel production (per inhabitant) in

Table A2 Population and steel production (1974) of six countries

		(1) Population (millions)	(2) Steel production	(3) Steel production (kg/inhabitant)
1	Indonesia	128	0	0
2	West Germany	62	53	855
3	Ethiopia	27	0	0
4	Romania	21	9	429
5	Peru	15	0.5	33
6	Australia	13	8	615

		(4) Steel prodn. (kg/in-habitant)	(5) Popn. (millions)	(6) Steel prodn.	(7) % popn.	(8) % steel prodn.	(9) Cumulative % popn.	(10) Cumulative % steel prodn.
2	West Germany	855	62	53	23	75	23	75
6	Australia	615	13	8	5	11	28	86
4	Romania	429	21	9	8	13	36	99
5	Peru	33	15	0.5	6	1	42	100
1	Indonesia	0	128	0	48	0	90	100
3	Ethiopia	0	27	0	10	0	100	100
			266	70.5	100	100		

Source: *United Nations Statistical Yearbook 1975,* Table 127.

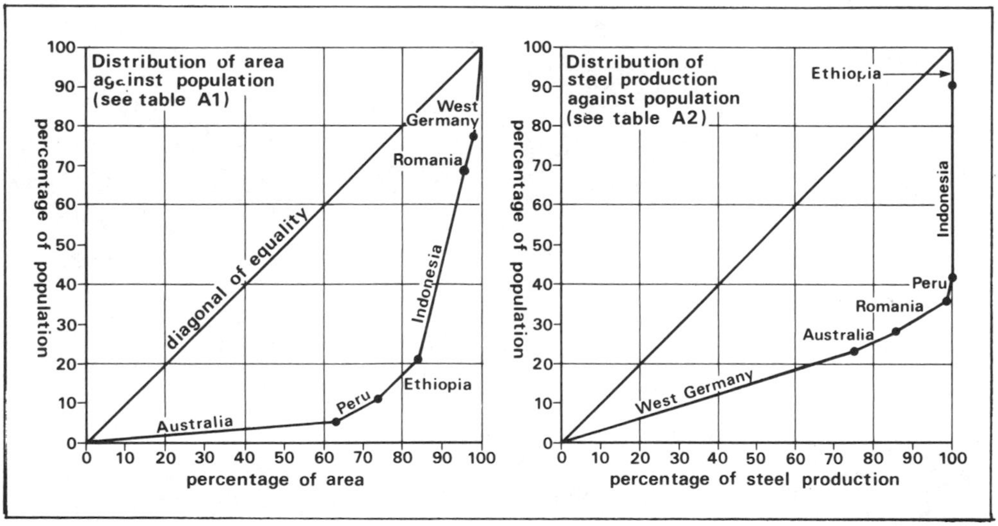

Figure A1 The construction of a Lorenz curve

West Germany. Each country (obviously) has some area but two of the countries produce no steel at all, Indonesia and Ethiopia. One hundred percent of the production is accounted for by 42 percent of the population.

Cell 46 Angola, Zaire, Congo, C. African Rep., Gabon, Cameroon
Cell 47 Somalia, Kenya, Uganda, Rwanda, Burundi
Cell 48 Ethiopia, Djibouti, Sudan
Cell 49 Ivory coast to Southern Nigeria
Cell 50 Nigeria except Western, Lagos, Mid-Western, Rivers, East Central States
Cell 51 Africa from Chad to Mauritania to Liberia
Cells 52-53 Cell 52 is Afghanistan plus roughly the northwestern half of Pakistan
Cell 54 Jammu and Kashmir, Himachal Pradesh, Punjab, Haryana, Delhi
Cell 55 Rajasthan and part of Madhya Pradesh
Cell 56 Gujarat and part of Maharashtra
Cell 57 Maharashtra excluding northwest
Cell 58 Karanataka and Goa
Cell 59 Kerala and Sri Lanka
Cell 60 Tamil Nadu
Cell 61 Andhra Pradesh
Cell 62 Orissa and part of West Bengal
Cell 63 West Bengal excluding southwest
Cell 64 Madhya Pradesh excluding northwest
Cell 65 Bihar, eastern two-thirds
Cell 66 Western part of Bihar and eastern extremity of Uttar Pradesh
Cells 67-68 Central and northwestern parts of Uttar Pradesh
Cell 69 Smaller divisions of Northeast India plus Bhutan, Sikkim, Nepal
Cells 70-71 North Bangladesh is Dacca plus Rajshahi, South is Khulna plus Chittagong
Cell 75 Malaysia, Singapore, Sumatra (Indonesia)
Cell 79 Vietnam, Laos, Kampuchea
Cell 81 North Korea is put with Liaoning province of China
Cell 100 Roughly the northwestern half of China from Tibet to Inner Mongolia plus the Mongolian People's Republic

In summary, the following countries (in order of listing in Table 6.16) are fragmented into the number of units listed in the left-hand column of numbers and join as indicated in the right-hand column of numbers:

Country	Cells	Joins	Joined with
U.K.	2	1	North Europe
West Germany	2	1	Netherlands
France	2	1	Belgium
Italy	2	2	Switzerland-Austria, Greece
U.S.S.R.	8	2	Romania, Poland
Japan	3	0	
U.S.A.	6	1	Canada
Brazil	3	1	Bolivia-Paraguay-Guianas
Mexico	2	1	Central America
Nigeria	2	1	Togo to Ivory Coast
Pakistan	2	1	Afghanistan
India	16	2	Sri Lanka, Nepal-Bhutan
Bangladesh	2	0	
Indonesia	4	2	Malaysia, Papua-New Guinea
China	21	2	North Korea, Mongolian People's Republic

References

Alexandersson, G., and Klevebring, B.-I. (1978) *World Resources, Energy, Metals, Minerals,* Walter de Gruyter, Berlin, New York.

Arnold, R. (1949) *A Yeoman of Kent,* Constable, London.

Bairoch, P. (1975) *The Economic Development of the Third World Since 1900* (in translation), Methuen, London.

Bairoch, P., Deldyke, D., Gelders, H., and Limber, J.M. (1968) 'The working population and its structure', *Statistiques Internationales Restrospectives,* Vol. 1, Université de Bruxelles.

Beckerman, W. (1977) 'A social science fiction' (review of H. Kahn's *The Next 200 Years*), *The Times Higher Education Supplement,* 6 May.

Beckerman, W. (1979) 'Small is stupid', *The Times Higher Education Supplement,* 23 November, 14-15.

Berri, L. Ya. (1977) *Planning a Socialist Economy,* Vol.2, Progress Publishers, Moscow.

Boyle, G., and Harper, P. (1976) *Radical Technology,* Wildwood House, London.

Brookfield, H.C. (1973) 'On one geography and a third world', *Transactions of The Institute of British Geographers,* No. 58, March, 1-20.

Brown, L.R. (1978) 'The worldwide loss of cropland', *Worldwatch Paper 24,* Worldwatch Institute, Washington D.C.

Brunet, R., Gay, F.J., Guermond, Y., Noin, D., and Preau, P. (1974) *La France, Maintenant,* Libraire Larousse, Paris.

Brooks, E. (1973) 'Twilight of Brazilian tribes', *The Geographical Magazine,* **XLV,** No. 4, 304-10.

Cabinet Office (1976) *Future World Trends,* London, Her Majesty's Stationery Office, 16.

Chatterjee, L. (1976) 'The Calcutta region: problems, planning and development', *Focus,* **XXVII,** No.1, 9-13.

Clark, C. (1967) *Population Growth and Land Use,* Macmillan, New York.

Coates, B.E., Johnston, R.J., and Knox, P.L. (1977) *Geography and Inequality,* Oxford University Press, London.

Cole, H.S.D., Freeman, C., Jahoda, M., and Pavitt, K.L.R. (1973) *Thinking About the Future. A Critique of the Limits to Growth,* Chatto and Windus, Sussex University Press, London.

447

Cole, J.P. (1979) *Geography of World Affairs,* Penguin, Harmondsworth, Middlesex.

Cole, J.P. (1981) *Geography of the U.S.S.R.,* Butterworth, London, in the press.

Cole, J.P., and Harrison, M.E. (1978) 'Regional inequality in services and purchasing power in the USSR 1940-1976', *Occasional Papers No.14,* Department of Geography, Queen Mary College, University of London.

Cole, J.P., and Mather, P.M. (1978) *Peru 1940-2000 Performance and Prospects,* Geography Department, University of Nottingham.

Datsiouk, B. (1976) *Causeries sur le Communisme Scientifique: Questions Théoriques et Pratiques, Première Partie,* Novosti, Moscow.

Davis, K. (1968) 'Colin Clark and the benefits of an increase in population', *Scientific American,* **218,** No.4, 133.

Eyre, S.R. (1978) *The Real Wealth of Nations,* Arnold, London.

Flower, A.R. (1978) 'World oil production', *Scientific American,* **238,** No.3, 42-9.

Forrester, J.W. (1971) *World Dynamics,* Wright Allen, Cambridge, Mass.

Freeman, C., and Jahoda, M. (1978) *World Futures. The Great Debate,* Martin Robertson, London.

Frejka, T. (1973) 'The prospects for a stationary world population', *Scientific American,* **228,** No.3, 15-23.

Gilbert, A.G. (Ed.) (1976) *Development Planning and Spatial Structure,* Wiley, London.

Ginsburg, N. (1961) *Atlas of Economic Development,* especially Part VIII, 'A statistical analysis', by B.J.L. Berry, University of Chicago Press, Chicago.

Hagerstrand, T. (1952) 'The propagation of innovation waves', *Lund Studies in Geography,* Ser. B. Human Geography No.4, Department of Geography, The Royal University of Lund.

Hirschman, A.O. (1958) *The Strategy of Economic Development,* Yale University Press, New Haven.

Jackson, H. (1979) 'The real cost of making oil from coal', *The Guardian,* 31 July.

Johnson, B.L.C. (1979) *India, Resources and Development,* Heinemann, London.

Kahn, H., Brown, W., and Martel, L. (1976) *The Next 200 Years,* Associated Business Programmes, London.

Kahn, H., and Wiener, A.J. (1967) *The Year 2000. A Framework for Speculation on the Next Thirty-Three Years,* Macmillan, New York.

Kesler, S.E. (1976) *Our Finite Mineral Resources,* McGraw-Hill, New York.

Keyfitz, N. (1976) 'World resources and the world middle class', *Scientific American,* **235,** No.1, 28-35.

Khachaturov, T. (1977) *The Economy of the Soviet Union Today,* Progress Publishers, Moscow.

Lau, P. (1969) *Suas Ilustraçoes,* Departmento de Documentação e Divulgação Geográfica e Cartográfica, Fundação IBGE, Rio de Janeiro.

MacLeish, K. (1972) 'The Tasadays — Stone Age cavemen of Mindanao', *National Geographic,* **142,** No.2, 219-48.

Macpherson, G.A. (1975) *First Steps in Village Mechanisation,* Tanzania Publishing House, Dar es Salaam.

Malthus, T. (1830) 'A summary view of world population', in *Three Essays on Population,* Mentor (1962), New York.

Manners, G. (1978) Paper presented at Anglo-Soviet Seminar, Ruislip College, May 1978.

McCulloch, J.R. (1816) 'Political economy', In *Encyclopaedia Britannica,* fourth, fifth and sixth editions, 1816-24.

Meadows, D.H., Meadows, D.L., Randers, J., and Behrens III, W.W. (1972) *The Limits to Growth,* A Report for the Club of Rome's Project on the Predicament of Mankind, Earth Island Ltd., London.

Merritt, R.L., and Rokkan, S. (1966) *Comparing Nations,* Yale University Press, New Haven.

Mesarovic, M., and Pestel, E. (1975) *Mankind at the Turning Point,* The Second Report of the Club of Rome, Hutchinson, London.

Mick, S.S. (1975) 'The foreign medical graduate', *Scientific American,* **232,** No.2, 14-21.

Mints, A.A., and Kakhanovskaya, T.G. (1974) 'An attempt at a quantitative evaluation of the natural resource potential of regions in the U.S.S.R.', *Soviet Geography, Review and Translation,* **XV,** No.9, 554-65.

Mitchell, B.R. (1975) *European Historical Statistics, 1750-1970,* Macmillan, London.

Myrdal, G. (1957) *Economic Theory and Under-Developed Regions,* Duckworth, London.

Nance, J. (1975) *The Gentle Tasaday,* Gollancz, London.

Nef, J.U. (1977) 'An early energy crisis and its consequences', *Scientific American,* **237,** No.5, 140-151.

Nippon: A Charted Survey of Japan (1975-6) Tokyo, 1975, Table 4.2.

Norman, G. (1975) 'Why we should measure happiness instead of income', *The Times,* 26 May.

Ophuls, W. (1977) *Ecology and the Politics of Scarcity,* Freeman, San Francisco.

Peiris, D. (1979) 'McNamara sees dark at the end of the tunnel', *Guardian Third World Review,* 8 October.

Population Reference Bureau (1979) *World's Children Data Sheet,* Population Reference Bureau, Inc., Washington D.C.

Pratt, C.J. (1965) 'Chemical fertilizers', *Scientific American,* **212,** No.6, 62-72.

Pryde, P.R. (1978) 'Nuclear energy development in the Soviet Union', *Soviet Geography, Review and Translation,* **XIX,** No.2, 75-83.

Rand McNally (1972) *Illustrated Atlas of China* (materials from U.S. government), U.S. Government Printing Office, Washington.

Revelle, R. (1976) 'The Resources Available for Agriculture', *Scientific American,* **235,** No.3, 164-78.

Richardson, L.F. (1961) 'The problem of contiguity', *General Systems* (Yearbook of the Society for General Systems Research), **VI,** 139-87.

Rona, P.A. (1973) 'Plate tectonics and mineral resources', *Scientific American,* **229,** 86-95.

Rostow, W.W. (1960) *The Stages of Economic Growth,* Cambridge University Press.

Rostow, W.W. (1975) *How it all Began,* Methuen, London.

Runova, T.G. (1973) 'A natural-resource regionalization of the U.S.S.R.', *Soviet Geography, Review and Translation,* **XIV,** No.8, 506-518.

Russett, B.M. (1965) *World Handbook of Political and Social Indicators,* Yale University Press, New Haven.

Schumacher, E.F. (1974) *Small is Beautiful,* Abacus, London.

Showalter, W.J. (1916) 'How the world is fed', *National Geographic Magazine,* **XXIX,** 1, 1-100.

Smith, A. (1776) *The Wealth of Nations,* Penguin, Harmondsworth, Middlesex.

Soboleva, L.I. (1974) 'Medical-geography aspects of the design of the Ust'-Ilimsk industrial node', *Soviet Geography, Review and Translation,* **XV,** No.7, 422-8.

Tinbergen, J., Dolman, A.J., and van Ettinger, J. (1976) *Reshaping the International Order,* Dutton, New York.

Ullman, E.L. (1960) 'Geographic theory and underdeveloped areas', *Essays on Geography and Economic Development,* University of Chicago Research Papers, No.62, Ch.II, 26-32.

United Nations (1949) *Mission to Haiti,* Report of the United Nations Mission of Technical Assistance to the Republic of Haiti, Lake Success, New York, July 1949.

U.S. Bureau of the Census (1975) *Historical Statistics of the United States to 1970,* U.S. Dept. of Commerce, Bureau of the Census, Washington D.C.

U.S. Bureau of Mines (1970) *Mineral Facts and Problems, 1970* (Bulletin 650), U.S. Dept. of the Interior, Bureau of Mines, Washington D.C.

Vico, G. (1744) *The New Science of Giambattista Vico,* third edition 1744 (trans.), Anchor Books, Doubleday (1961), New York.

Warantz, W. (1975), In R. Abler *et al., Human Geography in a Shrinking World,* Duxbury Press, North Scituate, Chapter 6.

Watson, J. Wreford (1967) *Mental Images and Geographical Reality in the Settlement of North America,* Cust Foundation Lecture, University of Nottingham.

Westlake, M. (1978) 'The growing legions of the world's poor', *The Sunday Times,* 25 June.

White, P.T. (1973) 'Calcutta, India's maligned metropolis', *National Geographic,* **143,** No.4, 534-65.

Williamson, J.G. (1968) 'Regional inequality and the process of national development: a description of the patterns', In *Regional Analysis, Selected Readings,* Ed. L. Needleman, Penguin, Harmondsworth, Middlesex.

Wolde-Meriam, M. (1972) *An Introductory Geography of Ethiopia,* Berhanena Selam H.S.I. Printing Press, Addis Ababa.

World Bank (1978) *1978 World Bank Atlas,* World Bank, Washington D.C.

Zeeman, E.C. (1976) 'Catastrophe theory', *Scientific American,* April, No.4, 65-83.

Index